A MUSLIM WHO BECAME A CHRISTIAN

Visit us online at www.authorsonline.co.uk

A MUSLIM WHO BECAME A CHRISTIAN

THE STORY OF JOHN AVETARANIAN

(Born Muhammed Shükri Efendi)

A translation of

Geschichte eines Mohammedaners der Christ wurde

By Johannes Awetaranian

An autobiography completed after his death

By Richard Schäfer.

And translated from the German into English with additional footnotes, appendices, indices, and maps

By John Bechard

An AuthorsOnLine Book

Published by Authors OnLine Ltd 2002

Copyright © Authors OnLine Ltd

Text Copyright for this English edition © John Bechard

Scripture taken from the NEW AMERICAN STANDARD BIBLE®, Copyright © 1960, 1962, 1963, 1968, 1971, 1972, 1973, 1975, 1977, 1995 by The Lockman Foundation. Used by permission.

The moral right of the author has been asserted

All rights reserved. No part of this publication may be reproduced, stored in a retrieval system, or transmitted in any form or by any means, electronic, mechanical, photocopy, recording or otherwise, without prior written permission of the copyright owner. Nor can it be circulated in any form of binding or cover other than that in which it is published and without similar condition including this condition being imposed on a subsequent purchaser.

ISBN 0-7552-0069-1

Authors OnLine Ltd
15-17 Maidenhead Street
Hertford SG14 1DW
England

This book is also available in e-book format from www.authorsonline.co.uk

ABOUT THE TRANSLATOR

John Bechard originally hails from Clay Center, Kansas in the United States. He studied at the University of Kansas from 1980 to 1986 (except for the 82-83 academic year) and has a Bachelor of Arts degree in German Language and Literature and French Language and Literature. He is married to Bobsie, and they live in London, England. She is originally from Jamaica. He has been employed as a bookkeeper/accountant for a local Christian fellowship in London since 1990.

CONTENTS

Original Forward		i
Translator's Acknowledgements		ii
Translator's Notes		iii
1	Childhood and Youth	1
2	A Sect of Islam	7
3	Like Sheep Gone Astray	15
4	The First Wrestling	23
5	Light after the Dark	28
6	Mullah and Christian?	35
7	New Way in the New Light	39
8	Trials of Faith	48
9	A Christian amongst Christians	57
10	Working for the Lord	61
11	Beyond the Pamirs	71
12	The Beginnings of the Mission in Kashgar	77
13	Hindrances	83
14	The First Baptism in Kashgar	89
15	Co-workers	95
16	Doctor Sven Hedin's Journey	98
17	My Last Stay in Kashgar	108
18	Travel Experiences	111
19	A New Acquaintance And Its Consequences	115
20	The Bible Translation	117
21	A Mission to Muslims in Bulgaria	122
22	All Sorts of Experiences and Blessings	136
23	Philippopolis. Years of Work and Struggle	144
24	After the Turkish Revolution	154
25	Struggle and Work. The Balkan Wars	162
26	The World War and Its Effects	184
27	The Conclusion of a Rich Life	189
28	Taking Stock of It All [Richard Schäfer's Original Summing Up]	194
29	The Translator's Summing Up	196
Appendices		199
Bibliography		248
Maps		251
Index		256
Photographs		264

[ORIGINAL] FORWARD

The Muslim who became a Christian, whom this book is about, died in 1919.

He told the story of his own life up to the year 1900 in the edition which first appeared in 1905. The story closed with the account of him joining the German Orient-Mission, in whose publications his later experiences were published.

The missionary John Avetaranian withdrew from the German Orient-Mission in 1918 and joined Doctor Lepsius' Orient-Mission in Potsdam. Along with Avetaranian, his life work also passed over to Lepsius' mission.

After Avetaranian's death, Johannes Lepsius, the man most capable for the job, wanted a new and complete history of Avetaranian's life published, but sickness and death prevented him from doing this. The task was left to his missionary society. As the mission's general secretary who was under Johannes Lepsius for 33 years and worked together with John Avetaranian from 1900 onward, the job fell to me. I am fulfilling a duty towards two men of great merit if only I do not shrink back from my task: to record what a German evangelical life of faith united with the devoted love of the Muslim who has converted to Christianity was able to accomplish in the past.

When the tired reapers set their scythes to one side, they did not throw them away but passed them on, because the harvest was the goal, and for that alone did they work.

Lord of the harvest, send workers into Your harvest!

Potsdam, 31 March 1930.

Richard Schäfer,
On behalf of Dr Lepsius' German Orient-Mission, Potsdam.

TRANSLATOR'S ACKNOWLEDGEMENTS

First to the Germans and the late Richard Schäfer in particular for publishing and preserving this wonderful story for future generations even through one world war and the rigours of a communist regime.

To my professors in the German department at the University of Kansas, in particular Professor Fullenwider and Professor Dick, who were so encouraging and who expressed a desire to see me carry on in my German studies beyond a Bachelor of Arts degree. There were times during this project when I wish I had.

To my late grandmother, Alice Luthi, who had more confidence in her grandson than he had in himself, for all her help and kind support during his years at university.

To my parents, Audrey and LaVern Bechard, for their unquestioning support even when it seemed their son was throwing his life away, and for the courage to give him the freedom to choose his own way and make his own mistakes.

To my wife, Bobsie, for continuing to love me, even though she may not always understand what I am on about, for putting up with my late nights in front of the computer and my spending ridiculous amounts of money on old books.

To Paul and Marcia Craig for their kind support and willingness to sit and listen to me rattle on about the translation work, and for some helpful feedback.

To Laura Kensington for some insights into Armenian names.

To Ute and Tillman Krueger and Uli Baker for their help with certain difficult German words and constructions, even though we might not always have arrived at a definitive answer.

To Nigel for his advice in regard to certain Turkish pronunciations and other suggestions and bits of information.

To Sandy Waldron for her generous help with proof-reading this work and getting it into shape to be published.

To Gordon Cowie and Gavin Dawson and the rest of my colleagues at work for putting up with the endless retelling of what I was doing and how I came about doing it.

To Rob Fathers and Mick Borrett for some invaluable information on publishing, book creation, and suggestions for the front cover.

To Dr Bruno Blaser for his information on the subsequent history of Dr Lepsius' Orient-Mission.

To Jürg and Marlis Heusser for their help and interest in this story.

And especially to John who has given me the opportunity of a lifetime in being able to take on a project like this and for the freedom to pursue my own way with it, for directing me into various lines of research that on my own I would certainly never have found, and for being patient with me and putting up with all my quirks.

And finally to God the Father and Jesus Christ His Son, Whose Great Story gives all of our little stories meaning.

TRANSLATOR'S NOTES

In translating this book (and as far as I can tell this is the first time it has ever been translated into another language), I have tried to keep the original text as complete as possible and deliver a full translation of the work. This means that I have preserved the comments of its original compiler, Richard Schäfer, even though I do not always agree with, if not his words, then at least his emphasis. In the interest of exactness, any footnotes in the story that I have added are followed by "Trans." to distinguish them from those belonging to the original text, and any text that I have included within the story itself or interjected into the original footnotes has been enclosed in brackets [] as is customary. What now follows are some of the rules and thoughts, which guided how I handled this work, and some of the problems I faced.

To begin with I had to decide on what to call the author of this book. In German he is called *Johannes Awetaranian*. As for his surname, I simply transliterated it using a *v* in place of a *w*; however, his first name was a different matter. I plumbed for *John* over *Johannes* on the basis of the story that Avetaranian relates in Chapter 7 in which his childhood friend calls him John after John the Baptist. This reference would only make sense if I used the English form of *John*. In addition, his first name would not have been *Johannes*, but rather *Hohannes*, *Hovaness*, or *Hovhannes*, which are the Armenian forms of the name *John*. Whether for convenience sake, or because it was already the common practice of those who knew Avetaranian, or for the same reason that I have done it, Schäfer opted to use the German form of *John* as opposed to the Armenian. Therefore I have taken the same liberty in using the English form as opposed to the German.

Some people (mainly British and American) with whom I have spoken and who have had greater dealings than I with Turkish people and all things Turkish, have cringed at hearing me use his Armenian name and have insisted on referring to him by his given Turkish name, Mehmed (Muhammed) Shükri Efendi. I must say I certainly would not agree with the old practice of automatically changing a person's name to that of one of those found in the Bible, as if having such a name makes you more of a Christian. In the Bible, name changes did take place in specific instances, but nowhere is there any indication that this should be a regular or automatic practice. But having said this, in Chapter 1 Avetaranian does make the best possible case for allowing his name to be changed, when he speaks of the pride he had had as a Muslim and a descendant of Muhammad in having the same name as the "Prophet". In this instance, putting away the name could be seen as going some way towards putting away the pride. And since he was content to go by the name

Avetaranian, which as he states means 'son of the Gospel' in Armenian, then I feel that it is right and proper to respect his decision.

To stay on the subject of names, I have opted for older spellings of place names and other references (e.g., *Koran* as opposed to *Qur'an*) to try to preserve the historical flavour of the story. One of the aspects of this book that I find striking is how much history (and quite a bit of little-known history) is touched upon throughout the story, though at the same time these historical events are dismissed or treated like a side-show in comparison to the greater importance placed on serving Christ and proclaiming His gospel.

In Appendices A and B I have listed out all the references, geographic and otherwise, and tried to give alternate historical spellings as well as the modern equivalents wherever this was possible. I have also included whatever additional information I could discover and what I thought might be helpful to the reader, especially pertaining to the various persons mentioned in the story. The use of *also* and *or* in the appendices refers to alternate spellings, and *possibly* indicates I could not find any adequate confirmation for the meaning or description of a certain item. Some descriptions simply come from the story itself. But deciding upon an appropriate historical spelling was not always easy. For example, the name for the city of Erzurum has several different renderings that changed over the period this story takes place. And for simplicity's sake I have used a basic alphabet, as opposed to the Turkish alphabet, for the modern Turkish place names in Appendix A.

The difficulties that arose in trying to identify all the places mentioned in the story were quite considerable, especially when I discovered how place names have changed in Turkey, China, and Bulgaria during and after Avetaranian's time. The problem was then compounded by Avetaranian making various references to small villages that were difficult to identify on modern maps let alone on 100-year-old maps. In Turkey the name changes came with the move away from the old Ottoman or Osmanli Turkish to modern Turkish, which also involved changing the old Arabic and Persian references to Turkish ones. In China there seems to have been a move away from using Turkish names to using Chinese names or renderings in what was known as Chinese Turkestan, though this is not true in every instance. And in Bulgaria there was a move away from the old Ottoman place names to Bulgarian names, though I have been told that the Turks there still refer to places using the old Turkish names. In the end I was able to identify all but 3 or 4 villages and have provided several maps at the back of the book to make it easier to locate all the places Avetaranian mentions.

In regard to maps, I have settled on four showing (1) the world centred on Central Asia, (2) eastern Turkey, Persia, and Caucasia, (3) the Tarim Basin in western China, and (4) Bulgaria and the Balkans. The difficulty in trying to draw maps of the region Avetaranian was in, at the time he was there, lay in the fact borders were constantly changing over the whole period. I decided to use as a basis a set of 1897 maps from *The Century Atlas*, which covered

Europe, Turkey, and Central Asia and I then consulted the 1907 map from Ellsworth Huntington's *The Pulse of Asia* and two maps from Sven Hedin's *Through Asia* for the Tarim Basin and Turkestan. With these as a starting point, I then inserted all the missing pieces and worked out where the smaller towns and villages needed to be positioned using modern maps.

In a number of instances I was not able to find an historical English equivalent or even a modern English equivalent for a place name, term, phrase, or person's name, so I had to transliterate. The big question was dealing with the German vowels which had umlauts: *ü*, *ö*, and *ä*. For simplicity's sake dropped the umlaut from the *u* and *o* for the most part, but with the *ä* I opted for *ae* in just about every instance.

I found it especially difficult where I was forced to transliterate a transliteration, like the Arabic quotations in Chapter 21: three quotes from the Qur'an and one from a ninth-century Islamic theologian which are written in Roman letters. In this case, since I do not know Arabic, I was afraid the effect might be something along the lines of a written "Chinese whisper", where what is finally said varies considerably from what was originally intended. But fortunately I was able to find several websites, one with a Romanised version of the Qur'an as well as a site on the Islamic theologian, which also contained a Romanised version of the same quote, so I had something to compare Avetaranian's quote with.

To pronounce certain Turkish and eastern Turki words, which have a vowel followed by *gh* like *Yologhli, Yolushaghi, Aghu-ichendi, Sung-Qaraghol, qum yaghar,* and *Darugham*, Avetaranian's *gh* (a combination you would not normally find in German) seems to serve for the *ğ* in modern Turkish. As I have been told, the *ğ* is silent and simply lengthens the vowel that precedes it. For example, *Yologhli* should probably be pronounced *Yoloali* with the *oa* having the same long *o* sound as the *oa* in *boat*.

I have used italics quite extensively throughout the story and in my appendices; I have kept the italics, which Schäfer employed to emphasise certain words and passages, and have italicised the foreign words and phrases only when they appear for the first time in the story.

Avetaranian refers to a wide variety of currencies (as a traveller would do). So to give the reader a framework to understand these currencies, I have provided a table of currencies and their US dollar equivalents from that period in Appendix H. I found the majority of these exchange rates in an old 1880s' American-English dictionary, which gives a table of some of the currencies and their US dollar equivalents. For the currencies not in that table, I had to use other sources like Hedin for the Turkestani *tenga* and Wilson for an estimate on the Persian *toman*. I have also included a small table giving a few examples of what a dollar could buy back then.

As I stated at the beginning of these notes, I have for the most part refrained from any excessive editing of the story itself. The only major change from the original 1930 edition is that I went back to Avetaranian's first autobiography published in 1905 to reconstruct Chapter 16, which deals with his adventures with the Swedish explorer, Doctor Sven Hedin. For some (I assume diplomatic) reason, this chapter was severely truncated in the later edition, large portions of Avetaranian's more critical comments about Hedin having been edited out. His comments were originally made in response to some rather caustic remarks about him in Hedin's own book published seven years before Avetaranian's first autobiography. Since I found some of Avetaranian's comments in the 1905 edition to be pertinent, I chose to resurrect them and have also included Hedin's own remarks in the footnotes to show what Avetaranian was responding to.

Because Chapters 21 to 28 (Chapter 29 is my own addition) are a patchwork of Avetaranian's missionary reports and Schäfer's comments along with a couple of reports or observations by Lepsius and one by Helene Avetaranian, the verb tenses especially toward the latter end of this section of the book were very erratic, jumping from the past tense to the present (possibly a historical present) and back again into the past. To smooth this out, I opted to put everything in the past tense, though reluctantly, because at times I found the present tense quite appealing as it does bring the events out of the past and makes them more immediate.

Finally I have capitalised some references to God and Jesus, especially in prayers and in conversations, but also in a few other places where I thought there might be some ambiguity concerning who was being referred to.

Many names, places, and terms will appear throughout this story; the appendices and maps are there to supply more information if needed, but if not, do not be troubled by them; just sit back and enjoy this very exceptional story.

John Bechard

I said, "You are gods,
And all of you are sons of the Most High.

Psalm 82:6

"I and the Father are one."

The Jews picked up stones again to stone Him.

Jesus answered them, "I showed you many good works from the Father; for which of them are you stoning Me?"

The Jews answered Him, "For a good work we do not stone You, but for blasphemy; and because You, being a man, make Yourself out *to be* God."

Jesus answered them, "Has it not been written in your Law, 'I SAID, YOU ARE GODS'?

"If he called them gods, to whom the word of God came (and the Scripture cannot be broken),

do you say of Him, whom the Father sanctified and sent into the world, 'You are blaspheming,' because I said, 'I am the Son of God'?

"If I do not do the works of My Father, do not believe Me;

but if I do them, though you do not believe Me, believe the works, so that you may know and understand that the Father is in Me, and I in the Father."

John 10:30-38

CHAPTER 1
CHILDHOOD AND YOUTH

I, John, was raised in the faith and teaching of Islam and propose to write the following history in order to praise the grace of the One who called me through His gospel and assured me by His Holy Spirit for the sake of the shed blood of His Son. To Him be the glory forever and ever!

In Erzerum in Asia Minor there lived a Muslim by the name of Suleiman Efendi; he was the keeper of the seal for Wali Assad Pasha. He had two daughters, Khadijé and Münifé. Münifé, the younger of the two, lost her hearing and speech at the age of twelve. Later on her eyesight also failed to such an extent that she could see almost nothing. The distraught father turned to many physicians, but they did not know what to do. Even the most renowned people whose efforts Suleiman Efendi could enlist by virtue of his considerable wealth were unable to help the unfortunate child. Khadijé was healthy and was given in marriage by her father to Zehni, the city secretary from Baiburt and a poet who was well known amongst Muslims. Suleiman Efendi wished for a grandson very much since he had been denied a son. That is why great was his joy when Khadijé gave birth to a son. But when death snatched this child away from his parents after only three years, there was nothing more to keep the grandfather at home. He left his house and his daughters and went away, never to return. A few years later Khadijé lost her husband as well and then stayed alone with her deaf-mute sister. However, after a short while she got married for the second time to a religious sheikh, Raejaeb Baba, from the village of Haidari near Erzerum. They stayed in Erzerum for a couple years. Then the sheikh with his wife and sister-in-law moved to Haidari.

While they were living there, one day a man by the name of Ghanizade Ali from the village of Avrenli came to see the sheikh to be initiated by him as a *murid*, that is, as his disciple. To this end he had to serve the sheikh several years according to the rules and customs of the dervishes. During this time the sheikh had the idea of marrying the unfortunate Münifé to his pupil. Ali complied with the wish of his teacher and master all the more willingly since the sheikh had prophesied to him that he would have a son, whose birth would make the whole family happy. This prediction was fulfilled. On 30 June 1861 Münifé had a son who was named Muhammed Shükri.

Then after a time the sheikh died, and Khadijé returned to the city [Erzerum] with her sister and the boy who was completely entrusted to her care. When Shükri was about three years old, one day his aunt went with him and his mother to the bathhouse, and something wonderful happened there. Münifé, who was sitting on the stone in the middle of the bath, suddenly began to speak and saw all the objects around her. She called her boy over, took him in her lap, embraced and kissed him, and promised to give him sweets as soon as they got home. After the final bath, they all lay down on cushions to smoke. Then after a while when Khadijé, who was extremely excited by her sister's sudden cure, went to wake her from her sleep, Münifé opened her eyes no more. She was dead.

The funeral was on the following day. Shükri stayed in Khadijé's care. His father quietly allowed this to happen; the aunt had certainly always taken good care of the boy. But after a time he came to take his son away. However, Khadijé was very resolute in refusing to let him have the child whom she loved as if he were her own. The father came again and again to demand his son but to no avail. The aunt finally barred the doors to her house to stop him from coming in. Then he seemed to give up in his efforts. He kept away from the house and even from the city, and Khadijé began to drop her guard. One day Shükri was playing in the street; suddenly Ali appeared, called him over, and took him along to his village. The child followed his father without any reluctance. Hardly had Khadijé noticed the boy's disappearance when she sent out a gendarme, who brought the child back straight away. Then the father turned to the *mufti* to gain his rights with the help of the law. However, Khadijé, who was friends with the mufti's wife, knew how to arrange it so the case was postponed again and again. When the mufti saw he could not bypass the law indefinitely, he advised both of them to get married. In this way the dispute was settled.

Ali was an odd man. He was filled with a limitless yearning for truth that was never quenched and made his life restless and unhappy. The ideas of the dervishes drove him to and fro. Today he would be with this sheikh, tomorrow with that one; one minute he was trading abroad, the next he was busy writing amulets and occasionally even earning some money by it. He also served in the army for a time. So it happened that often months and years passed by without him minding his son. If Khadijé had not watched over the boy with loving care, no doubt he would have been sent to a village and grown up in the home of his father's relatives without an education. He stayed at his aunt's house until he was sixteen years old, and his aunt earned the means to support herself and her charge by selling his inheritance which consisted of the houses left behind by her father, Suleiman Efendi.

From the age of six, Shükri attended a mullah's school. The mullah instructed him in the teaching of Islam until he was twelve. At this time the Muslim faith put down roots deep into the boy's receptive nature, and men would never have been able to exterminate these roots later on. In seven years he learned to perform the ritual prayer according to the rules of Islam. Every day at his aunt's house he had to repeat what the mullah had taught him because Khadijé wanted to stamp the religious regulations and principles deep into the boy's heart and memory.

When Shükri had completed his twelfth year, since his health could not take so much studying, his foster mother sent him to be an apprentice to an Armenian tailor by the name of Garabed. No doubt she hated the Christians immensely and loathed their religion, but since she knew *many of the customary sins amongst the Muslims did not occur amongst the Christians, she entrusted the boy to them*, admittedly under the stipulation he would be allowed to perform his prayers five times a day in the mosque. So Shükri learned the tailor's trade for two years and then recommenced his studies.

Meanwhile, during the war with Montenegro, Ali was called up for military service. In fact, his call up was on account of his love of the truth. Several years earlier he had served in the army during the war with Russia, but after one victory by the Russians he had run away with the rest of the troops whom he was with. Then everyone who had taken part in that war was assembled, and in front of a military court Ali was asked for what reason he had deserted the fight at that time. In accordance with the truth he answered he had run away. His former captain declared Ali had been enlisted to help in the hospital and intimated to him later, when they were alone, he would be released, if he corroborated this statement. Ali, however, stuck to the truth and as a result was sent off to fight. Incidentally, it went very well for him in the army. He was generally deemed to be a holy man on account of his quiet nature and his association with the dervishes. For the most part he was kept away from the fighting so that he could pray.

Khadijé was now at home, lonely and deserted. She therefore sent for Shükri and told him, "We have to get away from here. The Russians will certainly come to Erzerum and bring misery and poverty. We will go to Baiburt, to the home of my late husband Zehni, so no harm will come to you." Zehni had left behind a son from his first marriage who frequently visited his stepmother. This man had become a competent writer, and in his house Khadijé now found a home; Shükri learned much from him. But they had only been in Baiburt a year when Khadijé died, and her foster son mourned for her in a profound way.

Here the author of these lines must interject that he himself is this boy, Shükri, the son of Ali and Münifé, and he has thought about his aunt and foster mother with much love even throughout his later life.

After the Russians had taken Erzerum, I received the news my father was in Erzingan and wished to see me. So I made my way to that city. But when I arrived in Erzingan, my father was not there. Only when I found him in his native village of Avrenli did I tell him that Khadijé had died. Then he informed me of his plans for the future.

"We cannot stay here," he said, "because the Russians have taken our city." I heartily agreed with him since at that time I so hated the Russians it was dreadful for me to look at a Russian face. "We need to sell everything we have," he continued, "and move to Bagdad; there are many tombs of the *imams* there. Many dervishes also live in the city." I was not reluctant; after all I was young and inexperienced and did not know into what kind of life my father was leading me.

First we went to the city [Erzerum] in order to sell our house and exchange our clothes for the garb of the dervishes. We put on our green turbans, to which only the *saiyids*, the bodily descendants of the Prophet, are entitled. Up to that point I had worn it only once in my life: one day Khadijé had put it on me when I was going to school. But when the mullah saw me, he was astonished and asked how I had come by the green turban. I explained that my aunt had given it to me. Then he said very seriously, "Does your aunt not know that only the descendants of the Prophet are allowed to wear a green turban? Go and tell her what I have told you." When I came home I reported to Khadijé what had happened. She was surprised the teacher knew nothing about our family's origin, because where she was from, the descendants of Mohammed are recognised by the name, which no one bears except their family members. In other countries they only use documents, which establish the proof of a person's origin. The next morning my aunt accompanied me to see the mullah, and as soon as she had told him her father's name, his behaviour became obliging, even humble. From that day onward he would always rise whenever I came and even let me sit beside him. Nevertheless, he emphatically explained to me this attention and honour was not meant for me but only for my exalted ancestors. In my opinion these things do not really deserve to be mentioned because they are nothing, but they show what superstitions and kinds of prejudices the people of Islam are biased towards. It was no less with me. I placed my trust in futile things as long as I was without Christ, and it was exactly this, my ancestry, that in Satan's hand became a means to keep me away from Christ for a long time. But praised be the name of the Redeemer who has set me free!

My father had finally joined the sect of the *Bektashi Dervishes* and also drew me to them. These people, as do all dervishes, regard their body as their greatest enemy and would try in various ways to weaken it and restrict its desires. They take long journeys on foot, fast often, and give themselves over to smoking *esrar*.[1] In fact, with esrar the spirit is moved into a state of ecstasy and, in the opinion of the dervishes, gains quite a special ability to become immersed in the contemplation of divine things, which the dervishes see as the purpose and goal of life. They disdain forms and ceremonies like *namaz* ('the ritual prayer') and washings.

My father smoked esrar, and I likewise began to smoke it without knowing or considering that I was exposing my life and my youth to the very greatest of dangers.

We left Erzerum after a little while and came to Hassan Kala where, like everywhere on our travels, we stopped at the home of a dervish to talk with

---

[1] See Appendix B, *esrar*. Trans.

him. I heard many marvellous things there. The service to God I had faithfully performed all my life up to then did not count for anything. Many things against which I had guarded myself were supposed to be pleasing to God. Doubts and questions awoke in me, but whenever I smoked esrar, they quickly died away. Then I would consider this new life to be right and good. My pale complexion, the buzzing and the pains I soon felt in my lungs, I regarded as God's favour. I did not think about my future, what I should do and what I should become, rather I completely adopted the dervishes' way of life.

From Hassan Kala we came to the fortress of Khynis, then to Mush; from there we went on to Bitlis, from there to Sert and Jezireh. After we had stayed a few more days at the small town of Zakhu, we reached Mosul where we found many like-minded people. Especially in the surrounding villages, there lived many Bektashi Dervishes who, although belonging to different schools of thought, mostly to the *Yologhli*, differed only a little from each other in their teaching. Even in Arbil where we came to next we found many of these *kharabati* ('men fleeing the world'). In Altyn-kopri we stopped off at the home of one kharabati who seemed to me to be the most eloquent and worthy of all. He was an old man and in his small town he held the office of a Sunni priest. His congregation was certainly not familiar with his way of life and his views, which no doubt contradicted all that is holy to the Sunni. I confided in him concerning my doubts about the correctness of my present life, but he reassured me completely by explaining to me that the dervishes' way of life pointed to a higher level of enlightenment. To my question, why did he not encourage the members of his congregation into such a way of life, he answered they were not mature enough for it.

At Altyn-kopri my father fell ill, and we returned to Mosul. After he had recovered, we stayed on for two months at the cliff caves of Taz-Kharab, which on account of its good spring water is a well-known place of pilgrimage. We ran out of money there and then our difficulties began; moreover, my father became very sick again and came close to death. Meanwhile, I had copied out various religious books for the residents of the place, and they then tried to keep me in their village.

"Your father is dying," they said, "stay here. We will give you a house and everything else you need. Teach our children to read; then we will reward you in a special way." Few among them could actually read and these few only very poorly.

After several days my father recovered, and although the people repeated their request to me, I then moved back with him to Erzerum since the climate of the former region was very hot and unhealthy for my father.

Our stay in Erzerum was also only for a short time; soon we went on to my father's native village. But when winter came, my father continued on alone to see a 120-year-old dervish whom he regarded as his spiritual brother. Since the snow soon made the roads impassable, he did not return until spring. But I stayed with a relative by the name of Behjet Khanum, the sister of the sheikh to whom Khadijé had been married. This woman could read and write, and her eloquence made her very influential with the people she knew. After she had been converted to the Yologhli sect, she won over her husband to this teaching, her sons and daughters-in-law, one of my uncles, and a few of her neighbours. Through her great kindness she compelled me to stay at her home, although I had closer relatives in the village. She soon loved me like a son, and we often read and talked together.

My father embraced the teaching of the Yologhli as well, and I am now of the opinion that, for its part, I had led the life of a total wanderer with its pleasures and privations only to this end: to allow me to find peace in the teaching of the Yologhli.

CHAPTER 2
A SECT OF ISLAM

In the following chapter what I have in mind is to relate a few things about the worship and teaching of the Yologhli, a sect that leads a hidden existence within Islam while the various dervish orders, which all differ very little from one another and are closely related to the Yologhli like the *Kadiri, Nakshibendi, Rufai, Tarikh-i-Nazaenin,* and the *Bektashi*,[1] are generally well known. In particular, no one amongst the Muslims actually knows anything definite about the customs and practices of the Yologhli since their practices are not set down in writing but are only received in the way of tradition. Every now and then writings by them turn up which deal with their teaching, yet these are never printed, and a Sunni Muslim will never believe that they have such a teaching if he does not see it with his own eyes. Therefore the Yologhli are also called *Kitabsiz*, "the ones without the book".

The Sunni give the members of this sect a wide variety of names like *Chirasöndüren = extinguishers of the light; Kizilbash*[2] *= redheads; Rafizi = heretics; distant Turk = barbarian; Turkmans, Shabak, Shahsavan, Alallahi, Tsairakli,* and *the ones outside the seventy-two religions*.[3] They call themselves *Yologhli* or *Yolushaghi = sons of the way* or *children of the way,* that is, pilgrims or aliens, *Erenler = the brave men, Gerchekler = the truthful ones,* etc. A few communities of the Yologhli, who in teaching and ceremonies do not really differ from the others, bear particular names like the *Uryankhusurli,* the *Aghu-ichendi,* the *Baba-mansuri,* and the *Quraishi*. One stream which also differs from those mentioned in regards to worship are the *Inj-Yolli = the ones who go by the narrow way*.[4]

It is my conviction the teaching of the Yologhli came from Christian communities. Perhaps they were Galatians who returned to a righteousness

---

[1] See Appendix C, Established Dervish Orders Mentioned by Avetaranian. Trans.

[2] In a letter concerning the Kizilbash (Arabkir, 24 October 1854), George Nutting wrote to Rufus Anderson, the secretary of the American Board of Commissioners for Foreign Missions in Boston: "There [at Tchimishgazek; now Çemişgezek, Turkey] is a sect of nominal Moslems scattered through this region of whom I think you have not heard. They bear the name Kuzulbash [sic], which means literally 'readhead' [sic]. They never or almost never go through the Muslim forms of prayer; nor do they keep their fast. They are a people by themselves. A peculiar people and open to the Gospel [sic]. The Turks seem to regard them very much as they do the Koords [sic], as worthless heretics, and not worth caring for." ABC 16.7.1 (Archives of the ABCFM, Houghton Library, Harvard–this note was taken from an online article "Some Remarks on Alevi Responses to the Missionaries in Eastern Anatolia (19th-20th cc.)" by Hans-Lukas Kieser. Trans.

[3] See Appendix D, What the Sunni Call the Yologhli. Trans.

[4] See Appendix E, What the Yologhli Call Themselves. Trans.

based on works and then, on being threatened by the Muslims, professed their faith in a religious form adapted to Islam. Quite a few characteristics of their customs and ceremonies can hardly be explained in any other way than as a kind of concept of the Trinity, which emerges now and then when they call on the divine name.

The Yologhli call each other "brother". They recognise each other by small signs and habits, which are quite inconspicuous to the eye of the uninitiated. The men do not cut their moustaches, by which they distinguish themselves from the majority of the Sunni. When they greet one another, their eyes light up with joy, which again is only understood and reciprocated by the "brethren". When saying grace before a meal, they lay the index finger of the right hand on the table.

Towards the adherents of their sect the Yologhli show an extensive hospitality. If a stranger comes to the village—for the most part the communities stay away from the cities—first of all, he is greeted by the woman of the house of whichever home he stops at. She or her daughter washes the guest's feet and conducts him to a bed where he rests for a few hours. Meanwhile, the man of the house is notified, the villagers are assembled, and when the stranger wakes up, lively entertainment, music, and at times even dancing begin. The celebration goes on into the evening; only when the guest dismisses them do the villagers return to their homes. If the stranger stays longer, each morning the head of the household must obtain the guest's permission to be allowed to go about his work for the day. But each evening the social activities are repeated, the guest being honoured in the same way as he was on the first day. On his departure the head of the household sees the guest about a (English) mile out of the village.

As accommodating as the Yologhli are towards their own, their behaviour towards those of other faiths is reserved, even cold.

Amongst the adherents of this sect, divorce almost never occurs, polygamy very seldom. As well, it is forbidden to dismiss their wives as happens so frequently with Muslims; rather they are honoured and in the meetings are equal to men.

As to their position to worldly goods, the Yologhli endeavour to have all things in common.

Religious meetings are conducted by an elder called a *daedae* or *pir*, take place on Thursday evenings, and consist of a series of twelve ceremonies.

1. They begin with the *blessing of the bread*. The congregation lines up according to families. Each member of a family lays his hand on his relative's arm or shoulder so everyone, so to speak, forms a body. The father of the family holds the bread each family has brought with them, and the pir then speaks a blessing over it. Then all the loaves of bread are set down next to the leader of the meeting.

2. Then comes the selection of the *gözji*, the guards. Two men are chosen from the assembly. One of them receives a short thick baton and is sent to

stand in front of the door of the meeting room in order to stop any stranger from entering. The other one is given a long thin stick; he takes his place on the inside of the door and has to keep watch over those taking part in the service. If anyone is inattentive or falls asleep, he is reminded of his duty with one touch from the stick.

3. When these two men have taken up their posts, others line up next to the candles installed in the room and touch them with one hand while the pir speaks a blessing.

4. Then they all sit in a circle; if the assembly is large, they sit in two rows. What comes next is the *foot washing*. Everyone is allowed to take part. Whenever the elder performs this task himself, he demonstrates his great humility and devotion. But three women ordinarily carry out this act. First these women lay bare the feet of those present. Then they approach each one in turn but do not wash their feet, rather their hands. To do this, one of the women holds the bowl, the other pours water from a jug over the outstretched hands, and the third dries them with a cloth.

5. After the washing has been performed on everyone in this manner, the elder utters a *prayer of penance* on behalf of the congregation. He speaks without written notes, but for the most part the words are the same each time.

6. Then to the sound of the guitar a *song of praise* is struck up accompanied by continual hand clapping. From these songs, some of which have a beautiful spiritual content, the congregation receives doctrine and commandments and regulations for the way they should live.

7. Once the singing has finished, the elders of the congregation are allowed to smoke esrar, while any smoking by them other than in the service is strictly forbidden. Then five men stand and begin the *sema*, the holy dance, which again is accompanied by the guitar. They line up one by one inside the circle formed by the congregation with one of them in the middle and slowly begin to sway and spin while moving their arms. The accompaniment becomes faster and faster and more and more spirited and sweeps the men along until the elder finally motions to the person sitting next to him. He then touches one of the men who are dancing; the others immediately draw near, take one another by the hand, and make a low bow to the pir. Then the women's dance follows in the same manner.

8. Once they have all returned to their places, the pir has the loaves of bread brought to him, breaks them, and gives each person his share. The bread is received with such joy as if those present had not eaten anything for days. After the two gözji have also received their bread, the meal is eaten amidst lively, though purely spiritual, conversation.

9. Then everyone stands up and girds themselves like pilgrims who intend to take a long journey. What then follows is,

10. One of the most important ceremonies, the *dying for sin*. After making a low bow to the pir, two married men embrace one another and lay face down while a third assists them, making sure both of their backs form a

surface so they are again, as it were, one body. The two wives then kneel down at their husband's feet and cover them with their garments while putting a veil over their own faces. Then the elder takes from a chest a stick that has been carefully stored in many wrappings, a *tariq* or *aerkan*, which has served this same purpose for centuries. With this stick he strikes the ones lying there "dead" three times while shouting: "God, Mohammed, Ali!" After that, the "dead" rise again, that is to say, the two men stand up. One grasps the elder's garment with his right hand and the other with his left hand; this signifies a cry for help. Passing under the pir's arm, they then go back to the assembly, the wives following them in the same manner after the pir has touched their outstretched hands three times with the stick.

11. The dying for the sins concludes with the *zaki*, the drink. While the lament for the death of Husain is sung, the elder dips the rod, which he has just been using, in the water and then gives this water to those present to drink.

12. After this they strike up a final song of praise; with that the meeting is concluded. Everyone then bows to the pir and leaves the house.[1]

As far as the teaching of the Yologhli is concerned, it must first be stressed everyone believes in one God, however, in the sense God is all in all, meaning, the totality of all things in existence is God and everything else is nothing. The poet Salim Divana has explained this belief in his book in the following way: "God, or the Spirit, which is the same thing, neither goes out anywhere nor does he come in from anywhere. Rather you should understand him in this way: imagine a seashore, along which a number of barrels without bottoms are set up. If you place one of those barrels in the sea, it fills up with water; but if you pull it out, the water flows away. So it also is with the life and death of man. For the word of the Koran (Surah 15:29), 'and we breathed into him of our spirit',[2] means nothing other than exactly that." In another passage Salim Divana says, "Indeed, can something come from nothing? Never. Whatever is there has been there from the beginning, and the word, 'God made', can only mean that he made the thing into another form."

Just as there are a lot of contradictions found in the whole teaching of the Yologhli, so this view of the creation of the world contradicts the idea that the world has not been created at all, that it will not even have an end, as the following tradition shows:

> "One day when Solomon was walking in the country, he saw two large mountains of sand and between them a beautiful woman who barred his way with the words, 'You are mine, I will not leave you!' Solomon promised to marry her but asked her to let him go on. The woman spoke, 'If you will give me a pledge that you will come back, I will let you go.' Solomon gave her his

---

[1] Contrary to Avetaranian's comments on page 7 concerning the teaching of the Yologhli and the Galatians of the New Testament, the rituals recounted above are more reminiscent of the ancient pagan mystery cults. Trans.

[2] See Appendix J, Koran Passages 1. Trans.

signet ring and went on. When he returned he saw in the same place a very ugly woman whom he could hardly look upon. Solomon looked for the beautiful woman in order to have his pledge back. Then the ugly woman called, 'Solomon, son of David, come and take the signet ring you gave me as a pledge.' Solomon spoke, 'I gave you no ring. What am I supposed to take from you? Who are you?' She answered, 'I am the world. I first appear beautiful and charming to men, although I am not so; in this way I lead them astray. Come and receive your ring, if you recognise it.' With that she pulled her hand out of her purse. The purse was full of signet rings all engraved with 'King Solomon, son of David'. Quite astonished, Solomon asked, 'What does this mean?' The woman answered, 'Do not believe there are no other Solomons beside yourself. I have here thousands of signet rings which I have taken as pledges from such persons as yourself who are called 'Solomon, son of David.'—Do you see these mountains of sand? Each time when one hundred thousand years have passed by, I take one tiny grain of sand from one mountain and throw it onto the other. I do not remember how many millions of times these mountains have been transferred back and forth. They will be transferred back and forth forever.'"

The Yologhli believe after death a righteous man returns as a man to this world to a new life they call "paradise", but the evil man expects hell, a new life of agony in the form of an animal. The greatest punishment is if after his death a man is transformed into dust, then into stone, then into metal, e.g., iron. He must then work through the whole series of metals in order finally to become a man again and to begin the cycle anew of animal, man, or dust. These ideas are clearly expressed in the writings of Kaygusuz Abdal, Azizi, and others.

The Yologhli acknowledge all prophets beginning with Adam. They also hold Mohammed and Ali, Mohammed's cousin, in very high regard and say their salvation is in the hands of the descendants of these two prophets. Outwardly the two are equal. However, in the opinion of the Yologhli, on inner worth Ali outshines Mohammed. They compare the latter with the day, the former with the mysterious night. The book of Yamini provides the reference for this view in which it says:

"One day Mohammed was sitting in his place while Ali and the people stood by him. Then the angel Gabriel came to Mohammed with a revelation. When he noticed Ali to the right of Mohammed, Gabriel greeted him with a bow. Such a honour had never been shown to Mohammed. He was astonished by this and said, 'What does this mean, brother Gabriel?' 'O Mohammed, Ali is my leader,' answered the angel. 'When God created me,' he continued, 'he had not yet created anything else, but I had no idea about my existence. I had wings and soared in a vast expanse. I had flown for three hundred years in this way and had not found where I could land. Finally I became aware of a green dome and flew to it in order to rest there a while. But I heard a voice there asking, 'Who am I? Who are you?' I answered, 'I am me; you are you.' I had barely uttered this when my wings burnt up, and I plunged into the emptiness. I do not know how long I fell until my new wings grew back. After I had flown another three hundred years I came to the same dome. There I heard the same questions and gave the same answers. Again my wings burnt up, and I fell into the empty abyss. When my wings had grown and I again flew through infinity, I was deeply distressed as I remembered the earlier experiences. Then an old man with a white beard appeared to me and spoke, 'How long do you want to be ignorant and be punished? Come; I will teach you what you shall say when you come to the dome again and are questioned. Answer, "I am a creature; you are the creator."' So I did that the next time and was saved. After that, I looked into the interior of the dome and saw a bright lamp. Its light shone in three colours: white which is the colour of God, red which is the light (that is, the spirit) of Ali, and green which is the light of Mohammed. O Mohammed,' Gabriel said in closing, 'it was Ali who gave me that wise counsel; he guided me when nothing had yet been created. Therefore I honoured my teacher when I saw him just now standing next to you.'"

From this story the Yologhli conclude Ali has existed for all eternity. Furthermore, according to their teaching, the one in the Bible called Elijah was Ali, he appeared in the New Testament as John the Baptist, and he even met Mary in the form of a youth (the Sunni claim this youth was Gabriel). He looked at the virgin with such an impressive gaze she conceived at once. In the Koran he was then called Ali. Later he appeared as Hajji Bektash Wali; he would always be in the world. Also the *Mahdi* (see below) would be none other than him (the Sunni believe that the Mahdi will be born first).

All of these teachings are found in the book by Nirani Sultan, which a number of years ago was the only Yologhli work printed in Constantinople.

The Yologhli also believe in the twelve apostles but they regard them as the twelve imams who descend from Mohammed and Ali. The order begins with Ali himself, then come his two sons, Hasan and Husain whom his wife, Fatima, Mohammed's daughter, bore him. They were followed by Husain's son, Zain-ul-Abidin, then Mohammed-Baghir, Musa al-Kazim, Hasan al-'Askari, Mohammed-Tagi, Ali an-Naqi, Ali-Riza, Jafar-Sadik, and Mahdi-al-Hadi.[1] The one named last disappeared into a hole, but in the last days he is to return to take up the struggle with the Antichrist.

Another tradition relates that the souls of the twelve imams were called into existence before all the created beings, or they have always existed. Others ascribe an eternal existence only to the souls of Fatima, Hasan and Husain, and again others declare they are all only one soul and Hajji Bektash is also one with them. The descendants of Mohammed are also supposed to have that soul, and that soul is God.

According to the teaching of the Yologhli, God has sent five revelations to men: the Law of Moses, the Psalms, the Gospel, the Koran, and the book of the Imam Jafar-Sadik. The sect remains committed to following this last revelation. Besides that, they possess yet other writings called *The Commands of the Saints*. From one of these writings the sect establishes proof of its holy

---

[1] See Appendix F, The Twelve Imams According to the Yologhli. Trans.

descent, namely from the following account:

> "When Adam and Eve were expelled from Paradise and were living on the earth, Cain and Abel were born to them. Then they argued with one another: Adam said the children were from him; Eve claimed they were from her. In order to decide the question, they wanted to put it to a test and each one set out a jug. Adam was busy with the farming while Eve prepared the meal at home and carried it to the field, but she did not serve her husband well, and Adam was very dissatisfied with her. Then God sent to Adam's house a heavenly virgin whose name was 'the Redeemed One'. She said to Eve, 'Because your husband is dissatisfied with you, God has sent me that I shall be his wife. Where is your husband?' Eve spoke, 'Sit down a little while; I will call him.' She took the food, hurried to Adam who was in the field, and was extremely kind towards him so he was happy and grateful. Then Eve spoke to him, 'Swear to me that while I live you will not marry another.' Adam swore. But in the evening, when he came home and saw the Redeemed One, he was very grieved about his oath, and behold, Seth came forth from his jug. Since the jug had been too narrow, and Eve, angry her jug had remained empty, had shaken it violently, Seth was limping. Later Adam married Seth to the Redeemed One, and from these two all of the prophets are descended. For in Seth there is no portion of the sinner and deceiver, that is Eve."

The Yologhli now maintain they are the "Redeemed People", the descendants of Seth and the Redeemed One. They do not belong to the seventy-two religious communities and are called "half" because their first father was half, that is, he descended from Adam alone.

Finally I want to cite two more passages from the writing of Kaygusuz Abdal since these passages, in particular, show the peculiar style and the odd way of thinking of the Yologhli.

It begins with the following:

> "I was sitting under a tree when I saw how Moses led the children of Israel out of Egypt. Pharaoh prepared his army, but his zeal had died down somewhat. Then the Devil came and incited the Egyptians against Israel. When I saw Satan wanted to harm Moses, I got up to pursue him. I caught up to him and fought him, but he escaped, and I was left with only his cloak, his hat, and his cane. Then I returned to sit under my tree. Afterwards Moses came to me and spoke to me, 'Give Satan back his coat, his cane, and his cap.' I answered, 'No.' Then he asked, 'What do you want with them?' I replied, 'I will only give them back to him when he repents and promises to cause no more trouble for the prophets.' Then Satan came to me, repented, and promised he would no longer lead men astray against the prophets—I know who I am. I converted Satan that he will no longer lead my people astray against my Moses."

In another passage in this work it states: "I saw the dervish who went up to the place where Satan and the demons wanted to lead Solomon astray. But Solomon, whose eyes Ali looked out of, recognised them immediately. I know," the writer continues, "who I am, that is, I know I am the dervish, Solomon, and Ali looks out of my eyes. I beheld it in my body; therefore the demons will not be able to lead me astray. The whole universe is in me. Nothing at all which is from eternity and will be in eternity—be it Paradise or Hell, be it angel or devil, be it believer or non-believer—I am missing nothing at all. Everything is in me, if only I want to see it; the Last Judgement is also in me."

CHAPTER 3
LIKE SHEEP GONE ASTRAY

At the end of Chapter 1 it was already told how I spent the winter of 1879 in the home of Mrs Behjet, Behjet Khanum, in Avrenli, my father's native village, which was six hours away from Erzerum. My stay there was of the greatest significance for me. It was here I would hear for the first time the voice of God calling me to a new life.

The tool that brought me to a knowledge of the truth was a New Testament in the Turkish language. For several decades the Scriptures have been translated by Bible Societies into the Ottoman Turkish and Persian languages and distributed throughout Muslim countries, but these Bibles are seldom seen because they are kept hidden for fear of the Muslim priests.

The village of Avrenli was situated on the main road leading to Erzerum, the capital of our province. Behjet Khanum would show hospitality to many who travelled this way. It so happened the Yologhli chiefs as well as Sunni scholars visited and discussed the most important questions and concerns with her. She was a curious woman and possessed rare spiritual gifts. Over sixty years old, she was still an impressive figure. She wore no veil, which was very much held against her by the women in my family. When guests came to see her, she would first send food and drink to them and after a time would appear herself. At the beginning of the conversation she was always very cold and critical, but if the guests seemed to her worthy of consideration, she would soon become lively and charming. She had a wonderful poetic talent and many of the guests came simply to listen to her. She would often be asked for a song without her complying with this wish, but when she was prompted through witty conversation or through the poetry of others, an odd enthusiasm came over her. For hours she could improvise songs that sprang from her sprightly spirit into ideas, rhyme, and melody and aroused the admiration of her learned guests. Often we tried to write her songs down, but it was impossible because our quill was not capable of following the flow of her thoughts, and every disturbance immediately silenced her. She could read and write and owned many books.

One day I noticed among her books one I had never seen before. I looked inside and read the beginning—it was the Gospel in Turkish. I asked Behjet where she got the book from, and she told me her son had been a prisoner in Russia during the Russo-Turkish War. While there, a stranger gave him this book. Since he could not read himself, he brought it along as a gift for his mother.[1]

When I read the title of the book, I understood this much: it must be the *Injil*, that is, the Gospel as it is mentioned in the Koran. In the Koran it states: "God sent the law and the gospel to guide men." (Surah 3:2)[2]

For the Muslims both the Old and New Testament are sacred books, however, the contents of both are utterly unknown to them.

The beginning of the Gospel of Matthew with its register of lineage[3] had made so little impression on me that, dissatisfied, I put the book aside. After a few days, however, I picked it up again and read the tenth chapter of John's Gospel.

There it states: "Jesus answered them, 'Has it not been written in your Law, "I SAID, YOU ARE GODS?" If he called them gods, to whom the word of God came (and the Scripture cannot be broken), do you say of Him, whom the Father sanctified and sent into the world, "You are blaspheming," because I said, "I am the Son of God"?'"[4]

These words greatly astonished me because they firmly contradicted the Islamic view. Muslims reject in the strongest possible way that Jesus is the Son of God; on the other hand, the Koran teaches quite clearly that Jesus was one of the greatest prophets of all, and according to the Muslim view, all prophets are free from sin.

I thought about this again. If Jesus actually was a prophet and said of himself that he was the Son of God, then it must be true because as a prophet he could not tell a lie. Irrefutably the thought imposed itself upon me: if what is written here is true, then our Muslim religion is not true; if what is written here is not true, then Jesus is no prophet. But the Koran teaches and every Muslim knows from an early age: "Jesus was a prophet!"

When I read the words "Son of God" for the first time, I was so stunned, and my heart was stirred to its very depths. I said to myself, "What kind of a blasphemy is this! Son of God! Am I supposed to believe in polytheism? How is it possible Jesus could claim this about himself?" For according to Muslim belief, "Son of God" is understood as a son according to the flesh.

I asked God to make it clear to me and after I had calmed down somewhat, I considered once more how those words could be meant. As I carefully thought through the Old Testament passage Jesus cites and compared it with the words, "whom the Father sanctified and sent into the world" which Jesus added, it began to become clear to me there could be no thought here of

---

[1] In his *The Story of the Bible Society* (p. 293), Canton states: "In the Russo-Turkish struggle, 1877-78, there were 478,000 copies of the Scriptures distributed..." Bibles were distributed to those on both sides of the conflict. This makes it likely though not certain that the copy which Avetaranian found was produced by the British and Foreign Bible Society, though the American Bible Society also distributed and sold Turkish Bibles at that time. Trans.

[2] This is actually Surah 3:3. See Appendix J, Koran Passages 2. Trans.

[3] See Appendix I, Bible Passages 1. Trans.

[4] See Appendix I, Bible Passages 2. Trans.

fathering according to the flesh.

When the lady of the house saw me lost deep in thought and in response to her questions I communicated my doubts to her, she sought to distract me from my thoughts by taking the book from my hand and calling me to dinner.

With the beginning of spring my father came back. He told me, "My child, I have promised Ali Beg in the village of Perzor that you will go there and instruct his son!" I agreed to this, went with my father to see Ali Beg, and began to instruct his son. Many of the inhabitants of the village there asked me to become their teacher and priest. I accepted their proposal and stayed in that village at Ali Beg's home. He was the pir for the villagers who belonged to the Yologhli religion. After several days I went to see the chief mullah in Erzerum to attain from him the official appointment to my office. The people were really not bothered about this, but my conscience drove me to it. I went to see the mullah, at whose school I had studied, and asked him whether I was capable and worthy of holding the office of a priest. He gave me a written certificate of graduation, on which he pressed his seal, and dismissed me with a prayer and a blessing.

When I returned to the village, the inhabitants asked me to get married soon since they wanted to have a married mullah like most communities. In accordance with the Muslim custom, I gave no reply to their request. So the elders met to consider which girl would be right for me. Their choice fell to pir Ali Beg's daughter, and with that the engagement was concluded. I received the instruction to give a gift to my fiancée and sent her a gold piece on a chain.

However, I had not forgotten the word of the Gospel I had read, rather it often stirred in my heart. On occasion I told some educated people in my village that I had seen a translation of the Gospel, but they contested this.

To be exact, strange views about the New Testament have been formulated amongst the Muslims. Many say when God sent the Koran to earth, the Gospel was taken up by Him into heaven. Others claim that after Mohammed brought the Koran to the world, the Christians changed the Gospel in such a way that the correct Gospel actually no longer exists. Still others say the time of the Old Testament had passed when God sent the New Testament to earth; so likewise with the revelation of the Koran, the time and validity of the Gospel had passed.

I wrote repeatedly to Behjet Khanum to ask if she might send the Gospel to me, but she did not do it. She probably had the secret apprehension that I would occupy myself more with it than would be good for me. I then travelled to the capital of our province and asked the Armenian tailor, Garabed, where I could find a New Testament. He took me to an Armenian Protestant, and he told me where I could get one.

When I spoke with Garabed again about it, he became cross, although he alone had given me the good advice to consult the Protestant. Since he was a very fanatical adherent of the Armenian National Church, he did not want the

Protestants to sell me a New Testament. He went, as I heard later, to the bookseller and advised him not to let me have the book. I was a mullah and would bring the book to the police and report him. The bookseller was supposed either to say he had none or to ask for so much that I would not take it.

He really did ask me for around twelve [German] marks, which at the time was a great sum for my modest resources. I told him I heard the book only cost five *ghrish*.[1] Then God worked it out in such a way that right then and there an Armenian Protestant stepped into the shop. He heard the end of our conversation and said he knew precisely that the four Gospels with the Acts of the Apostles cost no more than five ghrish. In addition, he reproached the bookseller for demanding so much from me. With the persuasion of this Protestant the bookseller then sold the New Testament to me and, supremely happy, I returned to my village, which was two days' travel away.

An Armenian town was located at the halfway point along the way. I went to the home of a villager I knew and there met a young Armenian teacher who was visiting those people. He saw the New Testament I had and asked why I bought it. When I told him I wanted to study what was written in the Gospel, he showed me in the first chapter of John's Gospel the first and fourteenth verses[2] and asked me to think about these passages. He knew the Muslims' claim that it was impossible for God to have a son and referred me right to the point, which had given me the first occasion to think about the Christian teaching. The young man was a fervent, converted Christian. That very night he wrote down for me the Christian creed in Turkish as well as some other Christian teachings which seemed to him important for me. He lived in a room the inhabitants of the house also used for baking bread. For this purpose there was in the middle of the room a walled depression in which there were glowing coals. The sheet which he had worked hard to write out fell into this depression without the teacher noticing, and when he found it there the next morning, it was half burnt to a cinder. It was impossible to rewrite it since I had to go. So I took it as it was and continued on my journey. But the missing words and sentences were what especially prompted me later on to think things through and work things out.

On the road I was joined by two young men with whom I soon got into a conversation. One of them related he had married an Armenian girl, although he himself was a Turk.

"I had been fond of her," he said, "and soon noticed she was also willing to marry me. When I asked her to convert to Islam, she declared herself ready, provided I would carry her off from her father's house in order to protect her from her parents and the bishop. I promised her this; indeed, I knew the government would be on our side, but she was afraid nonetheless. Then I went

---

[1] See Appendix B, *ghrish*. Trans.
[2] See Appendix I, Bible Passages 3. Trans.

to see a friend who was cleverer and more experienced than myself and asked him for advice. He declared the matter to be very simple and advised me to bring the girl before the mufti, a higher priest and interpreter of the law, impressing upon her to relate to him the following story: 'I had a vision in the night. I saw a man sitting on a green stool; his face shone like the sun. When he saw me, he spoke to me: "O my daughter, you belong to my people; speak the word of testimony." At once my tongue was loosened and I said, "*La ilaha illa 'llah: Mohammed-er-Rasul-Ullah*," which is, "there is no God besides God, and Mohammed is his messenger." I then told him that I would have to suffer much if my parents and our priests heard this from me, but the man on the green stool ordered me to go to the mufti's home; he would protect me. When I awoke from my sleep, I walked out of the house. Then I saw this young man and asked him to bring me to you.' I liked my friend's advice very much. I brought the girl to the mufti, and she told the story in front of him and several witnesses. The mufti was very satisfied and married us after a few days. Her parents did not succeed in getting her back."

In brief this was the content of the story.

When I had parted from my companions, I began to think about the story and recollect similar accounts, which I had read in our religious books and were supposed to prove that Mohammed performed miracles. I told myself if this business was a deception, other deceptions could also be invented. In fact, I considered it possible that some stories were true and others were fabricated, but how was a person supposed to distinguish between truth and lie! For the mufti will have likewise written this story down long ago, and the Muslims will rejoice over the event as a miracle, and what an impression the story will make after only one hundred years! Meanwhile, I reproached myself in my heart and told myself, "What are these thoughts! How can I be allowed to doubt our holy books! Is this not falling away from faith and from religion?"

After I had returned to my village, my father, who in the meantime had been with friends in Bajavut and had been occupied with writing amulets, visited me for several days. He asked me to come with him to a quiet place since he had much to tell me. I was quite happy to go with him and took the Gospel with me to talk to him about it. We went out of the village and sat under some trees by the edge of a stream that was driving a mill. I gave him my book and asked him to examine it. He took it, leafed through it, laid it down, and with a deep sigh said, "My son, I am very distressed!"

"Why?" I asked.

"You see," he answered, "I have found no peace in my conscience up to this very hour, and I have come close to leading you down the same path. Who knows whether I have not already swayed you!"

"No, dear father," I said, "I do not feel it in my conscience."

"When I was your age," he continued, "I had doubts about our religion, about mullahs and interpreting the Koran, about all sorts of customs and traditions. Just the regulations about washings and prayers alone are so varied no one can fulfil them; the heart can never be at peace in the conviction one's duty is fulfilled. For it is written the ritual prayer, if it has been neglected once or not performed exactly according to the rules, must be repeated seventy times. If this does not happen, then a person must suffer seventy years in hell for it. Now I ask you, who can fulfil everything, and if a person cannot fulfil it, how is it possible God lays a burden on men which they cannot bear? When I was young, I disputed with the mullahs a lot about this and sought to gain clarity. Some told me we must simply be guided according to tradition. Others said we must do what we can; for whatever is lacking in us, Mohammed will be our mediator or God will exercise mercy. Still others said many of the righteous who have lived their whole lives according to the precepts of Islam would go to hell. On the other hand, sinners who on their deathbeds uttered the word of the testimony, "*La ilaha illa 'llah: Mohammed-er-Rasul-Ullah*", would go to Paradise. We disputed like this for five years, but no one helped to make it clear to me in a satisfactory way. The unrest of my heart just grew and grew, although I believed the Koran was true and regarded Mohammed and his followers as holy people. But when I saw the insincere lives of the mullahs and interpreters of the Koran, who forbid others and then violate the precepts themselves and whose teaching is full of contradictions, I had doubts about this as well.

"At that time I met the Emrah Khojah who had had the very same experiences, and we went together to the Sheikh Raejaeb Baba to confide in him about our doubts. He told us, 'What you have thought is correct. The Koran is true, but the interpretations of the mullahs are false, and the traditions for the most part are inventions. No one can go to Paradise through washings and fixed prayers unless he finds a perfect leader. For without the help of such a leader no one can please God.' Then he turned to me. 'If you want to attain perfection, you must serve me. When you gain my favour through obedience, you will realise that my words are truth.' Then I decided to stay with him, and in order to please him, I married his deaf-mute sister-in-law who gave birth to you, my son. But the sheikh came down with a severe illness from which he died after years of suffering. Our hope also sank into the grave with him because we saw him in doubt on the threshold of eternity.

"After his death I got to know many dervishes, however, with them I found neither peace nor clarity. Then I met a saiyid who belonged to the Yologhli. After long conversations he told me this: 'It really is true no one can please God without the help of a leader, but this leader must be a descendent of Mohammed so he can be worshipped. All the interpretations of the mullahs and all the traditions are lies, but in the Koran it is written man should be worshipped.' (See the Koran, Surah 2:32.)[1]

"Then I became a Yologhli and wanted you to become one as well. On our journeys I sought to prepare you for this, but now I have turned back from it

---

[1] See Appendix J, Koran Passages 3. Trans.

completely because I have heard much evil about the adherents of this sect and have had bad experiences myself. I previously believed the society of these people was spiritual and holy, but now I have experienced that this is not so—what am I supposed to do now? The Sunni religion in which we were born is empty and dissatisfying; the teaching of the dervishes is false and deceptive; the teaching of the Yologhli is unclean. Through all this my unrest has only grown, and now I only have doubts about faith and religion. Now and then I think: perhaps man is no better than a plant and every religion is an invention of men, but this thought frightens me very much because I consider it utterly impossible that God, the prophets, and the Koran are lies.

"Now I still have one hope. I want to visit my friend, Saiyid Ismael; perhaps he can provide me with clarity. If I do not find it with him, then I will flee from all men.

"Do not expect anything of me; use your reason and live well."

It still hurts me today that I had not yet grasped the truth of our Lord Jesus Christ at that time, although I held the Gospel in my hands. My eyes were still covered.

Nevertheless, I said several times, "Father, let's read in this book and see what it teaches," but he was weary of all books and would not listen to my plea.

After talking for three hours we returned to the village. He said goodbye to me and made his way to Saiyid Ismael's, but after he had gone a part of the way, he came back. This was repeated five or six times so the people of the village came to see me and said, "Your father has gone mad."

I was very ashamed, went to him, and said, "What are you doing? You are making us a laughing stock. Either go on, or come to me." Then he became angry so I had to keep quiet. However, it all distressed me so much I began to cry. Then his tears also flowed.

"Do not cry, my son," he said, "I am going and will never come again. Do not be surprised about my behaviour. I do not know where or to whom I am supposed to go."

So he left me. I returned home without setting much store by his words. Nevertheless, I was very sad and only calmed down after several hours. One morning a messenger brought me the news that my father was lying sick in Bajavut and was asking for me. I hurried to him, but he said, "My son, I am not that sick, and I regret I have disturbed you in your work, but since you have come, take my books and write an amulet for me; perhaps that will make me better. Your breath will help me." I took the books and did what he wished. Then I asked him whether he did not want to come back to my home.

"No," he said, "I am doing well here. Come tomorrow with a horse; then we will ride to your place."

I was delayed in the village and did not return for two days. Then I learned that my father had died shortly after I had said goodbye to him and, according to the custom of the people, had been buried the next day. So I could only go and visit his grave and return home in tears.

CHAPTER 4
THE FIRST WRESTLING

After I had returned home from my father's grave, I opened the Gospel and read in the book of John. When the Yologhli who were in my home heard the "truly, truly" which Jesus directed at Nicodemus,[1] they said, "Jesus must have been one of us" because they call their teaching the "truth".

Then I began to read the Gospel carefully from the beginning. When I came to the twenty-second verse of the last chapter I would like to have known whether there was a book of the prophets. I also did not understand the words, "all things which are written through the prophets [about the Son of man] will be accomplished" (Luke 18:31).[2] In our books there are no similar prophecies about Mohammed; what is cited there, for instance, is indefinite and unclear. So I thought through what I read: I liked a large part of it very much; *some of it annoyed me* because it contradicted the ideas which up to then had been holy to me. When I read the seventeenth verse in the fifth chapter of Matthew's Gospel, I was very astonished there was supposed to have been a law before our law.[3] Our books state the law was given to Mohammed and with the appearance of the Koran the Gospel became invalid, just as in the past all earlier religious books lost their validity with the coming of the Gospel, but here Jesus says he had not come to abolish the law or the prophets. When I came to the seventeenth verse of the eighth chapter where the fifty-third chapter of Isaiah is quoted: "HE HIMSELF TOOK OUR INFIRMITIES AND CARRIED AWAY OUR DISEASES",[4] I was astonished about the expression, "he carried". I had to accept that the prophet had lived before Jesus. Then why did he not say, "He *will* carry"? But if he was supposed to have lived after Jesus, how could it then be written: "This was to fulfil what was spoken through Isaiah the prophet"? Then it struck me again how great Jesus must have been since the prophet was able to say, "*Our* sorrows".[5] The word "our" must indeed include all prophets since the speaker himself was a prophet. I thought a lot about this and came to the conclusion that this must either be the honest truth or a mistake came in while it was being copied. If this passage really is stated in the book of the prophets in this way, then it must be concluded from this that no man has been as great as this Jesus.

---

[1] See Appendix I, Bible Passages 4. Trans.
[2] See Appendix I, Bible Passages 5. Trans.
[3] See Appendix I, Bible Passages 6. Trans.
[4] See Appendix I, Bible Passages 7. Trans.
[5] See Appendix I, Bible Passages 8. Trans.

My thoughts were occupied for more than three days with this passage. How was this verse supposed to be understood, if it was written correctly? It must be accepted that the prophet had died before Jesus. Even if he himself was still living at the time of Jesus, other prophets had died before him. Jesus took upon himself the sorrows of the ones who lived in his time. What about the ones who died before him? Had Jesus existed once before that the prophet could say, "He took"? What kind of mystery lay in this verse? "O God, make this clear to me if a truthful way lies hidden in it, and let me see the book of this prophet, if it really does exist!"

At this time an Armenian came to our village from the village of Karahasan to buy buffalo steers. The people had told him, "Our *khoja*[1] has bought a Gospel."

When I heard that he was here, I took the book, went to see him, and asked him, "What do these words of the prophet Isaiah mean? Are they written in his book exactly as they are here?"

"Yes," he answered, "they are correct, but come to our village; my older brother is a priest and will be able to tell you much about these things."

After several days I rode to see this priest. He honoured me greatly, and in the evening began to tell me many stories about Adam and the Patriarchs, which I did not yet know. When I asked him about Christian prayer and worship, he answered, "You can hear that tomorrow at church, but of course our prayers cannot be said in Turkish." Then I asked him to say it so I could hear it. So I heard the Lord's Prayer[2] in ancient Armenian and wrote it down using Turkish letters. In this I was reminded how we also place such great importance on the fact that our prayers are spoken in the ancient Arabic dialect.

Later I asked him, "Where are the stories written which you told me? Is there a Turkish translation of them?"

He answered, "Certainly, they are written in the Old Testament. You will find them in the Turkish language at the same place where you bought this Turkish Gospel."

He also advised me to buy a whole New Testament since mine stopped with the Acts of the Apostles. Afterwards he began to curse the evangelical Armenians, and it became clear to me that I was dealing with two parties here. Then he began to sing the praises of the bishops and their vestments, the churches and images, the saints, ceremonies, etc. When I heard him talk in this way, I liked the man less and less and lost all confidence in the words he had spoken up to then.

The following day we went to church together, and I saw how the images were worshipped. After that, the priest began to commend the vestments and the church's splendour to me. Finally, I could not take his talk any longer and

---

[1] See Appendix B, *khoja*. Trans.

[2] See Appendix I, Bible Passages 9. Trans.

asked him, "Do you not have anything else to tell me? What worth does this splendour have? We have more of it. Why do you praise these things? I am not looking for splendour, but for truth."

He answered, "A hidden power lies within this splendour." Then he gave me two pieces of the host on which a cross was imprinted and said, "Eat one piece; take the other with you and lay it down in front of you when you pray, make the sign of the cross, and in ancient Armenian say, "hanun Hor yev Vorto yev Hokuin Srpo" (which means: 'in the name of the Father and of the Son and of the Holy Spirit'). Fast two times a week; then you will see what power lies in these things." Although it had left me with an unfavourable impression and I had almost lost my delight in the Gospel, naively I decided to follow his advice in order to see whether he was right or not.

Several days after I had returned to my home, an evangelical Armenian trader came with whom I began to dispute about religion. I asked him, "Why do you not believe in the Koran and in Mohammed? We believe in the Koran as well as in the books that had come before, and in Mohammed as well as in earlier prophets."

He answered, "Please listen to me. I will pose some questions to you, and I only ask that you answer honestly. A man demands from someone a thousand [German] marks which he claims to have loaned him. The other man says, 'You have given me nothing, and I do not have to pay you anything.' How will the judge adjudicate when these men bring their case before him?"

I answered, "A just judge will ask the giver of the money for two witnesses or a promissory note."

"Fine," the Armenian said, "but if he does not have a promissory note or any witnesses?"

"Then the judge will say that the man can demand nothing without proof and will send both of them away."

"Fine, but what can the judge do, if the plaintiff really had given the money, admittedly, without asking for a promissory note?"

"What are you saying! In the first place, according to the law the judge can in no way believe the man is in a position to demand anything without a promissory note and without witnesses; and in the second place, the giver of the money deserves to lose it if he really was so careless. In this case the judge has done nothing wrong."

"Well, so it is also with Mohammed and the Koran on the one hand, and Jesus and the Gospel on the other. Mohammed and the Koran claim to be true; Jesus and the Gospel say the same of themselves. If witnesses or a note are demanded from both sides, Jesus points to the Gospel as the note and to Moses and the prophets as witnesses. Take the books of Moses and the prophets, read them, and compare them with the Gospel so you see whether or not they testify of Jesus. Now if witnesses and notes of proof are required from the Koran and Mohammed, the answer one gets is: I had them in the books of Moses and the prophets, but the Jews and the Christians stole them.

Who will we now admit to being right, if we place ourselves in the position of that judge? Do we not have to admit that the one who has the witnesses and the note of proof is right? How can we believe God will leave His own case without witnesses and proofs? Think justly!"

When our discussion was over, I considered everything carefully and came to this conclusion: in truth, the Christians will stand justified before God on Judgement Day. For the judgement of God is just as He Himself is just. The ones who follow the Gospel can then say, "O Lord, we have seen in the world that only the Gospel had testimonies for itself in the books of the prophets and of Moses which proved it was connected with the earlier books and is of divine origin. But the Koran had no proofs and claimed that they were stolen from it. Why, O almighty and just God, could we not see those testimonies and proofs for Mohammed, if You really had put such things in Your holy books? Are they destroyed as the Koran says? Who would have been capable of taking them away against Your will, if they really were Your testimonies? If You have allowed the testimonies which referred to Mohammed to be lost, what could we do then? How could we believe in a thing contrary to right and reason, having no evidence, since we ourselves testify You are wise and just and require it of men that they also judge sensibly and fairly? Can Your righteousness allow You to condemn us for what we could not believe, what had no reasonable and just proof, since You Yourself have given us good sense?"

I told myself as well that if someone in such a case were innocently punished, this suffering would be better than the happiness by which he could come to accept a teaching which conflicts with all reason and justice.

Why am I not supposed to read the Gospel? Why not explore whether and by what means its truth is proven? Why not compare ours and the Christian religion, one with the other?

After this, I began to read the Gospel with new eagerness. I read both in private as well as before the eyes of men and was so totally fond of the book that I took it with me wherever I went. Whenever I went for a walk in the area around the village, I always had it with me, and by reading it my enthusiasm grew for the ethics and divine demands of Jesus who requires our perfect love just as He sacrificed Himself for us and loved His own to the end. Then my conscience trembled because I understood the demands of Jesus more and more as orders which were also issued to me, like Matthew 11:28: "Come to Me, all who are weary and heavy-laden, and I will give you rest."[1]

About prayers in the biblical sense I still had no idea. Whenever my heart was especially filled by the influence of the Word, I read the Lord's Prayer according to the priest's words in ancient Armenian as I had written it down using Turkish letters, for the desire to pray came to me as soon as I became engrossed in the Scriptures. Of course, to read the Lord's Prayer in a

---

[1] See Appendix I, Bible Passages 10. Trans.

language unknown to me could not afford me any satisfaction, but whenever I read Jesus' words in the sixth chapter of Matthew's Gospel: "Pray, then, in this way" and after that the Lord's Prayer in Turkish, even then I was not satisfied because I thought a proper prayer must not be said in a common, intelligible language. Therefore, it seemed to me like only half a prayer, but later when I understood the compassion of God, it became clear to me that the Holy Spirit at that time was already interceding on my behalf with inexpressible sighing, just as the apostle says.[1] For I remember exactly that from my heart prayers and petitions ascended without my lips finding the words since I did not have any idea how I should pray. The Holy Spirit spoke on my behalf and came to help me in my weakness. I sighed from my heart, "O Lord, give me spirit and truth, for I am ignorant and blind."

---

[1] See Appendix I, Bible Passages 11. Trans.

CHAPTER 5
LIGHT AFTER THE DARK

So I read the Gospel from beginning to end for the second time and then carried on with the Epistles. I cannot describe what joy and love filled my heart as I read the first chapters of the Letter to the Romans because through them I became completely convinced that Jesus is the Son of God. Indeed, if many clever and learned men would have tried to convince me, it would have been impossible for them to affect me as profoundly as the words of Romans 1:3-4[1] did. For through these words God gave me faith and through them my heart learned of the power of God. When I had finished reading Paul's letters I was sad because I would have loved to have had even more of them. I did not know whether I was happy about what I had read or whether I was saddened because I had nothing more of his to read. I soon thought, "O how sweet it was, what I have read!" and then again, "Ah, it is finished." So my heart was divided between joy and sorrow. I consoled myself that it was not finished since I still had the book in my hand. Then I pressed the book to my lips, kissed it again and again, opened it up, read what was in it over and over, and said, "What shall I do? Shall I eat you, O Book?"

In this joy I continued to read all the way to the end of the book of Revelation. By reading this book I gained a lot because as I read about the throne of God, the images appeared in my mind's eye, and I believed everything from my heart; it was so new and unexpected. It was the first time I received an impression of the glory of God, and my heart spoke, "O Lord, my Creator, now I believe You have loved me, for You have given me this book. I believe this is Your true way and ask You: make me steadfast in this way. My spirit does well to believe this. Why should I look for another way for my spiritual life? Up to now my spirit has not found such a perfect peace in anything as it has in this faith. How this book has satisfied my soul, and I have much more spiritual food to look forward to! Therefore I want to follow You alone, O Jesus, Son of God, whatever may happen. I believe You are my mediator and will not let me go astray. Even if You should send me to Hell, nevertheless, I would obey You and worship You. My body and spirit shall be a sacrifice to You. I only ask You for strength to understand Your commandments correctly."

During that time I read the piece of burnt paper on which the young teacher, Petros, had written for me: "We believe in one God——", and then

---
[1] See Appendix I, Bible Passages 12. Trans.

further separate disjointed bits of the confession of faith. This aroused my attention, and I wondered what they might mean.

I wrote a letter to Mr Sevortian and asked him to send me a complete Bible so I could read the book of the prophet Isaiah. I wanted to compare it with the Gospels in order to be quite convinced they agreed. I enclosed the half-burnt pieces of paper and asked him to complete the words for me and to hand them to my messenger along with the Bible.

Around this time I moved from the village of Bajavut to Saribaba, which was two (English) miles away. Although I had to look after both of these villages as their teacher and preacher, it was better for me to live in Saribaba since I had more pupils there than in Bajavut. The pir Ali Beg also agreed to this change. I was barely at my new place of residence when tax officials came to the village. When they saw the Gospel in my room, they began to quarrel with me. "Is it right for you to be reading this book?"

When I asked after the reason for their reproach, they answered, "In this book it is written, 'Son of God', and that is a blasphemy."

I explained to them it was not meant as we had understood it, and I began to explain the Word to them to the best of my ability. They were people who thought a lot of themselves and so were not very easy to convince. But when they saw they were not able to argue against the truth, they said the Gospel was Greek and it could not be translated. To my claim that this book was translated from the Greek text, they answered, "No one understands ancient Greek. The Gospel could not possibly agree with this book." With mocking words they left me.

I then waited anxiously for my Bible, but instead of the book I received this answer: it would be better if I came to the city myself to get the book. Since the letter was written in good Turkish and most Armenians write very poor Turkish, I believed the letter came from an Islamic mullah who perhaps had read the Gospels and the books of the prophets as I had done. In order to come to know the writer of the letter, I decided to travel to the city.

Meanwhile, because a man had recently been murdered on the road to Erzerum, my people tried to stop me going, asking me rather to wait until some of them would be making the same trip. But my heart could not wait. That very evening I set off on my journey. On the way I considered whether I should not go to the village of Karahasan where my acquaintance, the Armenian priest, lived. He had invited me to come and see him again and promised to recommend me to the bishop who would answer my questions better than he had done. I was somewhat undecided, so I sat down on the side of the road, opened up my Gospel, and hoped God would show me through His Word whether I should go to see the priest or go straight to the city. I no longer remember the passage that I read, but it became quite clear to me I must go to the city without delay. Since at this time I was a little afraid to go alone, I asked God to let the trip be a success, if it be according to His will. My heart still entertained some doubts about the passage in Isaiah, and I wanted to have clarity about it before I died.

"God, send me a travelling companion for my safety," I thought. "Certainly to die for the sake of the faith cannot be difficult. If I am supposed to be killed on this trip, I ask that it would not happen in vain."

With such thoughts I came to Askala and called on a friend at his home. I had barely arrived there before twelve people whom I knew came. A gendarme was taking them to the city to be interrogated since it was claimed that the murderer was from their village. So now I had many travelling companions, but on the way, when I spoke with them about the Gospel, they showed me the profoundest contempt.

On arriving in the city I proceeded to Sevortian's shop and asked after the man who had written the letter to me. "You will find him at the school where he teaches," Sevortian said, "I want you to take along a message for him." As he was speaking, a rich Muslim came and joined him, so he said, "Come back a little later."

I came back for a second and even a third time but to no avail because the Muslim was still there. Finally I asked Sevortian whether he had written the message. The Muslim was curious and wanted to know what it was about, but he received no answer. After he had finally left, Sevortian wrote a short message and gave it to me. I went to the Protestant school and found a teacher there by the name of Sarkis [Effendi Kasabian] who turned out to be the writer of the letter. When he found out who I was, he was very glad and took me to his room where we talked alone with one another for a long time. He, who had learned from Jesus, was very patient with me and lovingly tried through the Word of God to remove any areas of uncertainty that I had. For my whole way of thinking and of expressing myself was like all of my behaviour: still like a Muslim and not suited to a Christian. Finally brother Sarkis read one chapter of the Scriptures in Turkish, and then we stood up to pray, but what kind of prayer was this! My heart melted and my body began to tremble, but my spirit was full of joy as he prayed to God for me, fervently and full of faith: "O God, wash this young brother with the blood of Jesus and guide him by the truth and by your Holy Spirit, until he finds his portion, that perfect peace."

After Sarkis had stopped praying, I said to myself he was a holy man and fell at his feet because I did not know what I should do. He lifted me up, grasped my hand, and said, "Brother, I do not despise the love you have in your heart, but I want to show you something." Then he opened the Bible and read to me about Cornelius[1] and from Revelation about the angel who, when John wanted to worship him, rebuffed him with the words, "Behold, our worship and adoration belong to God alone!"[2]

In the course of the conversation I then asked the teacher, "I have found

---

[1] See Appendix I, Bible Passages 13. Trans.
[2] See Appendix I, Bible Passages 14. Trans.

nothing in the Gospel about ceremonies and worshipping images. Why do I see images in your churches? It worries me very much." He smiled a little, although it was apparent the question hurt him.

"All those things are errors, contrary to God's will," he said. "Attend to the testimony of the Scriptures." Then he showed me everything the Bible says about it. Afterwards I told him about my conversations with the Gregorian priest, and he explained to me various things. In the end we spoke about the books, and he invited me to come that evening with Master Garabed, at whose home I was staying, to Baron Sevortian's shop. There he would buy the necessary books with me.

We met, as arranged. I noticed Sarkis wanted to keep our conversation a secret, so even I kept quiet about it. When Garabed heard that I wanted books worth thirty *piastres*,[1] he said, "Give them to him tomorrow; I will pay for them." In fact, he owed me a Turkish pound. In the morning when I appeared in the shop to fetch the books, Sarkis and Sevortian asked me just to pay the money myself as it would be difficult for them to get the money from Garabed later.

When I spoke with Garabed, he tried to persuade me not to take the books with me right away. He preferred to send them to me and he even thought it would be possible for him to get them without paying any money. I became angry and said, "It is indeed a shame to make a promise and not to keep it. Yesterday we told the people we would buy them, and today you are saying something different." Then I went to the shop and communicated Garabed's words to Sarkis and Sevortian. Sarkis asked me how much money I had with me. "Ten piastres," I answered. He said it would be enough and then took me along to see the American missionaries. They treated me with much love, and in spite of our short time together I felt I had come into contact with loving, Spirit-filled Christians. They led me to a room with numerous bookshelves along the walls and with me picked out the books I needed: a complete Bible, commentaries on Matthew and Mark, a book of Psalms in Arabic, a commentary on the Sermon on the Mount[2] and the Ten Commandments,[3] and a little book about evangelical doctrine. Later I received a Turkish hymnbook as a present from Hohannes Agha. Sarkis gave the missionaries my ten piastres, and when I asked about the remainder of what I owed, they said I may accept the rest as a gift from them.

On the way back Sarkis said, "We need several days together in order to be able to talk thoroughly about everything."

I saw his intention was to persuade me and thought, "He is a learned man who could overcome me by his eloquence so I would not know how to answer him, while the truth could indeed be on my side. To be sure, I love the Gospel

---

[1] See Appendix B, *piastre*. Trans.
[2] This is a collective name for chapters 5 through 7 of Matthew's Gospel. Trans.
[3] See Appendix I, Bible Passages 15. Trans.

and would not like to have any other faith than the one that is there. But I do not know what is written in these books and must first see whether their contents agree with its words." If I were to talk the man around to my way of thinking, I was afraid I would become more set in my religion, while the truth could be on his side. So I avoided this conversation.

I knew Garabed would prevent me from taking the books with me. Therefore I spoke once more with Sarkis about it. I intended to give evasive answers when Garabed addressed me and to take the books with me. That is to say, up to that point I had not dealt with the truth in a very exact way since for the Muslim the white lie is allowed. But Sarkis told me, "Our speech must at all times be so clear that not even the appearance of insincerity can be attributed to us." Then I was very ashamed of myself and made the resolution never again to speak what was not true.

In the evening I came to Master Garabed's house. He became very angry when he saw the books.

Since the next day was a Saturday, I wanted to spend the Sunday in the city in order to hear a sermon at the Protestant chapel just as Sarkis had advised me. On Sunday morning Master Garabed invited me to go to church with him. I agreed and attended the Gregorian church service with him. Afterwards we went together to the Protestant church where the preacher, Hagop Tashjian, preached in Turkish on Genesis 3:21.[1] After the service we three, Sarkis, Garabed, and I, stayed behind and spoke with the priest. The master, who beforehand had wanted to persuade me to leave the books behind, now also spoke with both of them about it, but they spoke Armenian, which I did not understand.

Finally the preacher told me, "The master does not consider it prudent for you to take the books with you. He prefers to forward them to you because he thinks it could be dangerous for you, if the books were found on you, a mullah. They would continue to delve, and it might become dangerous not only for you but for all of us. I am also of the opinion that it is better to leave them here, and I think the master speaks with good intentions."

I did not answer him but secretly asked Sarkis for his opinion. He answered, "Take the books with you. Whatever God's will is, so it will happen. We must be ready even to shed our blood for Jesus' sake." Since his words agreed with my desires, I did as he advised me, went back to my village, and began to read my books.

At that time I had about twenty pupils and lived in the home of Saiyid Hasan who, like my former landlord Ali Beg, was the pir of the village. At that time he was about thirty years of age.

I began to speak with him about the books I was reading. He was full of enthusiasm to hear about them and to dispute with me and asked among other things, "We say, 'Ali is God'. Are you saying that Jesus is God?"

---

[1] See Appendix I, Bible Passages 16. Trans.

"Yes," I answered, and went on to ask, "How do you come to know that Ali is God?" Actually, I knew the teachings of the Yologhli better than the majority of them.

He replied, "Ali performed miracles and raised the dead as you yourself know all too well from the books."

I said, "I have certainly read he raised the dead, but he had to ask God beforehand. However, Jesus gave the command and the dead got up." I tried to make this clear to him in various discussions we had, and after some time he was convinced.

At this time the Armenian priest visited me. He knew I, as a mullah and a representative of the government, had to supervise the delivery of the taxes, which consisted of the tithes on all agricultural crops. He took advantage of this to request one or two cartloads of hay from me. I remained silent—on that day he was a guest in our village. When evening came I went to speak with him. He began to talk about the sin of David against Uriah,[1] which at that time I had already read about. When he told how the prophet Nathan came to see David in order to reproach him for his sin,[2] I said, "*Kaeshish* ('priest'), I must ask you something. In a village there lived a man who knew very well the commandments of God and his duty to obey them. However, in another place lived a man who knew little of the commands of God and of obedience towards those commandments. The ignorant one wished to learn from the knowledgeable one. What then is the duty of the one who has much knowledge?"

He answered, "He must instruct the ignorant one, both in word as well as in deed."

I said, "Then if that one who knows much, instead of warning the ignorant one of his sins and teaching him the way of righteousness, urges him to sin for the sake of profit?"

Quickly the priest answered, "Then he is accursed of God."

He did not understand I meant him because he had asked me to supply him with hay in an illegal manner. So I said to him, "Please, think about it a little."

Then he answered, "The story is similar to the one of David and Nathan."

When I saw he had understood me, I left him and went home. He did not ask me for hay again.

On another day I saw the same Gregorian priest in the village wandering from house to house telling fortunes. I went after him and asked him, "Priest, do you not fear God? Sorcery is called a great sin throughout the whole of Scriptures. How are you then allowed to practise magic?"

He was startled but quickly composed himself and answered me with a smile, "What shall we do? We have to live too." From then on any association between us stopped.

---

[1] For this story see the Bible, II Samuel, chapter 11. Trans.

[2] For this story see the Bible, II Samuel, chapter 12. Trans.

I read continually in the Scriptures, thought about each passage I did not understand, and implored God to explain it to me. The Lord helped me and gave me understanding. My constant prayer was, "Lord, show me the truth and give me grace to grasp it and to abide in it, so I may praise You forever. Grant it to me that I might come to where Your people are. As You called Abraham, so he left his home and followed You, so also show me the way I should go. I am ready to leave everything and follow after You. I only ask of You that You would give me strength to stand when men ridicule, persecute, or kill me for the sake of the Gospel. I will gladly suffer, only give me strength to stand that I will not be put to shame before You."

CHAPTER 6

MULLAH AND CHRISTIAN?

Soon after, I began to tell my pupils about Jesus, that is, the ones who were able to understand. One 14-year-old boy named Kaya was especially attentive. I gave him the New Testament through which I had first seen the light, spoke and prayed with him a lot.

As I went on in this way, the people of the village took offence and began to speak ill of me because I kept the Sabbath holy and refrained from performing the *azan* (the mullah's call to prayer from the *minaret*, which occurs five times a day) or had my students perform it. I also no longer wrote amulets for the sick as is customary for Muslim priests. As well, regardless of where I was, I prayed before each meal with my head uncovered. Added to that, I preached the gospel to the people. All of this made them angry, but they could not dispute with me since they were uneducated people. On the other hand, Saiyid Hasan was quite in agreement with me and believed what I told him. He no longer wanted to take the tithes from the people to which the saiyids are entitled within the Yologhli community, but he taught, "The saiyids have no power to forgive sins, therefore you should not bring them any tribute." That is to say, the saiyids claim they can forgive sins.

At that time two saiyids came to the village in order to extort money from the people. However, Saiyid Hasan said to them, "Go! What right do you have to rob the people?" and drove them from the village with curses and swearing, for it is the custom of the Yologhli to curse, and Saiyid Hasan did not yet have enough understanding to recognise it as being wrong. Soon after that, guests from the city came to Saiyid Hasan's home, another saiyid and a man by the name of Ishmael Efendi, the son of a famous writer in Erzerum. Soon the three men were engrossed in a conversation about religion.

Saiyid Hasan said, "Our mullah understands many such things; he will come and answer you."

I was called, and Efendi, with whom I was already acquainted through my father, asked me, "How do you think we attain salvation?"

"If you want to know that, then let's read the Gospel; we will then see how things stand."

"The Gospel is incorrect."

"Your father wrote about the Gospel of John in his great work and praised it as correct and true. Do you now want to deny what your father has said?"

"No, I said nothing against the Gospel of John."

His father was held in high regard among the Yologhli because he had composed many spiritual songs for them. It is very curious that he named John in his book and praised his Gospel.

Efendi later asked me, "What does the Gospel teach?"

I began by saying, "Salvation is found in Jesus alone because He has offered Himself as a sacrifice." Then I went on to speak about the Ten Commandments.

He said, "Our way is *ael aelae ael haqqa*, hand in hand and hand to God", that is to say, our hand must be in the hands of the saiyids, so we obtain salvation through them, but the hands of the saiyids are in the hands of God.

I read to them in Arabic the words of the psalm, "If the godless also go hand in hand, they will not remain unpunished", and translated these words into Turkish. Then they kept quiet. For in their superstitions they thought each Arabic word came from the mouth of God. We also spoke of the teaching of the transmigration of souls in which the Yologhli believe, whereas they deny the Last Judgement and the resurrection of the dead. The Lord also helped me in this, so they could not answer me. Saiyid Hasan's faith was strengthened more and more.

After several days another saiyid came to the village. He threatened me with scornful words, but my spirit was cheerful.

Not far from the village was a cave into which I went every evening to read the Scriptures and pray to God there in private.

"I thank You, Heavenly Father, that You have had mercy on me and have shown me Your holy Scriptures, so I understand perfectly You and Your Son, the Lord Jesus Christ, by whose blood alone is there cleansing from sins. I now stand alone before You and ask of You that You make propitiation for my sins, O Lord, although I am very sinful. Whenever I regard my sins, I doubt whether or not You will accept me. But Your Word says, 'the one who comes to me I will certainly not cast out.'[1] Therefore, O Lord, give me grace that I will believe completely in this Word, which contains my deliverance. I believe salvation comes from You, but Satan confuses me with doubts, saying, 'Will Jesus accept you since you once spurned God?' I ask You, Lord, protect me from the evil one, from all sins, and from the impurities of youth. You know many temptations surround me in this land and some want to confuse me, but O Lord, as You kept Joseph, so keep me too. Father, You know how little of Your Word I yet understand, how many passages are still unclear to me. I ask in the name of Your only begotten Son that You give me Your Spirit, the Spirit of wisdom, so I can have a good understanding of Your book, which I love. I ask You, Lord, that Your kingdom would soon come and the righteousness, which is fulfilled through the Lord Jesus, would be accepted by all men, but especially by our people. I thank You that You have given me the spirit of forgiveness, so I can forgive all who despise and hate me, indeed, so I can love them. I ask You, have mercy on them, so they will

---

[1] See Appendix I, Bible Passages 17. Trans.

understand what they do and turn back to the Lord Jesus; for Yours is the kingdom and the power and the glory! Amen. In all of this let Your will be done, Lord, for perhaps I do not even understand what I pray, but You know best what is necessary. Therefore grant this to me in the name of Jesus. Amen." That was the content of my daily prayer.

Autumn was drawing near.

Usta Garabed came to the village in order to speak with the Armenian who was attending to his businesses there. He wronged the poor man by giving him no share of the profit, but said, "Such men like you only deserve two ghrish (*piastre = Turkish coin*) a day. You have eaten and drunk here for such a long time that you have already consumed more than you are worth; nevertheless, I will to give you something."

When the poor man saw that an injustice was being done to him, he said, "I will take nothing from you!" and went away crying.

Before leaving, Usta Garabed said to me, "Now we ought to see about getting you married." I said it would be better if we left it for this year. "Why?" he said, "you are healthy, and if it is that you do not have any money on hand, then I will cover all the costs."

At first I kept quiet. But on another day I said to him, "Perhaps the marriage will make my love for Jesus grow cold."

He answered, smiling, "That is childish talk. I took you for an intelligent man. Seek only what is comfortable for your flesh. Who has brought news about the hereafter?" So he continued with his mocking words, which are not worth repeating here. When he saw that for the sake of the Gospel I had lost the respect the people had for me, he said to me one day at Saiyid Hasan's house, "How can you be so ignorant that the people now hate you! Why do you teach them the Gospel?"

I answered, "Do you not know how much the apostles were persecuted for Jesus' sake? Am I greater than they!"

"The apostles were stupid people. Do you want to be the same?"

Then I understood that this man was no Christian, but rather an unbeliever, and I forbade him to speak further. "Silence," I said, "I will have nothing more to do with you."

I then wrote a letter to Sarkis concerning my marriage and asked for his advice on this difficult question: "Here they want me to get married, but I am afraid it will then become with me as with the seed that fell amongst the thorns."[1]

He answered, "I think so too. If it is possible, let this year go by; then we will see what the Lord will do."

Gradually it became clear to me that as long as I stayed in the village, my conscience would not leave me in peace. Therefore I decided to leave.

I gave my Bible and some other books to the Armenian whom Garabed

---

[1] This is a reference to the Parable of the Sower; see Appendix I, Bible Passages 18, 19, 20, and 32. Trans.

had treated in such a bad way and told him he should take them secretly to Sarkis. Indeed, I impressed upon him not to speak with Garabed about it.

At this time Garabed set off on horseback with Saiyid Hasan to the neighbouring town of Askala. At first Saiyid Hasan had refused, but Garabed knew how to persuade him. They were barely a quarter of an hour away when the news came: Saiyid Hasan had fallen with his horse and was fatally injured. He was brought back to the village on a cart; his spine was broken. When I went to see him, he opened his eyes and looked at me. I said, "Believe in Jesus." He answered, "I am dying now—I am sorry that my wish has not been fulfilled, but pray for me."

When he heard his relatives say that Usta was to blame for his misfortune, the good Saiyid Hasan opened his eyes, called those standing around nearer to himself, and said, "Listen and be witnesses to my words. Garabed has done nothing to me. I galloped and fell. If you love me, do nothing to harm him."

After I had realised the right way was only in the Gospel, I soon considered it wrong to be always proclaiming the honour of Mohammed outwardly as a mullah, while I lived only for Jesus in private. It became clear to me that I could no longer perform the Muslim prayer rites with a clear conscience.

At first I found some relief by getting my grown-up pupils to do the prayers for me. However, I soon recognised that this too was not right. Then I gathered my pupils together, told them how I had found the Bible and realised that Jesus was the only Saviour. Then I explained the Gospel to them. They told their parents about this, and it resulted in great agitation in the village. The people came to see me and asked me for an explanation. "Why do you not do your duty? You are our priest." I answered they must look for another priest for themselves because I could no longer perform their religious services.

To their question, why did I want to resign from my office, I read to them from the Gospel and explained to them that until now we had been living in blindness and the Gospel must be the only guiding principle of our life and behaviour. Everyone was surprised at this. For some it pierced their hearts, but others became very furious and tried to create trouble for me. At that time I expected every day that the government would send people to have me arrested.

CHAPTER 7

NEW WAY IN THE NEW LIGHT

It was now very important for me to explore how things stood with my fiancée, whether I might hope she would believe in Jesus, for I could only take her with me as a fellow believer. I went to see her on several evenings because, in contrast to the Muslim women who are kept in strict seclusion, the Yologhli allow the betrothed to see and speak with one another in the presence of the mother-in-law. I went to a lot of trouble to convince her and make the matter clear enough to her so that she could form her own opinion. I then asked her, "Now what do you think?"

She answered, "Do you want to turn me into a *giaour* ('unbeliever')?"

"No," I said, "I do not want that. The situation is the other way around", and I continued with my explanations.

However, she did not agree with my words but only said, "I cannot leave my father's path."

"If you cannot leave it, then you must stay in it," I replied, "but I can leave everything, even you, for the sake of the love of Jesus."

When she heard this she said, "No, do not leave me. To whatever faith you belong, I will belong as well." However, it was quite clear to me she only said this for my sake without any conviction on her part.

I tried to explain the matter to her in another way, but the result was always the same. I was convinced that if she would not come for Christ's sake but only for my sake, she would soon start longing for father, mother, and home. The situation would have made my conscience uneasy. In addition, her father would immediately come after us. The police would always be hard on our heels, quite apart from the fact it would be quite a difficult and serious business to travel with a woman, especially in Asia.

Soon God gave me the opportunity I desired to leave my village. It is a part of the civil duties of a mullah to deliver the tithes the country dwellers owe to the Turkish government. As a rule several respected people go with the mullah to the city. The mullah then hands the money over to the government and receives a receipt for his village.

Along the way I decided not to go back, come what may. I hoped the Christians would look after me and with them I would have the opportunity to continue studying the Christian teaching and then to preach; that would have been a gift from God for me. If that did not work out, I wanted to take the Word of God and wander like a hermit in the mountains and preach in the villages until the end of my life. I thought I would go to warm regions in the winter and to cooler regions in the summer. I would sustain myself on the plants and fruits that are found in the mountains or in the fields. I had once lived like that for four days as a dervish when I was returning with my father from Mosul. At that time the Kurdish villagers had moved to the pastures with their herds, while the others had fled and hid from the tax officials. That is why during four days of travelling we found no people and lived on plants.

Several days after my arrival in the city, I heard that Saiyid Hasan had died. When I had gone to say goodbye to him before leaving the village, he once again had said to me, "It is a pity I can no longer live to work with you for Jesus, but pray for me that the Lord Jesus Christ will accept me."

In the city I was reunited with a childhood friend, a young Armenian by the name of Arshak who was born in my parents' neighbour's home. As children we had played a lot together and loved each other very much. At that time I would often try to win my small playmate over to the Muslim teaching. I still remember one of these childlike conversion attempts very well. Our neighbour's little son frequently played with me in our garden, and each time I used the opportunity to speak with him about the "true faith" and about the necessity of accepting it. One day, when I had again summoned up all my powers of persuasion, my little friend finally promised me he would become a Muslim. I was extremely delighted and declared to him we were now brothers. In the evening I did not let him go home but took him along to our house and enthusiastically told my aunt what had happened. Strangely enough she acted rather disapprovingly at the whole affair. As we were eating supper together the neighbour lady came to collect her little boy. I explained very firmly he belonged to us now and must stay at our home. When no one listened to me, I began to cry bitterly, but it all came to an end when the mother carried home this brother whom I had welcomed with such delight.

Now I could tell this friend I had read the Gospel and believed in Jesus. I myself was now a confessor of Jesus Christ.

The young man was very delighted and said, "This is a miracle of God! You will now be to the Muslims what John the Baptist was to the Jews. You will prepare them for Christianity."

His mother came in and called me by my Muslim name of Shükri. He then said, "Do not call him that. He will now be called John. He has become a Christian, and John shall be his name!"

The Lord had given me such a love and fervency that I feared nothing. I was still in my mullah's garb and came to the evangelical meeting dressed that way. When I saw the brothers removing their hats at the door, I took my turban off as well since I believed it went with the duties of that religion. When I went to the bazaar, I visited the brothers whom I had got to know at the meeting and spoke out loud with them about spiritual things. But it is not allowed to talk so openly there about the deity of Christ, and the Muslims gave me dirty looks from every side. As soon as one of them addressed me, I used the opportunity to preach the gospel. It went so far that the brothers finally asked me not to speak so freely of Christ with all the Muslims; much danger and difficulty could result from it for themselves and for me. But I was so taken up by it all that I thought neither about life nor about danger and death. I saw nothing but Christ and His love. "Will Christ accept me?" That was my only thought. My confidence was His promise: "The one who comes to me I will certainly not cast out." Of whom should I be afraid? My life might gladly be broken to pieces for Him. If I gave Him my life, what great thing did I do? Was He not the Lord of my life as in all things? He gave up His life to bring me, and other sinners like me, to God. Why should I spare myself and not give myself up for Him?

Almost every day I would go to the evangelical Armenian preacher and he would examine me. Once he asked, "Why do you not believe in Mohammed and in the Koran? The teaching of Mohammed is also a good religion."

"But it does not have its roots in the Bible," I answered. "In the Koran it is written the Gospel and the Prophets tell about Mohammed, but I have found nothing of this." Then I showed him the passages of the Bible, which I had compared with the Koran.

To his question, "Are you not afraid that the Muslims will find and kill you?" I answered, "If they kill me because of my faith in Jesus, then I am afraid of nothing. The apostles in their time were killed by the Jews."

Along with Sarkis I visited the American missionaries who had given me the Bible and declared to them I wanted to become a Christian, but both could hardly believe that I had been converted.[1]

To their question, why had I come to see them, I explained to them I wanted to learn everything necessary to understand Christianity and to study theology in order that later on I could take the gospel to the Muslims. They thought I could no longer stay in Erzerum and asked whether they should perhaps send me to Russia or Bulgaria. I left this question completely for them to decide. Afterwards they suggested to me that I feed their horses and take lessons with them two or three hours a day.

I agreed very heartily to this. After I had come to know the truth, God very soon took the pride out of my heart which I had as a Muslim who was descended from Mohammed himself.

On the other hand, Sarkis expressed his misgivings to the missionaries: "If the Muslims discover that a mullah is with you and is performing the work of a stable hand, the situation will only become more dangerous. No one will believe he has agreed to do this kind of work without ulterior motives, and that above all else will betray him. We know with what eyes the Gregorians look at us, how they are very much looking for reasons to have the Muslims

---

[1] Mr William N. Chambers' letter in the June 1882 issue of *The Missionary Herald* (p. 231) states: "The converted Moullah, [sic] about whom you have heard, is making good progress in study. He manifests a true spirit, and has gained the confidence and regard of all the brethren. He writes that it is his desire to preach to his people, and that he is ready to give his life for his Saviour who had done so much for him." Trans.

take us to court. This would be a welcome reason for them. Then the Muslims will see that what the Gregorians say is true, 'The Protestants have come not only to corrupt our religion but also to wreck yours.' Our meetings will be raided and much harm done to us."

They decided to send me to another city and said, "Go to the village of Chevermeh in Khynis and learn Armenian there. Then we will find a good college where we can send you."

They wrote several letters of recommendation for me, but when I wanted to be baptised in their meeting before my departure, they answered, "Wait; it is not yet time."

Sarkis said, "Go and be true in your faith; we will see what the Lord will do." They advised me to exchange my suit for Armenian clothing in a village before I arrived at my destination, and that I did.

I came to Chevermeh safely and was warmly received by the Armenians. The missionaries' fear, that I would be recognised as a Turk since I did not have the Armenian language mastered, proved to be groundless because in Khynis many Armenians are from Kaisarieh and they can only speak a little Armenian or even none at all.

I was given a new name. To my joy it was the name *John*, which my childhood friend had also given me.

I spent half a year in this place, attending school every day and diligently learning the Armenian language both through study and through contact with the Armenians.

At this point I must say that after my departure from Erzerum, Usta Garabed had come to see the brothers in the city and had asked about me, however, without getting a response. Then he had gone with two Turks to the Protestant school and had cunningly asked, "Where is Shükri? Please tell me. These two gentlemen owe him money and will gladly pay it back." Again no one had given him any answer. Then he showed his true character and exclaimed, "You Protestants have taken him away and now will not say where he is, but consider this: he was a mullah. You will not go unpunished when he is found. When I learn where he is, then you will see what happens to you!"

Incidentally, with my arrival at Chevermeh the preacher as well as the other brothers had very nervously expressed what was on their minds: "It will be dangerous for you as well as for us if you stay here. It will be better if you go to Kharput; there you will also have more opportunity to study." I therefore suggested to them to write to the missionaries since I had promised them to act according to their orders. They did this, however, the answer they received was to the contrary.

So I stayed in Chevermeh for six months as a guest at the home of a respected Armenian, Malo Agha, who was an evangelical, and I learned a number of things there. I saw brothers full of the power of faith but also such ones who astonished me by their weakness because I had come with the illusion that all those who accepted the Gospel had to be devoted and full of faith in the same way. Then I remembered Sarkis' words, "We must never be respecters of men. All men are liars; only God is true. We must look to Jesus for our example so as not to stumble." So I only had the Scriptures as my guide and eagerly strove to change in such a way, as Jesus requires it of us.

In these six months I learned to read and write Armenian, only I did not like to speak it because I did not speak it correctly.

At that time in the village many disputations took place between Gregorian and Protestant Armenians. In the house where I lived many people often gathered in the evenings and disputed for hours with one another. This was a good opportunity for me to perfect my use of the Armenian language.

After half a year the missionaries wrote to me: I should go to another village, Alashkerd. There I lived at the home of a preacher who at the same time was the teacher in his village; he was a very good man. In his school I continued to study Armenian and taught Turkish. In the autumn a teacher by the name of Gegham came there for the Gregorian Armenian school which was in that village. He had studied in a monastery and was very competent in the ancient Armenian language. He wished to learn Turkish from me, so we helped each other for seven months.

Around this time Usta Garabed, using his cunning, once again tried to discover where I was staying. He sent an Armenian to Sarkis and had him say he had been in the village of Perza on business. There a young girl had come to see him and had asked him whether he knew anything of her fiancé. She was ready to follow him and accept his faith. But Sarkis gave no definite answer, and when he wrote to me about it, I knew immediately it was only a fresh act of malice on the part of Garabed.

At that time I got to know an Armenian merchant from Bitlis who had previously been a Protestant. Since he had had to suffer much from the Gregorians, he had gone to the missionaries and asked them to obtain an order from the government, which was supposed to protect him from the Gregorians as well as from the Kurds. The missionaries could not comply with his wish and that made him so disgruntled he gave up his fellowship with the Protestants and in the end became their opponent. This man bought a mill in Alashkerd and asked me to draw up the contract for him, which I did, but after several days the former owner of the mill wanted to call off the purchase. When the case was brought before the *kadi*, he simply looked at the document and said, "The matter is in order and cannot be overturned." Then he asked who had written this contract.

Someone answered him, "A young man by the name of John."

The kadi said, "We do not have a capable clerk who knows his business. Call this man over, so we can employ him." An Armenian trader delivered the message to me, but I explained that I would not go. The Lord had called me for His Gospel. How could I become a co-worker of one who practised bribery!

Several days after this, the kadi came with his officials to my village on account of another trial. Since my host, the preacher, had the best house in the village, they took up official residence there. In the evening they asked about me: "A John lives here who can write well. Where is he?" I was called. I came, however, I answered his questions in a cautious manner. Then I fetched my Bible and read to them about the birth of Christ. I wanted to do my duty as much as I could and to testify to the truth. In response to what I had read, he said, "That is very beautiful!" or "That is what happened!" The other officials as well as the Armenians listened tensely. So we, the kadi and I, spoke a good two hours about Christ.

On the following day he travelled back again.

One day the Armenian bishop in Alashkerd invited me to his place and asked me to write a petition on the people's behalf. To be exact, the government had arranged to buy wheat for the army in the Armenian villages, however, without paying for it. After I had finished the petition, the bishop was very friendly towards me and asked me whether I would stay on as a teacher in the Gregorian school teaching Turkish. He would give me whatever I wanted in regards to salary. I answered, "The missionaries give me whatever I need at this time of persecution, and I go wherever they send me. If you obtain permission from the missionaries for me to accept this position, I will gladly do so." He thought that would be impossible, and I said goodbye to him.

Around this time I wrote to the missionaries and asked when they would be sending me to school in order to prepare me for service in the Lord's vineyard.[1] I received the answer: "Travel back to Chevermeh; there is a new teacher there, Garekin Chitjian. Continue your preparations with him until we find out where we can best send you. At the same time give a few Turkish lessons at the school. That is the brothers' wish."

So it happened. I returned to the village and found there the young Armenian teacher, Garekin Chitjian. He was actually a student at the American college in Kharput,[2] but since his health was shattered, he had been sent to the village to recover and instructed to give several lessons while he was there. We lived in one room and soon became close friends. He was also the one who gave me the name I currently have.

One day he told me, "If you no longer want to be a Muslim, you must also accept a second name like all Christians."

I answered him, "Then I want to be called *Abrahamian* (that is, 'son of Abraham') because I am Abraham's son through faith."

"No," he said, "you are Abraham's son according to the flesh; according to the Spirit you are the son of the Gospel. Therefore you shall be called *Avetaranian*!" ('son of the Gospel')

---

[1] This is a reference to Jesus' Parable of the Labourers in the Vineyard in the Gospel of Matthew. See Appendix I, Bible Passages 21. Trans.

[2] See Appendix B, Euphrates College. Trans.

After six months a messenger came from the missionaries and asked me to return immediately to Alashkerd.

So we had to say goodbye. We very rarely heard from one another from then on and only met each other again years later. Here I would like to say more about my friend's fate.

Garekin Chitjian possessed a keen intellect and a farseeing spirit. He was also a Christian with deep foundations and filled with a heartfelt love for his unfortunate people. After he had finished his studies in Kharput, he was sent as a preacher to an Armenian village. There he had several years of fruitful labour, but since he took an active interest in the political efforts of his people, he incurred the hatred and persecution of the Turks. His life was brought into serious danger and in order to escape his enemies, he emigrated to America, leaving his wife and children back in the homeland.

In America he was given the preaching duties at an Armenian evangelical church. From there he then tried to gather his people, who were like the scattered children of Israel, and through speaking and writing worked towards their restoration. For this purpose he published a periodical, *Voice from the Homeland*, which was widely read within the Armenian community in America and earned him the recognition and admiration of all fair-minded fellow Armenians.

After he had worked in America in this way for twelve years, he made his way to the meeting of a revolutionary Armenian committee in London. He even had his family come there. Addressing the committee, Chitjian very convincingly propounded his view that a liberation of the Armenian people could only be achieved peacefully by way of a moral reformation, but not by violent rebukes or tricks and betrayal. Since he was by far superior to most of his fellow Armenians in gifts of intellect as well as of sentiment, no one could refute him. Indeed, a large number of the committee members came over to his point of view, and he was appointed to work amongst the Armenians in every country of the world along the lines that had been expressed.

With this mission Chitjian first made his way to the continent of Europe. In all the cities where Armenians lived he gave addresses. He even called on some at their homes and challenged them to come together and work together for the welfare of their people.

In this way he even reached Bulgaria. When he heard I had established a field of work in Shumla, he came to see me, and once again we spent several days together in a lively exchange of mutual thoughts, memories, and interests. Even in Shumla he spoke repeatedly on behalf of the Armenians, and his serious, urgent, and passionate words found many enthusiastic listeners, but at the same time the voices of his opponents asserted themselves more and more staunchly. A revolutionary Armenian newspaper declared him an enemy of the people and uttered threats against him.

I recognised the danger he was in and asked him to withdraw from the struggle of political parties and, as a preacher of the Gospel, quietly serve his people. He admitted my fears were justified and promised to follow my advice. He still wanted to bring about the conference planned to take place in Tiflis. Then, he said, his national duty would be fulfilled. Giving up his public activity, he would then return to me to give himself completely to working with individual souls.

So with a heavy heart I let him go to Odessa where he intended to meet a co-worker. The committee wanted to put this co-worker, a bold, powerful man, alongside him for protection but had sent him straight to Odessa since no one yet feared any danger for Chitjian in the Balkans.

Right after my friend had left me, I learned that the Armenian was no longer in Odessa. However, a telegram relating to this fact, which I forwarded to Chitjian, did not reach him.

After some time, I received a letter from Odessa in which he communicated that his companion had been murdered in the Caucasus by the party hostile towards them and that his life was also surrounded by danger. But he considered it his duty not to save himself where he could be of use to his people.

After the arrival of this letter, some time passed without any further news. Then I learned that he too had been attacked and murdered on the street in Odessa by Armenian revolutionaries. He died a martyr for the cause of his people.

The Armenian people were in profound mourning for him. In the churches they held funeral services and in the papers of the day they lamented the early death of the man who would have been well suited to lead his people towards a better future. —

The messenger whom the missionaries sent to me had horses ready for himself and me, and we rode over the mountains to Alashkerd where I met two missionaries, Mr Hargrave and Miss Van Duzee. With them I went over the Persian border to Urumiah. The missionaries had given this order since they had heard that someone was looking to seize me. When I was safely over the border, the government telegraphed concerning me, but it was too late. In Urumiah I stayed forty days as a guest of the missionaries. In this city I found a fellowship of Muslims who believed in Christ. This was a great joy to me because up to that point I had not seen anything like it.

At the time of my conversion, Husain Aga, a Muslim who believed in Christ, had been murdered in prison, and almost at the same time in Stambul, twelve Muslim students who had gone over to Christianity were drowned in the Bosporus. Another Muslim, Ahmed Aga, had escaped to Bulgaria where his widow, Fatma, still lives today. I have visited her many times in Philippopolis.

I frequently met with fellow believers in Urumiah. We read the Scriptures and prayed together; a heartfelt love united us. Since then that fellowship has unfortunately been scattered by persecution.

The American missionaries had a college in Urumiah, and it was the intention of the American missionaries in Turkey that I should take the exam there. But after the missionaries there in Urumiah had consulted with one another, they said, "Mr Chambers wants you to study here. But the lessons here are taught in Syriac, and until now you have been learning Armenian. Much time will be lost if only now you start to learn Syriac. That is why we consider it better if you travel to Tabriz since the lessons there are in Armenian. You will learn the same things there as you can learn here and will reach your goal quicker."

Then I said goodbye to the brothers and went with Mr Whipple to Tabriz where Mr Wilson admitted me to the school. I studied for a year with the Armenian students who had come there from various villages in Azerbaijan.

CHAPTER 8
TRIALS OF FAITH

I had not yet been admitted through baptism into the wider community of the Christian Church. When I came to see the missionaries in Erzerum for the first time, my desire was to be baptised as I had read about in the Gospel, that is, I wanted to confess my faith in Jesus publicly through baptism. If the Muslims had seen it and heard it and seized me, that would have been all right by me. They could only kill the body, and my death would not have been in vain. Rather the Muslims, especially the ones who knew me from childhood, would have asked, "What kind of cause is this for which he has gone to his death?" If they did not kill me, I hoped to be able to work in the Lord's vineyard.

However, I did not achieve my objective, rather I found *that the missionaries did not take baptism as seriously as I did*. They were also afraid, although the Lord's command is: "Go and baptise."[1]

During my stay in Chevermeh and Alashkerd I read many writings about baptism, which for the most part held the view that baptism was only a symbol or a sign. However, they did not convince me since I had gained a different view from the Gospel. This view was that *baptism, for me and for everyone who is not born a Christian, is a confession of Jesus before men and an act of faith through which a person is received into the Kingdom of Christ.*[2]

In Urumiah the missionaries put me off by saying I could be baptised in Tabriz. When I spoke to them there about it, I was told, "In the past we baptised many (that is to say, in secret), but many lapsed back into their old ways. That is why we have made it the rule for those who desire to be baptised to wait a year. Although for you this is not actually necessary, we would really like to stick with our rule." Towards the end of the year I asked them again, but they said, "Now it will be hard to baptise you. The people

---

[1] See Appendix I, Bible Passages 22. Trans.
[2] In the August 1882 edition of *The Missionary Herald* (pp. 310-311), a letter dated 27 May 1882 from Mr W. N. Chambers in Erzerum states: "The High School, which was established in the village of Chevermeh a year ago, has been doing very good service. Scholars from other villages were in attendance, and it continues through the summer with very good prospects. It is in this village that Shukri Effendi [sic] — the converted Turkish Moullah [sic] — is staying. He has given very clear evidence of true conversion, and has gained the good-will and respect of all the village by his modest, and gentlemanly, and consistent conduct. He put in a strong request for baptism, and his views on the subject are remarkably clear. He is attending school, and makes good progress in the Armenian. He takes every opportunity of preaching to his countrymen, and, though by no means obtrusive or offensive to them, he himself works without fear." Trans.

either think you are an Armenian—then they will be astonished that you are being baptised—or they know you were a mullah. Then there will be difficulties, especially because you want to be baptised in public."

I now considered whether it would not be better for me to leave Tabriz, and to do this for various reasons. Our maintenance was very modest, one and a half *toman* per month. In German money that is about six and a half [German] marks.[1] We were supposed to live on the money I had to earn by doing all sorts of work in the house and around the grounds of the mission school. To be sure, I would have gladly endured all of this, though physically I had become very weak, if I had been able to learn more and be baptised in Tabriz. Since this was not the case, I decided to return to the missionaries in my home town and asked Mr Wilson to have his servant sort out a passport for me and, if possible, to help me with the fare. I was turned down since he wanted me to stay in Tabriz. When I saw that I was to expect no help from him, I sold my bedding, hired a horse in a caravan, and said farewell to the good missionaries. When I came to see Mr Wilson, he prayed with me. The pupils from the mission accompanied me a part of the way, and one of them by the name of Ghazar came with me outside the city where we said a tearful goodbye to each other. In the afternoon our caravan arrived in Khoi.

In Khoi I developed a high fever because of the intense heat but I could not stay there since I had hired the horse up to the border, and the money I had on me was not enough for me to take another one later.

So in spite of my high fever I travelled on with the caravan. My fellow travellers were Persian Muslims, Shiites who do not eat together with Christians since they consider them to be unclean. They would not even permit a Christian to drink from one of their containers. Everyone took me for a Christian, an Armenian, because I had mastered the Armenian language so well that none of the Muslims were able to suspect me of being a former fellow believer.

At night we always camped in the open country in places where the horses found good pasture. One night the Persians who were driving the caravan were talking near to where I was. They spoke about me in Persian, believing that I would not understand them.

"This infidel (*kafir*) is sick," they said, "he will die. Is there no one amongst us who will kill him and by it render service to God?"

They called me over and said, "You are sick, very sick, and will die. But we do not want you to go to Hell. If you will believe in Mohammed and in the Koran, you will go to Paradise. Will you or will you not believe?"

In a steady and determined manner I replied, "I believe in Jesus Christ who is sent by God as the Saviour of men, and in the Gospel which is the truth. If you want me become a Muslim, you must first prove to me that Mohammed and the Koran really are of God."

---

[1] Probably closer to ten German marks at that time. Trans.

A merchant travelling with us who had some knowledge of Islamic literature offered to supply me with the proof that Mohammed was the only true prophet of God, but I very soon succeeded in confounding his reasoning, so he realised he could not find me guilty. Finally he shouted angrily to his companions in Persian, "He is an infidel and wants to stay that way. He deserves the sword!" They sent me away, and I made my way back to the place where my things lay. There I prayed to God and entrusted my soul to him because I believed they would attack me in my sleep and kill me. I was much too sick to flee; I would not even have known where to go. I was not afraid of death, *but I was very sad that I had not received baptism and had not been able to carry out my plan to preach the gospel to the Muslims.*

The Persians then deliberated over which of them should kill me, and they divided my things amongst themselves in advance. I understood every word they said. One wanted my watch, another wanted my clothes, a third wanted my horse, and another one my money, for they assumed I was carrying a large sum.

That night a man by the name of Mahmud joined our caravan. He had hostile intentions towards the Persian drivers. They had robbed and killed an Armenian several years before on the same journey without handing over any of the loot to Mahmud. Now they were afraid that this time he could report them to the police and so did not risk killing me.

On the following day we rode on and passed through a place that was very dangerous due to the bands of robbers in the area. From a nearby village the Persian caravan drivers fetched two well-armed men who were supposed to take on the night watches. They then wanted to get these two men to kill me, but the two men refused, saying Mahmud would be just as likely to report them. So God protected me that night too.

On the following day we stopped a day's journey from the border. Now my fever became so severe that I lay unconscious for several hours. When I revived, I suffered from a terrible thirst but had no water. Although I was near death, the Shiites refused to give me anything to drink since I would have thereby polluted their containers. Then I asked them to pour some water from their jugs into my hands, so I would not need to touch the jug while drinking, but they became furious, called me a dog, and chased me away.

Half dead from thirst and weariness, I dragged myself into the field to look for water there, but to no avail. After half an hour, I was near to collapse. In my distress I wept and prayed the Lord's Prayer. Only God saw my tears. After the prayer, I received enough strength to be able to reach the next village. In the door of the first house stood a Muslim woman. I asked her to give me some sour milk ('yoghurt'), which I would pay for. She promised to do this and went into the house only to return immediately with two ferocious dogs that she set on me. I jumped back apprehensively. A man who was cleaning wheat nearby called me over and promised to give me some milk. When I went to him, he set a dog on me too, so I ran from there, pursued by evil beasts. Behind me I heard the loud laughter of the people who mocked me as an Armenian.

When I saw that I would receive neither water nor milk in this village, I wanted to drag myself back to the caravan. Then a woman called out to me; she would bring me some milk. Naturally I believed she would do as the others, so I carried on, but she called me once more and swore she wanted to give me some milk. After a short time, she actually came to me with a container full of sour milk.

When I offered her money, she declined it, saying, "My brother is also in a foreign land; perhaps it is with him as it is with you." She suggested I take the milk to the caravan camp. When I told her I would not be able to bring the container back, she said her husband could collect it in the evening.

After I had quenched my burning thirst, I returned to the caravan invigorated and slept the whole night through. I had a wonderful dream and awoke fit, without a trace of the fever.

At the border I parted from the caravan and went to Alashkerd where I had been a year earlier. From there I went to Erzerum and paid a visit to the missionaries. They wanted to know how I had fared in the meantime, and I reported everything. To their question, whether I had been baptised, I answered I did not desire a baptism done in secret and had found no one who would risk baptising me in public. We spoke for an hour about the question of baptism; I told them on which quotations in the Scriptures my conviction was based, but when I saw that they too would not baptise me in public, I went to see a Baptist missionary. He tried to prove to me that baptism was not for children, rather only for adults. To my objection that this issue really did not need to create any problems for us, he said, "If you were to be baptised by us, we would send you to Stambul to study theology." This suggestion was in accordance with my wishes, but since he likewise did not dare baptise me in public, while it appeared very essential to me to confess my faith publicly, we could not agree.

I then returned to my old friend who suggested I travel back to Alashkerd where previously I had spent a year. I was supposed to hide there until they sent me news concerning which higher-level mission school I could attend.

I gladly went along with their advice and travelled to Alashkerd, but I was scarcely there a couple of days when a Kurd by the name of Kassim Bey came by chance to the preacher's home where I was a guest. He recognised me and told me the police would come after me. The joy of the man in having discovered me was great because naturally he himself intended to report me immediately to the authorities. Fortunately his intellectual ability was quite limited, so he was not able to conceal his plan from us.

On the same evening I received a letter from the missionaries, in which they advised me to escape to Russia as quickly as possible.

Crossing the border was a difficult matter for me since I lacked a passport. However, God worked it out in such a way that an Armenian border guard just happened to be paying a visit to his relatives in Alashkerd that night. At the preacher's request he offered to take me along secretly over the Russian border.

With the help of God this dangerous business was successful. Arriving in Russian territory, I hired a horse to Karakala, which is near the fortress of Kars. The missionaries had, as I knew, written two letters of recommendation on my behalf: one to Karakala and the other to Erivan. In Karakala I was warmly received. The Armenian evangelical brothers praised the grace of God towards me and did not tire of having me preach the gospel to them. I stayed with them for about ten days and was then sent to Erivan accompanied by one of the evangelical Armenians since it was not safe for me in that small village.

In Erivan there lived a converted Armenian brother, Daniel Bey, who held a high-level government post. He received me into his house with great joy and with loving care provided me with a home. In his outward appearance he was quite exceptional: big and imposing with lively, beautiful eyes and a piercing gaze. Above all, he was a loving, gentle child of God. It was a joy for him to see Christian guests in his home, and he did much good through his open hand and his open heart. The meetings were always at his home, and he himself was a preacher of the word without having been appointed to it by men.

I stayed with him for fourteen days and received much blessing from this time. In the afternoon, when he returned home from work, we had long conversations together, and he did much to instruct me. Through him I heard many things that no preacher had as yet told me. He read to me from all sorts of religious writings, and his prayers and songs were a tremendous refreshment to me.

He advised me to go to Tiflis and call on a friend whom he had known from his youth in Shusha, the evangelical Armenian preacher Abraham Amirkhaniantz. At that time he was occupied with translating the Bible into Ararat Armenian, which had been commissioned by the British and Foreign Bible Society.

It was winter when I came to Tiflis. Since I was a complete stranger there, I went to a café with an Armenian whom I had got to know on the way. After warming myself with a glass of tea, I left my things and called on the British Bible depository where I was supposed to find out Amirkhaniantz's address.

It was New Year's Day; the depository was closed, and I heard it would only be open again in three-days' time. So I returned to the café and asked whether I could sleep there. The response was I might do so if I could produce a passport. Since I did not have one, I went into the city in the hope of finding other accommodation. I saw many people all hurrying in the same direction and followed them. I came to a big Armenian church where the liturgy had just been sung in ancient Armenian. In front of me stood a youth who looked familiar to me. I leaned forward a little in order to see his face. Then he also looked at me, recognised me immediately, caught hold of my hand, and went outside with me. For eight months we had attended the school in Tabriz together and we were very happy to see each other again. When I told him I was without a passport and had no place to live, he advised me to fetch my things from the café. Then we went to the Asian quarter of the city to look for an apartment for me in the caravansaries.

The young man, a Gregorian, would liked to have brought me to his parents' home, but just that day the police had imposed a strict ban. According to this ban, no one must be admitted without a passport. We roamed from one caravansary to another but were turned away everywhere. Finally my companion left me to get his father. His father arranged for the porter of a caravansary to admit me; he would accept responsibility if it resulted in any damage. I received permission to stay there a couple of days, but it could not be for long. I was brought to a room in which no one could live: the walls were full of holes through which the wind whistled in, and neither stove nor bed, neither chair nor table, were to be found there. The young man got a blanket for me from his apartment, and I wrapped myself up in it at night. My few books made up my pillow. For five kopecks I bought an earthenware bowl in which I placed a few glowing embers to warm my hands.

The following day I went out to inquire about Pastor Amirkhaniantz's address. In the street I met an Armenian whom I asked for information. He said, "What do you want with him? Have you become a Protestant as well?" He took me for an Armenian. "I will be passing by his house," he added coolly, "if you want to, then come with me." It was a long way to my destination, and on the way he began to scold me.

"Why have you forsaken the religion of your people? Why have you become disloyal to your nation? Amirkhaniantz is a deceiver. What can you learn from him?" I let everything that he said simply wash over me just to get on and was happy when I reached Amirkhaniantz's house.

A servant opened the door to me, and I was announced. I found Pastor Amirkhaniantz in his study and greeted him in Armenian. He asked me, "Who are you? What do you want?"

I said, "Has Daniel Bey not written to you about a mullah who was supposed to be coming here?"

"Yes," he said, "but what does that have to do with you?"

"I am he."

"You, a mullah? Are you not ashamed to be lying to me in this way? I have no time to speak with deceivers. Go!" I tried to say a few more words to him, but he did not want to listen and showed me to the door.

As I was a few steps away from his house, his servant came running after me and said, "Come back tomorrow at the same time."

When I entered Amirkhaniantz's study on the following day, he asked me, "Are you the mullah?"

"Yes," I answered.

"What do you understand about being a mullah? How can you prove that you have been a mullah?"

"If you understand these things, then of course you can examine me."

"Fine," he said, brought over a Koran, and had me read a few lines while he watched me closely. When I had finished he said, "Fine, but now I will read, and you will listen." He read, and I noticed that he made a few mistakes according to the *tajwid* (that is, the exact regulations on how one must read and intonate; without this knowledge a person cannot become a priest). After he had finished, he said, "Do you see; I can read as well, but I am an Armenian."

"According to the tajwid it was not exactly correct," I replied.

"Well," he said, "let's assume you can read a little better than I, but that is no proof that you have ever been a priest. You lie and want to deceive me. Go on now, tomorrow we will speak further about this."

When I came to see him the next day, he asked, "How could you learn Armenian so well if you are not an Armenian? How long did it take you to learn the language?"

"I have been on the run for three years and have been with Armenians the whole time and have devoted myself to this language day and night."

"Are you not ashamed to lie in this way? I can speak twelve languages, but I have not learned one so well in just three years."

"Perhaps I have been a little more astute."

He replied, "Silence!" Again I went away, and again the servant said to me, "Come back tomorrow."

He treated me like this for a whole week. On Saturday he said, "Tomorrow we have an Armenian meeting in the German school at which I will be preaching. If you want, you can come there." I went. When the service was over, most of the people left the room; only eight or ten evangelical brothers stayed behind. Amirkhaniantz said to them, "Brothers, I have something to say to you. I want to tell you about a curious matter. Have you ever seen a deceiver? This man here is one. He is an Armenian and wants to make me believe he was once a Muslim priest." Then he addressed me.

"How did you come here? Do you have a passport? Where do you live?"

I answered, "I live at the Aslan Caravansary. I do not have a passport since I am on the run."

"I do not understand this," he said. "How were you admitted without a passport? Who knows what you have done and why you had to flee!"

"I have said which city I am from and which missionaries I know. Why do you torment me if you do not want to ask them!"

"You have deceived the missionaries as you now want to deceive me."

Sadly I went out with the thought, "Lord, help me get away from this man. I do not want to see him again."

One of the brothers, a Bible distributor by the name of Sarkis [Assadur], followed me and tried to comfort me. "Do not take him for an evil man because of what he has said," he urged me, "we know he is vicious. God has led you to Christ, and we are happy about this, but Amirkhaniantz has been deceived many times. That is why he is now so suspicious. Please go and see him again tomorrow. I will be there too."

I did as he had said. Amirkhaniantz then asked me what I had read and learned and what books I had with me. I brought them to him.

Now my money was finished, and they no longer wanted to keep me at the caravansary. I could not tell this to Amirkhaniantz since he then would have considered me a deceiver all the more. So I wrote to Daniel Bey and told him how I had fared. He sent me two *roubles* via the Bible Society, with which I was able to pay the rent and still had a few kopecks left over.

The next Sunday Sembad Bagdasariantz preached at the Armenian meeting. During his sermon, to my great joy, Mr Wilson suddenly entered. After the service, Amirkhaniantz greeted him and introduced him to the Armenian brothers. As he was just about to add in his own inimitable way, "This is a man who claims to be a mullah, etc.", Mr Wilson said, "This is Brother John. I know him. You do not need to introduce him to me." As we went outside, Mr Wilson asked me to go with him to his hotel. I followed him and told him all that I had gone through, even how Amirkhaniantz had treated me. He was willing to help me but said, "Unfortunately I have barely enough money to be able to travel to America. However, I have an extra suit that I want to give you. I will also speak with Amirkhaniantz."

After Mr Wilson had left, I went back to Amirkhaniantz but I soon saw that the missionary's explanation had not been able to change his views about my character. Perhaps he considered Mr Wilson to be a deceiver too. He then sent me to an Armenian merchant with whom I was supposed to talk. I visited this man and found him to be an unbeliever who told me, "These days religion no longer has any meaning. It is out-of-date stupidity. Why do you make so many sacrifices to the Christian religion?" So he tried to win me over to his views. That incident distressed me much more than anything Amirkhaniantz had done up till then. I said, "I do not want to listen to your words!" and went away.

It was a hard time for me; on the one hand, poverty and privation, on the other, the unkindness of Christians. Tiflis had become a very dark city for me. The young Sarkis came to see me and took me back to Amirkhaniantz. He told me, if I could no longer live at the caravansary, I should stay with Sarkis. The latter was very poor. He did not have any steady employment as a Bible distributor, rather he only sold one or two Bibles a day, keeping half of the proceeds as food money and giving the other half to the Bible Society. He shared his room with a blacksmith by the name of Hagop Arushanian who worked in a factory and only came home at night. I moved in with them, received a blanket, and lay on the floor.

I was very glad to be able to leave the caravansary and to find assistance, even if it was so modest. The young Gregorian and his father visited me frequently and went to a lot of trouble for me in the most loving way. They wanted to find me a position as a clerk in a large newspaper office where I would have been able to earn a good living, but since it was fixed in my own heart that I must not become anything other than a worker in my Lord's vineyard, I refused the offer. I was sorry to have to put up a steady resistance to their incessant pleas, which they did not understand.

That young man's father, Bses Assadur, was still alive in Erivan in the year 1905 at the age of 100. Whenever my path took me through that city, I would often visit him and always met with a warm welcome. Each time he showered me with presents from the fruits of his garden, and these fruits were certainly the most beautiful in the whole region. Our friendly relations were an object of amazement to the evangelical brothers because they regarded the old one as an odd, repulsive man.

Soon after I had moved in with Sarkis, my last kopeck was spent, but I told no one about this and ate nothing. When I woke up the following morning, the blacksmith had already left, and Sarkis was just about to set off. I intended to ask him whether perhaps he was able to give me a little money, but I refrained from this because I saw he, himself, ate nothing. So I continued to sleep until the hunger would no longer leave me in peace. After I had read several chapters in the Bible and prayed, the thought came to me that I could still sell my watch and use the money to buy bread, but when I stepped into the street I saw all the shops were closed; it was a holiday. I was very weak but went to Amirkhaniantz and said, "My last kopeck is spent. I ate nothing yesterday. Please lend me some money, if that is possible. I will sell my watch tomorrow and pay you back. Today is a holiday, and I can do nothing about it."

He answered, "Why do you want to sell your watch? What will you eat when your money is exhausted?"

"What am I supposed to do," I retorted, "since I am so hungry? God will help me along later."

"No," he said, "you must work." I wanted to do that very much and asked him to show me a job to do. Then he told me to wait, went into another room, and returned with one rouble and seventy kopecks. He said, "Take this and do not sell your watch. We will see how things go later on. Go to my wife. There you will get something to eat." Mrs Amirkhaniantz kindly received me and fed me well. Then I received several assignments for clerical work from her husband. I went to see him every day, and together we read the book, *Mizan ul-Haqq (Balance of Truth)*. With the money he had given me I lived very economically, so I would not have to beg from him again. It was enough for about two weeks. After one week he asked, "Do you have any money?" I told him I still had seventy kopecks. Then he asked, "How do you live, having only used one rouble up to now?"

"As economically as possible," I replied.

He gave me five roubles and said, "Feed yourself a bit better."

CHAPTER 9

A CHRISTIAN AMONGST CHRISTIANS

After several more days had passed, Amirkhaniantz said to me, "Brother John, you have had a great deal of patience. I have tormented you very much, but you have overcome everything." Then we spoke about baptism, and he asked me why I had not been baptised up to then. I told him the reason: they wanted to baptise me in secret, and I did not consider that to be correct. He said, "Now you can be baptised when and how you wish."

I was very happy, and when he asked, "Where do you want to be baptised: in the German church, or in our house in the presence of the Armenian brothers, or somewhere else? I am ready to baptise you. If you are not afraid, I am not afraid either," I answered, "If possible, I would like to be baptised in the Kur River because in respect to form I consider it correct to be immersed."

It was on 28 February 1885, after the Sunday sermon, when we went with the brothers to the river, which flows through the middle of the city of Tiflis. I took off my outer garments; he pulled off his boots, took me by the hand, and we went about ten paces into the water. There he asked me, "Brother John, do you believe that Jesus is the Son of God?"

I answered, "Yes, with all my heart."

He said, "Then I baptise you, John, in the name of the Father, and of the Son, and of the Holy Spirit!" Then he immersed me under the water. It was freezing, pieces of ice floated around us, but I did not notice the cold because of the joy I felt. During this time many people had assembled on the bridge and looked on in amazement.

After the baptism, we went back to his house and celebrated the Lord's Supper. When he later asked what ought to become of me, I answered it was my wish to be prepared, so I could preach the gospel within the Muslim community, but he dismissed me with the words, "It is written, 'Let not many of you become teachers.'[1] You must work and earn your bread."

"But I have been a teacher up till now," I objected, "it is my profession, and now I would like to practise it for the Saviour."

He stuck to his view, "No, you must learn a trade. Go to a factory and become a mechanic."

I raised one more objection, but to no avail. Reluctantly I finally said, "Fine, if it can be no other way!" although I did not have the least inclination for this work.

---

[1] See Appendix I, Bible Passages 23. Trans.

After a few days I met the Swedish missionary, Höijer, at Amirkhaniantz's home. Höijer spoke very warmly and kindly with me, although he had not mastered the Armenian language. At the close of our conversation he asked me, "Do you want to come with me and preach the gospel of Christ in the villages?" I gladly agreed. Amirkhaniantz also consented, so we went to Shemakha where Höijer was living at the time. He lived at the home of an old preacher, Sarkis Hampartzumian, who had studied at Dorpat and then had established an evangelical fellowship in Shemakha; he was a precious character.[1] Besides him, Pastor Kevorkian also had a fruitful work in Shemakha. We were often together and grew truly fond of each other. I especially learned to appreciate him very much on our joint preaching trips.

I stayed in Shemakha six months, gave Mrs Höijer lessons in Armenian, and began to learn some Swedish for myself. I often went to the villages, sometimes with Höijer, sometimes alone, and preached the gospel amongst the Molokans[2] and Armenians. Before I arrived, a young man from Shusha, Markara ter Asaturoff, had been at the Höijers' home for six months; he now intended to travel to Sweden to attend the mission school there. The old preacher Sarkis very much wanted me to travel with the young man to Sweden, but I did not have the fare, and Missionary Höijer could not obtain it. Finally the old Sarkis said, "Now I have found the fare for him! Many years ago a Muslim became a Christian and when he died he left to the evangelical fellowship the small amount of cash he had on hand. This sum consisted of seventy roubles and came with the request that they use it to spread the gospel amongst the Muslims. Now we have an opportunity through Brother John to use this money in accordance with his designation."

So Höijer brought both of us to Sweden where we arrived on 1 June 1886.

In Stockholm we were warmly received by the Swedish Missionary Society. The following year of my stay in Sweden will always remain a dear memory to me, as I was together with many fervent Christians whom I got to know there, even if on the other hand the Lord at this time was leading me back into the depths again.

The Swedish Missionary Society (*Svenska Missionsförbundet*), whose chairman was Doctor Ekman, had a school in Kristinehamn where workers for the missions in the Congo Free State, in China, and among the Armenians were trained in three-year courses. To this school we, my companion Markara

---

[1] In fact Hampartzumian was involved in an evangelical work amongst the Armenians that had been instigated by Count Felician Zaremba and the missionaries of the Basel Mission in the 1820s, a work that then centred around a schoolteacher named Arakel; according to Schlatter's *History of the Basel Mission* (pp. 96, 105), Sarkis actually studied at Reval (now Tallinn, Estonia); it was Zaremba who studied at Dorpat.

In 1866 the church in Shemakha was made up of around three hundred and thirteen people. It was later reported in the July 1882 issue of *The Missionary Herald* (p. 278) that a congregation of four to six hundred met every Sunday in Shemakha. Trans.

[2] *Molokans* (also *Malakans* = *milk-eaters*), a Christian sect without the sacraments and with a spiritual interpretation of the Scriptures.

and I, were sent. Since I had only learned a little Swedish through my day-to-day contact with the Swedish missionaries, I had to make a big effort at the beginning to be able to follow the lessons. However, the unceasing work in conjunction with the cold climate to which I was unaccustomed had such a detrimental effect on my eyes that I fell ill when they became severely inflamed. At first the doctor placed no importance at all on my condition, but as it grew increasingly worse, I was sent to Stockholm and from there to Kristiania to a famous eye specialist. However, he could not help me either. So I returned to Kristinehamn and was received into the home of an elderly lady, Mrs Sundqvist, who with great devotion cared for me together with Mrs Karlsson and the Bible-woman, Anna Nyström, who was then staying at her home.

The doctor had prescribed atropine for my eye inflammation. Through one reason or another some of the strong toxin had got into my throat and had caused a severe inflammation. The doctor had given up on me. One evening he said to Mrs Sundqvist, as was later told to me, he did not believe I would last through the night. When he had gone, Mrs Sundqvist and Mrs Karlsson stayed by my bedside and read to me from the Scriptures. From the passage they chose I recognised that they believed my death to be near. Even I felt my breath stop now and again, especially as soon as I was almost asleep. Therefore I asked Mrs Karlsson to wake me as soon as I should fall asleep. She faithfully carried out my request and woke me almost every two minutes since from exhaustion I kept falling asleep. Once I must have slept for a good few minutes before she noticed and in this short time I had a wonderful dream:

> I stood in a wide, green meadow. A beautiful white lamb drew near to me and then turned round and round in front of me, faster and faster, until it finally disappeared, and in its place I saw a lion. The lion likewise began to turn round and round and then transformed into a great millstone which suddenly divided, while an odd carriage, which had legs like those of a table instead of wheels, came forth from inside the millstone. The carriage stopped in front of me and out climbed a beautiful boy of about twelve years of age. He was wearing gleaming blue garments and had a staff in his hand. With a gentle voice he said, "Come, John," and had me climb in. Then the carriage drove away through the air. Inside I saw a second boy who was similar to the first, and both now began to speak very lovingly to me. They made known to me lofty thoughts about spiritual things. Then it suddenly became clear that earthly boys could not speak in such a way. I knew these were angels guiding me. At the same time I became convinced the destination to which they were leading me could only be heaven. In the first moment my heart was filled with joy that I was really adopted by grace, but then I sighed deeply in my thoughts, knowing I could now do nothing for my brothers, the Muslims. Then the angels spoke: "Why are you sad, John? Are you not happy we are with you and love you?" With their warm words they soon took my mind off things. It seemed to me we had passed through the clouds like this for a long, long time.

Then the carriage suddenly stopped. One of the angels climbed out, held out his hand, and had me climb out, saying, "We are leaving you here for a short time. Goodbye!" While the other from still inside the carriage waved goodbye, the carriage disappeared, and I found myself alone on a high mountain.

At that moment Mrs Karlsson woke me up. When I opened my eyes I felt better and consequently asked my nurse now to let me sleep and get some rest herself. When she explained she wanted to stay, I said, "I will not die. I cannot speak now; I will tell you tomorrow." Then she left me.

The next morning I awoke strengthened, and in a short time recovered. —

In June 1889 Markara and I, along with several brothers who were going to China and Africa, were consecrated at the Immanuel Church in Stockholm and sent out as missionaries to Caucasia.

CHAPTER 10
WORKING FOR THE LORD

A petition came before the board of the Swedish Missionary Society which contained the following: "We have formed a *German* association of young men in Caucasia with the intention of doing something towards spreading the gospel amongst Muslims. Allow us to help John Avetaranian and give something towards his support, so he might preach amongst the Muslims here in Caucasia." So I went to Tiflis in the autumn of 1889 and worked there; I also took missionary trips into the Caucasian villages and cities as far as Persia. Whenever the young men's gifts were not enough, Doctor Bädeker or my Swedish missionary society helped me.

When I came to Tiflis I did not find Pastor Amirkhaniantz there and heard he had been sent away to Siberia for four years. That is to say, before my departure the Russians had wanted to have some public discussions with the representatives of the various other confessions, and Amirkhaniantz had been very willing to attend these meetings. As I was to hear, a discussion had later taken place in front of the exarch in which Pastor Amirkhaniantz, as well as two Baptist missionaries, had demanded biblical proof for the use of images in churches. For this they were expelled from the country.

There are several memories to relate from the time of my three years spent in Caucasia. My chief aim was to preach the gospel to the Muslims there; I knew I was called for this, but I also worked amongst the Armenians and other tribes. Whenever I was in Tiflis, I preached every Sunday in different languages. The difficulties of a mission within the Muslim community do not only lie in the fanatical mind of the Muslim and in the persecutions to which every devoted convert is exposed. The inclination of the Shiites towards lying and hypocrisy is also a great obstacle for the mission in Caucasia and Persia. The basic evil is the *tagia*, the teaching that it is permitted to deny one's religion in cases of extreme danger. This teaching is not known amongst the Sunni. Many Shiites use this tagia at every opportunity, even the most insignificant. Whenever they come to a Sunnite Muslim's home, they put on an act and deny their Shiism because they consider it more convenient, and it is allowed according to the tagia. Both lofty and low use is made of this allowance, not only from fear but also to achieve some worldly advantage. Naturally a person's character becomes thoroughly corrupted by it.

Missionaries have to suffer very much under this tagia. While I was working in Caucasia, we baptised only a few Muslims, but although we had examined most of them in advance for a long time, there was still some deception. Once a saiyid was sent to me from Shusha. The brothers had sent him along with a letter of recommendation, informing me he had been instructed from the Word of God and wanted to become a Christian. He was a 60-year-old man. I kindly received him, spoke with him about salvation in Christ, and soon saw he was not lacking in the knowledge of the Scriptures; his speech could be quite edifying. He told me he had heard Pastor Amirkhaniantz preach several years ago in Shusha. Since then he had been searching the Scriptures and looking for Christ. After he had been with us for several days, my co-worker, Missionary Höijer, said, "We ought to fulfil his wish and baptise him." I asked to wait one more year, but Höijer stuck to his view: "We have no reason to keep him waiting. If he believes and confesses that Jesus is the Son of God, then we must not withhold baptism from him." Höijer then posed several questions to him through me since he could not speak Turkish, and the answers were so good that Höijer, quite satisfied, said, "Tomorrow we will baptise him." And so it happened.

After the baptism, Saiyid Ahmed—he had now received the name John—said, "My wife has died, but I have a son in Tabriz. I would like to travel there in order to sell my house and get my son. Please give me the money to make the trip." I decided to travel with him to Tabriz. So we set off and came to Akstafa where we stopped at a caravansary at which some Muslims were also staying. To my astonishment I saw Saiyid Ahmed stand up, carry out the Muslim washings, and begin to perform the *namaz*, the prayer.

When we were alone again, I asked, "What have you been doing?"

"I have done tagia," was his answer.

"Tell me which danger threatened you then? Indeed, we are in Russia, and besides, if you are a Christian, you must know that in Christianity there is no tagia. Our Saviour says, 'Whoever denies me before men, I will also deny him before my Father who is in heaven.'"[1]

So he thought for a little while and then said, "Please forgive me; I will not do it again."

I replied to him, "Before your baptism we spoke about all these things, and I told you that you must be ready to die for Jesus. But there was not even a danger here."

Subsequently we went through many more sad experiences with Ahmed, but no missionary is spared such disappointments. Such people were with us one minute and gone from us the next because "they were not really of us; for if they had been of us, they would have remained with us; but they went out, so that it would be shown that they all are not of us."[2]

However, such experiences did not discourage us and they will never be able to do so. For on the other hand, we have found very faithful confessors of Christ amongst the Muslims who for the sake of the faith suffered a martyr's

---

[1] See Appendix I, Bible Passages 24. Trans.

[2] See Appendix I, Bible Passages 25. Trans.

death.

I stayed in Tabriz over the winter and only came back to Tiflis in the spring. Some time after that, Missionary Högberg came to us; he had worked for six years in Kharkov amongst the Molokans. The Swedish Missionary Society gave me the task of accompanying him and his family to Tabriz, so I travelled there once more.

Högberg opened a mission school there in order to train workers for the mission amongst the Muslims, but later on it turned out he was not knowledgeable enough for such work; nothing came of it.

On my return to Russia we had a missionary conference in Shemakha. At this conference evangelical brothers from various cities in Caucasia gathered together. It was Höijer's intention to found a mission to the Orient. He formed a committee for this purpose; I was also one of its members. Our desire was to join up this Orient mission with the American mission in Persia and Turkey since the Americans would also have liked to work in Caucasia, however, they did not receive permission from the government. Admittedly, in Tabriz I had already satisfied myself the missionaries there would not agree with our suggestions, but we hoped the missionaries in Turkey would think differently. In order to communicate our plans to them, the committee was now supposed to choose a messenger from its own members, and the choice fell to me. To be sure, this undertaking was quite dangerous for me, but since no one else was willing, I took on the assignment. This trip was especially important to me since on the journey out and the journey back I would have many opportunities to proclaim the gospel to my people.

I arrived safely in Erzerum and stayed for six days. At first I kept myself hidden, but shortly before my departure I preached once in Armenian in the mission chapel. Several Turks came but did not recognise me. The missionaries kindly agreed with our suggestions, however, they set down several conditions. Höijer would not accept these conditions, so the committee was gradually disbanded again. The brothers considered such an association dangerous without permission from the government and preferred to spread the gospel, each according to his abilities, without an organisation of that kind.

During the "week of prayer"[1] in the last year I spent in Tiflis, we came together every evening at the home of one of the brothers. On the fourth evening we assembled at my apartment. After we had read and prayed, we began to sing songs of praise. All of a sudden a policeman stepped inside and said in Russian, "*Chto takoe*?" ('What is this?')

Brother Sembad answered, "We have been singing."

He asked, "Who is the landlord?"

I answered, "I am."

"Then you must come along to the police station," he said tersely. It was

---

[1] Traditionally this was the first week of January. Trans.

around eleven o'clock in the evening, but I had to follow him. The brothers stayed there, knelt down again to pray, and awaited my return.

The policeman brought me to the *pristav*,[1] and he asked, "What were you doing there?"

"We were just reading and praying."

"Why?"

"Because these days are holy to us, and we come together to pray."

He stamped his foot and said, "It would have been better for you if you had come together to drink wine." He sent me home with two policemen to have me fetch the brothers and my collection of books. Then he wrote down the people's names and let them go again but kept me back. He stuck my books in a sack and sealed it; then he sat and took down my statement until one o'clock. As he was about to leave, he said to me, "You must stay here. Do you want to sleep in the entrance or in the room?"

"It is cold there; I will stay here," I answered.

He placed an armed policeman next to me and a guard in front of the door then went. After just five minutes he returned, opened a cupboard, put the sack of books inside, locked it, and stuck the key in his pocket. Perhaps he was afraid I would be able to kill the two soldiers, take the bag of books, and run away. There was no sofa there; I had to sleep on the floor. I had a *yapunja* (a Caucasian coat) with me, and at my request I was given the police books for a pillow. I had hardly fallen asleep when someone woke me again and asked for my pocket knife.

The next morning the pristav returned and sent me with a policeman to the *sledovatel'*.[2] I had to carry the sack with my forty books on my back. When I could go no further with my load, I asked the policeman to allow me to take a porter, but he would not do this because he was afraid I would be able to run away. Therefore I suggested to him we might go the rest of the way arm in arm, and so we arrived at our destination with our arms linked.

The judge, an educated Russian, read the pristav's statement and said, "Your case is very serious."

"Not at all."

"You will see; you will be sent to Siberia."

"No," I said, "I have done nothing wrong and will never go to Siberia."

"What did you do?"

"We read the Bible and prayed to God."

"Was there an image of Christ or of Mary there?"

"No, we pray to God, not to images."

"How can you pray where there is no image!"

"We are evangelicals and need no images."

Then he went on to ask, "How many languages do you know, and in what

---

[1] See Appendix B, *pristav*. Trans.

[2] See Appendix B, *sledovatel'*. Trans.

languages are these books written?"

"They are my private books," I said, "in four or five languages."

"That is exactly why you have to go to Siberia," he said. On the whole he was much kinder towards me than the pristav had been. He gave the policeman my passport and ordered him to bring it along with my books to the *mirovoi sud'ia*.[1] I was allowed to follow on my own without a police escort.

The mirovoi sud'ia opened the sack, looked inside my books, and said, "I will send your books to the censor; your passport will stay here. Only when the books come back will we be able to hear the case. Now go home." I went to my apartment but stayed under police supervision for twelve days. Since the case dragged on and on, I went to the censor myself and asked him to examine my books as quickly as possible.

In a friendly manner he said, "Are these your books? Are you Avetaranian? Your books are very good. I would like to keep them a few days more, but because you are in such a hurry, I will send them in two days' time."

Two of the books were in Swedish, and the censor could not read them. I had to get an intermediary who could read Swedish and who could reassure the mirovoi sud'ia about the contents of the books. There lived in Tiflis a general from Finland by the name of Blumhard, a good Christian man whom I knew and who attended our meetings now and then with his family. At my request he came and gave a signed testimony that the books were all right. He said, "I do not know why you are making so much fuss. I know Mr Avetaranian; he is by no means a dangerous man."

The mirovoi sud'ia said, "Perhaps the pristav has made a mistake. I will investigate the matter. You can come on the day the court is in session and listen." On the following day we, all the brothers and I, received a summons: "It is claimed that Avetaranian has acted contrary to paragraph 128 of the legal code. On 19 January the inquiry will take place."

We looked it up in the statute book and found: "Whoever holds meetings without permission will be sent to Siberia for four years." The brothers were very afraid for me, but I was quite confident.

On the appointed day we all went to the courthouse. The mirovoi sud'ia first interrogated each one of us separately and afterwards all of us together. He only had one question, and we all gave the same answer, which the interpreter translated. He asked the Turkish brothers, "Why did you go there on that evening?"

They answered, "Because John is our brother. We read and prayed together."

The Armenians answered in like manner as did the two Swedish sisters, Miss Beckström and Miss Nyström. Since the Armenians and the Turks were

---

[1] See Appendix B, *mirovoi sud'ia*. Trans.

from different places, and the two ladies were also not from the same city, he said, "I do not understand you. Here a Turk says, John is his brother, and the Armenian from Caucasia as well as the one from Turkey, the Persian, and even the two Swedish women claim the same thing. How can he be the brother of all these people?"

After that, he threw on his ceremonial uniform, and we went into the large courtroom. The pristav and the policeman who had arrested me were also present, and many spectators from various nations had come.

The mirovoi sud'ia asked the policeman why he brought me to the police station so late at night and what he had really seen. He said, "I heard singing and went in."

"Did you understand what they were singing? Perhaps they were singing a secular song. Why did you disturb these people?"

"No," he said, "I was certainly able to recognise it was no secular song."

"What did you see when you went inside?"

"I saw the landlord standing in front of a table and singing with the others."

"How were the chairs placed? Were they standing in a row?"

"No, like in a private home."

The mirovoi sud'ia then continued to ask about every tiny detail: what lay on the table and so forth. Then he sent the policeman out and told the pristav, "I see now that it was no meeting in the sense in which you are charging them since not one of the chairs stood in a row. A person does have some freedom in his own home. Now be reconciled with Mr Avetaranian, for you have caused him much trouble and robbed him unnecessarily of his books." To me he said, "Give the pristav your hand and forgive him." Then he asked me to sign a paper that I would not hold a meeting without police permission; the brothers had to sign it as well. So we went merrily home, and I did not have to go to Siberia for four years.

I held my peace for one month; then I went to the mirovoi sud'ia and asked him whether there would be any possibility for us to hold meetings. He was a kindly old gentleman, a Georgian. "Why do you not go to the Lutheran Church?" he asked. "Those people are Protestants too."

I replied, "We do not speak German and must read and pray in a language we understand." Then he told me whom I had to consult in order to receive such permission, but all efforts were in vain.

I decided to make further missionary trips and preached in many places. When I came to Shemakha I received the unpleasant news that the Russian government had deported Pastor Kevorkian to his homeland, Turkey. He had worked for ten to fifteen years in the evangelical Armenian fellowship at Shemakha. God had richly blessed his work, and his expulsion was a severe blow to the fellowship. The missionaries in Tabriz wanted Kevorkian to come to them, but the Russian government did not allow him to travel to Persia. Only the route to Turkey via Batum lay open. Then he asked me to take his wife the direct way to Tabriz since the long way he was taking via Batum would be too arduous for her. His farewell to the fellowship was very emotional; they could hardly bear being separated from him. Sick with grief, the sexton became like one demented. We had to take him to the hospital. When the hour for his departure came, the whole fellowship accompanied their pastor out of the city; many Gregorians came along as well. On a hill outside the city he gave his last address, and I closed with a prayer for his journey.

On the first day we travelled together. Then our ways parted, and I proceeded with Mrs Kevorkian to Tabriz where she met up with her husband later. After I had preached several times in the city and in the villages, I returned to Tiflis.

When I had been in Caucasia for three years—it was 1892[1]—Pastor Amirkhaniantz came from Sweden with an assignment from the Swedish Missionary Society for me to travel to Kashgar and there set up a new mission station for Muslims. He came to Tiflis with Missionary Höijer, and I was delighted to see him again. Soon they were travelling on to Samarkand, but Amirkhaniantz got sick there and had to turn back. When he had arrived in Tiflis he told me, "I would have liked to have travelled to Kashgar, but because of my illness it is not possible for me. I believe the Lord is sending you there. They are your people, and you are called to work amongst your brothers."

So it was decided I should travel with Missionary Höijer to Kashgar. I had to commit myself to staying there one year and gladly did this because I was happy and confident that this was the way the Lord was showing me. Höijer advised me to leave my books behind so my luggage would be light, so I only took along my Bible and a songbook. I chose Ghazar, a young man from Tabriz, to accompany me; we had attended the school together. But in Baku he asked me to allow him to turn back since he wanted to attend a European school and was afraid he would not be able to do anything for his education in Kashgar. Mnatsagan, a young Armenian, accompanied me in his place.[2]

We travelled to Samarkand via Usun-ada, Kizil-Arvat, Ashkabad, Merv, and Bokhara. In Ashkabad and Merv we stayed several days and preached. In Ashkabad the *Babites*[3] hold meetings with the permission of the Russian government. I attended one of these meetings and got into a dispute with the leaders. When they could no longer answer me, they asked me to speak with

---

[1] Actually it was in 1891; see next footnote. This means he was only in Caucasia the second time for just over 2 years. Trans.

[2] In *Passion For The Impossible, The Life Of The Pioneer Nils Fredrik Höijer* by Ann-Charlotte Fritzon, Fritzon relates that the group left Caucasia for China in December 1891 and did not arrive in Kashgar until early in 1892 (p. 109). This also tallies with the opening line of Chapter 25 in this story (p. 162), which gives the starting date for the work in Kashgar (which must include the trip out there) as 1891. Trans.

[3] About the Babites or Babis, also called Baha'is, a branch of Islam, see R. Roemer: *Die Báb'í-Behá'í. Eine Studie zur Religionsgeschichte des Islams.* Reich Christi XIII. Nr. 2/9, separate edition. The publishing house of the Evangelical Society in Stuttgart.

Abdul-Fazl in Samarkand. I promised to do this and went to see him soon after my arrival in Samarkand. He was a tea merchant and lived in a caravansary. Previously, that is, before he had accepted the Babi teaching, he had been a famous *mujtahid*.[1] His name, *Abdl-Fazl*, means 'father of virtue'. The Babites consider him to be one of the twelve apostles of the *Baha' Ullah* which means 'light of God'. As I entered his home, he received me warmly, brought out the Bible, and our conversation began. First he complained a little about the mullahs; they would have the gate of the kingdom of heaven sealed to men. But then he explained that between Christians and Babites there was no difference since they believe in the same Christ. He showed me two Jews and said, "They are from the people of Israel who crucified Jesus, but now they have become believers in Jesus through me." The Jews corroborated his words.

I asked him, "Who really is Christ? We need to speak somewhat in depth about him."

In a friendly fashion he immediately broke off the conversation; I noticed he did not want to answer in front of the Jews. "It is getting late and the way is far to your hotel from our Asian quarter. I will come and see you tomorrow. Then we can talk further."

When he came the next day, I repeated my question: "What do you mean? Who is Christ?"

He answered, "Christ was crucified by the Jews and is, as you read in the Gospel, risen."

"I am happy you believe in Him," I replied, "for He has died for our sin, but what do you think of the Bab?"

"He is this same Christ," he answered and explained to me that in Abraham's times Christ had appeared as Melchizedek, then as the one whom the Jews crucified, and now for the last time as the Bab.

"How is it possible that the Bab is our saviour?" I asked him.

"The Jews also said such things to Christ."

Then I explained to him, "In the Gospel it clearly states that Christ will come again as He has gone into heaven, that is, in the clouds of the sky", and opened up the Bible to Acts of the Apostles 1:11[2] where it is written: "Men of Galilee, why do you stand looking into the sky? This Jesus, who has been taken up from you into heaven, will come in just the same way as you have watched Him go into heaven." Then I continued, "Therefore this Mirza Husain Ali, whom you call the Bab, cannot possibly be the saviour we are expecting from heaven. Jesus came and died for the sins of the world, but this one knows nothing at all about sin. Therefore he cannot be Christ. As well, Christ is coming to His own and not to the ones who do not know Him or who have a false idea of Him." Abdul-Fazl went to a lot of trouble to convince me,

---

[1] See Appendix B, *mujtahid*. Trans.

[2] See Appendix I, Bible Passages 26. Trans.

but when he saw it was impossible, he spoke of other things. Our farewell was very cordial.

For ten days we drove by carriage to Osh, the last city in West Turkestan. There we had to prepare ourselves for the journey over the high mountains. We bought coats, hats, and stockings made of longhaired fur, which were even lined on the inside with fur. The sleeves of our coats hung a full hand's width over our hands, and our hats had flaps that could be tied over the mouth and nose, so just our eyes looked out from under the longhaired rim. Our boots were made of felt, two to three centimetres thick. We tied belts over our jackets. Then we started our ascent on horseback. We had food with us for ten days. In fact, we ate big meals, except at the top of the Terek Davan, where for a day's journey the air was so thin it became hard for us to breathe.

On the seventh day we crossed over the pass and came to Irkeshtam. The Russian border officials received us as guests but did everything possible to deter us. They assured us we would not be admitted and advised turning back, but it was to no avail; they could not frighten us away. After we had spent the night with them—the first night since we left Osh that we spent under a roof—we rode on to Ulugchat, a Chinese fortress. This time we stayed the night in a Kirghiz tent in which the Kirghiz people assembled in the evening, so we could read to them from the Gospel. Although the Kirghiz language is more similar to my mother tongue than Kashgari, we could barely make ourselves understood.

I asked the *aksaqal* (that is, *white beard = leader*) what was supposed to happen with our passports, but he knew nothing about either passports or visas. I tried to explain it to him, but he said, "I heard once that there are such things in Russia, but with us it is unheard of." On the following day, after we had ridden for three hours, we saw three Chinese riders on huge horses behind us. When they had reached us, they dismounted, greeted us politely, and said, "The *amban*[1] invites you to come back." Naturally it was hard for us to turn back since we would have lost a day by doing that, so we asked to be excused this time. We would visit him on our way back. But it was to no avail. So, accompanied by one of the soldiers, I decided to turn back, taking along Höijer and Mnatsagan's passports. I mounted one of the Chinese riders' horses, so mine would not get too tired, and rode back to see the official. When I came to see him, he explained it would have been a dishonour to him if we had ridden by without having been his guest for one night.

I told him, "We were with the aksaqal and asked him, but he told us nothing about you, and he also did not know what to do with our passports."

"Ah," he said, "these people differ very little from the *qotaz* (that is, the yak)."

Incidentally, our passports were not very important to him either; he only wanted to pay us a courtesy and show his hospitality. Someone brought me some tea. After that, I excused myself by saying I could not stay long and

---

[1] See Appendix B, *amban*. Trans.

rode back to my companions.

On the following day we rode to Mingyol, likewise a Chinese fortress, where we visited the Chinese officials. They took our passports from us and sent them to Sung-Qaraghol, from where we were supposed to get them back. On arriving in this city we were greeted by a Chinese official who held a high-level government post. He asked us to be his guests for a day. He had an extremely active interest in our selves and especially in our clothing and amused us very much. He measured the length of our coats with his own hands and asked for the exact price of our clothes. He was a bird enthusiast and in particular owned many parrots that he had someone bring in and show us their tricks. When I saw how very much he was interested in us, I gave to him as a memento a beautiful Swedish pocket knife, which I carried with me. He took it, said thank you, and looked at it from all sides for about ten minutes. After that, he placed it back into my hand and said, "I have received your gift, and now I am giving it back to you again."

I answered him: "You will make us sad if you will not accept this small thing from us."

But he explained, "No, no, I have accepted it, but you are our guests, having gone to much trouble to come and see us from a distant land. We must give gifts to you and not you to us." It stayed this way in spite of our attempts to persuade him otherwise.

When we arrived in Kashgar, first we visited the Russian Consul General, Petrovsky. He urgently advised us to go back immediately; the Muslims were very fanatical and would never permit a mission to come into being here. As a result Missionary Höijer considered it advisable to turn back now and return later with other Swedish missionaries. However, I announced to him I would be staying since I was not afraid and was convinced that the Lord had called me to this work. After four days Höijer and Mnatsagan left me, after I had escorted them for a mile.[1]

---

[1] This could be a Swedish mile or a German mile. See Appendix B, mile. Trans.

CHAPTER 11
BEYOND THE PAMIRS

Kashgar belongs to the countries of the earth that until the beginning of the twentieth century were completely closed to Europeans. About half a millennium ago Mohammedanism came to Kashgar. After they had conquered Bokhara and Samarkand, the Arabs soon directed their attacks towards Kashgar. Their leader, Yussuf Kadrkhan Ghazi ('the victor') issued a proclamation to the people of Kashgar in which he said no harm would come to anyone who accepted Islam, but whoever refused was supposed to be immediately put to the sword. The people of Kashgar considered what they would do. It was clear they could accomplish nothing against the superior might of the enemy, so they decided to accept the new religion.

From Kashgar the victorious commander moved on to Yarkand and quickly conquered this city as well, but in Khotan he ran into serious resistance. The two kings of this country, Chokti Rashid and Nükti Dakshid, were very courageous, defeated the Muslim army, and killed the greater part of the soldiers. When the Kashgaris heard that the Arabs were beaten, they abandoned Islam straight away and went back to their religion. Tradition tells that the Arabs moved against Kashgar seven times, but each time they were beaten back. Finally a learned Arab came as a missionary to Kashgar, lived there as a peaceful merchant, and tried to teach the people to read and write. The crown prince of the country[1] took lessons himself, and the missionary succeeded in winning him for Islam, to the dismay of his old father. When the prince came to power he immediately introduced Islam into the country by force, but to this day this religion has gained no firm foothold in the hearts of the Kashgari people. Only the mullahs and scholars understand the religious system of Islam; the people for the most part are very uneducated. However, at the same time they are very kind-hearted. The Kashgaris do not trust the mullahs. They claim all Muslim priests are liars, and in most cases they are not wrong.

The first European who went to Kashgar was the famous traveller, Marco Polo, who died in 1323; he even tells about Kashgar in the great book about his travels. For many centuries no European entered the country, but several decades ago an English traveller by the name of Show[2] came there and wrote

---

[1] This was Satoq Boghra Khan, though there seems to be some chronological confusion, because traditionally Boghra embraced Islam in the tenth century, and Yussuf Kadrkhan came to Kashgar in the late tenth or early eleventh century. Trans.

[2] He probably means Robert Shaw. See Appendix B, Show. Trans.

a small English-Kashgari grammar.

In the year 1857 the famous German traveller, [Adolf] Schlagintweit, came there on his journey from India to Kokand. At Kokand he wanted to meet the emir of that place, Khan Khudayar, but was taken prisoner in Kashgar by King Vali Khan Tura. The king asked Schlagintweit why he had come to Kashgar. When he heard he was travelling to Kokand to see Khan Khudayar and he had letters addressed to him, the king demanded to see them. However, when Schlagintweit refused to surrender the letters, the king gave the order to lead him outside the city and behead him, after having had it repeatedly made known to him, though to no avail, that he would save his life by producing the letters. He was buried on the bank of the river, but the spot was later washed away. In my time France sent an iron monument to Petrovsky, a Russian consul who had been sent to Kashgar with forty soldiers, with the instructions to mark Schlagintweit's grave in memory of the famous traveller and his sad end.[1]

The king of Kashgar who had Schlagintweit executed was a very cruel man. In particular, he was a woman hater. As soon as a woman appeared on the street while he was out walking, he had her imprisoned and her head chopped off, showing no mercy. However, his reign of terror did not last long. A zealous Muslim, Yakub Beg, came from Tashkent and stirred up the inhabitants of Kashgar against their king by demonstrating to them that their king was a servant of the Chinese. In a short time Yakub Beg had many supporters. One day he and a crowd of his followers stormed the royal residence and took Vali Khan Tura prisoner. Since he was not allowed to be put to the sword because he was a saiyid and a descendant of Mohammed, Yakub Beg had him placed under a wall and had the wall turned over on top of him. Then all the Chinese in Kashgar were executed.

After Yakub Beg had conquered Kashgar, he moved on with his supporters to the city of Yangi-shahr, where there were Chinese armed forces and many Chinese inhabitants. He had the city encircled and was on the verge of starving them out. All attempts by the inhabitants to break through the enemy's line failed, and the hoped-for relief from Peking was a long time in coming. When the Chinese officers saw their food supply was finished, they assembled all the defenders of the city into several large buildings, set fire to them, and burnt themselves up with the buildings.

But Yakub Beg was soon just as terrible a tyrant as his predecessor had been. He had no less than forty wives, and his royal household devoured vast sums. Outside of Kashgar he built himself a palace with beautiful gardens. In order to gain the means for all this expenditure, he burdened the population with unbearable taxes. When the people now saw how Yakub Beg was bringing the country more and more headlong into disaster, their sympathy

---

[1] According to Hedin (*Through Asia*, p. 247) Petrovsky erected a monument to Schlagintweit in 1887. Trans.

turned back to the Chinese.

Whenever the farmers sowed their fields, they asked that God would let the wheat and other crops grow. Now they prayed that God would let the Chinese grow instead of the wheat. Finally they sent a message in secret to Peking; the Chinese might have mercy and set them free from the tyranny of Yakub Beg. Then the Chinese sent a large army that took Kashgar. Yakub Beg poisoned himself. His rule had lasted from 1864 to 1877. Several Muslims buried him, but when the Chinese had conquered the country of Kashgar, they took his bones and incinerated them. His sons fled to Russia.

Kashgar lies in the Tarim Basin and is bounded on three sides by the high mountains of the Kuen-luns, Pamirs, and Tyan Shans in such a way that the Indus, Amu, and Syr Rivers can only be reached by way of arduous mountain passes. Numerous small rivers flow from the high mountains to the surrounding area then disappear into the desert sand after feeding several oases on the edge of the mountain slopes. Only at a more considerable breadth does it become the Tarim River, the single largest river in the heart of High Asia and the confluence of the Khotan and Yarkand Rivers, both of which come from the Karakoram Mountain Range, and the Kashgar River, which comes from the Pamir Mountains. The Tarim finishes at Lop-nor. From the Tyan Shan Mountains it also receives tributaries, which feed several oases, and is then lost in fresh water reservoirs surrounded by salt deserts. East of Kashgar lies the Takla Makan Desert about which many odd things are told. It is said whole cities lay buried in the sand, and indeed, people often dig for silver, gold, and antiques there with success. The area of the desert is so great that a journey crossways through this desert takes fifteen days, while passing through it lengthways takes about thirty days. Now there is no water there, but watercourses from old, dried up rivers and the ruins of many bridges can be seen. The Kashgaris do not travel through this desert since they say it is a dwelling place of evil spirits.

In Kashgar it rains very seldom since the high mountains hold back the clouds. But the snow covering the highest regions partly melts in the spring and sends much water into the country. A developed system of canals conducts this water through the fields, vineyards, and fruit plantations and makes them very fertile. The rivers carry a lot of sand with them from the mountains, and in the middle of summer, when the water has dried up, the canals are completely filled with dust and sand. So that the water again has a free course to run in, the canals are cleaned out with earth banks being thrown up on both sides. But with the violent, frequently recurring winds, these mounds of earth are churned up; more sand flies down from the mountains, and this material is swept over the roads and fields. Clouds of dust often veil the sun for days. When the wind dies down, a shower of dust follows which sometimes lasts for ten days. The people there call this the *qum yaghar*, that is, "it is raining sand". In this way whole villages gradually become buried.

Afterwards the air becomes clean again, sunshine and lovely weather follow, and the people, who were so on edge during the qum yaghar that even the best of friends quarrelled with one another, heave a sigh of relief and become peaceable again. But storms and raining sand can be repeated even after one month.

The soil in the country of Kashgar is very fertile, especially next to the river courses. It grows cotton, rice, wheat, barley, corn, grapes, and other crops. Silk worms are also raised there.

The language of the Kashgaris is the actual mother tongue of the Turkish dialects. The reason why Turkish has been preserved there in such unusual purity lies in the fact that the country had no contact with foreign peoples since it is completely surrounded by high mountains. A written language did not exist previously. Whatever the Kashgaris heard from their forefathers was passed on to the children and to the children's children. A typical Kashgari never troubles himself to introduce anything new, rather he says, "In all things we want to keep it like our fathers had it."

The people dress very simply and go barefoot in the warm season since there are hardly any stones. A long white shirt held together with a belt, trousers under that, and a small cap on his head—this is what is worn in summer.

In the winter for most a fur hat makes up the headgear; a cotton-lined coat protects against the cold, and instead of stockings, long woollen bands are worn which are wrapped around the legs. Over these bands are pulled boots or overshoes, though it would be more correct to call them leather stockings.

In the morning they drink tea; however, it is prepared differently than in Europe. Cream, salt, and tea are all boiled together, and bread is eaten with it. At noon the rich people have *pilaf*, that is, boiled rice with mutton. This dish is prepared in the following way: grease from the broad, fatty tail of the Persian sheep is melted in an iron pan and fried for a short time, so it is as hot as possible. Then salt is poured in, and after that, finely sliced carrots, boiled onions, as well as the mutton, which has been cut into pieces, is added, and everything is fried together until the carrots and onions have almost disappeared. After that, just enough water is added as is necessary for boiling the rice. After the meat has been cooked for a short time, the washed rice is added and cooked in the uncovered pot until it is done. When the water is nearly soaked up, quinces and some saffron are laid on top of the rice in order to season the dish still further, and this is then covered and steamed for about another half-hour on a very low heat. Then the dish is served. The table consists of a clean, thin cloth, which is spread out on the ground. After all the occupants of the house have washed themselves in a most careful manner, they sit down next to this cloth and reach into the bowl with their right hand; for the most part this is performed skilfully and cleanly. Orientals never use the left hand to eat with.

The favourite dish of the poor people is the quite palatable *suyukash*. Finely cut meat, chopped carrots, peas, lentils, and herbs are prepared into a soup. Then a dough is made from flour and cut into long strips, and these noodles are poured into the soup.

In the evening, as in the morning, they drink tea and eat bread with it. The bread is baked according to the Asiatic way, in flat, round loaves.

Before the beginning of the meal the oldest man says grace. The women almost always eat alone.

The Kashgaris are a beautiful people and are reminiscent of the inhabitants of the Caucasus. Their physique is slender and of medium build. The men have beards, but they shave their heads almost bald. They also always wear a hat in the house.

The houses are low and most of them have two storeys; the walls are made from unfired brick. To construct the roof, large beams are placed on top of the walls, and on top of the beams are spread wide mats made from reeds; these are covered with hay and earth. There are no windows; however, there is a large opening in the middle of the flat roof through which the lovely sun shines in. If it rains at any time, then this is bad, but fortunately it only rarely rains in Kashgar. During my five-year stay there it rained only twice. Admittedly, I have seen over two thousand houses collapse during a single shower. The soil is very saline, and as a result the walls dissolve extraordinarily fast in rain.

There are no ovens, only fireplaces of a primitive sort with an open fire. The streets in Kashgar, as in all oriental cities, are narrow and winding since the houses have been quite irregularly built. Everywhere wild dogs run around taking care of the street cleaning. The rubbish from every meal is thrown into the street and is devoured by them straight away.

The bazaar is covered over with reeds and mats. Once a week it is market day in every city.

The city of Kashgar is surrounded by walls, behind which is a deep moat. The city walls are seven to eight metres thick at the base but become narrower at the top and reach a height of twenty metres so that from outside the city not a single house can be seen. The walls are built out of loam and at the top are fitted with battlements on which the Chinese sentries patrol. Kashgar has three large gates; there is a customs guardhouse at each one. However, custom is only raised from domestic business: wood, fruit, and suchlike, while foreign products pass without a charge. Two of these gates are closed in the evening around seven o'clock while one stays open until ten o'clock. In the morning all three gates are opened around six o'clock.

Hunting is not popular with the Kashgaris. They do not even like to carry weapons, a practice which is customary for all the other peoples of the Orient. They are a quiet, peace-loving people; once they get into an argument, they use their hands as weapons. They have lived for many centuries cut off from the whole world and consider themselves to be the best people under the sun.

They are a talkative people, addicted to chatting. Although there are no newspapers, everyone already knows by evening what has happened that morning in the city. Once a foreigner comes to the city it is discussed at great length: where he lives, what he looks like, what kind of clothing he is wearing, where he comes from, and whether he is good or bad.

In the morning and evening all the people go to the mosque to pray, then after the service they sit in the open square in front of the mosque to chat with one another. This pleasure is decidedly more popular than work, but it is not necessary to work as much as in Europe because everything is so exceptionally cheap.

In the summer the people like to sit in the beautiful gardens where they eat and drink, or read and sing to the music. For this the preferred choice of poems are the ones by Emir Shir Ali Nava'i. The instruments are quite different from those of other Oriental countries. The *qalon*, for example, is outwardly reminiscent of the European zither, but it sounds like a piano. The *setar* is similar to a stringed zither with ten strings, but only one of the strings is played with the bow; the others resonate. The Kashgaris also have a type of tambourine. Instead of the drum they have a peculiar instrument: iron chains fastened to a large pole. The pole is moved back and forth, so the chains slap against each other as if someone is clapping his hands or beating a drum in a monotone.

Wine growing is not important in Kashgar. There is only one kind of wine prepared which is drunk with water and serves the sick and the weak as a medicine and a means of refreshment. Drinking wine for pleasure is not customary in Muslim countries.

Opium by comparison is used as a means of pleasure and as a narcotic, though not as much as in China and India. Another typical means of intoxication is extracted from a plant known as *nasha*.[1] On the leaves of this plant are fine, dust-like particles, which grow along with the plant. These are collected, mixed with tobacco, and smoked. When this pollen is heated up it melts. It is hard as stone when cooled; heating it immediately softens it again. People are more easily benumbed by nasha than by the strongest wines. Quite a large export of the processed powder from this plant goes to India where the Buddhist priests and lamas are fond of smoking it.

The Kashgaris' most holy ones are the first preachers of Islam in that country who died as martyrs. Their graves lie in beautiful gardens and are adorned with monuments. The anniversaries of their deaths are celebrated in quite a special way. At those times countless bands of pilgrims make their way to their burial places and celebrate the day with food and drink, songs and games.

---

[1] See Appendix B, *nasha*. Trans.

CHAPTER 12

THE BEGINNINGS OF THE MISSION IN KASHGAR

When I came to Kashgar, the Russian Consul instructed his secretary, Mirza Fazel Beg from Darvaz, to back me up in both word and deed. He told me all sorts of frightful things about the city and advised me to live outside it.

"Look," he said, "there is a Catholic missionary here, Father Hendricks, who came here six years ago with a Polish man, Adam Ignatovich.[1] They dare not live inside the city because it is very dangerous."

I answered him that I was not afraid and must live in the city in order to become well acquainted with the people. If I really were to be driven out, then it certainly would be time to move out of the city.

"You do not understand me," he said, "the Kashgaris are not accustomed to seeing someone in their midst in European clothes."

"If that is the hindrance," I answered, "then I can dress differently."

"Then maybe it will work," he said. "I will see about getting you some Kashgari clothes." He did this then brought me into the city. At the Urateba Caravansary he rented a room for me, and when I asked about a servant, he brought me his cousin, Omar Akhund.

The caravansary in which I lived had about fifty rooms occupied mainly by people from India. The rooms formed a circle with the door of each facing the inside of the circle. Light came through an opening in the middle of the ceiling, which consisted of earth. In front of the doors, likewise running in the shape of a ring, was a corridor from between three and four metres wide in which the horses were tied up. The actual middle of the whole thing was lower down; the camels stood there.

The Kashgaris soon came to see me and were very curious to learn what had led me there. At first it was very hard for me to understand their language, but I soon learned it since Kashgari is closely related to my mother tongue, Osmanli Turkish.

From Samarkand I had brought along two large chests of Bibles in Chinese, Arabic, and Persian and set them up at my home. I told the Kashgaris, these books were translations of the Old and New Testament: those holy books the Koran states are from God. It was my intention to live here for some time and fulfil whatever God would give me to do, but the Russian Consul General, Petrovsky, told the people I had come to make them

---

[1] Hedin, in his *My Life as an Explorer* (p. 99), states that Father Hendricks came to Kashgar in 1885 and that Adam's surname was Ignatieff. Trans.

apostates to the religion of their fathers, and I dressed like the Kashgaris, so I would not be known. Now the Kashgaris regarded me as an enemy of their religion and believed Mirza Fazel Beg who was spreading outrageous rumours about me. They had not yet seen a devoted Christian because the few Europeans whom they had come to know had not made a favourable impression on them by the way they lived. At first my young servant was very anxious because Mirza Fazel Beg had warned him and said I was a pagan who worshipped trees and rivers. He did not want to eat with me, and when I tried to talk to him, I noticed his distrust and did not speak further with him.

When Father Hendricks, the Catholic missionary, saw that I fared quite well at my caravansary, he rented a room across from me, but his helper Adam stayed outside the city in their old apartment near the Russian consulate.

After my servant had been in my home for six months and had listened every day to the discussions I had with the mullahs about Islam and the Christian religion, one day he said, "Now I see that everything I have heard about you is not true. For half a year I have seen how you live and have heard what you say about the purity and holiness of God. I love your religion with all my heart. Please read to me from your book, so I might come to understand what is written in it."

I wrote down the Turkish alphabet for him and told him he should learn to read, but he did not trust himself very much since as a child he had had difficulty with comprehension. First he had been sent away from the Muslim school, and a later attempt at a Chinese school was also unsuccessful. He asked me to read to him and to translate because there was not yet a Bible in the Kashgari language. So I read to him several chapters of the New Testament every day and was very astonished that on the following day he could always faithfully repeat the contents of what had been read and in the end learned how to read.

At this time an agent of the British and Foreign Bible Society came to Kashgar, Mr Morrison, who later was the director of this Bible Society for Germany. He gave me the job of translating the New Testament into the Kashgari language for his society and to start with the Sermon on the Mount as a test.

He had a Bible distributor with him, Hagop Arushanian, a dear, devoted man from the Caucasus. I had stayed at his home in Tiflis previously, and I was able to cultivate Christian fellowship with him. We read the Bible in Armenian and prayed with one another. When he had left again, my servant asked me to pray with him just as I had done with Hagop.

I had rented a second room next to my previous one. Every morning before sunrise my servant would come, tidy my room, and put the copper Kashgari teapot on the fire. Then we would have breakfast together. The room had a fireplace. I would sit on one side of the fire and he, according to his curious custom, always knelt on the other side. Then we would pray together. I had translated the Lord's Prayer into Kashgari for him, and he repeated it every morning. Then we would open the door to our room, as everyone does there, and I would read to him from the Bible. I began with the book of Genesis, and in the course of one year we had read the entire Bible. With this it was my principle not to preach but rather to use simple words to make it clear what is written. At the end of the chapter I would let him tell me in his own words what we had read. If he had understood it, I went on; if not, then I repeated it until it became clear to him. In the morning I would ask once more, and on Sunday everything we had read in the week was repeated. While we were reading together, other people would also come in to see us, and I would continue my reading in front of them. Especially on Sunday I would have many guests since they knew I would be home the whole day and would always read something to them out of the Bible.

God gave me many friends among the Kashgaris. There was one who was a former minister of Yakub Beg, an old, learned man who now worked as a goldsmith. Another was a young merchant. Even several Kashgari *begs*[1] came, and a Manchu, the dragoman to the Chinese governor, visited me every day. In the Orient people have a lot of time since life is inexpensive and the needs of the people are few. So they would sit with me in the morning and afternoon and sometimes even the whole day. If they wanted to go away at lunchtime, then I would ask them to stay and would share my food with them. If it was not enough we bought more bread, which is good and cheap, and drank tea with it, which likewise is cheap and good and is drunk without sugar. With fifty *pfennig*, at most a [German] mark, I could feed a large company, and we did not need to interrupt our discussion.

In the meantime I had begun the translation of the New Testament into Kashgari. Even before Mr Morrison had assigned the job to me, I myself had intended to do it and consequently had been looking to talk with a variety of people, to speak with them about all areas of life and learn the appropriate expressions in their language. As a result I soon found out that Kashgari has two dialects; the one is spoken by native Kashgaris and the other by Muslims who have immigrated from Andidjan (West Turkestan). Admittedly, the dialect of the latter is despised since it has a harsh sound and is lacking in polite phrases. For example, the Kashgaris do not address anyone as "you",[2] rather they always use the third person plural; with the Andidjanis, on the other hand, the second person singular is the customary address. The politest form heard from them is the second person plural, which is only used by the Kashgaris with regard to a group of people. Much more value is placed on the observance of these customs in the whole of the country than is, for example, in Europe. The Kashgaris have a far more distinct national consciousness than the rest of the Turkish people with whom the religion of Islam is the only

---

[1] See Appendix B, *beg*. Trans.

[2] That is, *du*, the informal second person singular in German. Trans.

bond. Unlike the Kashgari Turkish, the Andidjani (Uzbek) Turkish lacks the vowel harmony, which is the main cause for the harshness of the language. For instance, in Kashgari you say, *ketgen* ('gone away') and *algan* ('taken'), while the Andidjanis say *ketgan* and *algen*. However, the older books of both dialects are written in true Kashgari, a proof that the Andidjani language has lost its original purity.

The Kashgaris in turn are divided into two tribes, the *Aqtaghliq* ('people of the white mountain') and the *Qarataghliq* ('people of the black mountain'), of which the former speaks the better dialect, even though the differences between the two are minor. Concerning the translation, I was advised only to speak with the Aqtaghliq. My first servant, Omar Akhund, also belonged to this tribe, while my later servant, Hashim, was Qarataghliq.

Besides the day-to-day occupation with the language, I also read a number of books, that is, manuscripts, which I had purchased here and there in people's homes, since there is not a single bookshop in Kashgar.

In spite of these preparations, it seemed to me necessary to do the work with help from the Kashgaris. I found a capable secretary in Mirza Abd-ul-Karim Akhund, the best pupil of the famous Kashgari scholar, Maksum Akhund, who himself was a Turkish language teacher. I now worked together with him every morning. In the afternoon I would go to see the *Daotai's* translator, Fushang Daloy, with whom I became such good friends that I visited him every day, provided he did not come to see me first. In his office, which was in the town hall, it was customary to employ the Kashgari begs as well. I always met with a friendly reception and lively discussions there. I read my translation to them and asked those present to correct the language mistakes that might occur. In the evening I read back what I had written to Omar Akhund in order to check whether he, who could not read himself, understood everything as well. The old mullah, Niaz Akhund, who was one of Yakub Beg's former ministers, gave the third critique. Whenever someone found it necessary to make an alteration, I would discuss the suggestion with Mirza Abd-ul-Karim. Some technical terms, which my friends could not have had any knowledge of, I learned from craftsmen, farmers, and others.

A considerable help to me were several very valuable translations from the Persian into Kashgari, for example, *Anwár-i-Suhaylí* and *Chartak*.

As I said before, through the translation work I entered into a very friendly relationship with Fushang Daloy. To my regret I soon noticed that at times he consumed a lot of alcohol, a habit he did not have in his homeland of Manchuria but had adopted from the Europeans. As often as he had to pass on instructions from the Daotai to the Russian Consul or to Mr Macartney, they would do him the honour of putting intoxicating drinks in front of him. And he had to drink it. So his fondness for the consumption of alcohol grew. Once I spoke with him about this, warning him such a habit would have harmful effects on his health, especially his mind. But he replied, "I see that the Europeans, who consume a lot of spirits, have much understanding. Therefore

I will follow their example." It was very hard to convince him that this view was wrong.

When I visited Mr Macartney on New Year's Day, I met Fushang Daloy there. Munshi Ahmed ed-Din, Mr Macartney's Indian secretary, was "doing the honours". It was known I would not drink alcohol, so none was offered to me. However, the Manchurian was handed a tea glass full of brandy. I saw from the brand on the bottle that it was a strong drink and warned Fushang, "Be careful; this is no ordinary wine."

He answered, "I am familiar with it." However, when I visited him the next day, he was sick and had red, swollen eyes. He lamented to me, "You were right; the wine was bad for me. When I get better, I will follow your advice and drink no more."

After fourteen days he had recovered, and I visited him every day as usual. In order not to make it quite so noticeable that I came so frequently only because of the translation, I kept my work in my pocket until there was an occasion to read it. Sometimes I waited in vain. Fushang himself had good books from which he recited now and then and translated at my request. One day he read from a collection of teachings on ethics, the author of which was the Chinese emperor, Shung-chi. It was only a small work but one which contained very good rules. They corresponded in part with the ethics of the Gospel.

Several passages from this book ought to be mentioned here:

"Whoever does good and gathers good, that one will have more than enough blessing and joy in his home. Whoever does evil and gathers evil will have more than enough troubles and tribulation in his home. Heaven has determined nothing in advance. Whoever does good, that one will be rewarded a hundred-fold good; whoever does evil, that one will be punished a hundred-fold.—A morally pure life or a bad life is bound up with the man like his voice and his shadow.—If someone by doing good does not achieve the highest rank, then no one is able to have a good reputation. Before the measure of evil is filled up, a person cannot be lost. Fools say, 'A little good is of no use,' and do not do good, and 'a little evil does no harm,' and do it. That is why evil increases and when it has increased, nothing more can be done about it. You should not say, 'What can come of doing a little good?' and have scant regard for it. When a person does not do the little good, then perfection cannot be achieved. You should also not say, 'A little evil is no sin.' The little evil accumulates and brings disaster on you.—Among good deeds there are no great ones; among evil deeds there are no small ones.—Whenever you see good, then you ought to be like one who is thirsty; whenever you hear evil, then you ought to be like one who is deaf. When you see good, then think that it is coming out from you; when you see evil, then think that it has come like an illness into your body.

"When a person lives appropriately, that is to say, does not want to go above his station, deceives no one *in secret* [literally, 'in a dark house'], practises good deeds, has mercy on everyone, sincerely changes his way of life, adorns himself with fidelity, mercy, and a sense of honour, concerns himself with the education of others, supports the defenceless, practises mercy towards widows, honours the elderly, kindly inquires after the condition of the young, does not harm either animals or plants, rejoices over the good deeds of others, helps the needy, delivers the sorely afflicted, rejoices over the fortune of others as much as over his own, grieves over the misfortune of others as much as over his own, does not talk about the faults of others, does not praise his own knowledge, does not complain about his misfortune, does not become proud in a higher position, does not expect recompense for a good deed, does not regret a gift given: such a person can be called a good man."

I asked Fushang why he did not translate these valuable words into Kashgari as I was doing with the Bible. My intention with this question was to occupy his thoughts with noble things and release him from the pleasure of alcohol. He said he could not do it alone, but if I would help, he was ready and willing. In fact, he had the means to write, but he could not read Turkish. I promised to help him. So the book was translated, and he forgot about alcohol. When the work was finished, we looked for a printer. Just at that time a Kashgari, Nur Hajim, who had learned lithography in India, had returned to his homeland to introduce the new art there. So the Manchu-Chinese teaching on ethics according to the manuscript of Mirza Abd-ul-Karim Akhund became the first book[1] printed in Kashgar. Since there was no printer's ink, the government issued the order that in every house soot should be collected from above the oil lamps and delivered to Nur Hajim.

Through the translation I also got to know Nur Hajim, and my secretary Mirza Abd-ul-Karim entered into an association with Fushang Daloy so that a coming together of Muslim and Chinese literary work took place.

---

[1] I would like to mention here that at the time of my stay in Kashgar, the first telegram sent from Peking arrived there [Hedin also mentions the telegraph from Peking to Kashgar as being in existence in March 1896 (see *Through Asia*, p. 841). Trans.].

CHAPTER 13
HINDRANCES

The greatest difficulty for the spread of the gospel in Kashgar lay in the fact that the few European Christians who lived there knew nothing of a living faith and by no means led a life of holiness.

So at that time four Europeans, all from different nations, were staying in Kashgar: the Russian Consul General, Petrovsky; an Englishman, Mr Macartney, the son of a Chinese mother; and finally a Dutchman, Father Hendricks, and his companion, Adam Ignatovich, a Polish nobleman. The last two named were Catholics, the others, Russian Orthodox and Protestant, although in name only. The Pole had been sent to Siberia by the Russians because he had rebelled against them, and Father Hendricks, who had lived in Mongolia for twenty years, had found him in Omsk as he was travelling to Kashgar. He had promised him, "What I receive from the Pope as a stipend shall also belong to you, but like me, you must be ready to be faithful unto death."

So they came as missionaries to Kashgar. Adam was a fine figure of a man, about sixty years old with a white beard and a forceful bearing. Father Hendricks was the same age, of medium build with a full, brown beard and a bald head, very thin, and of an excitable nature. Adam's clothes were very odd: he wore a fur without sleeves and with the hair to the outside. He always had with him a bag with keys, knives, locks, and brandy bottles as well as a cane. A rosary always hung around his arm and neck, and on his chest he wore a cross. The people said of him that he had sworn he would not die. Father Hendricks wore an old tattered coat, a hat that was just as bad, and Chinese shoes. Because of these he was called *kitaykafsh* ('Chinese galoshes'). He carried a cane.

When the two came to Kashgar they turned to the Daotai and asked him for an available apartment. They introduced themselves to him as teachers of virtue and asked him for his help, so they could serve the country. The good governor gave them a house outside the city next to the Russian consulate.

Adam then served as Father Hendricks' cook. He had brought along a little money with which he bought food for both of them. At the time of the grape harvest they made wine, which they drank all year round. The priest had some medical knowledge, and the sick came to see him, but his manner was so cold and fierce that the people were soon repelled. He associated with the Russian Consul and with Mr Macartney, to whom he gave German and French lessons. He did not particularly trouble himself to study the language and the character of the people thoroughly, and that is why he got nowhere as a missionary.

He was very thrifty. Several of his fingers were frostbitten because he had journeyed through the Mongolian mountains without gloves. Once when we were on a walk through a dense forest, he put his hat under his arm. I said, "Father, the branches are slapping us. Put your hat on, so you will not get hurt."

"No," he answered, "it does not matter. I have had this hat for seven years, and I must look after it." I looked at the hat from the side; it was old and riddled with holes.

When Adam's money ran out, he told the priest, "Give me some money and say what I am supposed to buy and prepare for us today."

Then the priest became furious: "We cannot live as we have up to now. We must economise even more", and only gave him enough money for him to be able to buy a little bread.

Since Adam had not led such a meagre existence, neither at home, nor in Siberia, this treatment became hard for him to take, and he said, "Father, you were to give me two roubles a day, and for this I promised to stand faithfully by you. Now give me my money, and I will support us both with it." The priest gave an angry response, took his things, and went to stay with Mr Macartney. This had taken place at the time of my arrival in Kashgar. As I have already said, after some time Father Hendricks likewise moved into the Urateba Caravansary and became my neighbour.

The room which he lived in was furnished in the following way: on one side stood an altar with a crucifix and pictures of saints; on the other side stood many wine jugs and bottles in addition to books, newspapers, and medicine bottles. On the third side stood a bed; some wood lay along the fourth side. In the middle of the room he had a small iron stove, the chimney pipe of which went through the ceiling. In front of the stove stood baking tins he used for baking the communion hosts. Once a year he cleaned his room. The dust always lay so thick that a person could write on any object with his finger. The Swedish explorer, Doctor Sven Hedin, once was at Father Hendricks' home and then wrote about him and his room in his book. As a result the priest did not let him back into his dwelling. The European travellers who came to Kashgar usually lived with Mr Macartney. To receive them at Father Hendricks' place was always very awkward. Whenever they came, they would find him sitting in front of the door with his mass book, but if they wanted to pay him a visit, then he would bring them to my place. He also wanted to bring wine there for them, but I did not allow it since the Kashgaris who associated with me would not come to see me any more if they had seen it.

Father Hendricks very seldom ate by himself at home. In the morning either he came to my place for tea or he went with a teapot to the Indians and got what he wanted there by begging. During the mid morning he stayed at home and waited on the sick to whom he gave medicine, but because he could not speak good Kashgari, the people often came to me and had me translate his words. Then he always became very angry and did not give any more medicine to those who did that. At noon he went to see Mr Macartney and gave him language lessons; he also ate lunch with him. In the afternoon he came to see me, and we read together for an hour. We communicated in Russian, Swedish, and Dutch, and he told me everything he had read earlier in Macartney's newspapers, but since his visits were of no use either to him or to me, I suggested to him he should give me French lessons. I wanted to teach him Arabic or Persian or whatever else he might want to know. He felt more at home with me than in his own home.

However, in the autumn the daily get-together stopped since he had to spend weeks preparing the wine. He bought the grapes and pressed them himself. One time the Kashgari priest had given the order that no one should sell grapes to the Catholic priest. Firstly, the Kashgaris do not like wine at all, and, secondly, the previous year he had thrown the pressed grape skins into the rubbish pit. Since the grape is considered to be a holy fruit, they wanted to punish him for the great sin of having thrown the skins into the filth.

Adam now suffered from great poverty. He came to see the priest, but he did not let him into the room. That morning before sunrise he appeared with his prayer book in his hand, knelt at the priest's door, and read for half an hour. He often came to my room and ate with me, but whenever I spoke to him of Christ and redemption, I met with little sympathy because he was a fanatical Catholic. When winter came, Adam's need became even greater. He turned to the Russian Consul and complained to him about what had happened. Then the Consul sent a soldier and had Father Hendricks called to the consulate. The father shouted at the messenger, "What do you want? Me?" He turned around quickly, took hold of an old rifle, and said, "Do you want me to shoot? I have nothing to do with the Russian Consul." Now the Consul asked me to make some suggestions to him. He should either give Adam money to live here or the money to travel to Omsk. As I was speaking with the priest in front of my door, he put his hand into his bootleg, brought out a hundred-rouble bank note, and said, "Please give this to Adam, so he will leave and I will not have to see him any more." On the following day I went to the Consul and brought the money to him, but he did not want to take it. "He will never get as far as Omsk with that," he said. Adam now decided to take his complaint to the Chinese government.

But before the case was decided, he became sick with a fever. The priest came to see him, felt his pulse, checked his reflexes, and said, "It is too late; there is nothing more to be done for you. I will give you the last rites." He brought a bottle of strong wine and gave him a good swig. This was necessary, he claimed, for him to regain his full strength. From the wine and the fever Adam went completely out of his mind. The priest told him, "Now you are dying, and after your death the Russian Consul will demand your salary from me and will spend the money on himself; this would be a great sin against our holy Church. If you testify with your signature that you have not asked me for anything, then I will give you the last rites; if you do not, then you shall pass away in your sins." Poor Adam did not know what he was doing and signed everything the priest wanted him to sign, but he did not die; rather he was well again in a few days and continued with his court case without knowing what he had done.

When the Chinese government called the priest before the court, he asked the men from the Russian consulate to be summoned and then said, "The whole case is a lie and a scheme on the part of the Russians. This man has nothing to demand of me." He brought out Adam's signature, the dragoman translated, it was established that the matter was correct, and with that it was concluded. Now the unfortunate Adam was at his wits' end. Nevertheless, he came to the priest's door every morning with his prayer book and knelt there for half an hour in spite of the winter cold.

I told him, "Adam, if you know this man has behaved badly, why do you then come to his door and pray there? You can pray at home. God is everywhere."

He answered, "I know he is bad, but in his room there are holy relics: a piece of the cross of Christ and a small bone from Peter. That is why I come here."

On the following morning he came back, and what's more, without his long white beard; he was clean-shaven. I was astonished, and when I asked him about the reason for this change, he answered, "Now I am young again. Now I can punish the father." He prayed in front of the door and then went away. After an hour I again saw him pass by my open door. Shortly after that, I heard the noise of punches, and when I ran to the doorway I caught sight of Adam attacking the priest. But the priest stood there stock-still and did not defend himself. I rushed in and took hold of Adam's hand.

"What are you doing?" I said. "You are making a mockery of Christianity in front of the heathen and Muslims." That is to say, from every door Hindus and other neighbours were approaching.

Adam cried, "*Davai dengi*!" ('Give me my money!'), and he said to the people, "You are good men, but he is a deceiver."

I took him by the hand, led him to my room, admonished and calmed him down, and sent him away. After that, the priest came to see me. When I asked him, "Father, did he hurt you very much?" he answered, "It does not matter even if he wounded me." But he really was afraid, and now whenever he went out, he took my servant along. I told him the Consul thought Adam would take the relics away.

"Is that so?" he said, startled. "Please tell him these things are worthless outside of my room and are nothing but wood and bone." I cautioned Adam he should now no longer come and pray at his door after he had beaten the priest in front of all those people. For the heathen were laughing and poking fun at the way the Christians were behaving. He listened to me and prayed at home.

Later on, with the accession to the throne of the new Russian Tsar,[1] Adam would not swear allegiance to him; therefore the Russians persecuted him, sealed up his door, and drove him away. He came to see me and complained to me, "It is winter. Where shall I sleep?" I gave him permission to sleep in my room that night, but he asked me only to give him a blanket; he preferred to lie in front of the priest's door. When the priest saw him the next morning, he kicked him: "Away with you! Why are you lying here?", went into his room, and locked the door behind him. In the evening Adam went to the Chinese man, Fungshang, to whom he had given Russian lessons, and asked him for a room, but the Chinese had already heard why the Russians were persecuting him and drove him out of the city. Meanwhile, Swedish missionaries had arrived, and he went to see one of them, Mr Högberg, but even he did not receive him for fear of the Russian Consul. So now the poor man stayed overnight in the Muslim cemetery. On the following day he came to see me, warmed himself, fortified himself with some food, and regained a little of his strength. I asked him to be reasonable and quietly take the oath. I would arrange the matter with the Consul.

"No," he said, "my fathers did not do it, and I will not do it either. I would rather die."

When the Russians saw that Adam was at my home, they put all of his things in a cart and sent them to my caravansary. I wanted to rent a room for him near to me, but the priest called me to one side and said, "I have rented an apartment for him with Haji Ali; send him there." So I did that. In the meantime the priest went from door to door in the caravansary and made the people apprehensive by telling them Adam ought not to be admitted without permission from the Russian government. The business with Haji Ali proved to be incorrect, and Adam returned again with his things, but now the gatekeeper did not want to let him into the caravansary. He went out of the city to the island in the Tuman River, pitched his tent, and lived there in the cold of January. The next day I sent him some food since I knew he had nothing to eat, and learned that he was sick. Then I spoke with a Kashgari beg who took pity on him and gave him an apartment without asking for any rent. He later died there.

As I said before, the Kashgaris visited me often, and I in turn visited them. Whenever I read the Gospel and talked to them about Christianity, they liked it very much, but they told me, "It is just as you preach; we have not seen any Christians. The Europeans who have been in Kashgar for the most part have not believed in God at all, or in an afterlife. Rather they have ridiculed all religions. We have seen no trace of what you have read to us from the Gospel. In Khotan (south of Kashgar)," they went on to tell me, "there were two

---

[1] Alexander III died on 1 November 1894. Trans.

Frenchmen, learned men, who after several months wanted to get married. But the priests would not permit any girl to marry a man who had not accepted Islam beforehand. Then these Frenchmen professed Islam and were married. However, soon they left their wives, travelled back to Europe, and were never heard from again. Thus we see that they deceived our people and were not sincere confessors of Islam. Even according to their own religion they must not behave in that way. If this is what the Christians are like, then Christianity cannot be a good religion. Islam must then be better."

I explained to them that not all those who call themselves Christians really are Christians. I also pointed out to them there were even many bad people amongst the Muslims, but I said to them as well that I knew many Christians who really believe what is written in the Gospel and who take the trouble to live according to it.

"Fine," they answered, *"but we have not seen these people, and although we cannot say anything bad about you personally, your testimony is really not enough to cause us to give up our religion and adopt another. It would be very good if we could get to know a few good Christian families."*

I replied, "I will ask our society to send some people here."

To this they said, "Very good! Please write, so the families will come, and we might become acquainted with their family life."

After some deliberation, I wrote to Stockholm to Doctor Ekman, the chairman of the Swedish Missionary Society. He placed my letter in the missions newsletter and wrote back to me that he proposed for the time being to send me two missionaries to help out, Raquette and Beklund.

However, in the meantime I received a letter from Missionary Högberg in Tabriz who expressed his desire to come to me. I wrote to Doctor Ekman: first, the work would require an experienced missionary who had already spent some time living amongst Muslims and was reasonably acquainted with their language and customs. Also it was important he bring his family along. I suggested to Högberg that Brothers Raquette and Beklund could come later. Doctor Ekman agreed with this and informed me that for the time being, Högberg would be the one to come. He had written to Shanghai for Chinese passports and hoped to take care of everything in the course of a month. I was happy about this news and looked forward to the missionary and his family with great anticipation.

CHAPTER 14

THE FIRST BAPTISM IN KASHGAR

Through the many discussions I had with Muslims about Christianity my servant's faith was strengthened more and more, and his knowledge of the Scriptures grew. One day he said to me he wanted to be baptised, though I had never spoken to him about baptism.

"How do you come by this idea?" I asked.

"You read it to me from the Acts of the Apostles," he replied, "that if someone had come to believe in Jesus, he was baptised. I now believe Jesus is my Saviour, and that is why I would like to be baptised."

"It will mean a lot of difficulties for you," I said. "If you are baptised, the Muslims will persecute you and perhaps kill you."

However, he was steadfast and said, "I am not worth more than the first Christians. They too were persecuted and killed." My response to him was we would wait until the missionaries had arrived from Sweden; then he would be baptised. He was a little dejected but said nothing in reply.

Now before I tell of my other experiences, I would like to relate several things about my servant's family and home.

Omar Akund's father, Khoja Baehav ed-Din (which means 'faith's splendour') was from the lineage of the Khojas that in the first half of the seventeenth century had given Kashgar its princes. His fellow citizens held him in especially high regard because of his strict observance of Islamic religious regulations. He was married to a woman from a wealthy, distinguished family, and for a while having one wife was enough for him, but then according to the Islamic way of thinking, it is regarded as commendable, if it is at all possible, to take the four wives allowed by law. In this way the numerous descendants made possible by this provision increase the number of Islam's followers. So Khoja brought along a new wife from each of his business trips he made over the Celestial Mountains (Tyan Shans) to the now Armenian city of Andidjan until the number of his wives totalled four. The consequence of this was that he not only was unkind to and neglected his first wife, but he even wore her out since she alone did all of the work in the house. By this she was in a way reduced to being the maid of the other three wives who had been taken after her. She had to wait on these women from early morning until late in the evening, cleaning and washing their clothes. Untiringly and with the greatest diligence, this most pitiful woman subjected herself to all of them with nothing else to do but weep in complete secrecy over her harsh lot, which came through no fault of her own. The little free time remaining to her she spent caring for her young daughter. As much as she slaved away and suffered to do right in all things, she did not succeed in pleasing her husband. He always had to find fault with her and with her work; he beat and abused her and finally ordered her out of his sight. The woman patiently and silently put up with everything. She even did without the solace of visiting her parents and relatives if only to keep her husband, whose permission she would have had to ask in order to go out, from thinking she was complaining to her relatives about his treatment of her.

Four years passed in this way. Meanwhile, Kashgar had been the scene of repeated radical changes in politics, as I have briefly mentioned before. In China itself there was an uprising amongst the numerous Chinese Muslims, and the revolt had also spread westward.[1] In East Turkestan the Chinese people, officials, soldiers, and merchants were massacred by the Muslims, and only a few saved their lives by accepting Islam. The power of the government in Kashgar as well as in the other cities of the country fell, partly through force and partly through the trust that the population placed in the hands of men who were distinguished but incapable of making the people recognise them in a popular or lasting way.

Yakub Beg put an end to this state of affairs. He had come from the khanate of Kokand, north of the Celestial Mountains, under the pretext of helping an offspring of the old Kashgari race of princes, the Khojas, to the throne. But at an opportune moment Yakub Beg pushed this man, who was incompetent and debauched,[2] to one side and founded his own kingdom, which covered the whole of East Turkestan. After he had snatched up power for himself, he knew how to weaken the Khojas in every conceivable way. He rid himself of some of them through assassination; others, among them Khoja Baehav ed-Din, were apprehended and were supposed to be executed. As soon as Khoja's wife learned her husband was in prison and what fate was in store for him, she hurried to her father, whom Yakub Beg held in high regard, and beseeched him to make his influence felt and save her husband. Then she prepared food for her husband, brought it to him in prison, and encouraged him. On his request, she pressed her father once more, so he went back to Yakub Beg that evening and persuaded him to set the prisoner free that very night. So Khoja Baehav ed-Din returned to his home. The first thing he did was to make his way to his wife's chamber, to the very wife he had so neglected, and thank her for his rescue. What followed was she bore him a son in addition to the little daughter she had already had. This son was Omar Akhund.

Several years after these events the Khoja fell terminally ill. As he felt his end approaching, remorse gripped him once again very intensely, and he asked his first wife to forgive him for all the sorrow he had caused her. Now

---

[1] This was the great Ttingani (Dungani) revolt, or insurrection, which broke out in 1862. Trans.
[2] This was Buzurg Khan (he ruled Kashgar from 1865 to 1867). Trans.

in his pain he only wanted to see her by his side. He was no longer interested in his other wives, and such a fierce aversion to them took hold of him that he chased them away with curses whenever they came to see him. Finally death delivered him from his suffering. His three younger wives married again, abandoning their children to their fates, but the first wife stayed faithful to her husband even after his death. She refused every proposal, even some honourable ones, and lived totally for bringing up her son and her daughter, whose marriage she lived to see.

When Omar Akhund had grown up, he married a woman who, like almost all Muslim women, was very fanatical.

About a month after my conversation about baptism with Omar Akhund, I went out for a ride one evening. Along the way I met Mr Macartney who likewise was on horseback. After we had ridden a little way together, he said, "Do you not see the two Europeans there?" When I replied that there were no Europeans here, he assured me, "They are riding across the street in front of us. Do you not see them?" With that he motioned with his hand in front of us. I then saw two riders. However, I could not quite make them out clearly since my eyesight is weak and the sun was shining in my eyes. Mr Macartney told me that one was the commanding officer of the Russian soldiers; the other was the Consul's secretary. When I heard this, a foreboding rose in my mind that this encounter would lead to something unpleasant. I knew the Consul would take offence if I had seen his men and had not greeted them. After I had arrived home that evening, I immediately went to see the commanding officer and asked him to excuse me that I had not greeted him; Mr Macartney had only told me afterwards he had gone past us.

He replied, "It is too late. I have already informed the Consul about it."

The following day was the day for the post to arrive. I went to the Consul to collect any letters and newspapers that had come for me. He gave them to me but at the same time said, "You do not know what favour you are enjoying here. This is no post office. The post is only for me, and you get your letters from my hand only by my good will. But you go for a ride with Mr Macartney, see my commanding officer, and do not greet him even once. From now on I am stopping this arrangement of mine for you to send and receive post. This is the last consignment."

I tried to explain to him that I had not recognised the commanding officer, and I turned to the commanding officer, who was also present in the room, and asked him whether I had not come to see him the previous evening and told him all about it. The Consul cut me off and remarked he would hear nothing more; no more post would be accepted for me. I should go to Mr Macartney and have him take care of my post.

On arriving home I considered I would hardly be able to stay here if I could no longer have any correspondence with Europe. That is to say, if my letters were supposed to be sent by the Chinese post, I would have to wait at least half a year for the response to one letter. If I had them sent by Mr

Macartney, they would still take several months because he received his post via India; and besides, it would not be reliable. There were only two solutions: either I had to leave Kashgar or I had to try and placate the Consul. I now wrote a petition in which I explained the true facts of the case. I also informed him I had bumped into Mr Macartney quite unexpectedly. With this petition I went to the consulate myself to present it to the Consul in person; however, I was not allowed in.

I now prepared to leave Kashgar. This was immediately communicated to the Consul through his spies. The following day I tried once more to present my petition, but in vain. Finally on the third day he sent for me and said, "What do you want me to do with your petition? I am not your Consul, rather I am the Russian Consul." I replied it was not actually a petition; rather it was an explanation about the true facts of the case. He asked me to read it out loud and then declared that he forgave me and from now on would go back to conveying my post. After I had thanked him for this, he asked me, "I have heard you will be taking a trip. When will this be?" I responded I would be travelling as soon as the Lord wanted it to happen.

At that time a torrential rain suddenly set in. The salty soil became soft, and the roads were destroyed, so it took a month before the paths were dry again. In addition, the horse I had bought for the journey was killed by a collapsing wall. Those were good reasons for me to give up the idea of travelling.

Meanwhile, my servant Omar Akhund asked me ever more urgently to baptise him. He said if I travel, then he would remain unbaptised, and I was responsible to God for him. He believed and was not afraid of death. When I saw he really believed in Jesus and had no fear, I took him and baptised him in the Tuman River, which flows past the city. In regard to baptism I asked him, "Which name do you want to have as a Christian name?"

He replied, "I would like to be called by the name of Lazarus who loved Jesus and who rose from the dead."[1]

When his wife learned that her husband had become a Christian, she betrayed him to the mullahs. They sent for him and threatened him with death if he would not come back regularly to the mosque and perform the Muslim ritual prayer every day as before. But he stood firm and told the mullahs many things from the gospel.

Another time he was led before a gathering of fifty mullahs. They placed a rope around his neck and threatened to strangle him immediately if he spoke about Jesus and the gospel. Although Lazarus was a strong young man, he did not defend himself, rather he declared to the mullahs he would die for Jesus. When they then saw he was not afraid of death and noticed as well that the Chinese government did not comply with their wish to punish him because of his conversion, they began to torment him anew during the month of fasting

---

[1] For this story see the Bible, Gospel of John chapter 11. Trans.

called *Ramazan*, a time when they are especially fanatically minded. I now arranged it, so he went to another village during the month of fasting and only returned after the people had calmed down again.

Before his conversion, Lazarus had been a rather careless young man who had shown little kindness to others, but the power of the gospel had produced a wonderful change. He was now honest, loving, patient, and kind towards everyone, even towards his enemies, so everyone was bound to grow fond of him. Even his wife, though she, as I have said before, was a very fanatical Muslim woman, regained her love and respect for him little by little. She was not as uneducated as most of the Muslim women; she could read and write which for women within Islam is a great rarity.

At this time the Swedish explorer, Doctor Sven Hedin, came to Kashgar and was living at the home of the Russian Consul.[1] I visited him, spoke Swedish with him, and because of the conversation, was invited by the Russian Consul to tea every evening. It was not pleasant for me, but I had to comply since I was indeed completely dependent on the Consul. He indulged in mocking clichés about religion and missions, and Doctor Sven Hedin would agree with him. The explorer stayed in Kashgar for several months. However, he finally told me he intended to travel to the Mustagh Ata and asked me to accompany him since of course he could not speak the language of the country; at the same time it would be a good opportunity for me to do missionary work.

I did not want to go with him and told him I was expecting some Swedish missionaries, but the Consul and Sven Hedin declared that this was no reason to stay here; the Chinese would never allow the missionaries to come. When I said they would be coming with Chinese passports and with the *Tsung-li Yamen's* special permission and the local Chinese would not be able to stop them, they replied the matter would not go through so quickly; they would not be able to get a passport from the Chinese government in less than a year. When I saw that neither the Consul nor Sven Hedin would forgo my going along and would have caused trouble for me if I had refused, I agreed to go for two months. On this journey I hoped to be able to study the character and customs of the rural population.

So Sven Hedin, his armed servant, Islam [Baï] from Russian Turkestan, and I (with my own horse) rode away from Kashgar and reached Yangi-hissar in two days. We spent the night at the home of a Hindu friend of mine. The Chinese commander had been informed by the governor of Kashgar about our forthcoming arrival. On the following morning, as Doctor Hedin was still sleeping, four of the provincial governor's servants came and brought a large

---

[1] This was Hedin's second trip to Asia, which lasted from 1893 to 1897; his first visit was from 1890 to 1891. In his book, *Through Asia*, Hedin mentions Avetaranian but only by his first name, Johannes or John. He states, "At the time of my visit to Kashgar he [Avetaranian] chiefly occupied himself with translating the Bible into Turki and the dialect of Kashgar, and with playing Swedish psalm tunes on a violin in the evening" (p. 232). Trans.

basket of food arranged in a similar way to the customary hampers of food, which are prepared in European hotels to take ready-made, midday meals to private homes. Forty different dishes on plates were inside the basket. In addition, the men brought a sack of rice and a sheep especially for our servants, who always suffered from huge appetites, as well as barley and hay for the horses.[1] Doctor Hedin sent the food back again with many thanks since it was so much that we would not be able to eat it. However, we kept the sheep as well as the rice, barley, and hay. At noon we went to pay him a visit, but the provincial governor informed us through his servant that unfortunately he was sick and could not receive us.

We then had an interesting ride in the direction of Mount Mustagh for several days, during which Doctor Hedin made geographical and geological observations. Although we were in the middle of July, it was very cold since we had gone higher and higher up into the mountains. The air became so thin that I got severe pains in my eyes and could no longer ride along with them.

---

[1] This was a common form of hospitality shown to travellers in the region. Trans.

CHAPTER 15
CO-WORKERS

After returning to Yangi-hissar, I found a letter from Sweden, which said, the missionaries would be coming; I was supposed to rent a house for them. One of them, Högberg, was already on his way from Baku.

In Kashgar there was only a single small house built with windows after the European pattern. A rich man had erected it for himself in the garden on the edge of the city. Every European who came to the city lived there. When I had arrived back in Kashgar, I told the owner of the house that missionaries were coming from Sweden; I wanted to rent the whole of the small property for them for one year. The man declared he would receive the men of God into his home rent-free. However, I told him it would be better if they paid rent. The Europeans would not be able to understand Asian hospitality and would wish to be independent and do as they pleased in the house. So I made a contract with him and rented the beautiful house with the garden for two hundred and forty [German] marks a year.

Then I discussed with my servant what was to be done in regards to the arrival of the missionaries and decided to go see the *Shaengaeng*, the [regional] head of the Office of Foreign Affairs, and sort out a passport for myself in order to ride out to meet the brothers at the border. The official was so friendly that he did not give me a passport but a letter of recommendation to take along, to the effect that I should be assisted in all my business wherever I went and should be helped to receive the guests in a respectful manner.

I then sent a messenger with a letter to meet the missionaries at the Russian border because I was afraid the Russians could deter them and tell them the Chinese would not let them in. I rode for three days as far as Oksalur to meet the brothers and sisters and there met Missionary Högberg and his wife, the Bible-woman Anna Nyström, and a Persian who had taken the name Yussuf at his baptism in Tiflis. It was a great joy for me to meet them since I had been alone for such a long time. Concerning the Persian, Mirza Yussuf, Högberg told me he had been teaching Persian to Anna Nyström in Tabriz. After she had left, he had come to Tiflis and been baptised there. He had brought him along from Baku to serve as physician since he had been a doctor in Teheran for quite some time.

I answered, "Fine, but is this Persian a true believer? How did you get to know him?"

He answered, "I can say nothing more about him since I have had no time to get to know him."

I was surprised he had been with him on the journey for three months and had not had any time to get to know him. I also had misgivings that he had brought him along to a new mission field without any knowledge of his character and position in regard to the faith. For nothing can be achieved in the mission for the Lord while working with unbelieving men.

The Chinese officials helped us on our way, and we did not need to make as many detours as when I came the first time. I urgently asked Högberg to keep silent for a while until he had got to know the people and their language. I also told him about the experiences I had had with the Consul, Mr Macartney, and others. The next day I told him we would first have to visit the Daotai[1] and then the Shaengaeng since it was the custom here for strangers to pay a visit to the officials, but he declared he must first visit the Russian Consul, afterwards the others. As a result I went with him to the Russian consulate and then to the palace of the governor who received him warmly. Tea was served in glasses according to the Russian custom as well as in Chinese vessels. I interpreted.

The Governor said, "Welcome! What country do you come from? What do you propose to do in our region?"

Högberg said, "We are teachers of virtue." To the question, whether he would travel on or make his permanent residence in Kashgar, he answered, "Just as it is entered in our passport, we intend to travel."

When he wanted to produce his passport to confirm what he had said, the Governor said in a polite but firm manner, "My department does not deal with these matters. You must consult the appropriate official. By the way, I am very happy to have been allowed to welcome as my guests, men whose profession it is to teach virtue. In the next few days it will be my pleasure to return your visit."

Before we went, he asked in passing, "Have you met the old Russian who is staying here?" Högberg replied that he had paid a visit to the Russian Consul. During the audience with the governor, the Swedish missionary, not familiar with oriental customs, had taken off his hat, although I had asked him beforehand not to do it. This offence against oriental custom, according to which uncovering the head is extremely inappropriate, obviously displeased the Governor, and he asked Högberg to cover his head. When the missionary answered that in Europe it is regarded as a mark of respect to remove one's hat, the Governor replied, "But we are not in Europe, rather we are in Kashgar", whereupon the Swede covered his head.

Then the missionaries moved into the house I had rented for them, but Yussuf did not want to live there and rented a house inside the city. He wanted to set up a hospital there, but the people sent a petition to the authorities to keep this man out of the city. As a result he rented a plot of land

---

[1] For more information about the Daotai, see Appendix B, Li Tsung-pin. Trans.

outside the city and built a house there on Högberg's instructions. The contract for the land had been concluded in such a way that after several years the house would belong to the owner of the land.

However, it turned out Yussuf was unsuited for the mission since he gave offence by his character and his manner. He was a drinker and an opium smoker and quarrelled almost every day with someone. This worried me a great deal. I spoke with him seriously about it but to no avail; he was deaf to every good exhortation. He had an odd idea of the mission: he said missionaries must only pursue politics; religion was none of their business. I told Högberg it could not go on like this; our mission would suffer from it if Yussuf would not change. Högberg promised me he would caution Yussuf. On the following day I received a letter from the missionary in which he wrote, "I had a talk with Yussuf. He has confessed all his sins and prayed for forgiveness, but he is a doctor; he knows what he is doing. He smokes opium because of his toothache. He drinks wine with Munshi Ahmed ed-Din because he has a stomach-ache. He has a reason for drinking spirits in the evenings: the newly built house is still damp."

After I had read the letter, Yussuf came to see me. Of course he knew what Högberg had written but he asked, "Have you received a good letter from Högberg? What does it say? Did I not tell you these people are not religious; rather they are political? I can do what I like, and you will not be able to take any action against me." I exhorted him in a brotherly way, but he just laughed.

Soon after, Doctor Hedin came back from the Mustagh Ata and was again a guest of the Russian Consul. He paid a visit to the Swedish missionaries and made a request for me to accompany him to Lop-nor as an interpreter. I declined. My time was too precious to me since I was devoted to the work of translating the New Testament and, besides, I had to teach the missionaries the Kashgari language. He lived at the Consul's home for three months and often spoke with me about his travel plans. One day, when Högberg had invited us to lunch, Doctor Hedin asked again since there were now three missionaries in Kashgar with a good command of the Turkish language, if one of them would like to accompany him as an interpreter. Högberg declined since he was too much tied down to Kashgar with the construction of his house and other things. The prospect of the Persian Yussuf travelling along with him foundered on the tears of Anna Nyström, his wife-to-be. Doctor Hedin told his fellow countrywoman, "Do not cry; your dearest shall stay here." Then Högberg suggested I go, but I refused since I would not be able to continue my translation work while on the trip. To this Doctor Hedin replied, "You can translate along the way just as well as you could here, for I also have to write. Besides, you can take along a servant so as to have more time and peace." Under these circumstances I was once again unable to refuse his request and promised to accompany him, though I was not happy about it.

CHAPTER 16
DOCTOR SVEN HEDIN'S JOURNEY[1]

Sven Hedin's plan was to explore the Takla Makan Desert. It was the beginning of the month of January, the most suitable time, when he planned this trip. In the spring or summer it is impossible to ride across the desert because of the heat. After I had made inquiries in the city about the Takla Makan, I advised him to buy camels in Kashgar, since no one would have hired them out for such a journey, and to ride via Khanarik and Terim to Merket, which we could reach in four or five days. The desert begins there. But Doctor Hedin said the Consul thought camels would be cheaper to buy in Maral-bashi, so he wanted to go as far as that town by cart and only use camels from there on. I had learned that Maral-bashi was a small town situated in the forest where there were no camels available. Camels can only be bought in big cities and in non-wooded areas, but Doctor Hedin persisted in his resolve, remarking that the Consul's aksaqal must really know what is best. I made no reply but asked him to let us set out as quickly as possible. However, he was expecting a letter from Sweden with the Consul's next consignment of post, and, since the post arrived at the consulate only every seven days, we were forced to lose several more days. However, since the letter did not come in either the next delivery or in the one after that, our departure was put off again and again until we finally left Kashgar on 17 February.

I left Lazarus back in Kashgar and took along another servant by the name of Hashim. Our journey from Kashgar to Maral-bashi lasted seven days. As we arrived in the city of Yangi-shahr, which lies about a mile[2] from Kashgar, a Chinese man came running up behind our cart and took away my dog, Haemrah. We stopped the cart. Hashim climbed down and wanted to take the dog away from the Chinese man. Then a big commotion ensued. Hundreds of Chinese and Turkish people came running up and gathered around our cart. From every side they were calling out, "What's the matter? What's the matter?" The Chinese man claimed the dog belonged to him and that it had been stolen from him. He wanted to have it back. But Hashim replied the dog

---

[1] I was very reluctant to publish the details about this journey. However, Doctor Sven Hedin has attacked me on several occasions in his writings. In one work about Kashgar he declared that I ('the missionary') deserted him as soon as difficulties arose. As an answer to the questions that have been addressed to me from several quarters because of this, I have described the facts in greater detail than I would have done otherwise.

[2] This could be a German mile but is probably a Swedish mile. See Appendix B, mile. Trans.

had been with me from when it was young. In order to bring this scandal to a close, I wanted to let the Chinese man have the dog, although it was a beautiful animal and very loyal, but Doctor Hedin advised against this. My dog was much better than his; Yoldash was its name. I should not let him go to the Chinese man. Therefore we climbed down from our cart and arranged that Hashim as well as the Chinese man should call the dog at a distance from the cart. Whomever the dog followed, that is the one to whom it should belong. The people standing around declared, "This is very good." Sven Hedin's servant, Islam, kept hold of the dog next to the cart until the two had moved off about two hundred paces. The Chinese man took a piece of meat out of his pocket and called the dog by a Chinese name. However, Hashim had nothing in his hand and only called, "Haemrah! Haemrah!" Immediately the dog ran to him. Then the crowd rebuked the Chinese man for wanting to steal the dog; he ought to be ashamed of himself.

On arriving at Maral-bashi we learned from the Chinese official there were no camels there. Doctor Hedin telegraphed the Consul and asked where he was now supposed to get some. He waited two days for an answer but none came.

At this time an old man by the name of Munshi Abdurrahman, whom I had got to know in Kashgar, came to see us. Many years before he had been sent by a king of India, the *Rajah*, to Kashgar to explore the country, but the king died, political circumstances changed, and he could not go back again. So he stayed in Kashgar and got married there. Later on I will give further details about this curious man. When he heard we wanted to travel through the Takla Makan Desert, he said now would be the best time; later on it would be impossible because of the heat. Doctor Hedin asked me to stay with our things until he had explored the surrounding mountains. In the meantime an answer from the Consul would no doubt have arrived.

So I found time to continue working on my translation. For while we were travelling I had almost no peace to do this. When we reached a stop, the first thing we did was to prepare food. Then Doctor Hedin would send for a man from the village who would have to give him information about the number of sheep, oxen, and people and also about climatic conditions. I translated since he himself could not yet communicate with the people in Turkish, but I noticed that in many cases the people deliberately gave him false details since they saw him writing and became apprehensive by it. I considered it my duty to draw his attention to the incorrect manner of his procedure and told him I could make more exact enquiries in his absence through completely harmless discussions. When this conversation was concluded, we had to boil water in order to measure the altitude of each place in turn. It was almost twelve o'clock at night before everything was finished, and at twelve o'clock the chronometers had to be wound up. Early the next morning we would get up, get ready, and move on again. It went on like this the whole time we were travelling.

After three days Doctor Hedin came back from his expedition, but we had not yet had any news from the Consul. We considered whether we should go to Aksu or to Yarkand to buy camels. It seemed to us more advisable to go to Yarkand since Aksu is a small city where perhaps no camels were available. Just as we were about to depart, a messenger came from the Consul bringing us letters and newspapers, however, no answer to the telegram. Doctor Hedin took the messenger with us. On the way we were both very distressed, he, because he had no camels, and I, because it was Sunday when we were travelling and I was thinking about the Lord's work. As we arrived in Aksakmaral in the evening, he asked me why I was so despondent. I told him that today I had not been able to do the Lord's work, as was my job. To this he turned to face me and said, "I have spoken with the Consul about you. It was foolish of you to give up the religion of your fathers and adopt Christianity."

These unexpected words seemed very harsh to me, and I answered him, "If you consider the forsaking of one's ancestral religion foolish, then it must be said that the Swedes and Russians were also stupid, as they gave up their ancestral religion and became Christians."

When we left Aksakmaral the following day, we did not say a word to each other all day long, even though we sat next to one another. In the evening he told me he had heard that I had written a letter to Sweden about him. I denied it and said I had been with him both day and night; if I had written anything, he would have seen it. "My servant Islam said you had written something," he retorted. I asked him to call his servant since I did not believe he had said this. He quickly replied, "It doesn't matter."

In the evening on the third day, as we were drinking tea in Lailik, he addressed me, "Colleague, we must now part company. It is better we do so on friendly terms. Therefore let's cheerfully drink our last cup of tea together." During tea he was very much in the dark whether he should buy camels in Yarkand or send the messenger to the Consul and have camels brought back from there. The messenger could reach Kashgar in three days, but for him to succeed in buying camels there and returning immediately he needed at least nine days to get there and back. On the other hand, Yarkand was situated only one day's travel away from Lailik; besides, camels could be found more easily in this city. That is why I advised him to send the messenger to Yarkand since the time was already very late. After some reflection, Hedin said perhaps it would be cheaper for the Consul to get the camels in Kashgar. Therefore he would ask him by letter to buy them and send them to him. In the meantime he would send Islam to Yarkand to get enough food for the men and enough fodder for the animals for fifteen days, as well as lead containers[1] for water. I was supposed to give him my servant, Hashim, to accompany him as he explored the Tarim Desert while the

---

[1] Hedin refers to these containers as "iron tanks" (see *Through Asia*, p. 466). Trans.

preparations for the great desert journey were going on. Until then I was to stay in Lailik; afterwards he would bid me farewell, so I could return home to Kashgar. Thus Islam went to Yarkand, and Doctor Hedin went with Hashim to Terim. After five days everyone was back again in Lailik.

Fourteen days had passed, but we waited for the messenger in vain. Doctor Hedin became uneasy and did not know what he should do. He now wanted to go over the Yarkand River to Merket, from where the desert starts. I remarked I had to stay in Lailik according to our arrangement, but he asked me to accompany him to Merket; he needed an interpreter to speak with the officials there. So I left my books in Lailik and accompanied him. The heat was already very oppressive. Receiving us in a very kind manner, the beg was very astonish to learn we wanted to go through the desert and explained it was now impossible to explore the Takla Makan because of the heat. If it had been properly prepared two months ago, then we could still risk it. However, the inhabitants, the *Dolang*, that is, 'people of the forest', said even for them the trip across the desert was now impossible, but Doctor Hedin was so learned that he could command the wind and the clouds. Perhaps he would be able to undertake such a hazardous business. Doctor Hedin was surprised at the superstitions the people held and did not notice the subtle mockery that lay in these words.

As I was about to say goodbye and return to my books in Lailik, Doctor Hedin asked me to leave him my servant for another four or five days until Islam had bought camels for him in Yarkand. He had since given up hope of obtaining them from Kashgar. I met the messenger from Kashgar just outside Lailik, but he had no camels. I asked him why he had taken so long and where the camels were. He answered, "I am the Consul's servant; I cannot come before my lord sends me. The camels in Kashgar are expensive. The Consul says they would be cheaper in Yarkand. Doctor Hedin should only buy them there."

The following day I received a letter from Sven Hedin in which it said, "Since you have to wait for your servant in Lailik, I suggest you come here with your books until Islam brings the camels." I took my books and travelled to Merket. At first he was glad to see me again and told me the Consul had sent him a letter of recommendation for the aksaqal in Yarkand. He had given this letter to Islam to take along, so the aksaqal would buy good and cheap camels. I replied if the matter was being taken care of by the aksaqal, then it would again drag on for a very long time. He said the Consul had written that it should happen quickly.

After two days Islam came back and reported that the camels in Yarkand were very expensive and asked whether or not he should buy them. Doctor Hedin insisted on purchasing them quickly, even though they cost so much.[1]

---

[1] At this time Hedin says of Avetaranian, "I did not find Johannes, the missionary, much of a resource. He was one of those morbidly religious people who imagine that true Christianity is incompatible with a sober joy in life, as well as with good spirits. This was no doubt partly due to his being a converted

In the evening, as I sat with my translation and he was reading the newspaper, he began a disputation with me over the Bible.

"The Bible is a book," he began, "in which much nonsense and many impossible things are written. I do not understand how you can be so delighted by it."

"Show me this nonsense and the many impossible passages."

"Paul says he fought with God. How could he fight with the invisible God?"

"The Bible does not say that."

"It is so written."

I gave him a Swedish Bible and asked him to show me the passage.

"I cannot find the passage now," he said, "you must know that. But that the Bible says this is a fact."

"When Paul was persecuting the assembly of Christ and was on the road to Damascus, the Lord revealed Himself to him and said: 'Saul, Saul, why are you persecuting me!'[1] Perhaps you mean this passage?"

He said yes.

"I cannot understand," I continued, "why this passage should be incomprehensible since even in the political world to persecute an ambassador is tantamount to persecuting the one who sent him. In this sense Jesus could also say: 'Saul, Saul, why are you persecuting me?'"

Then he railed against the mission: "The cause of missions is unjust because Christians have so much need and poverty in their own midst. Money that should be used for the poor at home is given for missions, and the missionaries use these funds for a foreign people who have nothing at all to do with them."

I replied, "The command Jesus gave to His disciples is not limited solely to one people but refers to the whole world. If you think rightly, then you will of course see that those who help the poor at home are the same ones who support missions, but the ones who have no heart for missions, have also not learned to feel for the poor of their own people. The truly compassionate people are only those who believe the Bible and seek to carry out the command of their Saviour with all their heart, be it at home or in a foreign land."

Our dispute dragged on for hours. Doctor Hedin spoke many things against missions, but it is not worth quoting them here.

The following day he got sick. He could hardly swallow and could only speak with difficulty. Therefore he said, "That I have now become ill is a punishment from your God for what I spoke against missions. You have won. Now you have no opponent." Every day I gave him four egg yolks with sugar;

Mohammedan: such proselytes are often ten times worse than their teachers. However, he was good-natured and helpful, though he always seemed to be depressed and in dull spirits." (*Through Asia*, pp. 471-472). Trans.

[1] See Appendix I, Bible Passages 27. Trans.

he could not eat anything else. As he lay sick, I looked after the instruments and took readings while he wrote them down, so the work suffered no interruption. At this time two *bakhshis*[1] got in touch with Doctor Hedin and offered to drive away the spirit of sickness with their musical instruments, according to Kashgari custom. He declared that it was pagan, however he let the men play for two nights in a row.

When he was well again after thirteen days he said, "Just think if you had stayed in Lailik! Would you have been able to answer to your God for leaving me alone in my illness?" I explained to him I had only been this patient with him for the sake of the gospel and would have been able to go with him that far.

Islam had not yet returned from Yarkand with the camels, and we did not know why he was so long overdue. Then one day in the bazaar I learned he had got married in Yarkand. Sixteen days after his departure Doctor Hedin asked me to travel there and look and see where his servant was staying. In the event he had not yet bought any camels, since it was now too late, perhaps he should no longer search for them. At the same time he asked me to make the trip through the desert with him. I replied it was now impossible. If it had been earlier, I would have done it, but now I would be facing death and, since this undertaking was not the Lord's work, I must not risk my life contrary to better judgement. I advised him as well to give up the journey for now. "Since you also intend to explore the surrounding mountains, I beseech you: do this now. In the autumn you can come here again and visit the desert then. Under those circumstances I would gladly be able to do what you ask of me now and later on."

He then had me travel to Yarkand and check whether any camels had been purchased. Afterwards we would consider what was to be done. Since it was hard to travel during the day because of the heat, I rode at night and reached Yarkand in the morning. I saw there were many camels available, but the aksaqal had not yet bought any. So I sent a messenger to ask Doctor Hedin whether camels should still be purchased. The answer was yes. I waited until the camels had been bought and were all outside the city; then I returned to Merket.

That evening Doctor Hedin tried again to persuade me to travel with him, however, I refused. Then he handed me three letters: one for the Consul, one for Mr Macartney, and one for Högberg. He gave them to me with the remark: "Take these letters along to Kashgar; all three speak against you. You will have no peace in Kashgar because you would not come with me, but if you change your mind, I will tear up these letters and write many good things about you in my book." I took the letters and told him I would have them delivered. Incidentally, I was not afraid, if only I did not act contrary to what I believed was better.

---

[1] See Appendix B, *bakhshi*. Trans.

Doctor Hedin got ready to make his departure. It was hard to find two servants to handle the camels. Finally, by making grand promises, he hired two men who were in debt. That is to say, it is the law that whoever cannot pay his debts is himself to be awarded to the creditor as property and may be sold. In the end Doctor Hedin asked me to give him my dog, Haemrah, since he was loyal and vigilant. I waited until he had departed and then returned to Lailik. On arriving there I wrote a letter to Högberg and sent it as well as the letters from Doctor Hedin to Kashgar via Hashim. Högberg wrote back that I had not acted rightly by not travelling on with him. Doctor Hedin had written to the Consul and to Mr Macartney and both were outraged at me. I would have no more peace in Kashgar and would receive no more letters from abroad since of course the mail was in the hands of these two men. Only Father Hendricks was on my side.[1]

I stayed in Lailik, but Doctor Hedin journeyed into the Takla Makan Desert. On the second day my dog abandoned him and returned again to me; on the fourth day two men and four camels were left behind and he lost much money and many instruments. He alone with his servant Islam loaded two camels with the things they needed most and rode on for another day, but then they even lost the last of the camels and could only save themselves. Half dead, they came to the road from Khotan to Aksu where some travelling Chinese looked after them. The loss was estimated at around thirty thousand roubles and cost the lives of two men.[2]

In the meantime I worked on my translation in peace at Lailik, a small village with about five houses. The inhabitants of the place are called *Dolang*, that is, 'people of the forest'; their language is a pure form of Turkish. Every

---

[1] Hedin's final observation concerning Avetaranian at their parting was, "The former [Avetaranian] had already said at Lailik that he did not really mean to go with me through Takla-makan. Now, when he saw the caravan ready to start, his courage completely failed him, and for the second time he deserted me in the moment when danger had really to be faced. I despised the fellow. Notwithstanding his pretended piety, he utterly lacked the courage which makes a man place all his reliance upon God. What a strange contrast to Islam Bai, the Mohammedan, the beau-ideal of a good and faithful servant, who throughout the days and months that followed never once hesitated to follow his master, no matter where I went, even when I rushed into dangers which prudence should properly have guarded me against!" (See *Through Asia*, p. 483). Trans.

[2] According to Hedin's account, they left Merket on 10 April 1895 heading northeast, parallel with the Yarkand Darya. They started across the desert on 23 April and that was the day that Haemrah disappeared; on the evening of 1 May Hedin abandoned two men at the "death-camp" and set out with five of the original eight camels, some equipment, and two servants; one camel died shortly after they left the camp. Hedin decided to abandon everything except his life early on 2 May and carried on with one servant, leaving Islam Baï to catch up. On 5 May he alone finally reached the Khotan Darya and found water, having left his other servant behind in the forest. He then took water back to that servant and they both made their way back to the Khotan Darya. He was helped by shepherds on the 8th and then met three merchants travelling to Khotan on 9 May who helped him and also instructed him that they had found and given aid to Islam Baï. After taking time to regain his strength and backtrack to recover some of his abandoned equipment, he arrived in Kashgar on 21 June 1895 by way of Aksu. Only three of the five men who started the expedition came out alive. Contrary to what Avetaranian asserts, Hedin states that he did manage to recover a fair amount of his equipment later on thanks to the diligence of the amban of Khotan who prosecuted several men who it seems had found the camps in the desert where Hedin had left his equipment and supplies. These men were required to pay 1000 tengas for the items it was believed they had stolen. Trans.

day they were at their work, and I sat on the bank of the Yarkand River and worked in the shade of the trees. In the evening they gathered around me and asked me to read to them. Then I would read from the Scriptures and explain the Word of God to them. I translated the Gospel of John there.

After a month, Munshi Abdurrahman, whom I mentioned earlier, came from Maral-bashi. As I said before, this old Muslim came from India. He was an odd man, a real character. Although he was seventy years old and had a wife, he wanted to get married again and did this in spite of my advising against it. He did not have a proper job; rather he earned his living by telling fortunes and writing amulets. After he had got married in Yarkand, he went back to Kashgar and for a time lay seriously ill in Mr Macartney's courtyard; Mr Macartney had just gone away on a journey. I sent him food and had my servant take care of him. After he recovered, he departed again, taking with him a Bible I had given him. He had two white dogs and a strong horse that no one but he could control. When he rode, the two dogs sat in front of him on the horse. He loved his animals very much, but since, according to Muslim law, dogs are unclean, he would often get rebuked by Muslim clerics, however to no avail. In order to excuse himself he said that the dog is descended from Adam and came into being when Adam sneezed. When he came to Lailik, he only had one dog still with him. When I asked about the other one, his tears began to flow. "He died and I buried him," he said.

He asked me for work and, since he could write very beautifully and artistically, I gave him my translation to copy. So he stayed a week with me and helped me. Afterwards he asked to be allowed to move to the town of Merket; he could live there more cheaply with his animals. Every week he would come, bringing his work and taking back fresh work with him. After two weeks he returned and asked me to go with him to the village of Shabchi near Yarkand. In Yarkand we could easily get paper and every other material that we needed for our work.

As I was departing from Lailik, the people, with tears in their eyes, asked me to come back and speak the "good words" to them again. Along the way we came to a village where two women came to see us. They had requests for Munshi. The one wanted an amulet, so a man who was already married would fall in love with her, and the other wanted a magic spell from him for arousing discord between a man and his wife. He promised everything they wanted, if they would give him two *tengas*, that is, twenty pfennig.[1] He asked me for some paper in order to write down what they wanted, but I protested to him in Persian that he should really abandon such deception once and for all, even more so since he now had been reading the Bible for such a long time. But he went on begging for the piece of paper. He wanted to earn money to buy barley for his horse. I said, "I will give you some barley for your horse, but

---

[1] It was probably more along the lines of 40 pfennig or US $.10. At the time Hedin put the tenga at about 2.75 British pence or US $.05. See Appendix H, Exchange Rates to the US Dollar in the 1880s and 1890s. Trans.

not paper for such things as this."

When we came to Shabchi, we were very warmly received, but the old Munshi fell ill with a fever and was laid low. Since he had a little knowledge of medicine, he wrote himself a prescription, and we brought him the medicine he wanted from Yarkand, but it did not help. After we had sent for his old wife and his father-in-law, he died after much suffering. After his death, his dog would not eat for days and his horse would let no one near him. I stayed in Shabchi at the home of the Darugham family and found peace and a good opportunity to resume my work. The people there were good and friendly and enjoyed listening to the Word of God. I also had a good opportunity, through daily contact with them, to hear all the expressions of their language from them.

One day when I rode to Yarkand to purchase some things, I learned Mirza Yussuf had come there after his marriage to Anna Nyström in order to build a house for our mission. I returned to my village without seeing him. After several days I received a letter from Högberg in which he asked me to come and see him at Khanarik for a meeting. At the same time a letter came from Yussuf who apologised and asked to be forgiven for the trouble he had caused me. I travelled to Khanarik and met Högberg who came from Kashgar. He was very distressed. He read a letter to me from Doctor Ekman in which was written: "I have received your two letters and compared them, and I must say that everything John has written is correct. There is no smoke without fire. You must live in agreement with him and talk over everything with him that you wish to do. Anna Nyström and Yussuf's behaviour can only hurt the mission. Therefore Anna should come back to Sweden immediately, and Mirza Yussuf should go to Persia."

"What should we do?" asked Högberg. "I have already married the two. We cannot force Mirza Yussuf to go to Persia, and we cannot force his wife to leave him. Anyway, I had a difficult time with him, and because of that I sent him to Yarkand. If he becomes hostile to our mission, then he can do us much harm. Write to Doctor Ekman as the situation now stands, that we can do nothing about it. As a Christian you must also forgive Mirza Yussuf now that he has humbled himself."

I said, "He has not sinned against me, rather against the work of the Lord, and you were to blame for the whole thing on account of your rashness."

But as he kept on pleading, I wrote to Doctor Ekman. Högberg advised me not to return to Kashgar now, since Doctor Sven Hedin had set the Consul and Mr Macartney against me and I would not be able to correspond abroad. So I gladly returned to Shabchi. One day Mirza Yussuf came with two people from Kashmir to see me and invited me to Yarkand. I rode to see him and saw he had rented a plot of land and laid the foundations. But he had many quarrels and troubles of all sorts, and they wanted to prevent him from continuing to build. He then asked me to be in charge there for a couple of days while he travelled to Kashgar to get some money, but he did not come back. Högberg wrote to me: since Yussuf could not come, I should finish off the construction. I stayed about half a year in Yarkand until the building was completed, then returned to Kashgar.

CHAPTER 17

MY LAST STAY IN KASHGAR

After I had finished the building in Yarkand and came back to Kashgar, I wanted to begin my furlough, which I had already intended to take the year before. I told Högberg he should write to Doctor Ekman for leave for me, since I had no contact with Europe. However, his response was that a letter would not be necessary since it was up to him to make the decision, but for his part he would not permit me to travel, as there was no money available. If I insisted on going, I would have to resign from the mission. After I had spent a day considering what was to be done, I told him, "Fine, I will step down." In response he wrote several lines on a piece of paper, the content of which was that he, Högberg, had not induced me to resign, rather I had gone voluntarily. I had to sign it. I then asked him for the hundred roubles which was the amount set for me to travel to Tiflis, the city from which I had come to Kashgar.

On the following day, when I was about to get the money to make the preparations for my trip, I saw that Högberg was also getting ready to travel. In fact, he was going to Sweden. As a result he had no money left for me. However, he promised to send it to me from Sweden. I asked him to wait a few days and take my translation with him; it first had to be checked through once more, but he declared he could not wait for it any longer. So I rode on ahead of him, and every evening when he arrived at a stop I was already there a few hours before him and had checked through a part of the translation. So I finished my work during three days of travelling. He took the three Gospels with him—Matthew's Gospel had been sent prior to this—in order to hand them over to the Bible Society.

After I had accompanied Högberg so far, I rode back to Kashgar. At that time my funds only just came to about ten roubles. Of course I could not live on that for very long and found myself forced to borrow money from Indian merchants. In the meantime I continued to work on the translation of the New Testament until I received the money from Sweden.

After three months Högberg sent my travelling money. At the same time he wrote to his wife that she should send for the Indian merchants to pay off the debts I had with them and tell them they should not lend me any more since I would not be expecting money from any source. The merchants did not accept the money, rather they explained they had not loaned the money to her. Besides, they had already known me three years before Högberg and his wife had come to Kashgar.[1] Furthermore, they said it was not necessary for her to know whether or not I was to expect any money. In any case, she did not need to worry whether I could pay. Then they came to inform me about this discussion and offered to loan me as much money as I needed.

So I was given the money, but after paying my debts there was so little left over that I could not travel. However, I was expecting the remuneration for my translation work. One day, as I was riding from Kashgar to a village to work there in peace, my horse shied at a Chinese cart. I fell from the horse and broke my right leg. I was brought back to Kashgar on a stretcher. The pain was very severe; the broken limb was swollen as well. On the following day Father Hendricks came and so did the English physician from India, Doctor Chragadin. They examined my leg and said it would be impossible for me to get better if the leg were not amputated. Since I could not make up my mind, I sent for a Russian physician who was staying in Kashgar on account of the Russian soldiers. He examined my leg, however, he said nothing definite since the English physician had decided on the amputation.

Afterwards I asked whether in Kashgar there was not a *sungaq-chi*, a man who, although he has not studied, possesses a practical knowledge in the treatment of broken limbs. They brought a 95-year-old mullah who then came to see me every third day, although he lived quite far away from me. After careful examination he declared the leg was not only broken but was also dislocated from the hip joint. If he succeeded in putting the leg back in its socket, the rest would no longer pose any difficulties since the break was not very threatening. It is true it would take a few months, but the leg would be healed. He then got two young men to help him and in a few minutes had the leg back in its socket, which admittedly, caused me much pain. Then he took twenty eggs and poured the egg yolk in one bowl and the egg white in another. He wrapped a linen cloth five meters long, which he had dipped in the egg yolk, around my leg and laid a second cloth soaked in the egg white over the first. Onto that he tied two very thin boards using a cord. Then he tied me up, so I did not sit for several days; I only lay there. Every third day he pulled the cord tight again, and every fourteen days he put on a fresh dressing. For a diet he prescribed only white bread and milk. After fourteen days I was able to sit and after two months I could walk supported by crutches. Four months passed before I was completely restored to health.

When the Europeans in Kashgar heard I let an old Turk treat my leg, they were very surprised and said it was really odd I had been in Europe and did not know that the European physicians understood more than these bunglers. It would be of no use; if I would not have my leg amputated, then the other one would also go bad. In order to persuade me, I was told about a Russian prince by the name of Kniaz Galitzin who had recently come from India and

---

[1] As stated previously in Chapter 10, Avetaranian probably arrived in Kashgar early in 1892, not 1891, and as Högberg came in the autumn of 1894, Avetaranian would have only known the Indian merchants a little over two and a half years prior to his coming. Trans.

had travelled to St Petersburg. He had also broken his leg. If it had been possible to heal him in the way I had been healed, it certainly would have been done that way. Instead he must now go around with a wooden leg. I told this to my old doctor. He answered, "I cannot show you *yarim-pasha* ('half-prince')—this is what they called Kniaz Galitzin in Kashgar—but I can show you people who had worse broken bones than yours but now walk about fit and well. You will get fit again, and it will not be easy for anyone to see that you walk with a limp." For his treatment he received one of my old coats, which was worth about thirty [German] marks, and was very thankful for it.

Also during these months I worked on my translation. After my recovery, I read the work out to Muslims and revised it. After it was finally finished, I departed from Kashgar in February 1897. Up to now I had not received the three hundred roubles that was promised me for the translation. Högberg, who had returned in the meantime, provisionally bought off me the translation of the Letter of Paul to the Romans for one hundred roubles. However, since this sum was not enough for my journey, I had to run up debts with Indian merchants whom I paid back from Baku.

CHAPTER 18

TRAVEL EXPERIENCES

If you want to travel from East Turkestan to West Turkestan, it is best to travel in winter. Admittedly, it is very cold then, but you can protect yourself by wearing warm clothes. Whereas travelling in spring and summer is very dangerous because of the raging torrents and frequent avalanches. We took along enough provisions for both man and beast to last fourteen days, although caravans travelling without hindrance usually reach Osh in nine to twelve days. On the fifth day we reached Irkeshtam on the Russian border where the actual slope of the mountains begins. It was raining and was very stormy. Since we had to wait two days, the Russian officials very kindly received me.

After crossing over the pass, we reached a Kirghiz village, Sofininki. Since we could not reach Osh in fourteen days, several people wanted to purchase some things there, but the Kirghiz had no bread, and milk was not going to help us very much against the cold. We finally managed to find a kilo of suet. Melted and mixed with rice, which we still had left over, this served as our food for the last two days. In three days I went by carriage from Osh to Kokand, a city of about two hundred thousand inhabitants. I stayed there several days at the home of an Armenian merchant so as to reach Samarkand as cheaply as possible.

Many Muslims were making the pilgrimage to Mecca. For six roubles I covered the seven-day journey to Samarkand with one of the pilgrims and his son. My companion was a very odd man from Margelan. When we arrived at a stop on the first night, I went with the *hajis* (pilgrims en route to Mecca) to the caravansary. But my travelling companion stayed in the carriage and there performed the *zikr* (that is, he continually shouted the word *Allah* with the characteristic articulation). With this he wanted to draw the attention of his fellow travellers to himself, so they would see his devoutness and send him some food.

On the third day we began to discuss things. I initiated the discussion especially since I noticed the father and son were living at odds with one another. The Muslim said he had been the custodian of a holy place in Margelan; they called him *ishan* ('religious leader'). For many years he had had the desire to make a pilgrimage to Mecca. However, since he had no fortune, the pilgrimage did not happen. Now he had sold his house, dismissed his wife, and so gained the means to travel. He had taken this son with him. They did not want to go back; rather they wanted to die at the holy place. I expressed my wish that God might give him a good outcome to this journey and asked whether he had left behind any other children. He said he had a 5-year-old girl, an 8-year-old girl, and a young son. Since he saw I made no response to this but was lost in thought, he asked for my opinion about his conduct.

I told him, "According to your law, you have not acted rightly. Islam has set five duties for men: fasting, prayer, confessing the faith, pilgrimage, and giving alms. The first three hold true for all men, the last two only for the rich. Since you are not rich, you have no right to undertake this pilgrimage. What will your wife do now with the three small children since you have sold her house as well?"

He retorted, "I have dismissed my wife. She has the right to enter into another marriage."

"Fine, but what will the children do? She can certainly not take them along with her into the marriage. Where will she leave them?"

He said, "*Allah karim dir.*" ('God is gracious')

Then I said, "But the Merciful One does not love men who are not merciful. In this harsh winter you take your wife's and the children's bread and shelter to give it to savage Arabs who are robbers. By such conduct would you bring about a work that is well pleasing to God? Consider whether your conscience will not condemn you."

As far as Samarkand I spoke with him in a gentle way about his actions. In the end I told him, "Your pilgrimage should be to where your wife and your children are; that will be well pleasing to God." The result was he thanked me and decided to turn back and take back his wife and children. With tears in his eyes he said goodbye and asked me to come and see him if I came back to Turkestan again; he had learned much from me.

At the Sino-Russian border the soldiers had given me a letter that I was supposed to deliver in Samarkand. Early in the morning, as I was about to make my way to the Russian part of the city with this end in mind, a pristav met me. He looked at me and said, "*Vy Evrei!*" ('You are a Jew.')

I replied, "No, I am not a Jew!"

"No," he said, "you are a Jew. Where do you come from? Where is your passport?"

I answered him I was a Christian; my passport was with my things at the caravansary. He may come and inspect it. However, he refused and took me with him to the police. On arriving there he left me at the door under a gendarme's supervision while he went in by himself. In vain I asked the gendarme to send me to the caravansary, so I could produce my passport. My train would be leaving at noon. He refused my request and told me I had to wait until the *nachal'nik*[1] came. I waited, hungry and thirsty, until he finally came at twelve o'clock. However, I was not allowed in. Via the people who

---

[1] See Appendix B, *nachal'nik*. Trans.

entered the police station, I had the nachal'nik asked to have me summoned and was finally led before the official. At the same moment the kadi from Samarkand also came.

The pristav then repeated his claim, but I said, "I am a Christian from Persia. Why have you kept me so long and not sent a soldier along with me, so I could show him the passport?"

"You are a Jew," was the answer.

The nachal'nik asked the kadi to investigate whether I really was a Christian and came from Persia. After he had spoken Persian with me for about ten minutes, he told the official, "I can testify that he has spoken the truth." Then the nachal'nik ordered me to bring my passport to the kadi in the evening; that would be sufficient.

As I thanked him and was about to leave, the pristav said bitterly, "He is indeed a Jew!"

From Samarkand I reached Krasnovodsk on the Caspian Sea in six days by train, after I had stopped along the way for two days to preach at various places. At Krasnovodsk I boarded a ship to go to Baku. Since there was very rough weather and our ship suffered quite a bit from it, instead of arriving at Baku after one day, we only arrived after three. Here the Russian officials checked the luggage. I was afraid for my books. Once when I was travelling from Persia to Russia I had books worth about one hundred [German] marks taken away from me on the grounds that they needed to be sent to the censor. I never got them back. Although the border officials were very friendly, I was still worried this could happen to me again, but the Lord arranged it so circumstances came to our aid. It was a *brazhnik*, ('holiday') so the officials were not all able to come. In addition, it was very windy and cold, so they did not spend a lot of time but only had a quick glance at my things. So I saved my books.

I stayed in Baku several days and bore witness to the Saviour in front of the evangelical brothers there. Then I went to Shusha where I stayed with friends for a week. My next destination was Shemakha where I had previously been registered to preach in the Armenian-Lutheran Church. I was warmly greeted but afterwards I was again brought to the police on account of my passport's visa application.

When the pristav learned I wanted to preach on Sunday, he told me, "Then I must send you back as a prisoner, escorted by soldiers. You must not preach, rather you have to depart before then. It is not allowed for foreigners to preach here on a holiday."

So I preached on Friday evening and went on to Tiflis on Saturday. There I saw my old friend, Pastor Kevorkian, and also called on Mr Steinbrecher, the agent of the British [and Foreign] Bible Society. After I had spoken with him about the printing of my translation, I wrote to London that, in accordance with the instructions of the Society, the translation of the whole New Testament was finished. The response I received was that the four Gospels would have to be printed first; it would more or less depend upon their good distribution whether the rest of the New Testament ought to be printed. I was not satisfied with this answer, firstly, because I had received written instructions to translate the whole New Testament; secondly, because I knew from experience it is better to distribute the whole Testament all at once instead of in separate pieces; and finally, because I regarded it as my duty to put the Scriptures as soon as possible into the hands of the people whose language I had learned so well with God's help. This was especially true, as I knew what a great longing for the Word of God there was amongst the Kashgaris. I would have gladly born the cost of the printing myself, had I possessed the means to do so. It was incomprehensible to me why the Bible Society now put the matter off. For the second time I wrote to London and expounded in my letter all the points mentioned above. At the same time I noted if the Society so desired, I would do the proofreading and take no money for the translation, only so that the Word of God would come to the Kashgaris as soon as possible.

CHAPTER 19

A NEW ACQUAINTANCE AND ITS CONSEQUENCES

While I was waiting for the response I was introduced to the German pastor, Hansen, with whom I spoke on several occasions about my business. He advised me to get in contact with Pastor Faber who was expected to be passing through Tiflis some time soon on his way to Persia. He had been the director of a mission to the Muslims. I took his advice. Pastor Faber responded to me in a friendly way, was interested in me and my business, and promised me he would write immediately to London on behalf of the Bible translation. Then he asked me to accompany him to Persia for two months since, apart from the young Armenian physician whom he had with him, he needed a man who was familiar with the circumstances there. Since he for his part had promised me active assistance and, besides, my stay in Tiflis was of no particular use at the moment, I consented and travelled with him first to Erivan. Here he had to wait until some money was sent from Germany. During this time he was going to write the letter, which had been put off every day until then.

In addition, he intended to acquire a stone with cuneiform writing that he had been told about. It was in Karakoyunly, near to Erivan. With this aim in mind I got in touch with a Muslim who promised to arrange the matter with the man in whose field the stone was located. However, he asked Pastor Faber not to meddle with it any further since it would only be to his disadvantage. I used the delay which our trip suffered to visit the fellowship near to Erivan in which I had previously worked. When I came back after fourteen days, my first question to Pastor Faber was whether he had written to London. He answered he would do it now and immediately began to write with his pencil. In the meantime the Muslim had bought the stone in Karakoyunly and had had the valuable part with the inscription cut off by two master builders. The slab of stone, several metres high and several metres wide, was then transported by cart to Tiflis in order to be taken from there to Germany by train.

During this time it had already become very hot, and Pastor Faber suffered so much from the insects that one day he declared to me he could now not continue with the journey but would return to Germany and come back again at a later date. Shortly after this, he left Erivan, having asked me to write to him in Germany.

I had received the same negative answer to my letter to London as I had the first time. As there was now no longer anything keeping me in Caucasia, and since several brothers were supporting me with funds, I was able to travel to Stockholm in the summer. One Sunday I stayed in St Petersburg and visited the representative of the British [and Foreign] Bible Society, Doctor Kean, who was there. He was very friendly and inquired specifically about Kashgar and the translation since the distribution of the Scriptures in Kashgar lay in his hands.

On arriving in Stockholm I discovered a telegram from Pastor Faber: "Come to Germany. I will get the translation printed." I went first to see Doctor Ekman and spoke with him about the whole business. He said he did not understand the business with Faber, but he advised me first to travel to London and, as soon as everything was organised there, to see to the printing in Germany. I followed his advice. In London I visited the Swedish missionary, Engvall, and went with him to see Doctor Wright, the director of the Bible Society, only after we had had a lot of trouble finding him. But all of my efforts were in vain. He told me, "We have decided to print the four Gospels. Before the remaining part is printed, we must first see what kind of reception the Gospels meet with. They are being printed in Leipzig now. It would be good if you travelled to Germany to do the proofreading."

So I went from London to Berlin in the autumn of 1897. Since I was completely unknown there, I called on Pastor Faber. He approached me in a very friendly manner as at our first encounter and was helpful to me in every way. At his instigation I gave lectures on several occasions on the mission in Kashgar, and to him I owed my first connections to the circles of believers in Germany. When I had gained a fair command of the German language, I also took trips and won supporters everywhere for the work. Through speaking and writing Faber himself looked for additional societies who would be interested in the work, especially in my Bible translation. Through him I also made the acquaintance of the linguist, Professor Andreas, with whose help I checked my translation once more using the original [Greek] text as a basis.

At this time Pastor Amirkhaniantz came to Berlin. When he heard I was in contact with Faber he gave me an emphatic warning. He told me Faber's financial circumstances were not straightforward; besides, he had "stolen" a stone in Russia. That Faber stood alone and was not, as I had believed earlier, a member of a committee, I had in fact already seen for myself. But since I had only experienced kindness from him, and, as far as the stone was concerned, I had seen the proper sale of it myself, I did not heed this warning.

Meanwhile, summer had come. Faber had intended to send me out to Kashgar in August, which admittedly, I only learned about later. He wanted me at the outset, because of the great distance, to take along the means to support myself for a whole year and was now collecting this maintenance from the circle of missions supporters. I was still busy with the proofreading for Leipzig.

CHAPTER 20

THE BIBLE TRANSLATION

In the midst of doing this work I was invited to Stockholm to an annual missions conference in June 1898. I went there for ten days and met many brothers whom I knew, so this time became a time of joy and relaxation. I was asked why I no longer worked with the [Swedish] Missionary Society, and in the event that the committee should approve my re-entry, I was asked not to turn it down. In one meeting Doctor Ekman got up and said, "The Germans want to have our Missionary Avetaranian, but we want him to work with us and be sent out by us. Do you agree to this?" Almost every member present agreed with this suggestion. Afterwards Doctor Ekman called me and asked whether I also agreed.

My answer was: "I have come to Europe on account of the printing of the Kashgari New Testament. Until now nothing has happened concerning it. These German friends want to stand by me. If you want to take on this business, naturally I would like to continue working with you, but if these German friends get my work printed, I will go along with them." I was promised they would take on the printing. After the conference, Doctor Ekman advised me to travel back to Germany and inquire thoroughly about the cost of producing the work.

When I informed Pastor Faber of the conference's decision, he was very delighted since, as he told me, it would have been impossible for him to obtain the necessary resources to send me out. In order to contribute to the work in Kashgar, he published a leaflet in which he asked for a sum of money for the founding of an orphanage in Kashgar.

As I learned in Leipzig, the cost for two thousand copies of the whole New Testament would come to twelve thousand [German] marks. I informed Doctor Ekman of this. He answered me he had written to London to the Bible Society and perhaps the Society would print the New Testament. However, if the Society were to turn down the offer again, then the Swedish Society would have it printed. I should just continue revising with Doctor Andreas. After several months, I received an invitation from Mr Morrison, the director of the British and Foreign Bible Society in Berlin, to come and see him. At the same time I got a letter from Doctor Ekman saying the London Bible Society had accepted my translation and now there was no further hindrance. In good spirits I went to see Mr Morrison.

"I had a happy announcement to make to you," he addressed me, "but just this moment I have received a telegram from London that I should wait a bit before making the announcement and the matter might perhaps turn out differently."

Light was shed on the matter later to the effect that Missionary Högberg had written from Kashgar: the translation would first have to be revised again in Kashgar. That was the reason why the Bible Society had put off the printing. This complaint on the part of Högberg resulted in a committee, which met with Mr Morrison in Berlin. I will let the lector, Doctor Waldenström, speak concerning it; he wrote in the Swedish newspaper, *Hemlandsposten*, on 7 January 1899 the following:

> "I never would have believed I would again be travelling abroad so suddenly, but the circumstances made it necessary, so I had to comply. Our missionaries in Kashgar had made several remarks against Avetaranian's translation, which caused the British and Foreign Bible Society not to want to go to print before the defects were eliminated. There was no other way than that I travel along with our Missionary Beklund to Berlin to investigate how things stand. On the way to Berlin we thought about the remarks made; some seemed to me to be very serious.
>
> "In Berlin we were greeted by Avetaranian, Landsmann, the Swedish Missionary Society's missionary to the Jews, and Professor Andreas, an especially learned man in the area of oriental languages who has applied himself to Avetaranian's translation work with great interest. Professor Andreas had spent six years in Persia studying oriental languages. It is quite special how our God manages things, that this man of science should come in contact with Avetaranian and immediately be gripped by an intense interest in this work.
>
> "At noon on Wednesday we were invited to the home of the representative of the British and Foreign Bible Society, Mr Morrison, an especially devout, refined, and helpful man. Our hearings began in the afternoon and lasted many hours. Beklund made his remarks, but it emerged from the discussion that these remarks for the most part were based on misunderstandings—indeed, it cannot be expected of missionaries who have only been in Kashgar three to five years to have a perfect knowledge of the language. Avetaranian, on the other hand, born in Asian Turkey and himself a former Muslim priest, showed during the whole hearing an exceptionally keen feel for languages, which was also testified to by Professor Andreas. The proposed objections were reduced to a few passages and only concerned such trivial details that Director Morrison told me, 'If the objections which could be made refer to such minor points, then Avetaranian's translation must be excellent.' Professor Andreas declared the same and put his academic reputation to it that no current oriental translation of the Bible could compare with Avetaranian's—and that says a great deal."

This was the extent to which my affairs concerned Lector Doctor Waldenström.

The result of this meeting was that it was decided to write to London, so the printing would not be put off. Doctor Waldenström told me he first had to travel to Sweden and see to it that the chairman wrote to London. As a result the Bible Society declared itself ready to print. Suddenly a letter came from Högberg to London, to the effect that he had handed the Gospels over to a mullah by the name of Arabshah to be checked, and he had declared the translation was not good. As a result the Bible Society once again put off the printing. Doctor Ekman wrote to me he was sorry the matter suffered such a delay, but there was now probably no other counsel than that I travel to Kashgar to clear the matter up with Högberg and then send the work back to Europe. I could not agree to this suggestion because it then would have been impossible for me to do the proofreading which had to be done at least six times. Then two months would have been needed each time to send it from Leipzig to Kashgar and back. Besides, I was of the conviction a stay in Kashgar would be of no use for the revision since in that respect everything I could do in Kashgar on my part had already been done. I informed Doctor Ekman of my opinion and suggested to him about writing to Högberg that he should write down the objections as far as it was possible for him and send them on. Then, whatever needed to be changed could indeed be changed. If necessary, Arabshah could also be sent to Berlin.

On one of the lecture trips I was making at that time I got to know Mr Andrae-Roman in Stettin. Through him I was introduced to the von Osterroht family. The Lord arranged it for me to get engaged to one of Mr von Osterroht's daughters.

In order now to have a clear view of the present position of things, I asked Faber for a balance of the amounts received for Kashgar up to then, as well as a statement of the expenses, which had been taken from them up to the present. However, he refused, just as he had also constantly evaded my and Professor Andreas' requests to form a committee.[1] The matter dragged on for a long time, and finally I felt myself obliged to sever my association with him.

Four months passed before the answer concerning the translation could come from Kashgar. After getting Doctor Ekman's consent, I travelled with Doctor Lepsius to the Orient via Russia to Persia and Mesopotamia, then via Constantinople and Varna back to Berlin.

When we arrived in Berlin, Doctor Waldenström was there as well as Missionary Högberg from Kashgar. Again a meeting was called, which lasted even longer than the previous one. Doctor Waldenström was selected as chairman and Doctor Lepsius as secretary. Högberg stated his objections, setting them down in writing. He queried forty passages. Afterwards he was invited to say more if he had anything else to mention. Since that was not the case, his objections were classified. Thirty-eight objections concerned synonyms; these were not counted as mistakes by the committee since Högberg could not have known which words ought to have been chosen. I was questioned in respect to the other two passages. In the first verse of the

---

[1] Doctor Lepsius had also refrained from associating his work with Pastor Faber, "since F. had refused to work in conjunction with a committee" (*Christlicher Orient*, 1900, pp. 3-4).

first chapter of Matthew's Gospel[1] I had used the Arabic word *ibn* ('son'), as opposed to *ogul* (which also means 'son'), which I used in the fourth chapter.[2]

"In the first instance," I explained, "I have used *ibn* because it is used in the Turkish language to emphasise the idea of proper names. On the other hand, I have used *ogul* in the fourth chapter to emphasise sonship."[3] The committee were in agreement with this. In the other case there was a misunderstanding as well.

Finally Högberg said, "Arabshah really has found mistakes in your translation."

The translation Arabshah had read lay on the table. Pastor Amirkhaniantz took the Testament and read what Arabshah had written at the end of each one of the Gospels, namely: "I have checked through this sacred writing all the way to the end. The translation of this work is remarkably correct. The translator, Missionary John Avetaranian, has translated with extreme care and great effort. According to what I know, I have indicated a few words that can be placed in front or behind. That is all."

Since Högberg could read little Kashgari then, he had not understood these words. The committee decided to have my translation printed. If the Swedish missionaries wanted, I could send a proof to Arabshah.

Lector Doctor Waldenström went with Högberg back to Sweden while I stayed in Berlin. Several months passed without me hearing anything about the printing of my translation. I went to Mr Morrison and asked why the printing had not been started. He answered I should send my work to Stockholm. It would then be sent by the committee in Stockholm to Germany and be printed there. I asked why the translation had first to make such a long journey, if the work was supposed to be carried out in Germany; that could be dealt with by letter. Besides, I knew no one in Sweden had a good command of Kashgari. For since Högberg, as the committee had seen, was incapable of checking it through, I could not entrust my work to him. So the translation remained unprinted at that time.[4]

During the eight-month trip through the Orient, Doctor Lepsius and I had given sufficient thought to the mission in the Orient. Since after these hearings in Berlin I saw I did not achieve my aim and it went against my conscience to leave the work in such hands, I decided to work together with Doctor Lepsius and join the German Orient-Mission.

---

[1] See Appendix I, Bible Passages 28. Trans.

[2] See Appendix I, Bible Passages 29. Trans.

[3] In his *Mizan ul-Haqq* (*Balance of Truth*), p. 164, Pfander states that the Arabic word, *ibn*, is suitable for use in a metaphorical sense, that is, the sense that he felt was needed in the title "Son of God", but Avetaranian has chosen to use the eastern Turki word for *son* in the phrase "Son of God" (at least in the fourth chapter of Matthew) and has used *ibn* to denote someone's son as in "the son of Abraham" in Matthew 1:1; but as Avetaranian has just stated, his use of *ibn* is in accordance with how it is used in Osmanli Turkish, so possibly not necessarily in how it is used in Arabic. Trans.

[4] For the final completion of the printing and its further fate, see Chapter 26, p. 186 and the footnote [1] in Chapter 27, p. 192.

In a committee meeting of the German Orient-Mission it was decided I should move to Varna in Bulgaria in order to work amongst the Muslims. But first the supporters of the mission would have to be visited to lay on their hearts the spreading of the gospel within the Muslim community. For about four months I travelled in Eastern and Western Germany and gave talks.

In June 1900 Pastor Israel married Miss Helene von Osterroht and I in the Matthäikirche in Berlin.

After a commissioning ceremony in the presence of the supporters of the German Orient-Mission on 7 November of the same year, I travelled to Varna in Bulgaria with my dear wife who became a great help to me in the Lord's work.

CHAPTER 21

A MISSION TO MUSLIMS IN BULGARIA[1]

In Bulgaria the Lord gave us an open door in the city of *Varna*. Hagop Shahveled, the preacher at the Evangelical Armenian Church, as well as Theodoroff, the Bulgarian Methodist preacher, were united with us and were glad a work was being started for the Muslims. Up to that point the Christians had shown them so little consideration.

My activity in Bulgaria was organised in the following way: I preached every Sunday in Turkish, and my listeners were Turkish-speaking Armenians, Bulgarians, Greeks, and one or two Muslims. All of these different nationalities understand Turkish. On Sunday afternoon several men came to see me for a Bible study, and we prayed and delved into the Gospel of John together. In the process a very curious scene would develop because each one read his Bible verse in his mother tongue: Greeks in the original text, Armenians in Turkish and ancient and modern Armenian, Bulgarians in Bulgarian; in front of me lay the German and Swedish Bible commentaries, but the discussion took place in Turkish.

I visited Muslims in their shops and mosques in order to get to know thoroughly their particular way of behaving here in Bulgaria and to see how the Muslim clerics kept their people fettered. Perhaps it is not known that Muslims only have thirty-three sermons a year, thirty-two of which are given during Ramazan, the month of fasting, and the final one is given two months later during *Kurban*. Once, when Ramazan was just coming to an end, I met two Methodist brothers while on my way to the mosque. They wanted to go with me but in the end shied away from accompanying me. So I went alone.

The floor of the mosque is covered with mats, and every one who enters takes his shoes or overshoes off at the entrance, so he does not bring in any dust from the street. He places them with the soles facing each other and puts them in front of him in the spaces that are designated for this purpose. No table or chair is to be seen. There is only a pulpit for the preacher, which stands along the left side, and on the right is the *mimbar*, that is a flight of stairs with ten steps. Between the mimbar and pulpit is the *mihrab*, which more or less takes the place of our altar and is where the priest stands during the *namaz* ('service'). The mihrab is built in such a way that the priest must turn towards Mecca, and the people in turn stand behind him. The mimbar is

---

[1] The following chapters are taken from the author's hand-written accounts that he published in the monthly periodical of the German Orient-Mission, *Der Christliche Orient*, from 1901 onwards [Schäfer].

used every Friday and holiday. The priest climbs up to the seventh step, turns to the people, and reads *khutba* ('the address') in Arabic.

In the afternoon, when the service had ended, I went to hear the sermon. I left my overshoes at the entrance and sat *à la Turka* next to the door. That is the most unassuming place. After several minutes the *muezzin* noticed me, came over to me, and quietly said, "Please, come to the front and take a better place." I thanked him for his kindness but stayed in my place because that was the best place from where I could observe. But the kind muezzin still did not let up. He went to the door, took my overshoes, laid them beside me, and whispered, "I am afraid the gypsy children could steal them at the entrance."

The preacher got into the pulpit, which only had a low border because the priest sits, as do all his listeners, in the Turkish manner with his feet crossed. The spiritual food he offered was very meagre. After the Arabic prayer was read out, he began to declare to the people it was a sin to go to any other mosque than that one which was in each one's respective district. Afterwards he spoke about prayer and said the Koran cannot be read as the Koran, but as a prayer. He justified this odd assertion in various ways. "Whenever you want to pray," he said, "then recite from memory as much as you know from the Koran. God will count these words of yours as a prayer. You do not need to think about the meaning of the words. However, you ought also to pray in your usual way of speaking and ask God for something, be it food, money, clothing, and other such things, but it is best to pray for salvation because God likes to hear this prayer. The holy and learned men, when they prayed using their own words, expressed their prayer in seven words; any more than this is unnecessary, and unnecessary words are not acceptable to God. If you cannot be content with seven words, then repeat them as often as you like."

"It is now Ramazan," the preacher continued, "and we are fasting. The time most pleasing to God for prayer is in the evening before supper; without a doubt this prayer is most certainly heard by God. Indeed, if anyone doubts this, he is a blasphemer. My dear friends, do not forget and do not neglect this time for prayer." He reinforced this exhortation with several legends.

The next morning around six o'clock I visited the largest mosque in the city. It was full of listeners, so the preacher did not need to urge them to attend as his less fortunate colleague had to do the day before. His text was the word of the Koran: "He is saved who cleanses himself." (Surah 91:9)[1] He gets saved and is saved, not that he was saved!! He said no one comes into the world as a believer or an unbeliever; rather God gives him a free will and leaves him free to decide. That one cleanses himself who believes in God and gives no room in his heart to unbelief.

Then he asked the people to say in a loud voice: "God protect us from unbelief", and immediately the whole congregation echoed the response back to him. Afterwards he said, "God protect us from disobedience", and everyone

---

[1] See Appendix J, Koran Passages 4. Trans.

again repeated his words. Then he described how exact a person must be in washings, in forms of prayer, etc. He commended prayer performed at midnight and said, "Whenever someone gets up at midnight and does *namaz* ('prayer') three times, this is especially agreeable to God, and our Prophet and Lord, Mohammed—God's peace be upon him!—has entrusted it to his friends. He did not make it compulsory, like namaz performed five times a day, because he was afraid Muslims would be burdened by it. He had no instructions from God for this, therefore he could leave it to the free will."

After that, he told how Muslims should greet one another. This was a duty, like prayer five times a day. Whoever sees a Muslim and does not greet him, that one sins. If the other does not greet him back, then he sins. The right greeting is "Peace be with you", and the reply is "And the peace be with you". The "and the" must not be left out because by it the thanks becomes a little longer than the greeting. Made-up greetings like "Good morning, good evening" are no good. Also there must be the right greeting in every letter, and the recipient is obliged to respond to the greeting even if he does not want to respond to the contents; otherwise the guilt stays with him. Also in every prayer a greeting must be spoken to the prophet. "In this world," he went on to say, "there are many holy men of God, but we do not see them because our eyes are darkened by sin and evil. Among them is one of the Supreme Beings. At the time of Bayaziden Bestam—God's mercy be upon him!—there were seventy thousand holy men in the world, and the greatest of these was a blacksmith, and Bayaziden Bestam—God's grace be upon him!—asked God to show him that man. Then God revealed to him in a dream that he should visit the blacksmith; he was the one. When he came to see the blacksmith and saw how his hands were dirty, that he was occupied with his work and was weeping, he asked him, 'Why are you crying? Is the work so hard?' He said, 'No, rather sin and unbelief have become widespread in this world, and I fear God's punishment will come upon us.' This is the way of God's holy ones; no one can know them because they do not reveal themselves, but this blacksmith was the greatest saint of his time."

The preacher also talked about fragrances. With great seriousness he advised every Muslim always to carry some perfume with him, "because our Prophet," he said, "loved it very much. But only natural, pure, unadulterated things ought to be used, not those European fragrances,"—he said with an expression of the greatest contempt—"which are prepared with alcohol. These things are shameful and impure. God protect us from impurity," he called out to the congregation, and the whole assembly echoed the response back to him.

Following these words came fresh exhortations to pray: "Prayer five times a day must not be omitted. If you are sick and cannot stand, then you must do it sitting down. If you cannot sit, then you must make gestures with your head. If you cannot move your head, then you must move your eyes; and say the prayer in your heart, if you cannot speak with your mouth. Cleanliness is absolutely necessary for prayer. The place where you pray must not be dirty.

If you are forced to be together with unbelievers in a dirty place, then you ought to pray only in your heart. Every place where Jews, pagans, and Christians pray is unclean. Not only do they defile themselves with idolatry, but they also come polluted by alcohol or sit with dirty boots."

He went on to say, "Whoever 'commands his beard' (that is to say, lets it grow), should stand up." About ten men rose in response to these words. After that, the preacher spoke the *beard prayer*: God bless the beards of these Muslims and make them worthy to see the *Kaaba* and touch the black stone with their beards. God make them worthy to wash their beards in the *Zamzam* (the spring where Hagar gave Ishmael a drink)[1] etc. The congregation raised their hands and accompanied each sentence with a solemn "Amen".

With these visits to the mosque I made several good acquaintances. Even from these sermons a person can learn a good many ways of getting closer to Muslims. The place for holding meetings must be chosen in such a way that the Muslims will really want to come there and hear the Word. For Paul says in Romans 10:17,[2] "Faith comes from hearing."[3] It is difficult to get them into a hall where Armenians or Bulgarians have their meetings because *Muslims simply find the old Greek or Gregorian churches with all their ceremonies and outward appearances repulsive.* As, for example, their Christmas celebration: with much ceremony the priests take this cross and throw it into the water. After that, young men, who have warmed themselves with strong drink and give the impression of being half drunk, jump into the water and bring the cross back out. This ceremony is supposed to be a symbol of the baptism of Christ. A childhood memory in connection with this comes to mind: wherever there are Gregorians, even where we were in Erzerum, this ceremony would take place, and when I asked my [step]mother what it meant, she answered me, "The unbelievers are immersing their idols in water."

How obscured the picture of Christianity is, which such Christians present to Muslims. *Although so many within the Muslim community are looking for the truth, what they see in such instances puts them off so decidedly that they say they themselves have more true religion and purer worship than the Christians.* And the evangelical brothers amongst the Armenians and Bulgarians are so small in number compared with the large churches, that unfortunately the Muslims pay little attention to them. That is why all Christians are accused of the mistakes of the Gregorian and Greek churches since Muslims do not go to the meetings of the evangelicals and do not even understand their language. Every Muslim admits he is sinful, and praying five times a day and all his religious exercises remind him again and again of his sin. He will never be able to find complete satisfaction since he does not have the Redeemer. We must bring the teaching of God's redemption to the

---

[1] See Appendix I, Bible Passages 30. Trans.
[2] See Appendix I, Bible Passages 31. Trans.
[3] The verse that Avetaranian cites from the German Bible actually reads: "So kommt der Glaube aus der Predigt" ("Faith comes from the sermon"). Trans.

Muslims, but at the same time we must avoid everything that could keep them from coming to "hear the word of Christ".

In 1901 I spent eight days in *Rustchuk* where I was able to preach every day. Soon after that, I went on a four-month trip to Persia on behalf of the mission's leadership. My wife stayed behind at the mission post in Varna. My journey went by way of Constantza in Romania where on one Sunday I preached the Word of God several times in various languages. Then I went to Baku on the Caspian Sea.

When I had Mount Ararat behind me,[1] I went across the Aras River where all traces of civilisation stopped with the exception of telegraph poles, but these have to be set upright about once a week, so letters often arrive sooner than telegrams. Since the way there could not be negotiated by carriage, the journey had to be continued on horseback.

In a remote Muslim village I was warmly received. We had a meeting that actually lasted from noon until around nine o'clock in the evening. The people came and went, so we sat quite informally and read the Gospel. Among the different visitors there was also a sheikh who came; he was accompanied by a dervish. The latter was twenty-five years older than the sheikh. Nevertheless, he honoured the sheikh as a holy man and followed him wherever he went. The sheikh sat next to me, and while we continued to talk about religious things he often looked me in the face, and with such a trusting look, as if he were expecting something from me. I looked at him again, and our eyes so spoke to one another even before we began to talk.

Finally he asked me, "Why are you looking at me?"

I said, "I see that you have not yet seen yourself for who you are."

"Well, do you mean to say you have seen yourself for who you are?"

"Yes," I replied.

"Then tell me; what are you, if you have seen yourself for who you are?"

I answered, "I am a sinful, weak, unworthy man before God. Of myself I have nothing good, holy, or well pleasing to God."

When he heard this, he was silent for a while and then said, "I have not yet seen myself in this way."

My answer was: "If you do not know yourself as I have known myself, then you have no part in the righteousness of God nor in his salvation."

He was lost in thought; then he said, "You are my father and master; I see that I am a sinful man."

"I am not your father and master. There is only One who is master; I am your brother."

Afterwards he again sat there a good while with his head bowed. Then he said goodbye and went. After a couple of hours, as we were still sitting together, he came back a second time, again in the company of a dervish, and

---

[1] He had travelled from Baku to Erivan and then from Erivan to the Persian border. See Lepsius' *Ex Oriente Lux*, p. 84. Trans.

said, "My relatives were very much astonished that I confessed I was a sinful man." I replied this was a test for him he would just have to endure. Then I had a 16-year-old boy who came from a respected sheikh's family read Matthew 13, mainly the Parable of the Sower,[1] and after that the Sermon on the Mount, as well as several other passages. When he had read a section, I let his older brother repeat what was read in his own words and in between I also posed several questions in order to see whether it had been correctly understood. In everything the sheikh was an attentive listener.

The men as well as the women, who of course turned up heavily veiled, were affected by the teaching of our Saviour and said, "We have never heard such words."

The father of the boy who had given the reading told me, "I am sending my son along with you, so you can tell him these words of Jesus, and afterwards he might return to teach us as well." I promised, and everyone rejoiced over this, especially the women.

After my return from Persia, I visited *Shumla* and *Sofia*. The vast majority of the inhabitants of Shumla consisted of Muslims, and after I had preached and shortly before my departure, many were sorry to have known nothing about the fact that a gospel message had been preached for their sakes. In Shumla I had a large audience of Muslims. The city is also the centre for other Muslim towns. In addition, the food there was much cheaper than in Varna, and for the time being, since our brothers from Asia needed more assistance, we moved to Shumla in October 1901.

Saying goodbye to Varna was difficult for us because we had to part from our dear brothers, Pastor Theodoroff and Pastor Shahveled, with whom we were closely involved.

At first our activities were restricted to literary work (printing), Bible distribution, proclaiming the gospel in Shumla and the surrounding area, and educating and preparing four grown-up boys for the work of our mission.

There were thirteen of us all told, young and old alike. Several of the believers who had been Muslims had come over from Asia and formed the foundation of our first congregation in Bulgaria, in addition to the one already mentioned, young Mirza.

The 16-year-old youth, whom his father had handed over to me, had come with me to Varna.

During one whole year, which he spent with us, the seed of truth grew in him, and after he had been in Bulgaria several months, he surrendered his heart to the Saviour. This youth also had to go through many struggles. Through outsiders and false Christians the spirit of darkness tried in every way to hinder the young believer in his growth, but the Lord watched over him. For four months he asked me to baptise him. I could not quickly come to a decision about baptising him before being absolutely convinced he believed

---

[1] See Appendix I, Bible Passages 32. Trans.

in Jesus, the Son of God, with his whole heart and was ready to carry his cross.[1] *For the baptism of a Muslim is not the same as a baptism amongst Christians; it can lead to grave perils and a martyr's death for him, which is why it is important to be clear about all of these points.* When he declared to me, in front of witnesses, he was ready to be faithful to his Saviour unto death and his only aim was to glorify the name of the Lord, I could no longer refuse. (Acts of the Apostles 10:47)[2] I instructed him thoroughly about the meaning of Christian baptism and showed him every passage in the Scriptures dealing with this subject. We gathered together in our meeting hall, and I posed questions to him in front of witnesses about the doctrine of salvation. After this, we prayed and sang a song I had translated into Turkish. It begins:

> Do you know the power of the blood?
> Are you washed in Jesus' blood?

Then we each put on long white shirts and went to the edge of a pond located in our garden. As for witnesses, there were fifteen Christians and a Muslim mullah present. Among the Christians were three Bulgarian brothers, the leaders of the local Methodist congregation, and the old blind pastor, Krekor Kevorkian from Rustchuk, with his wife; then from amongst the Muslims: the Bible distributor, Mirza Yahyah who had been baptised thirty years before, Mirza Ibrahim who had been baptised three years before, and Mirza Mukhtar who had been baptised twenty years before. We sang another Turkish song:

> I was a lost son,
> But now I have come home,
> My Jesus has delivered me,
> From the world I have turned back to God.
> Now I have come home, now I have come home,
> Glory to God, now I am home!

After that, we both went into the water (Acts of the Apostles 8:34),[3] which reached to our waists, and I again asked, "Do you, Vadia, believe Jesus has died for your sins?"

He answered, "Yes, I believe it!"

Then I said, "Heaven and earth and these men are witnesses that you have confessed Jesus and that I baptise you in the name of the Father and of the Son and of the Holy Spirit." Saying this, I immersed him in the water as a sign that he was buried and would rise again with Jesus (Romans 6:3-4).[4] The whole act was very quiet and solemn and made a profound impression on those present. In the evening we celebrated the Lord's Supper with eight men

---

[1] See Appendix I, Bible Passages 33. Trans.

[2] See Appendix I, Bible Passages 34. Trans.

[3] It is actually Acts 8:38; see Appendix I, Bible Passages 35. Trans.

[4] See Appendix I, Bible Passages 36. Trans.

and boys and two women. *Since we work amongst Muslims, it is doubly important for us that even in the outward forms we follow the apostles' example exactly and do not fastidiously keep to the rules of Western ecclesiastical practices.*

I was sick for six months and only in the spring of 1903 did I feel well again.

The work in Shumla developed in the following way: first there was the *literary work*. To start with we had a small printing press we had brought with us from Germany and which served us well. I had begun to publish a Turkish newspaper under the name *Shahid-ül-Haqaiq*, that is, *Witness of Truth*, and had also printed several other things in Turkish and Persian. With God's help we translated all sorts of good reading material, books and tracts for the Muslims. This literary work was an important part of our mission because through it we created something lasting.

An Armenian from Constantinople, a dear man by the name of Nerses, worked as our typesetter. He had previously worked at the American "Bible House" and fled to this place with his elderly mother at the time of the massacres[1] and earned a meagre living as a greengrocer. In addition, we had several young men from Persia who were being educated in our house. They likewise helped with the printing and folding and received lessons from us every day.

The second part of our work, in my opinion the most important part, was the *personal contact with Muslims*. Before the first issue of my newspaper came out, it was quite hard to make contact with them. In the first months not a single Muslim visited me, but after that, many came to see me: clerics (mullahs), teachers, tradesmen, Young Turks, people from every walk of life. In almost every instance my little newspaper formed the first link. These people often expressed their joy to me that such a periodical was being published in their city and in their language. Then I would speak with each of them in accordance with who they were and what they understood, and many opportunities presented themselves to bring the Scriptures nearer to them. I spoke with learned men first about the works in their literature of which I possessed a fine collection. I showed them all sorts of things that interested them and most of the time ended our discussion with *the one thing needful*.[2]

A Muslim teacher came to see me once. He was one of the most able men of his profession, and we spoke with one another for several hours. Before he went, three other respected Muslims arrived on the scene; they belonged to

---

[1] The first campaigns conducted by Sultan Abdul Hamid against his Armenian and Assyrian subjects were in 1894-96. Over 300,000 people were murdered in that time. Trans.

[2] The italics are mine. *The one thing needful* was a phrase used by Comenius (1592-1672), a bishop of the Bohemian Brethren, in his book of the same title (in Latin, *Unum Necessarium*). In his book, he compares the world to a labyrinth and shows that the way out is by leaving what is needless, and choosing *the one thing needful*—Christ (see Broadbent's *The Pilgrim Church*, pp. 138-140). This can also be a reference to the Gospel story of Mary and Martha (see Luke 10:38-42) where Mary chooses the one thing that is necessary: to sit at Jesus' feet and listen to Him. Trans.

the party of the Young Turks. They stuck together like Pharisees and Sadducees,[1] but as long as they chatted with me, they got along quite well. They stayed quite a while, giving the impression each one wanted to be the last to leave in order afterwards to complain about the other party. The apostle's word in 1 Corinthians 9:20-22 holds true on such occasions: "To the Jews I became as a Jew, so that I might win Jews...I have become all things to all men, so that I may by all means save some."[2] Shortly after that, the teacher came back with another mullah and expressed his desire to continue studying the Persian language with me; he already knew a little. I asked him to come to see me every Thursday afternoon, and these lessons gave me a good opportunity to talk with him about what was on my heart.

The third part of our work were *lessons* on which we laid much stress, and my dear wife devoted herself to this task with all her might. The three young Muslim men whom we had received into our home saw us as parents. My wife taught them German and the other subjects, and I gave them lessons in religion. We were greatly delighted by this, but the main thing for us was to give them a Christian education.

The fourth part of our work was *Bible distribution*. Dear old Mirza Yahyah travelled around the country distributing the Holy Scriptures as well as work from our printing shop. He faithfully used every opportunity to testify for the Saviour, and I have found indications the Lord has been blessing his efforts.

The fifth part of the work was *preaching*, which I did three times a week. I preached in Turkish every Sunday morning at our home and in the afternoon at the Methodist chapel; on Wednesday evening I preached alternately in Turkish and Armenian, likewise in the chapel. Although we had plenty of room in our house, it was no real substitute for a church hall, which serves only spiritual purposes. The people found it easier to come there, but going to a preacher's home, to many, seemed questionable. That is why we also paid twenty francs[3] a month for the use of the Methodist chapel, but it remained my deepest desire to get our own chapel.

Two of the Persian brothers who had accompanied us to Shumla with their wives caused us much grief. Love and exhortations were of no use with them, and they finally returned to their homeland. The months in Bulgaria were a time of testing for them, and it turned out they were not of us, though they had come to be with us.[4] Such elements can do much damage, but our distressed hearts were comforted by the fact the Lord gave us a cheerful boost in the

---

[1] The comparison seems to be that on the surface the Pharisees and Sadducees appeared united (especially in their opposition to Jesus) but were in constant conflict with one another over a variety of issues both great and small. Trans.

[2] See Appendix I, Bible Passages 37. Trans.

[3] Bulgaria had joined the Latin Monetary Union with France, Switzerland, Belgium, Italy, and Greece in 1867; this gave its currency, the lev, a value equal to that of the French franc, which at the time was worth about US $.196. See Appendix H, Exchange Rates to the US Dollar in the 1880s and 1890s. Trans.

[4] See Appendix I, Bible Passages 25. Trans.

work after they had gone. Without our having a hand in it whatsoever He had sent us new tenants who helped us diligently and joyfully in our work. One of them, a young mullah and student from Constantinople, had made efforts to continue his education with me. He had read my newspaper, heard the preaching, and felt he could trust me. He sent me a written request in which he entreated me to instruct him, so he could be of service to his people later on. He wanted especially to study Western languages, and we fulfilled his wish. He was very modest, well mannered, and talented. I hope the lessons and our discussions have helped him to find the Saviour.

In addition, a young man came quite unexpectedly from Persia to Shumla. At Tiflis he had met the people who had left us to return to Persia. They wanted to put him off in the way the spies had done,[1] but he had not believed them and had come anyway. As a child, he had gone to the American school in Urumiah for three years at a time when his parents were still Muslims, and he told us since then he had stayed in contact with his Saviour through prayer. Since it is hard for converts to earn a living in Muslim lands, he had been in Russia for several years and had missed the fellowship of Christians very much. He listened to the preaching with great eagerness and never failed to write it down afterwards.

On a Thursday, 5 February 1903, I went to Rustchuk. In a very small waiting room there were Bulgarians and Armenians ordering food and drink. A Muslim mullah with a white turban came in, sat next to me, and ordered a glass of tea. While he drank his tea and I ate my soup, a conversation developed. He told me he lived in Shumla and was now going to the villages to write amulets and the like, so he would have something to live on.

"God has given something to everyone," he went on to say, "and he has given me this gift by which I can live."

I asked him where he had studied. He answered, "Both in Shumla and in Constantinople, but I am not one, as you perhaps think, who has had a good education; rather I have only learned enough, so I can read and write, and I live by that." I then gave him a copy of the *Shahid-ül-Haqaiq*, the Turkish journal I published, and another small tract, which we had printed on our small printing press. After he had read a little bit, he said, "You must be very well acquainted with our religion." He then posed several questions about the gospel and Old Testament, which I answered. Our conversation lasted more than an hour; in the end he thanked me and said he would come to see me in Shumla. In addition, he asked me to forgive him if he might have said anything impertinent.

During this whole conversation the Bulgarians and Armenians listened attentively since of course they all understood Turkish well and were happy where it was a question of bringing Christ to the Muslim.

In the train to Rustchuk a Romanian Jewish woman and a young Jewish

---

[1] See Appendix I, Bible Passages 38. Trans.

man sat in my compartment. In addition, there was also with us a nice Bulgarian man, a factory owner from Rustchuk. I had the *Reichsboten* with me; the Jewish woman asked me in German if she might borrow the newspaper for a little while. Finally she asked me whether I was a Jew.

I said, "No, I am a Christian. Are you a Jew?" She said yes. "But you speak Romanian amongst yourselves?" I asked.

"I am from Romania but have lived in Varna for two years and am now travelling back to Romania."

"Do you know Doctor Rosenberg in Varna?" I asked.

She said, "Yes, he has become a Protestant (Doctor Rosenberg had been baptised in the Methodist chapel in Shumla in the spring of the previous year). Do you think he had his wife and children baptised as well? One Sunday I was at his home on account of my teeth. He no longer works on Sunday, but on the Sabbath. He is now no longer a Jew."

I said, "On the contrary, only now is he a proper Jew since he has recognised the fulfilment of the hope of Israel in Christ."

She said, "But what has he gained by it? It has gone very bad for him and he has lost his Jewish patients. He will no longer be able to stay in Varna."

I said, "But if he has peace in his heart, then that is worth more. And I do not believe that anyone would believe in Christ without a sure conviction in his heart." I then told her the life stories of several Jews who later went over to Christianity. I had known them for some time: for example, Pastor Rosenstein, Pastor Gordon, the Missionaries Toff and Landsmann, formerly scholarly Jews, but afterwards devout Christians. Up to that point she apparently had not yet heard of such men because she paid close attention and, as I believe, had clearly been very impressed.

She then said, "Rosenberg and his wife almost compelled me to go to the Protestant church to hear the sermon, but I did not go."

"Why did you not go?" I asked.

"Then the Jews would have said I had become a Protestant too," she answered.

Although the Bulgarian man understood nothing of what was said, he became very attentive. Afterwards he asked me what my profession was. I answered him I was a preacher. He asked many questions in respect to religion. Among other things he regretted the condition of the Orthodox Church, that it had so many festivals and ceremonies but no correct knowledge of the gospel; on the other hand, the Protestants had everything so simple and the Gospel in a comprehensible language. He was Bulgarian Orthodox, believed in Jesus, and wished for the reform of his Church according to the Gospel. My conversation with this Bulgarian man moved me very much. I told him a lot about my experiences in Central Asia and about the mission in general.

In Rustchuk I was the guest at the home of my old friend, Pastor Kevorkian. The meetings at which I was supposed to speak and which were taking place at the Bulgarian Protestants' chapel had already been publicised in the city beforehand. I preached on Friday evening. Among my listeners were Bulgarians, Armenians, and Jews, but the majority of them were Muslims. I preached on the text: "Examine everything and hold fast to that which is good" (1 Thessalonians 5:21).[1] *I endeavoured to remove the Muslims' prejudices and misunderstandings towards Christians because until these points are cleared up, Muslims remain deaf to every word.*

The following evening I had more listeners than the night before. That evening I spoke about the Parable of the Good Samaritan.[2] At the close several prominent Muslims and mullahs came and thanked me. Through this lecture I tried in a gentle way to broaden their narrow horizon, which commands only to love one's fellow [Muslim] believers. On Sunday I preached twice in Armenian for the Armenians who were there. On Monday and Tuesday I preached again to Muslims and explained the fifth chapter of Matthew's Gospel. There were so many people attending that not only the main hall, but also the side rooms were filled up to the last seat. Through the explanation of the Sermon on the Mount I declared to them how Jesus had not abolished the law but rather had fulfilled it.[3] On Wednesday I opened my sermon about the Parable of the Sower[4] by presenting and explaining to them the prophecies concerning Jesus from Adam to the Prophets, so I could tell them that Jesus alone was the deliverer of mankind. Although the sermon lasted a very long time, the Muslims listened very attentively.

I cannot describe the joy felt amongst the brothers that so many Muslims had come. Many Muslims showed their most heartfelt gratitude, and many things happened that could be regarded as miracles brought about by the Lord. For example, a young Muslim, a grammar school student in Rustchuk, had a vision in the night after the first sermon he had heard. After he had woke, he shouted, "We read the Koran, but we must also read the Gospel." He shouted this out loud over and over several times, so his parents woke up. The next day people tried to stop him from coming to the meeting, but since they saw he was neither ill nor mentally disturbed, they had to let him go. Another of the listeners went to a different part of the city, into a café, and in front of the mullahs he gave an account of what he had heard. One man who was present went again to another part of the city and, likewise in front of the mullahs, said a man in such and such a café had said this and that.

Then a 70-year-old man stood up and said, "What you are saying here is true; I was there myself. Whatever you need for your soul can be found there."

Thereupon he was asked, "Have you become a Protestant? What will be

---

[1] See Appendix I, Bible Passages 39. Trans.
[2] See Appendix I, Bible Passages 40. Trans.
[3] See Appendix I, Bible Passages 6. Trans.
[4] See Appendix I, Bible Passages 32. Trans.

your answer when we carry you before the mufti?"

He answered, "What does the mufti have to do with me? I am old and what is left of my life is only the lifetime of a fly. I am going to where I will find deliverance for my soul."

This old man came every evening with his son, a shoemaker, always sat at the front, and listened very attentively. It was remarkable as he was very poor and provided for himself by selling sweets, which he offered for sale at the taverns in the evenings. During those evenings he sold nothing.

He was told, "You poor man, why have you refrained from selling your wares and lost the time that is so important for you just to go to that place?"

He answered, "Food for the soul is worth more than food for the body. As I said before, I am so old; I must have this." On the last evening he came to me and we prayed together. Since he could not read because of the weakness of his eyes and also because he had no money to buy glasses for himself, I ordered a pair for him and gave him the Holy Scriptures.

That night three learned Muslims came to see me. One of them was very proud since he had already been to see so many preachers, but no one was able to give satisfactory answers to his questions.

He said, "I have not attended your lectures because what would I get out of a sermon which is certainly for people who know nothing! That is why I came to speak with you in person." *His most important question first of all concerned the divinity of Christ.* "He ate and drank," he thus argued, "became tired and, as it states in your Gospel, was crucified; how could he be God? Furthermore, God is one, and if Jesus is also God, then that would make two out of God!"

The main content of my reply was, "Jesus was a perfect man: he ate, drank, and was crucified for the sins of mankind, and afterwards God raised him from the dead. Concerning his humanity, we say of him that he has a beginning, but he is eternal and is like God as the only begotten Son of God and as the Word of God because God has revealed himself in the person of Jesus. The Koran also testifies of the Word of God in the same way: '...Jesus the Messiah, the son of Mary, is the apostle of Allah, and His Word...' (Surah 4:169).[1] In addition, your traditions also say: the Word of God is not a created thing. This also concurs with our Gospel: 'In the beginning was the Word, and the Word was with God, and the Word was God...And the Word became flesh...'[2] And if you say that we are worshippers of two gods because we assert that Jesus is the Word of God, then according to your traditions you have nine gods. Because your traditions ascribe eight attributes to God that are eternal (one of these is the Word, and it has already been stated this is not something created), and besides, it is written: *Wa hiya walaahnawa laghaiyrahi*, that is, and these (attributes) are not he (God) himself and not

---

[1] It is actually Surah 4:171; see Appendix J, Koran Passages 5. Trans.
[2] See Appendix I, Bible Passages 3. Trans.

other than he himself.[1] I ask you, how shall these things be understood? If these attributes are eternal, like God, and not God himself, then it must be accepted there are nine gods. But if it is said they are not other than God himself, then it must be accepted that they form a party of all the same nature. I tell you this that you should not look down upon Christians out of hand and dismiss the teaching of the Gospel without a careful study of it. Incidentally, I know these traditions of yours also conflict with the Koran because the Koran only speaks of one personal, eternal God."

To this he said nothing; rather he went over to another question: "Can you prove to me that the Holy Scriptures you have are genuine?"

"*For you as Muslims I can bring many proofs and, since you are Muslims, I do not need to take many detours.* In the Koran, Surah 10:94 states: 'If thou were in doubt as to what we have revealed unto thee, then ask those who have been reading the Book from before thee.'[2] You know that Mohammed lived around six hundred years after Christ, and this passage testifies that the Christians at that time had the genuine Holy Scriptures. Otherwise how would God have been able to say to Mohammed he should go to the Jews and the Christians if he was in doubt about something? And if some people have falsified the Scriptures, then this had to have happened at or after the time the Koran was written. But we have many manuscripts and translations which were written several hundred years before Mohammed, and they are the same as those at our disposal today."

He was satisfied with this explanation. Our conversation carried on until one o'clock. In the end he asked me to send him three copies of the Scriptures that I print. One of the others, the son of a sheikh who is the head of an order of dervishes in Rustchuk, conveyed greetings to me from his father; unfortunately he was sick, otherwise he would liked to have come. My three guests went away after thanking me kindly and expressing the wish that, if I ever came to Rustchuk again, they might visit me.

The trip was a great joy to the brothers and me *because up to then no one had yet seen so many Muslims seeking the Word of God with sincere hearts.*

---

[1] See Appendix B, *wa hiya walaahnawa laghaiyrahi*. Trans.
[2] See Appendix J, Koran Passages 6. Trans.

CHAPTER 22
ALL SORTS OF EXPERIENCES AND BLESSINGS

In the spring of 1903 one of our Persian friends, Mukhtar, our printer, died of consumption after he had been with us for about a year. He knew his end was drawing near and was happy to die amongst Christians and to be buried with them.

American missionaries in Constantinople wrote to us and asked us to receive a Turkish Christian woman and her young daughter. *But since her husband remained a Muslim and did not dismiss her, I had to answer that we might receive her only with her husband's permission.*

Meanwhile, at our printing shop *Maghrabi* (Persian), *The Thirty-two Disputations of the Artisans* (Kashgari), a tract in Turkish, which I wrote, and the *Shahid-ül-Haqaiq* had been printed. In addition, there was the translation of Bunyan's *Pilgrim's Progress* in Turkish, which the American missionaries intended for the Turkish-speaking Armenians and which employed Armenian characters. I revised and printed it with Turkish characters for the Muslims. As well, there was *Kalilah Damina* in Armenian that I had already partially translated in Kashgar. We also printed a Turkish songbook. The songs were taken partly from the collection of songs (printed with Armenian characters) that the Americans had, and partly from what I had translated from the German and Swedish.

In 1903 the state of affairs in the East was very bad, not only in Bulgaria but also in Persia and Turkey. The Muslim newspapers wrote in the deepest desperation about the future of Islam. The *mujtahids*, the chief mullahs, were extremely agitated and feared for the continued existence of Islam. Mullahs and scholars were very embittered against the government and administration. The people were embittered against both the mullahs and the government. Everywhere they were shouting: we are perishing; we have no training, no science; how will we be able to exist? The clergy put the blame on the government, that it was not fulfilling its duty to promote the education and advancement of the people. The government in turn criticised the priests, that they were a hindrance for the education and advancement of the people. In Teheran an alarming situation prevailed which threatened the Shah's throne. The situation in Turkey was no better. It was an important time for us.

What was interpreted as Islam's declaration of war was a publication, which came out that year in a French journal under the slogan: "Islam's Final Word to Europe". The author who signed the work was a Sheikh Abdul Hagk from Bagdad, a member of the Holy Islamic League on whose expressed order the declaration was made. Here is an excerpt:

"Christian people! It is time to listen to us. Islam's hatred towards Europe is irreconcilable. After centuries of trying to make friendly overtures toward us, in these days the only conclusion which remains is this: we abhor you more than in any other time in our history. Understand this, you clever Europeans, in our eyes a Christian appears to us like a blind man who has lost all human dignity, as his position is based solely on the fact he is a Christian.

"We know exactly what we are. It is absolutely necessary for you at least to find your way into this fundamental truth, that the whole structure of Islam is founded on the unity of one God who is infinite, immeasurable, eternal, who is never begotten and has begotten nothing. This article of faith is especially directed against Christians. Through this article the Christian Trinity becomes the sworn enemy of the Islamic God. The conflict of these two basic ideas is the most awful and consuming trial of patience for every Muslim soul. You Christians, brought up from your youth in the teachings of your Church, you cannot at all imagine what shudder and horror grips us solely at the naming of your Trinity. At least permit the admission of this indisputable fact: *between your faith in the divinity of Jesus and us there is an eternal, unbridgeable abyss*. Know this, it is absolutely impossible for us, we who are filled by a boundless faith in our one God, to permit anything, to tolerate anything, to forgive anything that from far or near could do even the slightest harm to the absolute unity of our immeasurable, eternal, infinite God.

"We have not forgotten your Crusades. They continue now under a hundred dastardly forms. You have fought and humiliated us through every means at your disposal. You have pushed back the borders of Islam at every point on the globe, and you unceasingly seek to subvert what remains through your diplomats and missionaries. Your plan is complete. You pursue it openly, systematically: the ruin of Islam. Instead of any apology, you reproached us for being rebels against your civilisation. Of course we are rebels! And we will be rebels to the death! But you, you alone are to blame for this! No, you diplomats, we have paid too dearly for our naive trust. We know quite for certain that your civilisation, united in solidarity with your churches, knows and wants nothing else than the destruction of Islam.

"There is no doubt that you have brought great material benefit to India, Africa, and Central Asia, but with the infinite greatness of Islam's God, *is it at all possible we could excuse for even a single moment the lordship of a crucified God*, a God who wants to proclaim the degradation of our infinite God, the almighty Lord of the world? Know this, Christian conquerors, that no mathematical trick, no hoard of gold, no miracle can ever reconcile us to your godless rule. Know that just the sight of your banners alone fluttering in our land is a torment for the soul of Islam. The greatest of your good deeds are just so many blots with which our conscience is besmirched, and do not doubt what our most burning desire is: that the happy day would come when we can blot out the last traces of your cursed rule.

"Incidentally, we must also admit today that in the first place we are grateful to your acts of violence. They have taught us how to get to know ourselves better. We know now there are three hundred million of us. We have lacked organised concentration; you have taught it to us with imperious necessity.

"Islamic unity is rising up from one end of the world to the other, and a mysterious being is driving us to our holy purpose. Do not threaten us with your weapons. *What can the things of this world take away from us? Victory or defeat: that is the work of God. Our duty is to die well, and through thirteen centuries the world remembers that we know how to die.*"

This movement within the Muslim community showed that a vigorous resistance on the part of Islam was to be expected. Everywhere amongst the Islamic peoples of the earth the believers had been worked up into a rabid state.

This aim was also served by the message being trumpeted that Mohammed the Prophet had risen up with the call: "Allah, save your people."

Before every war that Muslims have waged against Christian peoples, similar messages were circulated, not every one as short as this one. As a rule they would come in the form of a tract under the title: *Vasiyadt* ('Name') or *Berat* ('Testament Letter'). These tracts would be circulated amongst the people, always with the introduction that Mohammed the Prophet in his tomb in Mecca asked for paper and ink from the sheikh[1] and the sheikh placed both of these items on Mohammed's grave and went away. In the morning when the sheikh returned, he found written what he reproduced as an introduction in the tract.

Although such a view conflicts with the fundamental teaching of Islam and Muslim scholars attach no belief to these fantastic stories, nevertheless, these tracts are still circulated among the people because one word from the Prophet is always the quickest way for superstitious and fanatical people to become fanatical for a "Holy War"—it is well known that such a tract was circulated at the time of the Crusades and before the last Russo-Turkish war. But the tract mentioned above is much fiercer and more spiteful than the earlier ones. Whoever is acquainted with the circumstances must say we will live to see much Christian blood being shed by Muslims because what gives the Muslims courage is the following:

1. that so many Christian Armenians were murdered by the Turks without the murderers being punished in any significant way;

2. that not only now but even in earlier times quite a few consuls of Christian governments fell victim to Muslim fanaticism—which likewise went unpunished—and in every case the apologies of the Sublime Porte were regarded as sincere and satisfactory. A learned Muslim told me: our former rulers were much too merciful in allowing their Christian subjects to live. If they had been forced to eradicate all of them, then we would have peace today.

A mufti with whom I spoke on the trip to Philippopolis told me: we have

---

[1] The chief mullah.

until today shown consideration to the Christian governments, but now we have come to see how far the governments are willing to go, and it will not go on like this much longer. Then everything will become how we want it, not how the Christian governments want it. Naturally what he meant by this was that the Christians would first have to be eradicated from Turkish lands (that was in 1903).

I must say: if the Lord, through the firm steps of the Christian governments, does not warn Islam, a hard time is coming for the Christians in the Middle East, a time like there has not yet been up to now. O that the Lord would have mercy![1]

On the other hand, Muslims are again very worried, indeed, they are almost in despair, regarding Islam's continuing existence. Any promises the Muslims have ever made to the Christian peoples in regard to reforms have never been kept. They cannot even keep these promises because, by doing so, they would offend the laws of Islam. If anything, which they ought not comply with, is ever really vigorously demanded of the Muslims, then nothing remains for them but the sword and violence, the *Holy War*. Muslims tell themselves: since the Christian governments are in disagreement amongst themselves and are always ready to give credence to what we tell them, we can still make the final attempt to bring Islam back to power. If we succeed, fine; if we do not succeed, then we have nothing to lose because disagreements between the Christian governments leave no danger for us to face.[2]

In Rustchuk, in 1904, I again preached to Muslims for three days in a row. The listeners were not as numerous as the year before. However, I had the impression that everyone who came had followed a real need in their heart. The 70-year-old Muslim who had accepted the word of truth the previous year came with his son, even though he had had to endure scorn and derision from fanatical Muslims throughout the year.

From Rustchuk I went up the Danube to Sistova. It had been announced that on the following day a sermon for Muslims would take place. It was just a few minutes before the appointed hour, but no one had appeared. We were already thinking the Muslims had completely refused to come. The mufti could have forbidden them from coming, but at four o'clock on the dot the Muslims poured into the chapel, and after a few minutes there were no more seats available. The ones who came later took their places, Middle Eastern fashion, on the floor or stayed standing in the doorway. The large room could

---

[1] This foresight became a sad reality through the events of the World War [WWI]. The Turkey of today is almost completely rid of Christians. The deportations exterminated hundreds of thousands; the Turkish government expelled the rest from the country. Cf. *Deutschland und Armenien. Diplomatische Aktenstücke des Auswärtigen Amtes in Berlin und der Deutschen Botschaft in Konstantinopel.* [*Germany and Armenia. Diplomatic files of the Foreign Office in Berlin and the German Embassy in Constantinople*] Published by Johannes Lepsius, 1928. Tempel-Verlag, Potsdam. [Schäfer].

[2] The development of Islam just as the development of Turkey after the World War [WWI] seems to have to be assessed differently; but its further development remains to be seen. [Schäfer].

not hold all the listeners and many had to turn back again. I spoke for one and a half hours. In the large crowd a deep silence and eager attentiveness prevailed.

After the close of the meeting, many Muslims came and expressed their gratitude for what they had heard. Several wanted to kiss my hand, but I did not permit it. This is an honour which Muslims are not allowed to show to a Christian, if they do not have the impression that the Christian knows the truth better than they do themselves. Even the mufti was among the ones who thanked me. In the evening he sent two messengers, elderly men, in order to give me his regards and to ask when and where he could speak with me. I fixed a time for that same evening. At eight o'clock he came with five educated Muslims, and we spoke until twelve o'clock about spiritual things. They told me about a book (*Mudafea*, that is, *Refutation*), which a pasha had written and which deals with a disputation he had with an English missionary. The Muslims posed several of the traditional questions to me concerning the divinity of Jesus and similar things. I answered them in the same way as I had done the year before in Rustchuk.

The mufti said, "We can understand the phrase, 'Father and Son', only in human terms; but it must have another meaning. A translation cannot convey the exact meaning of the original text at every point. That is why an explanation is required to arrive at a complete understanding of the text."

In response to this I gave a short explanation, but it was not enough. *We must give Muslims a translation of the New Testament with explanations addressing the particular difficulties they have. In addition, we need the help of theologians who are believers and thorough experts of the original biblical text as well as the circumstances in the Middle East.*

The next day I met a Muslim, Hafiz Effendi (*hafiz* is the title of those who know the Koran by heart). He greeted us with a beaming cheerfulness and asked us to come in and have a glass of tea. In the course of the conversation, which he kept bringing round to the previous day's sermon, he offered to take me to see the khoja, the teacher at the seminary. He was a venerable man with a white turban; he greeted us very warmly. The students greeted us by getting up from the ground, and, according to Muslim custom, they did not sit again until I asked the teacher to give them permission to do so. After several more sentences had been translated into Turkish from the Arabic religious book with which they were occupied at that moment, in order to give me a sample of what the students knew, the teacher began to talk with me. He regretted that he heard about the meeting too late. He had not been there, but he told me that on the previous evening there was great excitement amongst the Muslim women. One of them had been to the lecture and had told the others about it. Then they said, "Why were we not able to hear these words too?"

Just as we were just getting ready to make the return journey back to Rustchuk, Pastor Todoroff said to me, "There is talk amongst the Muslims that they want to invite you to preach at the mosque. Would you speak there?"

"With pleasure," was my answer, "only I would not enter the pulpit but would sit, as is the Middle Eastern fashion, in front of the mihrab and preach from there."

"Why not from the pulpit?"

"Because then one of the long prescribed prayers would have to be read out loud. I would not like to do that. On the other hand, I would not offend anyone from the mihrab if I were simply to begin the sermon with the name of God."

"It would be better if you preached in the church and not in the mosque."

"Why?"

"Because it would be more to the glory of Jesus than if the Muslims were to hear the truth in their mosque."

I had to tell him I was of a different opinion: "Here in the church the Muslims will bring along their mistrust if they were even to come at all. But in the mosque it would be easier to win them for Jesus."

On the steamship taking us back to Rustchuk there was a Muslim from Sistova who was bringing to Constantinople eight hundred rams for the *Kurban Bairam* ('Easter'). He had been to the meeting and immediately began to talk about it. He also told me the Muslims had spoken a great deal about the lecture in the cafés the previous evening.

In Shumla we had gained official permission for the printing shop and had even found a very useful pressman who took on the job of the deceased Mirza Mukhtar.

At home I found our Bible distributor, Daedo Petko, who had many good things to report about his three-month trip. In Dzhumaia, Osman Bazar, Oryekhovica, Tirnova, Sevlievo, Lovatz, Plevna, Somovit, Oryakhovo, Lom Palanka, Widdin, Nicopolis, Sistova, Vrtsel, and other cities and villages he distributed Scriptures and had discussions with Muslims on several occasions. He advised that I visit these towns as well and preach the gospel. Alas, I cannot go into his trip in greater detail.

There was all kinds of work for me to do. A new issue of the *Shahid-ül-Haqaiq* and a few small tracts had to be completed, so Daedo Petko could take them with him on his next trip. While I was busy with this, Pastor Hagop Shahveled paid me a visit. We decided to travel together to Baltchik on the Black Sea, a city of twenty thousand inhabitants.

The city belongs to those towns in Bulgaria where no American missionaries work, presumably because the inhabitants are mostly Muslims, whereas the activity of the Americans is restricted to Bulgarians.

The first evening a hafiz came to see us. I chatted with him for several hours and gave him a copy of *Shahid-ül-Haqaiq* and some tracts, with which he was very pleased. After we had had a time of worship together the next morning, which was a Sunday, we tried to organise a meeting for Muslims and Armenians, but we could not find a suitable room, and besides, it was a *day for competing* (see Genesis 32:25). In a courtyard, in the middle of the city, many Muslims got together to sing, and all of their fellow believers seemed to be gathered there to watch.[1] So we contented ourselves with me visiting several cafés accompanied by the old preacher in order to hand out Turkish tracts and the *Shahid-ül-Haqaiq*.

On Monday we paid a visit to the governor and asked him for permission to use the stock exchange building as a venue to preach to the Muslims. He was very friendly, chatted with us for a long time, and showed a lot of interest in the mission to the Muslims. Unfortunately, in regards to the stock exchange building, his answer to us was no. However, he advised us to hold our talks in the function room of the Hotel Denchov. So that is what we did. The *balaban*[2] announced it in the city that in the evening a lecture in Turkish would take place to which everyone was invited.

To begin with, many Bulgarians assembled in the hall at the appointed time; however, the Muslims were late. But since I proposed to speak just to the Muslims, I was somewhat embarrassed about what I was now supposed to preach to the Bulgarians. Pastor Shahveled began to speak quietly with them and tell them that I had a lecture to the Muslims in mind, and that was why I still wanted to wait and see whether the Turks would come or not. We waited half an hour, but the Muslims did not come. Then I began to draw a comparison between Christian and non-Christian peoples in order to explain to my audience in this way what a new life the gospel and the words of Jesus have brought to people and what these things have in store for them. While I was speaking, numerous Muslims and Armenians appeared. The room was not big enough, many stayed standing in the courtyard, and the windows were opened, so they too could hear. After I had spoken for an hour, Turkish tracts and the *Shahid-ül-Haqaiq* were handed out. Of the two hundred copies I had brought with me, there were almost none left. Since they were still asking for more, I asked Hafiz Effendi to give me back the tracts he had received the day before, and I promised to send him more from Shumla.

"No," he replied, "I cannot give them back. I am travelling to Constantinople the day after tomorrow and must take them along to give to my sons who are at school there."

The verdict, which the various listeners had on the meeting, was very odd. The young Bulgarians who had been to university and whose views were no doubt influenced mostly by the socialists said we must be Christian socialists since we preached love to all men; it would be good if they were also to spread these ideas amongst the Muslims.

---

[1] The italics are mine. Aveteranian uses the German word, *Ringtag*, which I have translated as *day for competing*; the German word *ringen* used in Genesis 32:25 means "to wrestle", that is, Jacob wrestling with the angel. See Appendix I, Bible Passages 41. After much deliberation I think Avetaranian means that by holding this gathering on a Sunday, the Muslims were looking to *compete* with the Christians or possibly that the Christians were being forced to compete with the Muslims. Trans.

[2] A *balaban* is a trumpet. If the government wants to announce something to the inhabitants of the city, the *balabandyi* goes around, blows his trumpet in every square and on every street in order to get the people's attention, and then passes on the government's instructions.

The Bulgarian-Orthodox pope who likewise had been present at the meeting said, "Do not listen to them. They are liars and deceivers." To the reply that everything we had said was true and good and beneficial for all people, he had declared, "Yes, in the beginning they will preach such things, but later on they will lie and deceive you." The Muslims had kept the word that had been spoken and had passed it on; the Armenians also rejoiced over it.

On this trip it became very clear to us again what thirst for the truth prevails amongst the Muslims who until now have not seen writings and tracts with such spiritual and moral content.

When I came home I found on my table various questions written down by Muslims, for example: "What is the difference between Christianity and Islam?" "What is the difference between the Holy Spirit and the Spirit of Truth; between the role of the prophets and the office of teachers of the Word of God?"

CHAPTER 23

PHILIPPOPOLIS. YEARS OF WORK AND STRUGGLE[1]

Aside from the substantial measure of work, the following years in Avetaranian's life were taken up with many struggles. Avetaranian not only had the work of the mission station in Bulgaria; at the forefront of this was his literary work, which formed the tools for his whole missionary activity. The "fruit" from this work was that he had to reckon with the resistance of those who were the official representatives of the Muslim religion in the country, the leaders of the Muslim population. Furthermore, he constantly had to try and win sympathy for his work within the German missions community. For in the societies that were otherwise involved in religious and missionary activities, the knowledge of Islam within Christendom and the understanding of the Muslim's psyche was itself such that he would not have been thought of as a missionary if he had not continually and with ever fresh reasons elicited support and had not shed light upon and provided an insight into the nature of Islam by way of countless individual reports. This insight always followed on from his most recent experiences that came from his travelling and lecturing in the mission field as well as on the mission's German home front. He reported on every new issue of the *Shahid-ül-Haqaiq* that came out and on the contents of his tracts, which he himself had composed and printed in his own printing shop. He showed how the concept of sin being testified to by the conscience is far removed from the Muslim for whom the precepts of Mohammed are regarded as the sole commandments of God.

Avetaranian translated John Bunyan's *Pilgrim's Progress* into Turkish, so the Muslim did not have to look upon the works of a Voltaire, Rousseau, or the French novels as products of Christian literature. He had his bookshop work along the same lines, kept his Bible distributors equipped, and continued to learn from their experiences. Of his pupils, Sahak and Hagop Arakelian, he had one learn a trade, and the other he had trained in Germany for later service within the Muslim community.

He reported on evangelistic trips which lasted several weeks and which continued to bring many Muslim listeners to him, besides the Christians who were friendly towards him. He reported on discussions and Nicodemus-like

---

[1] From this point on in the story, the passages that refer to Avetaranian indirectly in the third person were written by Richard Schäfer, the General Secretary of Dr Lepsius's Orient-Mission in Potsdam who published the 1930 edition of Avetaranian's autobiography eleven years after his death. Schäfer seeks to maintain the flow of the story by filling in the chronological gaps and connecting up the various reports that Avetaranian wrote detailing his life and activities at this time. Trans.

conversations but at the same time sensed everywhere, and also let his friends in Germany know, that no step in his work could be taken without it resulting in hostile opposition, threats, and attacks. Avetaranian's refuge was the *Lord* and *Him alone*. In his simple and heart-rending way he invited the *Church*, which stood behind him, the community of believers, to strengthen him and his fellow workers and encouraged them to take the next step forward with him. As their exhorting and entreating fellow helper in the Lord's work, he clothed everything in the word of the Scriptures.

In the spring of 1906 Doctor Johannes Lepsius, the chairman of the German Orient-Mission (Potsdam), visited his friend and fellow worker, Avetaranian, in Shumla and travelled with him and his wife to Cairo (Egypt) to the Muslim Missions Conference. In Bulgaria Lepsius found a congregation of Muslims and Christians, though not organised as such, which gathered around John Avetaranian and listened to the proclamation of the Word: the promising basis for a sound, faithful missionary work done according to the Scriptures.

The Cairo conference was the first attempt to make the task of the mission to Muslims a subject of international importance, to bring about consultation and agreement amongst the evangelical missionary societies of every country.

Twenty-nine missionary societies with sixty-two delegates were represented at the conference, and about sixty other persons with an interest in the subject were there as guests. In five days of consultations an excellent perspective was gained on every issue connected with the mission to Muslims. In an appeal to the Christian Church, the impressions of the Cairo conference were summarised as follows:

> "The need of more than two hundred million Muslims and the current problems of the mission to Muslims which concerns so many areas of missionary work were the reasons for a meeting of delegates from the missions in Islamic countries. The conference met in Cairo from 4 to 9 April 1906.
>
> "The consultations covered the whole of the Muslim world, their ethnographical, social, religious, and intellectual circumstances, the missionary work accomplished up to now, and the questions and problems which Islam poses to the Christian Church. The main methods of missionary work amongst Muslims with regard to preaching, literature, medical missions, and training were mentioned.
>
> "The facts put across to us, the great need of the Muslim world, the first fruits of Christian preaching, the unstoppable advance of the gospel in the countries of Islam, had the effect on us of a solemn call of God to His Church in our time.
>
> "Although we have come together from many Muslim and Christian countries and have come to know Islam from very different quarters, we unanimously and urgently call upon the Christian Church, as it is represented by its missionary societies, to tackle the work of the mission to Muslims with fresh vigour. We ask that this work be increased and supported in this way: 1. that more workers for this particular purpose be trained and sent out, 2. that a

literature for the Muslim world be systematically created and circulated, 3. that important centres of the Muslim world be reoccupied, the existing work be firmly supported, and the advance of Islam in areas, which until now have still been heathen, henceforth be prevented.

"May God make us able to do His will."

Avetaranian received considerable encouragement from this conference. Until then his method of working lay along the same lines as had also been taken by other experienced men who had extended life works like Doctor Zwemer, Reverend Jessup, Reverend Herrick. Avetaranian was already of the impression that all Muslims who had come in contact with secular civilisation had encountered a certain contradiction to the Islamic philosophy of life and with that, an approximation of what Christianity is. Extracting the individual from this way of thinking was to him first and foremost, and he named the channels, which would lead to this:

1. Distributing literature. Bibles, tracts, and pamphlets containing spiritual messages.
2. Preaching.
3. Private conversations about religious issues.
4. Care for the poor and sick.
5. Educating children.

He was quite certain "not everyone who preaches the gospel in Germany is a suitable missionary for the Orient; rather they should be believing men and women who are thoroughly prepared and experienced, whose good way of life is also an outward testimony, and who devote themselves purposefully in the love of Christ." He would have liked all missionaries to have a medical background.

It was a great joy and encouragement for Avetaranian that his German missionary society sent a missionary to the Muslim Kurds that year. He no doubt had all of these qualifications: Pastor Detwig von Oertzen who first of all created a reader in the Kurdish language for Kurdistan and began with the translation of the New Testament into Kurdish.

In September 1907 Avetaranian transferred his work from Shumla to Philippopolis.

About the origins of the work in Philippopolis, Avetaranian reports:

"After we had born witness to our Saviour, both through preaching and writing, at Varna for one year and at Shumla for six years, we transferred our mission station to *Philippopolis*. Through this change we moved a step closer to the centre of Islam [Constantinople]; our new place of residence is situated on the great connecting railway between East and West, and the Orient-Express reaches Constantinople, the capital of the Ottoman Empire, in a couple of hours. In many respects in Philippopolis we came by facilities for the work of our mission printing shop, which we had to do without in the remote city of Shumla.

"When the decision was taken, all our things were sent on, and the train brought me nearer to my new destination with each passing minute. The Lord Himself gave me a sign of encouragement.

"Several Muslims were sitting opposite me in the compartment; among them was a mullah. The attention of the latter was drawn to the *Shahid-ül-Haqaiq*, which I held in my hand. When he asked what kind of writing it was, I only answered, 'Please, read it', and handed it to him. When he had read several pages, he said, 'Who wrote this? Where can I get it?' I answered, 'You can get it from me, as many as you like.' He made a note of my address, asked to visit me in Philippopolis on his return trip and to be allowed to take at least twelve copies with him. Then we chatted until the train reached Philippopolis.

"At one point our conversation was interrupted by a Greek man whose interest was aroused by our words. He was a young man with clearly a lot of knowledge about Christian things. He was employed as an agent for a tobacco factory in Tatar Bazardjik, a city near Philippopolis. He told me that quite a few Muslims gathered at his home every evening; he would read to them from the Holy Scriptures and translate. He asked me to send him pamphlets now and then to distribute amongst the Turks.

"The mullah had studied in Constantinople and was a *muderis*, that is, a teacher of religion in Bosnia. He wanted to have the *Shahid-ül-Haqaiq* read in his classes. He already had some writings sent to him from the American mission in Beirut in order to gain an insight into the Christian teaching but said the printing shop in Beirut, a Turkish city influenced by the Turkish censors, could not express itself openly like the *Shahid-ül-Haqaiq*. He asked me if he might take with him the copy I gave him, though with permission to tear off the front cover since he was making a pilgrimage to Mecca via Constantinople and was afraid having the paper might be dangerous for him.

"It took us several weeks to finish setting up our home and the printing shop. After consulting with the American missionaries, Marsh and Haskell, who were working amongst the Bulgarian people, I decided to preach in Turkish to their congregation every Sunday afternoon in the chapel. We invited the Muslims to the worship service by means of handbills. It seemed to me the Muslims in Philippopolis were friendly towards us, so we had an open door. I enjoyed calling on the Turks in their cafés and establishing personal relationships with them, even visiting the surrounding villages and cities. But so much of my time was taken up with writing and running the printing shop that we urgently needed two co-workers, one to stand in for me and help me, and the other to be preparing himself while the Kashgari New Testament was being printed in order to go to Kashgar as a missionary.

"Our printing shop had the following works in progress: *Durra i Munajia i Massihia* (*Pearls of Christian Salvation*), a very good little book whose anonymous author must be a converted Muslim scholar. His aim is to bring salvation in Christ closer to Muslims. I found the small book as a single copy in Cairo. It was published in Constantinople, but no one knows anything about it. Presumably it has been forbidden and suppressed. Furthermore, we are printing *Pilgrim's Progress* in Azerbaijani-Turkish (that is, in the Turkish dialect which is spoken in Caucasia and Persia). At the same time the printing of my Kashgari translation is going ahead, a new issue of *Shahid-ül-Haqaiq* is also in the offing, the contents of which is a comparison of the conception of God between the Koran and the Holy Scriptures."

The next reports by Avetaranian give an insight into the progress that was being made and also the resistance, which was beginning to be encountered in the city of Philippopolis.

"On 15 December 1907 a Muslim priest was among those attending the worship service. He had probably been sent by other Muslim clerics with definite orders. After five or six weeks he published in the only Turkish newspaper in Bulgaria a lead article under the title, 'A Muslim Can Have No Religion Other Than Islam', which was followed two days later by a continuation of the piece. In brief, the content of the article was this:

> 'Everyone knows the Protestants spare no money and send preachers into every country in order to increase their following. One of them who has set up shop in our city invites Muslims to hear him preach. In order to learn what the difference is between Protestantism and Orthodoxism and what kind of evidence the Protestants have to convince a Muslim of the truth of their religion, I attended one of these sermons. In his sermon the preacher, John Avetaranian, spoke about various vices and showed that everyone acknowledges the same things as sin. Afterwards he described the contrasting virtues and closed with the claim that no one could be set free from their vices and blessed with virtue merely by the human will alone. For this freedom and blessing it was necessary to be born again; that is what Jesus taught. At the end of his sermon he said: let us pray. The Protestants stood up. *At first our Muslims were about to get up, but they quickly came to the conclusion they were standing before a Christian preacher and stayed seated.* With this invitation to prayer he had as his intention nothing other than to bring the Muslims under his command and so gradually to get them used to Protestantism. Such unfounded and inane preaching makes no impression on us. We learn the principles of ethics in our homes and primary schools from early childhood and endeavour to live by them.'

"In the next instalment he moderated his words in certain respects by saying:

> 'The words "unfounded" and "inane" ought to be applied to the teaching in the sermon. For in the Koran, in the traditions, and in our most distinguished books on religion, vices are called vices and virtues are called virtues. The claim that a person can be completely set free from vice and blessed with virtue through Christianity by being born again is simply unfounded and inane. So far as being born again is concerned, we call it *ilham* ('revelation' or 'vision') and *hidayat* ('divine guidance'). The path to rebirth is broad. That is to say, if a person believes in God, in his angels, in his holy books, and in his prophets, then that person has attained it. We are not ones who deny Jesus Christ, rather we are obliged to honour him as one of the greatest prophets and

beseech him for his help, and we do this every day. Whoever is blessed with this hidayat does not ask about such dubious and meaningless things as being born again. The preacher may be assured that a Muslim can have no other religion than Islam.'[1]

"I wrote a detailed response to this article and sent it to the editor. He promised me in a very obliging letter to print it, but that same evening he asked me instead to publish the reply myself in a pamphlet since he really feared trouble as a Muslim and the son of a Muslim. If I were to insist that the article go in the newspaper, then he would have to ask me for one hundred and fifty francs as compensation. I did not want to take on such an expense and therefore only wrote a short response as follows. I propose to publish in a pamphlet my own detailed refutation and line of reasoning that Muslims can become Christians.

'We Christians, who receive enlightenment of our minds, purification of our conduct, and cleansing of our hearts through the heavenly books that have been mercifully given to us, do not keep these things solely to ourselves. In order to bless our fellow men as well with these divine gifts and spiritual treasures, we have up to now translated them into four hundred languages and are getting them to our brothers in every country of the world. That we are mocked by the children of the world because we sacrifice our money and our lives for this cause can never make our hands lax. For we know we have come through from death to life and have experienced the truth of the verses contained in our books that "the Light has come into the world, and men loved the darkness rather than the Light for their deeds were evil. For everyone who does evil hates the Light, and does not come to the Light for fear that his deeds will be exposed. But he who practices the truth comes to the Light, so that his deeds may be manifested as having been wrought in God" (John 3:19-21).[2]

'Wanting to honour our Muslim brothers, we have invited them to hear the holy Gospel being preached which the verse in the Koran: "*Musaddiqan limaa maAAakum*"[3] affirms, and in which the verse: "*Wa maa unzila min qablika*"[4] makes it their duty to believe.

'We are very sorry to be shown so little esteem with words like "unfounded" and "inane" for this demonstration of our love, instead of being greeted with the verse from the Koran, "*Ilaah'naa wa Ilaah'kum waahidun wa nahnu lahu muslimun*"[5] and that the rebirth referred to in the Gospel verse, "unless one is born again he cannot see the kingdom of God" (John 3:3)[6] is

---

[1] These two articles appeared in numbers 362 and 364 of the *Balkan* authored by Khatib Djahid Efendi. Trans.

[2] See Appendix I, Bible Passages 42. Trans.

[3] Surah 2:38 [actually verse 41] states that the Koran was sent down in order to affirm the Bible. [See Appendix J, Koran Passages 7. Trans.].

[4] Surah 2:3 [actually verse 4] states that those ones who are led by God believe not only in the Koran but also in the Holy Scriptures. [See Appendix J, Koran Passages 8. Trans.].

[5] Surah 29:45 [actually verse 46] translated literally states: (O Muslims, say to the people of the Book:) Our God and your God is one God and it is to Him we bow. [See Appendix J, Koran Passages 9. Trans.].

[6] See Appendix I, Bible Passages 43. Trans.

judged with expressions like "dubious" and "meaningless" without anyone inquiring into its nature.

'But since they and we believe in one God, we nevertheless hope that the mistrust between us be done away with and an appropriate friendship between the sons of the book be achieved.

John Avetaranian.'"

This statement appeared in the *Balkan* accompanied by an additional remark from the editor, Adhem Ruhi, in which he praised and declared, among other things, Islam's freedom of conscience, that every Muslim can listen and read whatever he wants; in this he [Avetaranian] (*nota bene*) serves our work in the best possible way.

It gave rise to a very lively controversy that brought various religious leaders into the arena on the Muslim side until well into the month of April. The discussion grew more and more in scope and intense public interest. Avetaranian was able to fill up an issue of his *Shahid-ül-Haqaiq* with it in order to have the questions being discussed and the remarks from both sides together. By using material from the Gospel in his response he had at least earned a consideration and a regard, which went far beyond the framework of a momentary disturbance.

Concerning his disputation with the Muslim scholars, Avetaranian himself wrote:

"In the beginning I did not know the matter would assume such proportions. I am currently bringing the entire subject together into one issue of the *Shahid-ül-Haqaiq*. Now the scholars want to retreat, as can be seen from their articles, only they would like to have the last word. But since they themselves started it, justice demands that something written by me be the final word. I am thankful to God that He has opened this way for us to carry the truth of the gospel into wide sections of Muslim society. The authority of Islamic theology has been powerfully shaken in this way, *the common ideas the Muslim people have about Christianity have changed*, and my responses are read everywhere with great interest. Even people who cannot read ask the newsagent whether there is a reply in the newspaper. When there is, they buy a paper and have it read out to them. One day two mullahs met in front of an evangelical Armenian's shop in the narrow bazaar. Two of my articles had just come out, yet without any reply on their part. The one asked the other, 'What is going to happen if our scholars can no longer respond? The thoughts of the people are confused. This must not be left like this; an answer must be given.'

"Now they want to help themselves out through lying by spreading various reports. Because the atheism of their greatest mufti, in whom they had placed their hope, is clearly evident, they say the article did not come from him. Because such a learned mufti could not be an atheist, another has written using his name. Concerning this, people were saying in the cafés: 'How could he allow something like this to be written in his name?'

"Cleverer men gave the following explanation: 'The bearer of the title, his Excellency Ali Ziya, is not actually a mufti. He was first a teacher, then a priest—of course he has studied in Constantinople—but he is now the acting representative of the mufti in Rakhova who died. For a mufti cannot be an unbeliever. This is how the people are being bewitched.'

"They speak differently with regard to the Christians: 'Our scholars do not talk about religion. The writers of these articles are insignificant men. That is why they cannot overcome Avetaranian. Our true scholars do not consider it worthwhile to write about these things, otherwise forty of them would have taken it up.'"

In March 1908 it became possible for the missionary society to send a new, larger printing press to Philippopolis through the self-sacrifice of Miss Henriette von Blücher. The need for printed material was growing; the Kashgari translation of the New Testament was now finally to be printed. Also the translation of Mark's Gospel into Kurdish, which Pastor von Oertzen had set about doing, was expected.

The Turkish Revolution of 1908 gave the work a new momentum and its most promising prospects. That Avetaranian followed the Young Turks' political movement with the greatest interest goes without saying. His native country, Turkey, lay in the bonds of Islam. He, as a former Muslim and Turkish subject, could not live in his homeland if the severity of Turkish law, the death penalty, was not to catch up with him. Within the laws of the Turkish state there was still the association of Abdul Hamid's bloodthirsty despotism with the *Shari'ah*, the Islamic religious law. The "bloody" Sultan was a caliph, a holder of the highest religious rank and a successor to the Prophet. Neither political nor religious freedom would be granted as long as the state laws of Turkey were not established along modern liberal lines. The rule of the Young Turks, which wanted to bring about such a turnaround, was therefore sure of the sympathy of all those who wanted a cultural and economic resurrection for the people of Turkey. Above all, they even had the approval of all these peoples: the Armenians, Greeks, Arabs, Kurds, and Turks.

When the Young Turks' Revolution of 1908 forced a democratic constitution out of the Sultan, a marvellous prospect presented itself to all friends of liberty. Even for John Avetaranian, the way now finally seemed to be clearing to be able to preach the gospel freely and openly to his Turkish people and for him to return to his homeland.

Already the long-suppressed desire was surfacing to move to Constantinople with the mission work. Indeed, censorship had disappeared, and even the printed material being published in Philippopolis was making its way unhindered into the Turkish land and to the Turkish people, much sought after and closely heeded.

In view of this situation, Avetaranian asked his friends for help. He wanted to meet the need for Christian literature, a need which had suddenly become enormous. The dawn of a new age seemed to him to have broken; the time for a mission to the peoples of the Ottoman Empire seemed to have come. Even the reports from within Turkey left no more doubt that with the revolution something incredibly new had happened, and Christians and Muslims had "buried the hatchet" between them. Avetaranian and Pastor von Oertzen from Kurdistan were already preparing to travel to Constantinople.

"God has done a great thing in our time," wrote John Avetaranian in August. "The iron doors of Turkey, which until now were closed to the preaching of the gospel, now stand open. I, who left my homeland thirty years ago, had not thought it would be possible for me in my lifetime to see my native country again and bear witness to the love of Christ there. But the Lord has made all things possible. I can now travel there as well as anywhere else in Turkey and proclaim the glad tidings through writing and speaking. All of this seems to me like a dream, the reality of which one might doubt.

"How did the Young Turks, the leaders of the revolution, operate, and what kind of men were they? For the most part they were young men who through their studies had come in contact with some Christian ideas and could now no longer remain slaves under the laws of Islam. They wanted to be treated justly, but the reverse happened. They were thrown into prison and regarded as hostile elements to Islam, even though they confessed no teaching other than Islam. Many of them succeeded in escaping from prison or exile and in finding a place of refuge in a free Europe. For twenty-five years they had worked from there by means of several newspapers, constantly criticising the injustices of the Turkish government and other such things. The Sultan did his utmost through strict censorship, spies, and bribery to prevent their influence, all to no avail. The newspapers of the Young Turks came into the country, if only a few copies at a time. They went from person to person, were read in secret, and finally, in a completely worn-out condition, were torn up or incinerated. However, the ideas and views that these newspapers disseminated stuck in the minds of the readers, gained more and more ground, and like a leaven, quietly pervaded the army as well as the people. The result was the ruler who was persecuting the Young Turks had to give way. He had to follow their counsel and comply with their wishes, even showing that he trusted them more than he had his former officials. He was forced to give the people a constitution if he did not want to lose his rule and perhaps indeed his life.

"Now freedom and equality reigned in Turkey as in other countries, even freedom of the press and freedom to teach. When I think about these events, I find that they signify nothing other than a victory of Christian justice over that of Islam. The foundations of Islam are being shaken. A superficial revolution has no purpose; that would be like pouring new wine into old wineskins or putting a new piece of cloth on an old garment. Islam cannot tolerate that. The strength of Islam consists in three things: force, pride, and fanaticism. Through the constitution these three things are broken. In Muslim statute books it states that a Christian's house must not be of the same height as that of his Muslim neighbour. If the Christian wants to increase the height of his house, he must wait until the Muslim next door is in a position to raise his own house. The Christian must not be treated as equal to the Muslim in court and other such things as these. Now the constitution puts an end to all that. At present the Christian has equal rights and the same freedom as the Muslim. At last God has cleared the way for the preaching of the gospel.

"Now and then our periodical, *Shahid-ül-Haqaiq*, was also read in Turkey, even though it, like the Young Turks' newspapers, was often forbidden by the strict censors. Now this ban has been lifted, and quite a large stock of written material, which contains the seed of life, is ready to be sent forth. Today it is more necessary than ever to do the work."

CHAPTER 24
AFTER THE TURKISH REVOLUTION

In November 1908 Avetaranian wrote to his friend, Johannes Lepsius, that in view of the growing Turkish spiritual life, the publication of a newspaper for Muslims seemed an urgent necessity. Everyone in Turkey wanted to read newspapers, and the papers published by Muslims were clearly intent on ignoring the influence of Christianity, which is included in what is valuable to every culture and apparent even to Muslims, as well as intent on attributing to Islam all the recently adopted cultural assets that are advantageous to mankind. Avetaranian was in Constantinople in December, exploring the situation and seeing the best prospects for his work in the Turkish capital. He was also confirmed in his plan to publish a newspaper, which was set up by him shortly after.

After the *Gunesh* (*Sun*) had come into being as a weekly paper for the first time in January 1909, he wrote to his German friend [Lepsius] in March:

"The publication of a newspaper was now very necessary, but I still had other jobs to carry out. My *Kashgari* translation was being printed and required the greatest care, for I felt accountable to my Saviour who has entrusted me with the task of conveying His Gospel by way of a translation to a people of twelve million. Nevertheless, I believed I must begin the publication of this weekly paper; it would not have been right to lose any time. This newspaper was not supposed to do any direct missionary work. As far as possible, it was supposed to set burning issues of the day in the light of the truth. The *Shahid-ül-Haqaiq*, my purely religious monthly periodical, and other writings, which deal directly with missions, are not to be displaced by this weekly paper. Rather the different papers shall complement one another. The weekly paper ought to prepare the reader for accepting the truth of the Gospel, and the remaining writings to proclaim the truth itself. Perhaps it seems optimistic when a person takes on so much, but we know that Paul with Timothy and a few other co-workers undertook and executed far more than all the missions workers of our time. How urgently I need co-workers like that now!

"Recently a local Turkish paper out of jealousy came out with an article which was supposed to cast suspicion on our newspaper, *Gunesh*. It said the *Gunesh* wanted to convert Muslims to Protestantism, propagate paganism, and so forth. In the beginning this statement was quite serious, for whenever Muslims hear such things, they do not see for themselves what the true facts really are, rather they are frightened and do not read any further.

"Then in a wonderful way the Lord *sent two Muslim scholars, mullahs from Macedonia*. After much searching, these two men have come to a knowledge of the truth of the gospel and are now ready to work together in spreading the truth. They have a thorough knowledge of Islam in all of its forms, but they are still lacking many things needed to be true disciples of Jesus. It would be good if other Christians, full of wisdom and love, could help them achieve this. Then their great knowledge would likewise be utilised for the work of the Lord."

Then came the first reports of political setbacks, indeed, of a repeat of the massacres. On 13 April a reactionary coup took place in Constantinople; on 14 April the mass murder in Adana began. Twenty thousand people were killed, and the troops of the Young Turks had a part in this killing. An icy dew fell on the seed of hope, but Avetaranian still looked upon the slaughter of Christians as a product of the old Islam and expected only good things from the Young Turks. He writes (in May 1909):

"Now this great ruler,[1] the caliph of Islam, sits in prison. He has become the most despised man in the world. All of his secrets and disgraceful deeds are exposed before the eyes of men. Who has achieved this? Obviously it was the Young Turks, but who are they? They are the tools of some European ideas, and these ideas are nothing other than the product of the Christian culture. To be sure, they are not purely Christian, but they were capable of giving a severe blow to Islam, of snatching the sword from the hands of the tyrant and destroying his good reputation. To the nations condemned to servitude and extermination under Islam they promised freedom and equality.

"It is easy to understand that under these circumstances the spirit of Islam is offering the greatest resistance to the truth of the gospel and will try as much as possible to destroy any Christians who are under its political power. Islam is not acquainted with justice, mercy, and love towards non-Muslims. When compelled by necessity, a Muslim will flatter Christians; Mohammed himself ordered his followers to do such things, but this good-natured behaviour only lasts so long until a convenient opportunity presents itself for exterminating the Christians.

"Through the newspapers we are acquainted with the most recent massacres in Cilicia and Syria. The Muslims violated and murdered numerous Christians there in the most dreadful way. In Alexandretta many flung themselves into the sea in order to escape the hands of their inhuman persecutors. Others took refuge in the churches, but they set fire to these buildings and everyone died in the flames. Nineteen evangelical Armenian pastors who had come together from different villages for their annual conference were attacked at church during worship and tortured to death. From his window a missionary saw how innocent women and children were ill treated and killed in the most hideous way; women had their breasts cut off.

---

[1] Abdul Hamid, the "bloody Sultan".

Their screams and their pleading to be spared were not heard by men nor by God; this missionary's faith in the omnipotence and righteousness of God was severely shaken by this. Both native evangelical preachers as well as foreign missionaries were killed. In one village all inhabitants were butchered; only one teacher saved his life and the life of his family by accepting Islam at the last moment. The spirit of Islam that dwells in Muslims is to blame for these atrocities. It sees it is losing its influence more and more over men and that is why it commits these atrocities."

Meanwhile, the wave of freedom once generated was not to be held back. In Bulgaria, outside the Turkish borders, the spiritual debates in the form of public discussions continued unhindered. *In the Gunesh the two Muslims scholars, who had joined with Avetaranian, began to speak out and aroused the greatest sensation through the frank style of their criticism of Islam and not less by their dignity and holiness as Muslims, which had been recognised up to that point.* If their appearance on Turkish soil during the first days of liberty had already caused commotion and disturbances in the centres of Turkish Islam, then their constant literary activity became an outrage to the Bulgarian Muslims. By their activity as well as by the political situation, which had changed completely, Avetaranian's plan to go to Constantinople had to be put off; indeed, the whole work of the mission to Muslims was being forced into other channels.

In July 1909 Johannes Lepsius wrote:

"In February Avetaranian had reported that two mullahs were received into his home at Philippopolis. Meanwhile, he has satisfied himself to the sincerity of their faith and the purity of their motives and, to his own surprise, has found out what unusual effectiveness these two men had already exhibited in the foremost seats of Muslim learning. Without the knowledge of the living Islam as these mullahs and our Missionary Avetaranian were able to acquire as Muslim clerics, the most scholarly study of the Koran based on our European literature remains but a dead knowledge, which is unproductive for the active work of the mission. God has now sent from Islam to our mission three Muslim priests of the rarest type. All three came to a faith in the Son of God without human assistance and without the contribution of any mission, rather only through the work of the Holy Spirit, Who shone the light on them as they inquired into the Holy Scriptures.

"*Muhammed Shükri Efendi* who adopted the name *John Avetaranian* at his baptism in 1885 had been designated from childhood to the priestly class as a saiyid, that is, as a descendent of the Prophet, and was trained to be a cleric in the *medrese* of his home town up to the age of eighteen. It was as a mullah that he came to realise the truth of the gospel.

"*Sheikh Akhmed Keshaf* was still sheikh of the foremost order of Rufai dervishes in his home town in Macedonia up to 1907. He had attained to the highest levels of the teaching and religious practice of the dervish orders, of the knowledge of mystical, esoteric doctrine, and of the philosophy of the

Sufis.

"*Muhammed Nesimi Effendi* is a muderis, that is, he has the professors of theology's certificate of the highest degree, from which the *Sheikh al-Islam* is chosen. On his travels he was celebrated everywhere as one of the foremost scholars of Islam, and no one was in a position to overcome him in public debates."

Meanwhile, in Bulgaria the situation intensified. The press took up the struggle against Avetaranian and his two champions. Even the editorial staff of the *Balkan* were among the hostile attackers and now laid bare their Islamic fundamental philosophy. The rise of the political liberation movement and the open criticism by men, who had come out of Islam and where mindful of religion, threatened to loosen the bonds of religious tradition within wide sections of the population. The fanaticism of the worried friends of Islam was aroused. Removing Caliph Abdul Hamid from a national assembly to which even Jews and Christians belonged, the equal status of non-Muslims (*raya*) to the Muslim master race, and the doubts expressed publicly about the Muslim religion all gave reason enough to allow religious hatred to rage against exposed individuals. The joyful approval amongst the wider population that was given to the work of the three men could not dispel the fact religious hatred was looking for a way of expressing itself. Threatening letters, returned issues of the *Gunesh* accompanied by the rudest of insults, and caricatures, which very clearly expressed the wish and intention of killing those who were hated, arrived at the editorial office of the *Gunesh*. For the time being, no notice was taken of these threats, and they devoted themselves to the positive tasks. A Muslim village wanted to be instructed by the two mullahs and be prepared for conversion to Christianity.

In the end it was learned that an attempt on the lives of the two mullahs was being planned. An inquiry into whether the Bulgarian government would protect the two men yielded the notification that the murderers would no doubt be punished but a guarantee to safeguard the lives of those endangered would not be undertaken. Several friends reported that in Pashmakly, the two mullahs' home town, a secret assembly had resolved to kill the "apostates". A further report came in that a fanatical Muslim had publicly sworn by everything that is holy to Muslims to "beat to death like dogs" the two teachers within the week. *The endangered men themselves had no fear, rather they wanted to be baptised in public.*

Avetaranian considered what loss the death of these two men would be for the cause of the mission, how, under the given circumstances, little would be gained if they were to fall as martyrs. Therefore he decided to leave Philippopolis with them and get them out of harm's way. On 2 July he arrived with them in Potsdam, the headquarters of the Lepsius mission.

In the more than thirty years of the mission's existence there has been a peculiar state of affairs which has happened again and again to the German Orient-Mission led by Doctor Johannes Lepsius and which has clearly manifested itself as providence and guidance: *at the moment when the mission to Muslims is supposed to be being firmly tackled, the society is forced to devote itself to another task.* So it was in 1895 when the mission was founded, in the days of the massacre instigated by Abdul Hamid, which gave rise to the Armenian relief work. This work was set up to rescue from Islam the Christian nation of Armenia wounded by Islam. So it was in 1908 and 1909 when [the province of] Adana again required a fresh relief work for the Armenians, and at the same time the two Muslims, who had come to believe in Christ, were forced to escape the fury of Islam. Finally on an incomparably greater scale in 1915 and 1916 came the years of the Armenian deportations. Again the work of the mission to Muslims had to be postponed, and in this trouble, international Christendom has been giving itself over to a tremendous rescue work in the Middle East for the past fifteen years, saving from annihilation by Islam what remained of an ancient Christian people. Here again for more than a decade the German missionary society was pushed away from its original task and towards disaster relief for the Armenians.

So contrary to all plans, the managing of the Bulgarian work and the editing of *Gunesh* and *Shahid-ül-Haqaiq* had come to Germany and to Potsdam. The missions board came to the decision, made easier for them by the arrival of the three former Muslims, to set up a kind of seminary in Potsdam from which not only the two newspapers would continue to be edited, but also European theologians and missionaries would prepare themselves for the work of the mission to Muslims. Besides men like Doctor Johannes Lepsius, Doctor Paul Rohrbach, and Pastor Paul Fleischmann, the current chairman of Doctor Lepsius' Orient-Mission, the winter semester of 1909 to 1910 included the names of Avetaranian and the two mullahs. Avetaranian lectured in the Persian, Turkish, and Armenian languages, Muderis Nesimi Effendi in the interpretation of the Koran and Arabic, Sheikh Akhmed Keshaf in the dervish orders and the Sufic philosophy. The German theologians lectured in religious history.

In August Avetaranian was back in the Turkish capital. The impressions he received were very discouraging: the people dreamed of freedom, but they did not obtain it. Even freedom of the press was restricted. Bans on newspapers were the order of the day. Whenever Avetaranian spoke with Young Turks about prospects for the future, he met with evasive answers. He heard the Turkish press had asked the Sheikh al-Islam to work towards cessation of the publication of the *Gunesh*. In short, a work in Constantinople was not possible.

In the St Nicholas Church in Potsdam the two mullahs were baptised by Avetaranian on 10 October in front of a packed church. In spite of every hindrance from outside, Avetaranian again lived to see an answer to his prayers for his brothers, the Muslims. He moved with his wife to Berlin-Steglitz in order to be able to look after the work in the seminary and maintain his association with the two mullahs.

On 15 November the Muslim seminary in Potsdam was opened. An area almost unknown to the Western world opened up for research, and the eleven participants very soon got the impression it was one thing to explore Islam in its history and in its book, the Koran, as our orientalists do, and yet another thing to explore the living religion of the Muslims and the popular beliefs as they are taught and preached in the schools and mosques of Islam. An immense amount of material opened up. The chaotic mass of tradition and the whole jumble of the oldest and later traditions of religious history in the Middle East had to be tackled and begin to be put into order.

In February 1910 Avetaranian with his friends were at the missions conference in Halle (an der Saale). Conducted by the venerable Professor Warneck, the tasks of Christendom, which the situation in regard to Islam had given rise to, were discussed. Avetaranian did not see any practical results from the conference, even though the necessity of seeing the missionaries better equipped with the knowledge of Islam than they had been up to that point was strongly emphasised. *With regards to all "planned" methodology, Avetaranian declared that Islam would only be dealt with by eliminating the Shari'ah law*, and this law can only be criticised in a fair way, and in a way that people understand, by those who have an intimate knowledge of it. The people's confidence in this religious law, which stands above every state law, can be shaken. With the setback in Turkey, Avetaranian saw the emergence of this Shari'ah law and its victory over the reorganisation of the state. The line of attack recommended by him was the same one he took in his newspaper, *Gunesh*, and which had given rise to so much trouble in Bulgaria. It was just this "fruit" that was proof to him of the rightness of the way he had adopted.

While he worked in Germany at the seminary for Muslim outreach, edited his newspapers, and was eager to have them circulated by a new co-worker sent to Philippopolis, he attentively followed the Muslim press. He assimilated everything he found out from Turkey, Persia, India, and Egypt: the awakening of the whole of Islam and its becoming active in the form of pan-Islamism and the question of whether Africa, which was under threat, would fall prey to Islam. To his German supporters he gave an insight into the necessities that were becoming more urgent by the day. In addition, he travelled around Germany, giving his engaging lectures in churches and to supporters from the colonies. Apart from the requirements of his literary work in Bulgaria, which he presided over from Germany, he likewise did not evade his duty to impart to the German missionary fellowship a full understanding of the urgent tasks. All of this took its toll on his physical strength as well.

Meanwhile, in Constantinople his weekly newspaper, *Gunesh*, had been banned. In the beginning this ban led to a greater distribution. Orders from almost every part of the Muslim world could not be filled sufficiently; more and larger runs had to be printed. At the same time resources were running out. Further publishing was stopped for the time being. Besides the fierceness of the Muslim press over the criticism from the two mullahs, it continued to be an encouragement that men could be found in Turkey who would work for the ideas of the *Gunesh* and would circulate the paper in spite of the ban. Muslims, who recognised the great importance of his two co-workers, agreed with their critical articles, and wanted to support them in their struggle, declared their approval. News of this reached him, convincing him of the need to continue in the way to which he was committed. Along with the *Gunesh*, the other works were now finding a circulation as well: the *Pilgrim's Progress*, *Shahid-ül-Haqaiq*, and the small books and tracts.

The question of the mission to Muslims, which bombarded them so heavily, brought differences into the ranks of the committee members of the German Orient-Mission. The departure from the mission of the three gentlemen, along with Director Johannes Lepsius, was only narrowly avoided. The board stepped down, a new committee was formed, and the three men were able to continue with their work. These experiences did not pass Avetaranian by without a spiritual struggle, although in all the work during that time no one ever noticed any despondency with him. With a charming, smiling cheerfulness, behind which you could always see working the childlike naturalness of his desires and purposes—the unshakeable faith in his work—he spoke about the difficulties and about the differing views existing amongst his friends.

From Philippopolis the effects of his literary work, which now was being resumed from Germany, went on undisturbed. Kevorkian, a missionary who travelled around Bulgaria and evangelised there, apart from Bibles, also distributed the critical, enlightening, and edifying writings from the Philippopolis mission station. From Tiflis the works which Bible distributors circulated went to Persia, Central Asia, and even as far as Siberia.

Before the second (summer-) semester of the seminary for Muslim outreach could begin, Avetaranian's publications gave expression to the complaint that no more missionary-minded participants could be found for the task of the mission to Muslims. For only two foreign missionaries and two German missionaries had enrolled for the second semester, and Johannes Lepsius wrote:

"I understand if the preliminary work which we would like to do in our seminary for Muslim outreach is considered superfluous and judged with contempt. There are always some people who have a supremely mechanical idea of preaching the gospel and, if the talk is of missionary work, want to hear of quite large numbers. How many missionaries? How many have been baptised? How many applicants for baptism? You barely have begun to think about missions to Muslims before such questions are thrown up. The fact is we will make no substantial progress in the area of missions to Muslims *as long as we do not develop a new form of representing the gospel from the New Testament alone and have it clothed in the garments of the Oriental imagination. The work which Paul did for the Greek-thinking world must still be achieved for the Muslim-thinking world.*"

Avetaranian stayed in Bulgaria for three months at the beginning of 1911 and found the way the work was going there satisfactory. He preached again amidst large crowds and was welcomed by all well-meaning Muslims. Khayri Bey, a member of the military tribunal in Constantinople, turned up at one of the first talks he gave and wrote the sermon down. He had a discussion with him afterwards in which he [Avetaranian] answered his questions and for his part raised the accusation with the envoy, that although the new Turkey had proclaimed European freedom, it did not have the spirit of freedom and did not accept it.

CHAPTER 25
STRUGGLE AND WORK. THE BALKAN WARS

"The reader will recall," so wrote Avetaranian in November 1911, "that I proclaimed the gospel to the Muslims in Kashgar from 1891 to 1896[1] and also translated the New Testament into their language. The British and Foreign Bible Society had the four Gospels of my translation printed in Leipzig, and I went to Germany in 1897 in order to do the proofreading. After the Gospels were sent to Kashgar, I undertook in Bulgaria a greater task in the mission to Muslims in association with the German Orient-Mission and as a result could not return to Kashgar. But it was very important to me the *whole translation of the New Testament* should come to the mission to the Kashgari Muslims as soon as possible. Up to March of this year [1911] I had completed the reprinting of the Gospels and the printing of the remaining parts of the New Testament in our mission printing shop in Philippopolis, with the Epistles up to the tenth chapter of the Second Letter to the Corinthians ordered especially for it. As I was then in London in the month of July, I consulted with the secretary of the British and Foreign Bible Society, Reverend Ritson, and also later with Doctor Kilgour, the head of the publication department, on the distribution of my translation in Kashgar. Since the first edition of the four Gospels of my translation has already long been out of print and there existed in Kashgar a pressing need for a new edition, a meeting was arranged by the British Bible Society for 6 October in London for the purpose of discussing this question. Doctor Kilgour sent invitations to the Orient-Mission and to the Swedish Missionary Society, which is working in Kashgar. I was deputised to this conference by the committee. The aim of the meeting above all was to bring about an agreement between the Swedish Missionary Society and us, so they would undertake the distribution of the translation in Kashgar. To my joy my former co-worker, Mission Doctor Raquette, had come from Kashgar to London for the conference with the director of the Swedish Missionary Society, Doctor Waldenström.

"The conference took place on 6 October in the rooms of the British and Foreign Bible Society. Professor Tumayan had been consulted as a specialist and translator.

"There existed differences of opinion between the Swedish missionaries and myself with regard to some of the details of my translation, concerning

---

[1] As I pointed out in Chapter 10 (footnote [2] on p. 67), Avetaranian actually reached China in early 1892. And at the end of Chapter 17 (p. 110) he states that he left Kashgar in February 1897, which is probably more accurate than 1896. Trans.

which an understanding was supposed to be reached. Raquette shared that the Swedish missionaries in Kashgar were thankful for the translation because through it an invaluable service was being done for the Kashgari people and the mission. Several linguistic questions were reserved for a special meeting with Doctor Raquette in order to arrive at a complete agreement before finishing the printing. On these conditions the translation was accepted by the Swedes and taken on by the British and Foreign Bible Society.

"It was decided that as soon as the run of two thousand copies, which were currently being printed, was used up and a new edition was necessary, the revised edition would be carried out in agreement with the Swedish Society. The Bible Society has agreed to pay the costs of printing the translation.

"After one year has passed, the latest news is the printing of the New Testament, with the help of God, will be completed, and they will then set about distributing them.

"We had now been residing in Germany for two years, and this time for us was not wasted. We learned much and collected many experiences, which we could not have gained in the mission field and which would be useful to our work. At the time, the question of a seminary for Muslim outreach was also being revived once more. We opened a missions seminary and ran it for one semester, but as at any time, the most important undertakings always meet with difficulties, so our missions seminary fared in like manner. Theologians or orientalists ready to enter into our work as missionaries have up to now not yet been found. That is why only the primary and most important job of the seminary could be worked on: to investigate the Islam of today and prepare the literary tools for the mission to Muslims. Time will show that for this great purpose it is necessary from year to year to send out several missionaries into the Muslim world equipped with the spirit of faith and the necessary knowledge.

"Now circumstances resulted in my dear wife and I being able to go back to Philippopolis. From the Bulgarian border onward, in Rustchuk, in Rasgrad, in Shumla, and in Sofia, wherever we had mission stations, the evangelical brothers who were quite well acquainted with the circumstances amongst the Muslims voiced their anxieties for my safety. They were afraid Muslim fanatics in Bulgaria could do me harm. In addition, our friends from amongst the Bulgarians and Armenians also expressed the same reservations, but like Paul in his time, I too did not consider my life as dear.[1] Since the Lord had protected me for thirty years under much more difficult circumstances, He would protect me even now if that be His will.

"On my journey I was able to proclaim the Word of God in the cities mentioned above. In Rustchuk, where our dear Missionary Pastor Kevorkian works with great blessing, I had much joy. On Sunday I preached there four times, twice in the church, once at the youth group, and in the evening at

---

[1] See Appendix I, Bible Passages 44. Trans.

Kevorkian's home. Accompanied by Kevorkian, I went to Rasgrad for a day where there is a small evangelical fellowship.

"We stayed in Shumla for three days, and every day I had visitors. Several old housewives especially enjoyed coming to see me; they needed the comfort of the Word of God. I also had to have plenty of time for our old friend, Khachadur Agha Kurian, who manages our Bible depot in Shumla and carries on evangelism work. In fact, he is seventy-five years old, but nevertheless, he is as fit as a fiddle and takes great pleasure and enthusiasm in the work. He is bold in his struggle, especially against atheism, which is spreading amongst the youth at school. Several high school students gather at his home in the evening and enjoy listening to him, and he knows how to win young hearts for the Saviour. I also stayed several days in Sofia, was able to preach there twice, and even celebrated the Lord's Supper at Brother Shahveled's church."

And on Christmas Day:

"When I think of the great joy prevailing amongst the children of God at this time and at the same time cast a glance into the Muslim world, nothing is left for me but to join in Jeremiah's Lamentation[1] for the sake of my people, the Muslims. Why do worry, anxiety, and woe hold sway today in the land, since Christ became man?[2] The population in Turkey is now in constant fear of massacre. The Ottoman press reports bad news from every region in Turkey. In Armenia and Kurdistan and other places, murder and robbery are being resumed. In Ishtib in Albania, one hundred and forty-eight Christians were massacred by Muslims on Kurban Bairam (as Easter is called) and more than five hundred were injured. At the same time only three Muslims were hurt. It was claimed members of a Bulgarian committee had dropped bombs at the entrance of a mosque, but in actual fact the building was no mosque, and at the time of the attack there was no one inside. Besides, Christians did not throw the bomb; rather it was reactionary Muslims who did this. Also unpleasant news is coming from Lebanon, out of Beirut, Damascus, and other cities. As a result the hearts of the Christians in Turkey are full of worry and fear, even more so as they know from bleak experience that the Christian governments will not concern themselves over the internal affairs of Turkey.

"'Holy War' was declared against the Italians *as Christians*. The Turkish daily papers are thoroughly occupied with Tripoli, and the columns in their religious newspapers are full of bitter curses against the Italians as Christians. These things they read are well suited to arouse the fanaticism of the Muslims and incense them against those fellow citizens of theirs who are Christian. In this respect Islam knows no difference between politics and religion and does not ask about the differences in confessions amongst the Christian peoples, and so directs its hatred against *all* Christians.

---

[1] This is a reference to the book in the Bible by the prophet Jeremiah who laments the suffering that befell Jerusalem when Nebuchadnezzar captured the city in 586 BC. Trans.

[2] "Christ...became man" is from the Nicene Creed (325 AD). Trans.

"The Turkish newspapers report atrocities by the Italians in the Tripolitanish War, and the Italians lodge the same complaint against the Turks and Arabs, so it is not known which side has committed greater atrocities. But one thing is certain: the atrocities, which in recent years were committed in Turkey itself, in Macedonia, Armenia, and Arabia, on its own subjects, on Christians as well as Muslims, are much worse than anything now heard from Tripoli. How long is this state of affairs going to go on? How much longer shall fanaticism hold sway in Turkey and make well-ordered relationships impossible? There is only *one* salvation for the Islamic peoples, and that is the acceptance of the gospel. As long as they remain under the control of the ideas of the Prophet Mohammed, they will be a disaster for themselves, for their state, for their country, and for the world, but especially for the Christians who have the misfortune of living under their power.

"My newspaper, *Gunesh*, is now published under the new name, *Khurshid*,[1] and we are convinced it is even now being read with good results by many seekers of the truth in the Muslim world. The reader will recall when the Turkish government banned the *Gunesh* most rigorously and did their utmost to have the newspaper suppressed even in Bulgaria and Russia, but it did not succeed. After that, the local Muslim clerics boycotted the *Gunesh*; no Muslim was supposed to pick it up and read it. But they did not have much luck with this either because even then I kept receiving letters from Muslims, to the effect that they wished to read the *Gunesh* because the truths which they read in it they did not find in the Muslim papers."

The two learned mullahs, who meanwhile had published their confessions and their life experiences, had not returned with them [the Avetaranians] to Bulgaria. As teachers in Potsdam at the seminary for Muslim outreach, they were able to offer valuable help in the service of missions for all the missions working amongst Muslims. Johannes Lepsius wanted to see their practical and theoretical knowledge of Islam preserved as a living source of information. He did not want to leave a former teacher of Muslim theology like Muderis Nesimi and a dervish sheikh like Akhmed Keshaf to the uncertain mechanical workings of an ignorant time without any backing. So with several friends he personally undertook to raise the funds to support the two gentlemen. In 1912 in Potsdam, after a painful illness, Akhmed Keshaf succumbed to tuberculosis, which he contracted while preaching in the open-air during the Greco-Turkish War. Lepsius assumed the responsibility of providing for his physical needs until his death, just as he did for his brother Nesimi up to the year 1917.

"On the day after the first issue of the newspaper, *Khurshid*, was published," Avetaranian goes on to write, "it was reported in the *Balkan*, the local Turkish voice for Bulgaria, that the publisher of the *Khurshid*, Muhammed Shükri, was none other than Pastor Avetaranian who only

---

[1] Both names mean 'sun'.

intended to smuggle his Christian ideas into Islam, as previously he had done in the paper, *Gunesh,* which the Sheikh al-Islam had banned with a *fatwa*[1] as hostile to Islam. At the end came the following warning to me: 'O Efendi, you servant of God, formerly you were a Muslim; you became a Christian and have cast off your connection with Muslims! What do the Turkish parliament and the Turkish nation have to do with you? Why do you come out with these exhortations? If we were still living in the Middle Ages, then you could perhaps persuade some Muslims and bring them as trophies into the tent of Jesus! Who is stinging you that you arise again and go after the Muslim world?'

"To this I answered in the *Khurshid* that no one could deny me the right, as a person from the Middle East and as a Turk, to speak my opinion freely, and that faith was a matter of conviction and of the heart.

"Two days later it appeared in the *Balkan* that a great and holy scholar from Caucasia had come to Philippopolis in order to defend Islam against Avetaranian since the local scholars were unable to refute him.

"I went to see this man at his hotel and found him to be sensible and educated. He told me he had submitted an article against me to the *Balkan* and his intention was to establish and expound the truth without fanaticism. But the *Balkan* preferred not to publish his article, probably for fear of promoting the circulation of the *Khurshid* more than hindering it.

"However, the *Balkan* printed a lecture translated into Turkish which a Bulgarian teacher, Ilieff, had given in Shumla. Ilieff is a native of Ishtib and, taking up the subject of the last massacre of Christians in his home town, he had claimed the Turks had always been bloodthirsty and the Koran contained words which prevented the Turkish people from living in normal relations with the civilised world. He had quoted various passages from the Koran in order to explain from which causes the hatred of Muslims towards Christians originated and had argued that the Koran judged the teaching of the Trinity and the divine sonship of Jesus as polytheism and forbade Muslims from being on friendly terms with Christians. The *Balkan* responded to this lecture with a long article that was not very clever.

"The Efendi from Caucasia who had wanted to write against me in the *Balkan* now for his part wrote an article against Ilieff and asked me to publish it in the *Khurshid*. His article was in its own way good and factual and gave an explanation of those verses in the Koran from the standpoint of Islam. He said the verses had nothing to do with the Trinity; rather they were written against certain Christian sects which were in Arabia at the time of Mohammed and, like the Persians, believed in two gods—a God of good and a God of evil—from whom Jesus was supposed to have been sent into the world as the third person. Even the Christian Church had fought and overcome these sects.

---

[1] *Fatwa* = highest ruling of Muslim religious law; only for very important cases. *Sheikh al-Islam* = title of the highest priest ('Grand Mufti') in Constantinople.

After that, he tried to demonstrate in great detail that the Christian teaching of the Trinity did not contradict Islamic theology and the teachings of the Koran.

"While I was publishing this article in numbers 2 and 3 of the *Khurshid* with the necessary comments, an odd man turned up. He was a tall man in Circassian clothing with dagger, cartridge belts, and revolver. In his hand he carried a riding whip and on his back was the emblem of Islam with the star and crescent. He came to see me accompanied by Nuri Bey, the assistant editor of the *Balkan*. While we were talking, he put his whip on my desk. He recounted his travels in Turkey and Europe, knew many languages, and had much knowledge but was posing as a pronounced atheist. When he recounted his stay in Paris, I asked him whether he had seen Sherif Pasha, the former Turkish ambassador in Stockholm who now published a newspaper, *Mécheroutiette*, in Paris, which severely criticises the politics of the Young Turks.

"'Yes,' he said, 'I saw him in the park and I intended to shoot him dead like a dog.'

"Saying this, he pulled out his revolver and described to me with animated gestures in what way he had threatened him. I had the impression he only related this whole scene in order to intimidate me, and therefore I asked him in quite a friendly way: 'Was Sherif Pasha afraid of you?' whereupon somewhat embarrassed he replied, 'Yes', and stuck his revolver back away.

"The day after his visit, the *Balkan* printed an article about him in which he explained that he himself was a Circassian from Caucasia; however, the other man who published articles in the *Khurshid* was no Circassian at all, rather he was none other than a Christian, a Protestant, and the Protestants were endeavouring to cause divisions in Islam.

"He went on to say, 'There is no argument whatsoever about the Koran and its teaching. I command you that you ought to listen only to what your mullahs tell you!'

"On Friday he preached in the mosque and again wrote a strongly worded lead article in the *Balkan*, to the effect that he had come to Philippopolis with the task of speaking and exhorting on behalf of the thirty million Muslims (of Russia), that all Turks in the Balkan states as well as in the land of the Caliph should work both financially and personally for the fulfilment of the pan-Islamic idea. 'In the case where you do not do this and do not hold to the unity of all Muslims but give room for divisions, then we will call you to account,' he further wrote, 'together with the three hundred million Muslims throughout the rest of the world, and the day of reckoning shall be bitter for you!' Afterwards this odd man, an apostle of pan-Islamism, went back to Constantinople from where he had come.

"The circulation of my newspaper, *Khurshid*, is progressing nicely in spite of all the hostility. Three thousand copies are being sent off to Turkey and about three thousand are being distributed in Bulgaria and other Islamic countries. I am also pleased to be printing articles by Doctor Lepsius that have been translated into Turkish.

"Nearly a month ago the editor-in-chief of the *Balkan*, Adhem Ruhi, travelled to Turkey, and I hear on good authority that he had the expressed intention of preventing the *Khurshid* from entering into Turkey. He did not have much luck with this in Constantinople; however, he gave lectures in and around Adrianople with considerable success. He claimed the *Khurshid* would turn the whole Muslim people into Protestants and warns Muslims not to pick up this paper. He is even proposing to go to Monastir and to the other cities of Macedonia, where the Young Turks have a grip on power, and is looking to set the people against us by giving lectures and sermons in the mosques. It is striking that this man, like the rest of our Muslim opponents, is by no means a believing Muslim but rather an atheist, and yet he acts as a defender of Islam. Curiously enough, his deputy during his absence is an old friend of mine, the Muslim school inspector of Philippopolis who visited me on several occasions. The day before yesterday he came to see me with the local mufti's secretary. Both are sensible and educated men and do not agree with the hostile tone of the *Balkan*.

"Since the first issue of the *Khurshid* came out in January I have been getting letters of appreciation with almost every post, from Muslims as well as from Christians, from Turkey, Bosnia-Herzegovina, Caucasia, Bokhara, Turkestan, and Romania, as well as from Bulgaria. From Bosnia a distinguished Muslim has written a long letter which contains these words: 'After reflecting on your newspaper, I have been completely convinced that its contents are highly moral in every detail and in accordance with the truth; it has a character which is educational.' He has taken out a subscription. From St Petersburg an Efendi writes his appreciation of the *Khurshid*, at the same time sending me a book written by him that holds to the idea of reforming Islam along the lines of Luther and asks me to discuss this book, either for or against, in the *Khurshid*. He further writes, 'Since your newspaper supports true freedom and proceeds earnestly and rightly, you can be certain that all will be well. I am trying hard to bring about a wider circulation for the *Khurshid*.' His book is a proper academic work and aims to liberate Muslims from the pressure of outward customs. From Uskup a friend of the *Khurshid* writes that in his neighbourhood there is a great demand for my newspaper in spite of all the shouts of those who oppose it.

"From Constantza in Romania an educated Muslim writes in a detailed letter: 'We read your newspaper, *Khurshid*, with serious approval and favour, desiring that such an inspired newspaper continue to be successful, and we ask God to give you strength and endurance to carry on in the direction you have taken.'

"From a Bulgarian city a Muslim writes: 'I and my friends received much light through reading your *Khurshid*. Later on some other friends came in order to read with me, but unfortunately, when I looked into the drawer, I found that I had loaned the *Khurshid* to someone else, so the people went away disappointed. Honourable sir, I draw your attention to the fact that there are many villages in our region where there are those who want to read the *Khurshid*. Farmers come en masse to the newsagent in order to read the *Khurshid* or listen whenever it is being read out loud, but unfortunately it is already sold out, and they go back home again sad', and so forth. Again another Muslim, a secondary school teacher, writes: 'It will be superfluous to write to you that your newspaper brings to us what most do not these days. With all my heart I hasten to wish you luck while I remain your faithful brother', and so forth. Again a Muslim writes: 'By chance I read your newspaper in a café, and I ask of God the Most High that your newspaper be spread about and not held up. I regard it as my duty to mankind to subscribe to your newspaper.'

"Naturally I cannot count on covering the cost of the newspaper for the present, but it is already deserving of thanks that the paper is read and enjoyed in spite of all the hostilities of the fanatics. In this way Christian ideas and the truth of the gospel are finding circulation in the Muslim world in a most far-reaching manner." (March 1912)

"Recently the Muslim priest, Khatib Jahid Efendi from the large local mosque, 'Juma', came to see me, accompanied by Mohammed Zeki Efendi, the first secretary of the Grand Mufti in Sofia, and we spoke with one another for two hours. He was friendly and open, and I hope this conversation will not have been without use for his soul. Previously this same Khatib Jahid was one of my greatest opponents among the Muslim clerics. In Philippopolis, when I began to preach the gospel of salvation through faith in Jesus, he attacked my sermons with scorn and derision and published some angry articles against me in the local Turkish newspaper, *Balkan*, in which other Muslim clerics from Bulgaria also took part until they were silenced by the truth of the gospel. Later I published this whole episode, their attacks as well as my written defence, in my newspaper, *Shahid-ül-Haqaiq*, for distribution amongst the Muslims. I do not know what led this man to seek good relations with me, but it is clear he could not expect any material advantage from it.

"An incident again drew the attention of the Muslims in quite a special way to the work of our mission. It was at the beginning of the year when a learned Muslim who had read an issue of my newspaper, *Gunesh*, in a city in Asia Minor came to Philippopolis to see me, stayed with us, and wrote articles for our newspaper, *Khurshid*. Soon after his arrival it was written in the Turkish paper, *Balkan*, he had come in order to defend Islam against the attacks of Avetaranian since the clerics in Bulgaria could not cope with him. This man had already been baptised and since then had become an open confessor and a faithful member of our fellowship.

"The rule of the Young Turks lasted four years, but then Turkey once more faced a new radical change.

"In order to win the confidence of all Muslims and guided by the idea of organising Islam in all countries into a political world power, naturally the

Young Turks would have to come into fierce conflict with the efforts of the Christian nations in respect to Turkey and all the missionary work. They demonstrated this through the press as well as by their conduct in public. They sent emissaries to every part of the earth, wherever Muslims were to be found: to Russia, Bokhara, Afghanistan, China, India, Egypt, and Africa, entrusted with the tasks, depending on circumstances, (a) of acquainting Muslims with the new plan, (b) of opening schools so that the younger generation everywhere would receive a standard education, (c) of collecting money everywhere for the acquisition of a mighty fleet of ships and for the caliphate's other preparations for war.

"A reform of basic justice and a reimbursement of their estates which were taken by the Kurds at the time of the massacres were promised again and again to the Christian subjects of Turkey, but this was never kept. Rather, in a systematic way, life was made hard for them, and it was made easier for them to emigrate. Previously the Muslim press had never struck such a proud and provocative tone toward the Europeans and Christianity in general as the Young Turks' newspapers did at this time. They not only called for the releasing of Turkey from the *Capitulations*[1] but also proclaimed loudly in the whole Islamic world that the Christian governments wanted to bring Muslims completely under their influence and turn them into slaves and the time had come for all Muslims to unite and be liberated from each and every influence of Christian Europe. Religious newspapers, supported by the Committee[2] and published in the Caliph's city, made it their chief duty to stir up the Muslims against the Christians, especially against the missionaries and their work. They spread all sorts of slanderous rumours about their way of life, their writings, and their schools.

"I read newspapers and find in each issue one or more articles which attack in the coarsest manner the Christian religion and the mission and use the name 'missionary' as a term of abuse. Of the hundreds of such articles from Turkish newspapers, here are a few lines as a sample: an army priest in Adrianople, Alei[3]-Muftisi-Fakhred-din, an avid defender of the Young Turks' pan-Islamic idea, who for four years has written articles for the weekly religious paper, *Siratul-Mustaqim*, and also for the daily local paper, *Balkan* (in his time he also wrote against the *Gunesh*), has for some time directed his attacks against the *Beyan-ul-Hakk*, a Muslim religious weekly newspaper in Constantinople whose line is not pan-Islamic like the Young Turks' newspapers but strives in a practical way for the equal rights of Christians in Turkey. In the nineteenth edition of *Siratul-Mustaqim*, dated 11 June 1910, Fakhred-din writes an open letter to Javad Sami Bey as an answer to his article in the *Beyan-ul-Hakk*. In

---

[1] The exemption of all foreigners from the law of Turkey. No foreigner was allowed to be judged by Turkish courts for the duration of the *Capitulations*.

[2] That is, the Committee of Union and Progress, the official name of the Young Turks' organisation. Trans.

[3] *Alei* is ten thousand [I do not know where Schäfer or Avetaranian gets this from. The Arabic for *ten thousand* is *ashera alef*, unless this is Ottoman Turkish. Trans.].

this letter it states: 'You say, "The writer of these lines has never seen a missionary in his life and has neither studied in a foreign-run school nor in a school outside the country. Why do you call him a 'missionary's pupil', only because he is not of your opinion?" But I answer you, if you were a Muslim, how could you then say: "If we do not acquire the European civilisation for ourselves, then there will be no salvation for our people?" Do you not know the Cross does not love the Crescent and savagely treads it underfoot wherever it vanquishes it? The missionaries' pupils claim Islam is a hindrance to culture and progress. How would you support this opinion if you were not a pupil of the missionaries? *Turkdom* and Islam are one; if Islam disappears, then you can no longer speak of nationality. Missionaries are the cholera germs that poison the existence of our nation. — — The writings of the dumb European philosophers, of the scholars who are in love with women and who drink wine in the name of their goddesses and write while under the influence of lust, how might their writings meet with our approval? Yes, the attempt is even made to make them acceptable to the twenty million Osmanlis by referring to freedom of conscience and freedom of speech. But if the defenders of Islam and of *Osmanlidom* step forward and describe all the ignorance and nastiness of the Europeans, then they are accused of fanaticism. Is this not madness?'

"On 9 July Fakhred-din wrote in the *Balkan* to the editor of *Beyan-ul-Hakk*: 'O you evil spirit, you accursed one! You say I am a friend of the Patriarch Joachim. Who are you then? What are you? You are missionaries, the evilest of mischief-makers, the fathers of all curses...'

"The Young Turks' newspapers showed an increased hostility towards me and my work because they not only detested the spreading of Christian truths amongst the Muslims but also saw in this a hindrance to the realisation of their pan-Islamic plans. That is why they induced Fakhred-din, referred to above, and others to speak out against my *Gunesh* three years ago [1909] and fight it in the Turkish press. But when the truth, which the *Gunesh* brought, met with approval in many regions and they did not succeed in disproving it, they then found it necessary to apply stricter measures. No newspaper was so harshly persecuted as mine. Any person who was discovered with an issue in their possession could expect prison and a fine. A typesetter who had worked with us for some time went to Constantinople in order to look for a job, but an issue of the *Gunesh* was discovered in his bag. He was arrested and was not released before he had paid a twenty-franc fine, even though he was not a Turkish subject.

"A moneychanger in Constantinople, a Greek man who bought the *Gunesh*, was arrested by the police and brought before the military tribunal. He was sentenced to six weeks in prison and fined four hundred francs, and his excuse, that he knew nothing of the ban on the newspaper in question, was to no avail.

"After our paper, *Khurshid*, was published, there was no reason to ban it according to the existing laws governing the press, but the influence from the *Khurshid* soon seemed more dangerous than that from the *Gunesh*. First the *Balkan* repeated its attacks against the *Khurshid* in order to warn Muslims. (The editor of the *Balkan*, Adhem Ruhi, receives four hundred francs a month from the Young Turks' committee as a defender of Islam and of the Young Turks' policies, but he is, like them, an atheist and does not live according to Islamic law.) Nevertheless, the *Khurshid* made its way to Turkey and found a greater following amongst the Muslims than the *Gunesh* had done. Muslim newspapers cited quotations from it, Christian ideas were circulated, and fanaticism was weakened, but that was not in accordance with the inclination of the governing body, which wanted fanaticism increased and intensified in order to make use of it as the best and most powerful means of realising their pan-Islamic ideas. Since no reason was found to ban the *Khurshid* openly, the Turkish postal officials on the Bulgarian border were instructed to send the *Khurshid* back and not let it into Turkey. I protested against this with the Bulgarian post office. The matter went to the ministry in Sofia and from there to Constantinople, but only one to two months later did the Bulgarian post office receive the reply from Constantinople that the *Khurshid* was banned *at this time* and that is why it had to be turned away from the border. However, that did not correspond to the truth because no one in Constantinople knew about the ban.

"Even the Muslim religious press considered it necessary to have a good look at the articles and ideas of our *Khurshid*, even if for the most part they did not refer to it by name and did not say where and by whom these Christian ideas were being published. It is my conviction that here the Word of God is having an effect as well, the glad tidings of the gospel working like a leaven. Islam has no power of resistance against this. It cannot prevent the growth of the divine seed by cursing and swearing.

"I would like to tell of two more incidents which have given rise to great excitement in the Turkish religious press since the Proclamation of Freedom. The first instance is the agitation resulting from the distribution of *History of Islam* by Professor Dozy.[1] In this book Dozy had made a series of critical statements about Islam. After the Proclamation of Freedom, Doctor Abdullah Jevdet had translated the book into Turkish in Egypt, providing the necessary explanations (printed in 1908 in Cairo), and had it distributed in Turkey in the view he was doing a service to his people. Until then the Muslims had no history book that was summarised and founded on an academic basis; the history books in existence were rather one-sided, implausible, and full of fables. This translation struck like a bolt of lightning into the Muslim world. The clergy in Constantinople were extremely annoyed and had it banned. However, more than ten thousand copies had already been distributed prior to

---

[1] Professor Reinhart Dozy, who died in 1883 in Leyden, was a professor of history, orientalist, and Arabist at the University of Leyden and one of the best authorities on Islam.

this ban. Some Muslim scholars who understood the matter in the right way tried to defend Abdullah Jevdet, but this had bad consequences for them because they too were now condemned as *kafirs* ('infidels') and, since the fanatics had the greater strength, the former preferred to keep quiet. The fanatics found it necessary to refute the book if they wanted to make it innocuous; but they found this task difficult since it depicted Islam as it really is, and it was convincing. Nothing factual was actually said against the book because Dozy had drawn from the best Muslim sources. So the only thing that remained for the fanatics was a personal attack against the person of the author and of the translator, and the two religious papers, *Siratul-Mustaqim*, now the *Sabil-ur-Rashad*, and *Beyan-ul-Hakk*, undertook this task. For four years one of the most famous Muslim preachers at the Hagia Sophia, Ishmael Hakki from Monastir who at the same time was a member of the high counsel in Constantinople, wrote articles in the *Siratul-Mustaqim* against Dozy and his translator, and the *Beyan-ul-Hakk* also published a series of such articles that year.

"The writing style of Ishmael Hakki is characterised as early as the beginning of his first article in which, opening with the coarsest abuses, he calls the book 'an accumulation of slander from start to finish' and 'a book of insults, bad-mannered attacks, damned prattle, a forged work, unclean pages, a conceited work'. After starting in this way he goes on to say, 'After having relieved our astonishment somewhat over these villainous attacks by way of the preceding remarks, we now come to the facts.' But in reality he sticks to cursing and does not go over to the facts. In almost every article words like these find plenty of space: 'O, you lunatic, O, you lunatic, O, you man, prejudiced by carnal lust, without proof and without a clue, O, you devil, veiled in deceit; a work mingled with hypocrisy, a work that brings about ruin, a book that consists of "phantasms" from top to bottom, a writing which misleads, slanderous pages, the sparks of damnation...' Further on he calls the translator a kafir and a cursed one and finally associates him with the publisher of the paper, *Gunesh*, in Philippopolis. He says if Abdullah Jevdet were not a supporter and colleague of the *Gunesh*'s editor, then he would not have dared to translate such a book that wants to shake the foundations of Islam, etc.

"I do not know Abdullah Jevdet and do not even write along the same lines as he or Professor Dozy because they do not base themselves on Christianity and criticise Islam without being able to offer the people something else, something better.

"The second subject on which I would like to report concerns a small essay about Mohammed which was published in a Turkish newspaper as a tramslation from a work by the well-known German Professor Häckel. Häckel wrote Mohammed had portrayed God like a powerful, mighty man and had received his knowledge of God through a Nestorian monk; as a result he had been wrongly informed about Christianity. These words by Häckel had again extremely infuriated the Muslim clergy, and for several months the newspapers previously mentioned were also occupied with refuting Häckel's propositions as attacks against Islam.

"Actually the Muslim biographers themselves say, as a boy, Mohammed spent some time with the Nestorian monk, Buhaira, and Buhaira had paid homage to him and told him he would become a prophet. Indeed, he is even supposed to have interpreted a passage in the Gospel as a prophecy pointing to Mohammed. Until then the Muslims had taken pride in this story and had made it a reason for praising their prophet and, in the event they could not establish the proof of the prophecy concerning Mohammed in the Gospel, had established the claim that the Christians had distorted the Gospel and suppressed the passage because, they said, 'Buhaira himself showed it to the prophet.'

"But now Häckel's word, that Mohammed had learned much from Buhaira and had given an account of him in the Koran, is painful to them because they think everything in Islam is not from man but is direct divine revelation. To refute Häckel, they say, if it were true that Buhaira knew all that Mohammed taught, why did Buhaira not act as a prophet himself?

"If Muslims are powerless against Dozy and Häckel's words, which only criticise Islam and are not able to offer anything better, what will they do if they are faced with serious Christian writings which not only explain the errors of Islam but also show the few truths which the Koran contains are drawn from the Bible?

"That is the reason why Islam is so obviously afraid of Christian missions and makes such desperate efforts to shut itself off still further from every Christian influence."

Mrs Helene Avetaranian writes in November 1912:

"In September, when no one in Bulgaria was yet thinking of war, my dear husband lined up a trip of about two months to Stockholm in the matter of his Kashgari Bible translation. This trip had already been arranged and scheduled the year before, but hardly had my husband begun his work in Stockholm with the Swedish missionary from Kashgar when it appeared that this time things were becoming serious in the Balkans. The Balkan League was made public, armies were mobilised, postal and local passenger services restricted, and Philippopolis became an absolute army camp. But how calmly, how orderly the Bulgarian soldiers behaved! When thousands of people were situated in the centre of our city for weeks, the Armenians, with whom coincidentally they were mainly billeted, praised their modest and quiet conduct. 'We had fifty Bulgarian warriors, soldiers, in the house, and it was hardly noticeable,' they said. Even in the streets complete order prevailed. There was no drunken merriment, no excitement, no loud enthusiasm, only a calm, steady humanity conscious of the sacrifice it is making because, as it now stands, there is no other way. This war is not a 'raid' as some European newspapers have called it; rather it is a people's war in the truest sense of the word. 'The Russians liberated us; now we must free the Macedonians' was the foremost thought dominating all these thousands of men down to the last soldier. 'It is beautiful to fight for the liberation of others' and 'we feel God is with us', a young Bulgarian cavalry captain whom I know wrote to his family in Philippopolis. An old American lady missionary who has known the people and their language for more than thirty years told me that now in the Bulgarian church services, where it otherwise often gets so noisy and superficial, deep emotion and a real spirit of prayer prevails."

With the *outbreak of the (first Balkan) war (October 1912)* the tasks that confronted Avetaranian diverted him from his domestic work. Among the casualties and prisoners there was now a great number of Muslims. Avetaranian was in Sofia and visited the wounded. They admitted to him that they were better off here amongst the Christians, once they had escaped death, than in their own homes. They were given the Gospel; the more mature ones received the religious periodical. One of them who read the Gospel exclaimed he would not be here in this situation if he had seen this book earlier. The Muslim prisoners admitted they had become suspicious of the good care they were receiving from the Christians in the prison camp. They did not accept any food at first because it was believed that the Christians would poison the Muslims. Avetaranian also met such ones amongst the Muslims who asked him for some bloody war stories, such ones who boasted of having killed Christians (Armenians). Avetaranian was not able to visit the fourteen thousand prisoners who were not wounded; he was refused on account of the [Bulgarians'] mistrust of Germany.

Even within the Bulgarian Christian community there was pastoral care for Avetaranian and his assistants. The Christians' fear, that if there were an unfortunate outcome to the war they would have to suffer dreadfully, was only too well founded; the fanaticism of the 600,000 Muslims in Bulgaria made them a dangerous population.

Here too Avetaranian was a help to both Muslims and Christians. He preached at the Bulgarian evangelical church in Sofia, and his sermon was published in its entirety by the daily paper, *Utro*, in Sofia. He also served as an interpreter to the English doctors who were sent by the Indian Red Crescent, and there too he had opportunity to serve with his word. In March 1913 Avetaranian heard that in Pashmakly, the home town of the two mullahs staying in Germany, all the Muslims had gone over to the Christian Church.

"In this year of war," reports Avetaranian, "our mission-house and often even our lives were threatened by dangers, and over several months we were cut off from the outside world on all sides. We could neither travel out nor could anyone come to see us; even our correspondence was impeded and uncertain. Either we did not receive our post at all or at best only twice a month via Odessa. For Serbia and Romania did not let our post from Bulgaria through their region during the second Balkan War. However, what we saw and experienced from day to day at this time was quite exceptional.

"During the first war of the Balkan League against Turkey our city, Philippopolis, was repeatedly at risk from attacks by the Turks who were trying to advance over our national boundary, which is only about five hours away from here, and into the nearby Rhodope Mountains. Yet our situation was more dangerous *during the second Balkan War* after the Bulgarian troops had been called back from Tchataldcha and sent to the Serbian border. As the next largest city on this side of the old Bulgarian-Turkish border, Philippopolis was at no time safe from the Turks, especially since they had won back Adrianople without a shot being fired. It so happened that the Romanian army, which moved into Bulgaria and inflicted much damage and injustice on a defenceless country devoid of troops, advanced in individual cavalry units over the Balkan Mountains as far as Tatar Bazardjik, a railway station situated north of us. The population was terrified of them day and night, no less than of the *bashi-bazouks* who threatened from the south. From Thrace and Macedonia as well as from northern Bulgaria the number of refugees, who in their thousands were seeking protection and assistance here, increased day by day, and the need of the local poor families, whose breadwinners were off fighting, and of the many widows and orphans, became staggeringly great. At this time the price of food rose to almost double, and for days bread often could not be found. Added to all this misery of war, it happened that, shortly before the invasion by the Romanians, the poor Bulgarians were struck by a terrible earthquake. Thousands of poor, frightened people did not know where to go but wandered around the country and came here as well. From the beginning of the war, as I sought to remedy the spiritual need, so my wife cared for the poor, sick, and needy who often knocked at our door in droves. She was also able to give religious writings and many good words along with her ministration.

"Towards the end of July the fear and excitement in Philippopolis became enormous. To protect the city and also to guard the many prisoners of war, we only had a garrison of at most one thousand men because the greater part of the army was fighting in Macedonia against the Serbs and Greeks. Refugees from Thrace told of outrageous acts of cruelty by the bashi-bazouks. In order to calm the inhabitants of our city, the local commander, General Stoïleff, a kind and capable officer, used wall posters to circulate news coming from Sofia via the telegraph, the contents of which were that no danger existed for Philippopolis and the Turks would not cross the old border. One after the other, he sent for several leading personalities from the various denominations and several newspaper editors and asked them to do whatever they could to work towards calming the frightened people. Nevertheless, they soon heard that Turkish armed forces from Mustafa Pasha, having crossed the old border, had burned down Harmanli and the surrounding towns, and fresh bands of refugees from that region, wounded and maltreated, Bulgarians, Armenians and others, confirmed the terrible news, so the turmoil in our city was again on the increase. In the morning they heard: today the Turks are coming, they are advancing, and then it was said: tonight the Romanians will come. Many churches and churchyards were full of refugees who were seeking shelter there. The local Bulgarian national bank sent their cash boxes away from here. Everyone was looking for protection for life and property and did not know to whom they should turn. The government could not help since it was in danger itself, but it let weapons from its armoury be handed out to those who wanted to protect themselves. The Armenians thought of the massacres and feared the worst. Some asked me to hoist the German flag over our mission-house, so it too might provide protection for them and even to ask the American missionary, Mr Marsh, who was on his deathbed, whether or not the American flag could be raised over his house and over the Bulgarian evangelical church. I told them I would discuss it with the evangelical brothers and do whatever was possible, but basically in such cases most of the danger for our mission printing shop and especially for me, known in that country as a missionary to Muslims, would come from the Turkish side.

"With the start of the first war, when I was still in Stockholm, my wife, who was here alone at the station, had asked the local Austrian consul, who also represented the German consul, to put our mission-house and the mission printing shop under the protection of the German flag in the event of an emergency. I also turned to him with the same request. After I had presented my case to him, he answered, 'If the regular Turkish troops come here, there is nothing to fear, but if the bashi-bazouks come, then I am just as much at risk as everyone else.' To my question, whether in such a case I might raise the German flag over our mission printing shop, he answered, 'But not before I tell you to do it.' I was astonished by this answer because the consulate is located far from us, and if I was only able to speak to him after three visits, how might I count on him if I had to notify him quickly in the event of an emergency?

"That week the Turkish officers amongst the prisoners of war were confined to their quarters, and I got permission to visit them. I found them also concerned for their lives and safety because they were again afraid the Bulgarians would kill them since they had heard all sorts of disturbing rumours. They asked me to take steps for their safety. At this critical time I went to see the commander three times. The first time he, himself, had sent for me, and the third time I went at the request of the officers. He talked with me in the friendliest way and gave me his word of honour that, as long as he was alive and in Philippopolis, the Bulgarians would not touch a hair of the prisoners of war. I brought this reply to them, which pleased and calmed them.

"One day the local English consul, a dear Christian, asked me to stand in for him with the prisoners while he had to travel to Macedonia. That is to say, he wanted me to visit the prisoners at the mosque and give them the necessary clothing, shoes, soap, and so forth. This task and these gifts he had received from the London Balkans Committee. Conducted by the English consulate's *kavass* and by a Bulgarian gendarme, I went from mosque to mosque, and while distributing the gifts I was also able to speak with the men and give them God's word. After the Turkish army had reoccupied Thrace and had at times crossed the Bulgarian border, even the officers amongst the prisoners of war were confined to their quarters, but I obtained permission to visit them in their rooms.

"At the same time the Lord gave me strength to publish two important works and a tract, and these were likewise distributed amongst them. One of these pamphlets in particular expounds the fact, demonstrated by the current historical events, that there would be no deliverance and no true progress for the Turkish nation without the gospel. The other is the Turkish translation of the book entitled *Herzbüchlein* by Gossner, with ten symbolic pictures I translated into Turkish and published.[1]

"*From experience, all of our writings are written in a fashion that not only presents the truth of the gospel about salvation in Christ but also the prejudices towards the gospel and towards Christian teaching, which Muslims assimilate from childhood. The writings refute these prejudices in a way that is comprehensible and convincing to Muslims and encourage them to search the Holy Scriptures for themselves.* The evangelical Bulgarian preachers and other brothers, who likewise distributed written works, observed on several occasions that the Muslims, who in the beginning had repeatedly refused the Holy Scriptures which were offered to them, as soon as they had read one of our works, asked eagerly for the Holy Scriptures of their own accord. A Bulgarian evangelical pastor, who likewise had handed out some of our works to prisoners of war, after several days asked one of them whether he had read any of it and whether he had liked it. The pastor received the reply: 'I have not only read it but I will also preach to others what I have read.'

"Not only here in Philippopolis and the surrounding area, where the majority of the Turkish prisoners of war were housed, were Gospels and our writings distributed by me, my wife, and the Bible distributors whom we employed during this time of war, but also in Sofia and Adrianople by our co-worker, Pastor Shahveled, and in Rustchuk by our dear friend, Pastor Kevorkian. Even in Shumla our evangelical brothers handed out quite a few so that the prisoners everywhere received something good to read and take away. We must thank the Lord for what did take place because *if there had been no evangelical missions and no evangelical Christians in Bulgaria for*

---

[1] I would like to make a few comments about the publication of *Herzbüchlein* [*Little Book of the Heart*]: after my conversion, I read this small book, which was in Armenian, for the first time in Caucasia and was greatly blessed by it. From then on I always had the desire to translate it into Turkish. When I came from Kashgar to Berlin fifteen years ago, I spoke now and again with brother Johannes Warns about it; he was kind enough to draw eleven pictures for the little book in accordance with Middle Eastern taste. This summer I presented these pictures during a conversation with the Turkish officers, explained them to them, and noticed what deep impression they made on them, and one of them asked me to translate the little book; he would gladly serve me as a secretary in this.

whom the spreading of the gospel was a matter of the heart, then perhaps neither the prisoners of war nor the Bulgarian soldiers would have received God's word.

"I learned through the evangelical Bulgarian Pastor Furnadjieff in Sofia that the Bulgarian Holy Synod had refused a large consignment of Holy Scriptures in Turkish, which the British and Foreign Bible Society had sent for the prisoners, and had even induced the commander in Sofia to forbid the distribution of Scriptures amongst the prisoners. So the commander even refused my request for permission to do this, which King Ferdinand's secretary, Mr Genadieff, a brother of the future minister, was so kind to arrange. But the Lord showed us other ways, so we were at least partly able to supply the prisoners in Sofia with spiritual writings as well.

"From Stara Zagora, Sofia, and Tatar Bazardjik I received letters from officers who had only received a single piece of our writings or one issue of our newspaper and asked for all of them in order to be able to take them home. Naturally there were also many fanatics amongst the prisoners of war. One day I received an invitation from a Turkish officer to visit him at his hotel. I went there and heard he had received all the editions of my *Shahid-ül-Haqaiq* and had begun to refute me. He read several lines to me which he had written in this fashion, and I told him, 'I am glad you are applying yourself to this and, since my goal is nothing other than the truth, I am even ready and willing to publish your objections and give the necessary response to them. When you have finished writing your criticisms, then send them to me.'

"After we had spoken together for several hours, he changed his mind and said to me, 'I will not write anything more against you, rather I will only honour you.' As we were saying goodbye, he kissed my hand, a mark of the deepest respect in the Orient.

"From Sofia an Arabic gentleman who, as a supporter of Kiamil Pasha, had fled from Constantinople to Bulgaria, wrote that I should send him a copy of all of our writings. He had read about my life and activity in Arabic Muslim newspapers and came to see me in order to get to know me. Later, when I travelled to Sofia and saw him again, he told me, 'O, Muhammed Shükri Efendi, I did not order the writings for myself but for one of my friends, a learned man who wants to take them along to Constantinople and give them to his teacher, a famous *ulema*, and you will receive a proper answer from him. Not such an answer as the local ulemas have written, rather he will prove you wrong with logical reasons.'

"'I will be very glad,' I replied, 'if he responds, whether logical or not, because I am convinced, whoever explores these things with all seriousness will come to the same conclusion as I have, but, Haji Ali, if he does not answer me accordingly, then you can be sure you will not get rid of me.'

"One day I received a Turkish letter from Tatar Bazardjik, likewise from an officer. He wrote to me among other things: 'I am forty-five years old and have studied all the works of the greatest writers of the Sufis (pantheistic teaching). Now I have read your writings and am at peace with all men and will endeavour that all men be at peace with me as well. My intention is to visit you in Philippopolis as soon as I receive leave to travel because I want to get to know you personally. For the time being send me more of your writings.' So one morning he arrived here, stayed with me for four hours, and went straight back again—a learned man and leader of a Bektashi order. He related among other things what great influence the Sufi teaching had at present in the Muslim world, that among their followers the ground was especially ready for receiving the gospel, and of all the dervishes, the Bektashi orders stood closest to Christianity.

"After the retaking of Adrianople by the Turks, many Armenians who had fled here from Thrace attended my Turkish service and asked me to preach to them in Armenian as well. Although it was not easy to find the time, I naturally could not turn down such a request, and in addition to the service in Turkish, I arranged one more Sunday service in Armenian.

"One week before the prisoners of war left Bulgaria, I heard about the illness of our old faithful evangelist, Khachadur Kurian, who managed our Bible depository in Shumla. And the day before their departure, I became sick and had to lie down exhausted, so I could not accompany the departing officers to the train station. Many came to see us and said goodbye with tears in their eyes. Some who were prisoners of war here have notified us of their arrival in their homeland. We are of the conviction, and thank God for it, that in essence the prisoners' attachment was not to us personally but was meant for what they had seen and heard of the gospel's truth and of Christ's love in us and in what they had read in our writings.

"Fifteen years ago I went to Germany in order to have my Kashgari translation of the New Testament printed and then to return to Kashgar. But the Lord arranged it, so it became impossible for me to implement this intention. He led me to Bulgaria and called me to write and work. I wrote, translated, and worked but often sighed that this work did not meet with sufficient consideration. The ground was hard. I cannot speak of 'many individual conversions'; the effect of the sown seed cannot be seen. From year to year our stock of writings multiplied, but the distribution was not able to keep pace with it and that worried me. If at that time someone had said to me: you are preparing everything for the year 1913; then 100,000 Muslims will come from Turkey and they will read and take much away with them, then I would not have been able to believe it. For how could anyone expect that little Bulgaria would take 100,000 prisoners of war? But it was a fact; the Serbs and Greeks together did not take as many prisoners of war as our small state. But in Serbia and Greece there are no evangelical missionaries, and no stock of writing in Turkish was waiting for them there! Yes, God's ways are marvellous, and He wonderfully guides our missionary work.

"It is really a miracle of God that in spite of all the difficult circumstances our mission to the Orient was able to maintain its existence as an active missionary society. The time had come when the mission had to take its work forward with ten times the power because the Lord prepared the way, and we must walk in it in obedience.

"On Ascension Day 1914 we were again allowed to lead a Muslim through baptism into the Christian community.

"Husain Nasifoff was born of Muslim parents in Philippopolis and was a healthy and happy child, but when he was three years old, his parents emigrated to Turkey and, since it was troublesome for them to take the child along, they left him to his fate. A barber by the name of Nasif Husseinof, likewise a Muslim, out of compassion looked after the boy, raised him as his own son, sent him to school, had him work as his apprentice, and instructed him thoroughly, so at the death of his foster father, Husain possessed his guardian's knowledge. At the same time our Husain also occupied the post of a muezzin at the local mosque, 'Mullah Hassan'. That is to say, he had to give the call to prayer five times a day from the minaret. One day someone offered to sell him a New Testament, which he bought, and after he had read some of what was in it, he would occasionally show it to the Muslim priests who warned him about it, so as a fanatical Muslim, he considered it his duty to put the book to one side and no longer read it.

"When in 1908 the two brothers, Sheikh Keshaf and Muderis Nesimi whom I was to baptise a year later in Potsdam, came from Macedonia to Philippopolis, they initially lived near to Husain and even visited his shop. Since he noticed they were well-read and well-informed men, now and again he would show them his Gospel and ask them what they thought of it.

"'This is the book,' they answered him, 'that turns men into men; read it and take no notice of what is said to you against it.'

"With these words he got his courage back to continue reading the Gospel and also came to hear me preach. One day, as I was going home from the church, I saw Husain was following me. We talked all the way to my house, and I spoke with him about the Gospel.

"Later, when Nesimi and Keshaf came to see me and lived and worked with me, he visited them at my home, and they suggested I should give him a job in the printing shop as a typesetter. And so it happened; he learned quickly and became our typesetter, but not only this; he gradually came to understand more of the gospel and of Christianity, eagerly attended our meetings, and gave up all sorts of youthful foolishness and sin. When his friends in the city saw this, they spread the rumour that he had become a Protestant. He confessed he was quite open to the gospel and gave an earnest and friendly reply to anyone who questioned him.

"Five years earlier, around the time when the two mullahs were baptised, he also wanted to be baptised, but I considered it better if he waited a while. *At this time he went through some serious trials, experienced and learned many things, which, regarded from a human point of view, if he had had no faith could have caused him to relapse.* He also saw many Muslims who came to us for some external reason or other and because of that they would soon desert us again.

"After that came the Balkan Wars. The Bulgarians forced the *Pomaks* to convert, and we had to wait and see what would become of it, but that too passed. The Bulgarian government gave the Pomaks freedom to return again to Islam, and so even in this respect normal relations were gradually resumed.

"Among other things there was a serious test for our young friend which was as follows: even though it was commonly known by the Muslims that he stood by the Christians, many thought they could win him back through cunning, even more so as he was not yet baptised. Therefore he was betrothed to a Muslim girl and, since I was not present in Philippopolis when this happened, I could not warn him in time. When I learned of this, I asked him whether the girl's family knew he was a Christian, to which he said yes. As the time for the wedding drew near, the relatives of the bride-to-be demanded the wedding ceremony be Muslim and he should be quiet about his Christian faith—afterwards he could do what he wanted. Naturally they thought if he were to give in to them to that extent, once he was married he would be unable to assert himself in anything whatsoever. But he stuck with it. He could never be quiet about his faith if he were asked about it, and he had to confess openly that he was a Christian wherever that might be. After that, they declared they did not want to give their daughter to any Christian; he would have to give her up. And so it happened; he gave her up, although she was very dear to him.

"In the spring of 1914 he gave a joyful and clear testimony to his faith in Christ at the local Bulgarian evangelical church. He told his story in Bulgarian, which he speaks quite well, and his words were published in the *Zornitsa*, the local voice of the evangelical Bulgarians. The evangelical Bulgarian and Armenian brothers had a good and lasting impression of him and asked me to baptise him, so the baptism was arranged for the German Day of Ascension, 21 May. We had discussed with Husain beforehand what new name he would adopt, and my wife had suggested to him *Nathanael*. At first he thought the name would be too long, but after my wife had explained to him why she wished for just this name for him, how Jesus had said, 'Behold, an Israelite indeed, in whom there is no deceit',[1] and for her there was a profound significance in it, that this word would also become true in him, then this set him to thinking. We did not press him any further but were very glad when he asked for the name *Nathanael*.

"I invited our dear co-worker, Pastor Shahveled from Sofia, to come to the baptism, as well as the local evangelical Bulgarian Pastor Tzakoff, an old retired pastor, Kazandjieff, and some of the older evangelical brothers of the local fellowship, *and we went to the bank of the Maritza River*. Various Bulgarian workers and soldiers who were heading home to the city came to

---

[1] See Appendix I, Bible Passages 45. Trans.

see and listened to what took place, initially with great amazement, and afterwards with deep solemnity and visible emotion.

"After I had again stressed the importance and meaning of Christian baptism to our baptismal candidate, I asked him at the end whether he would stay faithful to his Saviour Jesus Christ to the end of his life, and he answered out loud and with joy, 'Yes, to the end of my life; He will help me in this.' After he said this, we both went into the river until the water was over our knees and, immersing him, I baptised him in the name of the Father, and of the Son, and of the Holy Spirit, and he received the name *Nathanael*. When we had come out of the water and changed our clothes, we four preachers laid hands on him, and Pastor Shahveled in Turkish and Pastor Tzakoff in Bulgarian spoke prayers and blessings over him.

"Shortly after that, I received letters from evangelical Christians in Smyrna concerning a young man, an army cadet from Constantinople, who was leaning towards Christianity and for that reason was being persecuted by Muslims. I have made the necessary preparations, and he knows he can find a place of refuge with us. Also the American missionaries in Constantinople have asked if they may send another Muslim youth from Trebizond to us. The Muslims in Turkey are being stirred up; the scattered seed of truth is having its effect. My friend in Constantinople, Professor Krikorian, a preacher and an editor of an important Christian newspaper, writes to me that there is much desire amongst the Muslims for the preaching of the gospel. They would very much like to come and hear the gospel, but unfortunately under the current Turkish government there is less freedom than under the old regime."

CHAPTER 26
THE WORLD WAR AND ITS EFFECTS

With the World War [World War I], clouds of tragedy drew near, spelling for the German missions work a destruction, which had hardly been foreseen. At the head office of the German Orient-Mission the resources for the whole work soon dried up. The Persian stations were closed and destroyed by the Russians; the missionaries were expelled. Bulgaria remained neutral, and the sympathies of the population remained on the side of the Germans, even those of the Bulgarian Muslims. That is why Avetaranian's work experienced no real interruption at first, although it suffered from the travel restrictions and the meagre rations. When Turkey entered the war on the side of the Central Powers, the uncertain hope was revived that with a favourable outcome to the war for the Central Powers the mission might be left free to build up its work. But it happened differently. At this dangerous time for its existence, Turkey prepared itself for a blind domestic policy which during the years of 1915 and 1916 led to an almost complete expulsion or eradication of its Christian subjects: Greeks, Armenians, and Syrians. The peasantry, the working population, was diminished to the point that feeding the army became impossible because behind the front line the greatest persecution of Christians in history was being orchestrated by an inner circle of Young Turks. The Turkish people, who had been steered in such an utterly conservative direction in the old Turkish kingdom, were lead by a Young Turks' government which wanted to have a pure Osmanli state and people by liberating national territory from the Christian population. Fanaticism geared to Islam was whipped up in order for them to rid themselves of the non-Islamic elements. It was a hopeless situation for a man like Avetaranian and for his work.

The peoples of the East were all mixed together. Individuals came to see him and made him realise again and again the time was near in which even in Islam the question of the gospel was moving from being hidden away to coming into the bright light of the public eye. The question of Holy War, which indeed became something of a problem because of the alliance with the Central Powers, was being dealt with by the written and spoken word. The facts being picked out were those favourable to all the Turks. For even with the Muslims, an experience and a hope had indeed developed through the camaraderie with Western Christians, a camaraderie having its roots in poverty and death. But Avetaranian felt that with the war God had bolted the door his servant so very much wanted to go through.

At the beginning of the war he was in his fifty-fourth year. His health was not the best. Kidney disease caused him a lot of trouble, especially when travelling. The war with its food shortages also weakened him and interrupted his hopeful work at a time when, according to human thinking, it would have needed to remain protected from any disruption.

On a trip to Constantinople where Johannes Lepsius wanted to find out exactly about the suffering of the Armenian people, he also called in on Avetaranian. He got the impression something serious must be causing Avetaranian's suffering. On his return trip he took Avetaranian with him to Vienna to get reliable medical treatment there. On the Viennese doctor's advice, Avetaranian had to begin a cure in [Bad] Nauheim, which he then continued in Wiesbaden.

At the end of December 1915 Avetaranian was back in Philippopolis. His health had improved, and he was supposed to repeat his treatment in Nauheim for several months each year in order to be completely back to fitness. In the spring he felt very weak. The work of the mission was, so he wrote to Germany, obstructed from every side: his printing shop was closed, and the printer was called up for military service. He still had enough to do. He turned to the Armenians to comfort them; indeed, masses of them fled to Bulgaria, many who only understood Turkish. The two evangelists Kevorkian and Shahveled also continued to work enthusiastically. In 1917 Avetaranian took on the German worship service, but since he missed his prescribed summer cure in Nauheim, his illness set in again. He was not even able to leave Bulgaria until Lepsius managed in 1918 to supply him with the exit permit for leaving Bulgaria so that he arrived in Nauheim on 7 August.

On the board of the German Orient-Mission disagreements had arisen from the *Armenian question*; the director of the mission, Johannes Lepsius, had published the truth about the Armenian suffering, within the limits of censorship, and was being hindered in his relief action for the Armenian widows and orphans by the board of his own missions society who wanted to take the interests of the [German] nation into consideration. Lepsius left his mission in 1917; his co-worker of long-standing, General Secretary Richard Schäfer, went with him. They founded a new society, which in the first place devoted itself to the task of saving the Armenian orphans.

In July 1918 Avetaranian also left the old German Orient-Mission and joined his friend Lepsius whom he did not want to abandon for the sake of his responsibilities in the mission to Muslims. He was then no longer doing any work in the field in the service of the new society. His final report from the spring of 1919 reads:

"In the fall of 1915 I was obliged to take my treatment in Bad Nauheim, and by the Lord's grace I was back on my feet and more or less fit for work. As chairman of the German Orient-Mission, Lepsius opposed my desire to return immediately to Bulgaria to the mission field and proposed an extension of my furlough until my health was thoroughly restored, and this was also granted. Although I was thankful for so much love and care, I was so powerfully drawn to the work in the mission field that I nevertheless asked to be allowed to leave, and this is what I did. My doctor in Nauheim made it a condition that I return to Bad Nauheim in six months' time to repeat the treatment.

"My dear wife and I returned to Philippopolis on Christmas Day and took up the work again which was waiting for us. The edition of the Kashgari translation of the New Testament, which I had translated and which had been printed and bound under my supervision, was packed in fourteen crates and ready to be dispatched to Kashgar. I tried once again to post them, but the war made everything impossible. I could not send them either to Odessa or to Stockholm to be forwarded on.[1]

"A large mass of Armenian refugees had come from Turkey to Philippopolis and other cities in Bulgaria, especially women and children. Some had lost their parents and other relatives through murder or forced conversion to Islam. Others had been sent by their husbands and fathers to Bulgaria for their safety's sake, but all needed to be consoled. Since among them were also such Armenians who only spoke Turkish, not Armenian, as the people from Kaisarieh in particular, I preached in Turkish and Armenian every Sunday. The worship service was well attended. Many were in distress, needing care and support, and we helped them as much as we could. Apart from them, there were still many refugees from the actual war zone, as, for example, from Dedeagach and various regions of Macedonia. It must be taken into consideration that Bulgaria had been at war almost non-stop since 1912, that fresh misery was then being added to what had come before. People of Bulgarian, Armenian, Greek, and Turkish nationality who had good livelihoods for themselves back home, widows with their children who told us about their own property, now long since destroyed by the war, were driven out by the various armies, hungry, cold, and pursued by all kinds of misfortune. They had wandered from village to village until they came to the Bulgarian cities, exhausted, without hope, stripped of all belongings and, more often than not, sick. Therefore all our hands were full with things to do and our strength was not enough. With great thankfulness we remember the German doctors and nurses from the German medical mission[2] who, besides their immense work with the sick and wounded soldiers in their hospital, also faithfully helped us with our poor people. Often, whenever my wife went with her charges to the clinic and saw the crowd of sick people, the mass of wretched and most miserable people, waiting for the doctor who was still busy in the operating theatre, it would seem almost impossible that our requirements could still be given time and consideration as well. Nevertheless, she made the attempt; in some cases admission into the hospitals was even

---

[1] For the continuing fate of the fourteen crates, see Chapter 27.
[2] That is, the Deutschen Sanitäts-Mission. Trans.

possible and saved many young lives from infirmity and an early death.

"My efforts in the summer of 1916 to return to Germany for treatment unfortunately came to nothing, and an attempt to recuperate in Sofia came to an unfavourable end because I took ill with influenza there. In the summer of 1917, when I had been suffering very much from the heat in Philippopolis, I wrote to the German Orient-Mission and asked for their help to get out of the country and go to Germany, which was becoming ever more difficult. For I was told an invitation from Germany with the reasons why the journey was necessary would make getting permission to leave the country easier. The reply I received was I had to wait until the committee's next meeting. In the meantime autumn was approaching, and before the next meeting took place, the requirements in passport matters were increased, and it became more difficult to leave the country. With a great deal of trouble and much expense we collected the necessary permission slips and sent them to the ministry in Sofia via the commander, who was the proper channel. They were supposed to be returned after a short time, but in spite of all our queries and reminders, winter went by without them coming. We were forced to wait until spring, the relevant officials changed, and the new officials explained to us our papers had not reached Sofia at all; rather they had been lost in Philippopolis, and we had to begin afresh. I was endeavouring to travel to Nauheim before the intense heat came on, which we in no way felt ourselves up to facing, but it was not in our power to conclude the matter quickly because the difficulties with the papers began again.

"With expense and much trouble we acquired the eight lost certificates again which were needed and had them sent with the photographs to the ministry in Sofia, for sending or taking them there ourselves was not allowed. Now the same business began as in the winter, that is to say, the papers were not returned, and in the end no one no longer knew where they were. Whenever our German friends in Sofia inquired at the ministry department, they received the answer that the papers had not yet arrived or had long since been sent back again. In Philippopolis at the police bureau it was said again and again that they would be coming soon.

"Finally we sent a telegram to Doctor Lepsius and asked him for help, and on his part he cabled the Bulgarian prime minister, Radoslavov, in Sofia about the situation and asked for his mediation. He immediately took up the matter, but before he was able to conclude it, he was overthrown. At any rate he had cabled the police bureau in Philippopolis, which was the relevant place, and emphasised the necessity of attending to our case, whereupon an official came to see me with Doctor Lepsius' telegram in his hand in order to convince himself of my illness. Then our papers finally came back from Sofia.

"Meanwhile, our residence had been sold, and the new owners, Jewish people, wanted us to vacate the house. Since it was impossible to find a new place to stay because there were many refugees in the city and house rents rose in an alarming way, they promised us that we might store our things in one room of the house and they would help to lighten the load regarding our leaving the country. Through personal sacrifices they got the travel permit to Sofia for us, so we could do the work on our case ourselves there and prepared various things for our departure. After they had obtained this permit, our papers came back from Sofia as well, but the passport was still missing. We then took care of everything we needed to do at home in a few days; our German friends kindly helped us with this. Accompanied to the train station by the Jewish gentlemen, who helped us to endure the final difficulties in the departure at the hands of the train station commander and did everything in their power to make things easier, we finally left Philippopolis.

"In Sofia we had to go to a hotel, and now our work to leave the country began anew. The secretary of the *gradonachal'nik*[1] was still not satisfied with our papers; one thing was missing. At any rate it went better for us than in Philippopolis. The secretary himself sent a telegram to Philippopolis, but several days went by during which my wife inquired again and again but to no avail; the reply had not come. Finally the matter came to a satisfactory conclusion with the help of our former foster son, Sahak Arakelian from Khoi who is married and living in Sofia. He knew the gradonachal'nik and his secretary personally and took care of the passports for us. Then the work began at the Austro-Hungarian consulate, and we were told that it would take another ten days since it was necessary to make an enquiry in Vienna. It was just as well because the permission to take the Balkan Express had to be obtained which again took several days and much futile running back and forth. Finally, even these difficulties were dealt with; then the German permit had to be obtained, which happened reasonably quickly. When we believed everything was ready, we still lacked the stamp of the commander in Sofia on our passport, without which we could not get a train ticket. Again Sahak Arakelian and other Armenian friends came to our aid, and through them we got the stamp and the tickets for the Balkan Express to Munich.

"Without changing trains we went to Munich via Vienna. With delays we then finally arrived in Frankfurt early on 7 August and a few hours later were in Bad Nauheim, the place so dear to us.

"After I had finished my treatment in Bad Nauheim, we accepted an invitation from Doctor Lepsius to go to Holland."

Avetaranian had started printing his Kashgari Bible translation at the beginning of 1915 in his own printing shop and was still completing it. The last form was barely printed when his machinist died as a result of the war.

---

[1] See Appendix B, *gradonachal'nik*. Trans.

CHAPTER 27

THE CONCLUSION OF A RICH LIFE

Many have been granted the privilege of meeting John Avetaranian in real life, but few got to know his character and his serious attitude towards life, which was conditioned by his life work. He was and remained thoroughly oriental; the West with its often nervous, unhealthy influences could not disturb the balance of his inner man nor his different way of Eastern thinking. How could he be a messenger of the gospel to his brothers if he had become a Westerner who, along with the message of the Son of God, had at the same time also brought along views and opinions that could only survive on Western soil? With simple wisdom, indeed, with a special gift, he associated with people of the Western world. It was unheard of for him to have caused conflicts anywhere that would have offended the Christian convictions of others.

The man, small in stature, was so simple in his dealings and conversations with people that the children who came in contact with him quickly became his friends. In a religious discussion he never imposed his opinion on anyone, but whatever he said so came across with the strength of certainty and with a peace adverse to any agitation that one could not escape the impression that here stood a firmly established conviction. The word of the Bible reinforcing his replies was always at his disposal, as we also saw in his disputations, which were free of any fanaticism.

That is not to say in him you would encounter a man who always went around with a grave expression on his face. His extraordinary kindness, which was simple and sincere, not only won over every heart but also instilled in everyone a sense of respect and admiration. To a special degree he knew himself to be of one mind with his friend Johannes Lepsius concerning the Kingdom of God. A twenty-year friendship bound him to Doctor Lepsius, a friendship, which was founded on mutual trust. For two decades Avetaranian was the most loyal co-worker associated with Lepsius in the mission to Muslims. Lepsius found sympathy for his unique ministry with Avetaranian, the believing Western theologian who had studied Islam during his time as a young priest in the Holy Land and later viewed the matter of his overcoming Islam as the purpose of his mission. Both men were completely clear and fully in agreement with one another that their goal stretched far beyond the bounds of individual conversions and serious academic questions were being resolved. Lepsius once wrote to his friend: "I am convinced more and more that the analysis of Islam must get to the bottom of the truth and at the same time we must not show any consideration for the conventional ideas of pietism and orthodoxy." Along these lines, Lepsius' work on the Trinity, the divinity of Christ, and other similar subjects also had an influence on Avetaranian's work. If God had granted the two friends a longer life, the mission to the Muslims would have received the academic tools it needs to confront Islam.

God had bestowed upon Avetaranian a magnificent sense of humour. Whenever he recounted one of the numerous funny stories of Mullah Nasreddin, every listener was under the spell of Middle Eastern merriment, and the storyteller himself laughed the most heartily of all. Even the various one-sided attitudes he encountered in his contact with earnest, believing people never troubled him. A smile of certainty appeared on his naturally friendly features whenever the doubts and overwhelming caution of others would see only hindrances. In such discussions one had the feeling that the experiences of this man in religious things—in his wrestling for insight, long before he was a Christian, he had passed through all the stages of Islam—went far beyond our experiences. This man had sacrificed his secure position in life, indeed, home, homeland, bride, and profession, all in all, to his religious conviction in order to fulfil his difficult life's commission. Compared with that, all external things had to come second.

What an incredible amount of difficulties he had to overcome in his work! He reported on them without complaining, no doubt asking for help and support, but he was never discouraged. A patience, which few men possess, armed him to stand his ground and to stay the course. He knew that not he, the weak man, not even with his best strength and plans, was capable of doing this important work; rather there is One over him who showed His child every step of the way. And his conduct was in keeping with this inner stand in all situations: if against his will he had to interrupt his incredibly important work on the New Testament for a long time in order serve an explorer as a companion and translator, he went along with it. But his resistance was aroused whenever he saw his task threatened in a real way by those who were supposed to be supporting him, yet would force on him strange methods for missions along the lines of their own preconceived ideas.

So his journey through life remained a certain one, and he was able to impress his mission to Muslims on Western Christendom, which he did painstakingly and with great patience.

Through the many journeys, in changing climates and changing circumstances, Avetaranian's body was exposed to severe attacks, to say nothing at all of the obvious privations and strains of primitive Middle Eastern travel. As a result of a cold, which he brought home with him from his Persian trip in 1901, he had chronic nephritis. He was restored to health at St Elisabeth's Hospital in Berlin and returned to his field of work. About twelve years later, as a result of his diseased kidneys and high blood pressure, he had several minor strokes that at first only temporarily interrupted the course of his work. There was also a severe dilation of his heart, which required treatment at Bad Nauheim and Wiesbaden in 1915. He was able to go back to Philippopolis. The next hot summer aggravated his condition again. In 1917, on account of the war, Avetaranian could not manage the journey from Bulgaria to take his essential annual treatment in Bad Nauheim. Only in 1918, through the intervention of Johannes Lepsius with the Bulgarian prime minister, did he receive permission to leave the country and reached Nauheim again. The food situation in Germany made a follow-up treatment in Holland necessary, which reunited him with his faithful friend Lepsius who was staying there on account of his health.

But his strength was already broken. He could only be led slowly along on his wife's arm. "He loved it," so writes Johannes Lepsius about those last days together, "spending the whole day in the open air. He lived quite near the *Bosch*, the large, lake-filled royal park with its marvellous trees. He would sit there for hours or be led around. He enjoyed thinking about the past. I lived through his rich life work once again with him. The travelling adventures we had had together in 1899 while visiting our stations in Persia and Mesopotamia appeared before us with their changing images. How for weeks we crossed through Armenia, Kurdistan, and Mesopotamia on horseback, camping out in tents and on rooftops under the starry sky, staying in Khoi, Urumiah, Van, Jezireh, Diarbekir, Urfa, Antioch, Tarsus, Ephesus, and on the island of Patmos, spending sunny days on the Mediterranean Sea and stormy nights on the Black Sea. Every solemn and cheerful hour was still clear in his mind.

"But it was not only the issues of the Orient and the problems of the mission to Muslims that concerned him; he also showed a lively interest in my theological work. In his life he had had many friends in pietistic circles and among people from various denominations but had never been shaken in his natural manner nor allowed limits to be placed on his sober judgement. He was much too good as an expert of the Scriptures, and with his translation of the New Testament into Kashgari he had looked much too deeply into the problems of searching the Scriptures to have allowed the freedom of his judgement to be restricted. Even in his conversations in the final year I could only admire again and again his uninhibited and agile mind. Although I no longer reckoned on his participation in the work on the mission field, I did hope his personal assistance and his profound experience in all areas of the spiritual life of Muslims would be preserved a while longer for me. It is hard to part from a loyal friend.

"One impression comes back to me every year. Avetaranian was a Turk, he grew up and was educated as a Muslim mullah, and in our friendship I never felt a difference of race or background between him and me. In spite of his energetic will, he had such a considerate, tender manner to feel and to give expression to his feelings. He had such an unwaveringly distinguished way in his basic convictions and had such a golden heart that I think of him just as a

German friend. In the end the human heart is neither European nor Asian; when it is at its best, then it is simply human. On the other hand his almost mischievous sense of humour was a humour of a quite special kind, a particularly thoroughbred species of Turkish humour. He remained true to it even through the hardest days of his illness. When he could hardly speak any more, he amused us with priceless observations. He was true to himself to the last hour because he had remained true to his God and Saviour."

In the summer of 1919 Avetaranian and his wife travelled back from Holland to Nauheim. With extreme care the treatment was applied there, and afterwards the follow-up treatment was applied in Wiesbaden, but it was no longer effective. The sick man suffered from insomnia. His faithful wife read to him. He lived near to the Wiesbaden health spa, so he could enjoy the music he so dearly loved. A bronchial catarrh in Holland had already made his condition more serious. The heart condition so weakened him that as far as we could foresee, there was no chance of recovery. In Wiesbaden he suffered from such a high fever he had to be placed under constant medical supervision in the hospital.

His lively spirit still took a full interest in everything that was happening. He dictated letters to his wife. When he heard of his friend Lepsius' accident which had a fortunate outcome, he had a letter sent to him: "It was the greatest joy for me that God has watched over you in your misfortune and has given your life back to you and given you afresh to us and restored your strength. I approve of all your plans (about the mission). God bless you in this."

One of his final joys was the news that his Kashgari translation of the New Testament, which could not be sent to Kashgar during wartime and was ready and waiting in Philippopolis packed in fourteen crates, could finally be sent off to Stockholm to the Swedish Missionary Society, and with that they could be put to their intended use. On this occasion Avetaranian dictates: "We have prayed day and night that God would open a way to send them to Kashgar and have learned He will now do it in this way."[1]

On the evening of 11 December 1919 the Lord called his servant home. His wife had read the one hundredth Psalm[2] to him. "When I finished," she herself writes, "he turned a little towards me and said with an unusually clear voice: 'That was beautiful!' It sounded so sure and so heartily contented. Then he stretched himself a little and closed his eyes. I continued to read, as he loved it so, the one hundredth and first Psalm[3] and after that 1 John, chapters 4 and 5.[4] His eyes remained closed, and up to his final breath he no longer regained full consciousness."

---

[1] And so it happened. We heard later from the Svenska Missionsförbundet that the fourteen cases with the Kashgari New Testaments arrived in Kashgar and became a source of blessing in the hands of the Swedish missionaries [Schäfer].

[2] See Appendix I, Bible Passages 46. Trans.

[3] See Appendix I, Bible Passages 47. Trans.

[4] See Appendix I, Bible Passages 48. Trans.

Fifty-eight and a half years God had granted to him to live and to work. Then the Master called him home, relieving him of his life's burden and work. God's word, which caught hold of him in the seeking and wrestling days of his youth, accompanied him throughout his life, even staying with him as the final sound in his ear and consciousness. Over his death stands the word of Scripture: 'Overcame by the blood of the Lamb'.[1]

Avetaranian's grave is at the Südfriedhof cemetery in Wiesbaden. He was laid to rest there in German soil on 14 December. His place of rest still lacks a worthy monument as a testimony for future generations. He himself erected a memorial in the life of the people of the East, an everlasting one, his translation of the New Testament into Kashgari.

Avetaranian's burial in German soil is no significant episode in world events; just as insignificant is his life and work and his association with the German evangelical missions communities. The resting place of the quiet sleeper speaks of the great task which was given to him in his lifetime and which others shall now take up after him.

---

[1] See Appendix I, Bible Passages 49. Trans.

CHAPTER 28

TAKING STOCK OF IT ALL

[RICHARD SCHÄFER'S ORIGINAL SUMMING UP]

Perhaps such was the will of God that with the completion of his translation of the New Testament, Avetaranian's work on the earth was finished.

Avetaranian's friend, the most sympathetic and understanding Lepsius who immediately after Avetaranian's death expressed publicly it would be up to him to acknowledge and continue Avetaranian's work, was called home five years later. It belongs to the incomprehensible aspects of the history of missions that these two men had to leave behind an important work unfinished.

But the significance of the life and work of John Avetaranian goes far beyond a missions work supported by a single nation. The question cannot be avoided: *what will become of the work of the mission to Muslims?*

Or does such a work go with men to their graves? Are the experiences, which are presented in this book to today's generations, the experiences of one called by God from amongst the Muslims, of a transitory nature meant only to sink into oblivion?

We surely do not need to wait until a man once again approaches Christendom from the Turkish people with the call: "Come over here!"[1] *The life of Avetaranian has made the task of the mission to Muslims irrefutable.* From his experiences—and this book will serve that end first and foremost—valuable clues can be gained and mistakes avoided. Whenever we are reminded how again and again this Muslim or that one has taken his [Avetaranian's] path through life, who has gone the same way of struggling for the gospel, then today we can also reckon on countless unknown people who in their lives feel the same burden which has as its purpose faith in Jesus Christ for every Muslim who has become a believer in Christ. If only the doors, which today are closed through political hampering, are open to the Orient, then witnesses for the service of the gospel will appear before us and be known to us by sight. We must hold out our hands to them; we must include them in the fellowship of those who believe in Christ to strengthen them to struggle and to testify.

The world is a different place today. Islam is in a state of crisis, the development of which no man can predict. It is threatened in its position in the life of the people, though not by missions, in which today there is hardly

---

[1] See Appendix I, Bible Passages 50. Trans.

any agreement in theoretical terms about the methods of a successful mission to Muslims. The religion of the Prophet Mohammed is threatened by the dwindling of its government support, by the complete isolation, which has come into being because no longer will any head of state or state laws protect and carry out its precepts. Even in Muslim countries, secularism, which is deliberate and more or less propagated, is the greatest threat to the Muslim religion; countless supporters have abandoned it because the severest economic and national requirements make its absolute control over people impossible.

Since the Great War [World War I] has stripped our much-praised culture of its Christian character and given the non-Christian peoples their own independent way of thinking, whatever winds that blow through the international community in our day will also introduce sharper attacks and criticism against Islam. *The religious debate between faith and unbelief is today catching hold of all zones and peoples. Our century will be the century of the unarmed religious struggle in which even Islam must be a comrade-in-arms, as a representative of two hundred million Muslims, or sink into atheism.*

Christianity, the most hated opponent to Islam until now, must first stand its ground alone in the struggle. It must also fend off Islam, which still has sufficient strength.

The mission to Muslims means that, in this struggle, the one who currently opposes the gospel will be won for the gospel and, if possible, will come to fight for the gospel.

CHAPTER 29

THE TRANSLATOR'S SUMMING UP

I feel that I cannot leave Avetaranian's story with the ending Richard Schäfer has given it. Apart from the fact he seems to be tacking on conclusions that are not well thought through and out of step with the rest of the story as Avetaranian tells it, Schäfer also seems to be limiting his readership to a small group of Christians with specific interests. Consequently, he narrows the scope of the book to a simple vindication of Avetaranian's work and the wider work of the mission and missions in general. This is a shame because it moves away from the true reflection of who Avetaranian was: a man from a very elite background who as a follower of Jesus was brought to a point where he could deal openly and honestly with anyone, be it one of his own people or a member of his own dervish sect, a young Jewish woman on a train, or Christians from a variety of denominations and backgrounds. Just the fact that this Turk could be brought not only to have dealings with Armenians, but also to have such close fellowship with them, at a time when the ground for a long-lasting enmity between them was being laid through the atrocities committed, is a wonder in itself. Schäfer's insistence on trying to see the "bigger picture" of the mission to Muslims ignores the little things making up Avetaranian's life, and any child of the Kingdom of God should know the importance of small things like the tiny mustard seed in the parable (Matthew 13:31-32). So in this respect the most powerful statement is Avetaranian's life itself, told in a simple and honest way, left to stand on its own merits as a witness to the truth of Jesus, a statement which speaks not just to Muslims, but to everyone.

But what has happened in some of these areas where Avetaranian once lived and worked? The havoc of World War I (to use Fred Goodsell's words) forced the American Board of Commissioners for Foreign Mission to abandon their work in Asia Minor, though certain medical missions carried on, and they have maintained a presence in Turkey up to the present day. More recently I have discovered there is a Christian organisation, which sends groups to Anatolia in eastern Turkey every year to pray with the hope of one day seeing the gospel preached freely there.

In spite of insurrections by both Muslims and communists, the Swedish missionaries continued with their work in and around Kashgar (including a medical mission in Yarkand) until the last of them were finally forced to leave Kashgar in 1939. By then there were over two hundred Christian believers in the region, not including children, almost every one a convert from amongst the Turkic people. They continued to update and print the Kashgari New

Testament as well as other literature in the local Turkic language. A project was started in 1938 to publish the whole of the Bible in eastern Turki, which was finally completed in the early 1950s. The intention was then to have local Chinese Christians make it available to those who could read eastern Turki.

The eastern Turki, or more appropriately the Uyghur, translation of the New Testament, a new translation, was started in the early 1980s, but for some fifteen years made very slow progress, in large part due to arguments over scholarship, a problem amazingly reminiscent of the difficulties Avetaranian had with the same project. These problems have been rectified, and there is hope of seeing the New Testament published in this language very soon. Sadly I have been told that, because Avetaranian's Kashgari New Testament was printed using the old Arabic script, scholars are the only ones who can read it now. And Avetaranian's translation, as well as subsequent work done by the Swedish missionaries, has not been used or consulted to any great extent for this latest translation of the New Testament into Uyghur.

It is Avetaranian's mission in Bulgaria, which seems to have contributed to, or at least helped, sow the seeds for a wonderful work of the gospel amongst the Turks in that country, a work that has continued up to the present day. The American and German missionaries were active in Bulgaria until the Second World War and the subsequent communist takeover brought what they were doing to an end. Although the work of the missionaries was thwarted, the work of the gospel progressed. It is known that churches amongst Turkish believers, which took the form of meetings in private homes, started as early as the late 1950s and carried on in spite of the communist regime. And in the 1990s there has been a tremendous increase in the number of Turkish Christian believers in that country.

Liane Mistele relates the story of the formation of the first of these "house churches" amongst the Turks in Bulgaria (see *Christliche Gemeinden unter der türkischsprachigen Minderheit in Bulgarien. Ein Beitrag zum ökumenischen Lernen im Religionsunterricht*, pp. 110-112). A 13-year-old Muslim boy, whose eye was injured by a stone while playing with his cousin, was totally healed even after the doctors had told his parents he would probably have to be fitted with a glass eye. His father had already been a believer in Jesus for several years, but his mother was not. His father prayed with his mother in Jesus' name for the eye to be healed, and it gradually got better, so after twenty days he was able to leave the hospital. Years later, when the boy went in for his physical for his military service, his eyesight checked out at 100 per cent. On the back of this healing and the interest it provoked in the neighbours, a church was formed which met in his parents' home (though it must be said that the boy himself, at the point when the story was related, had not become a Christian).

As for myself, I do know how much I appreciate the story of Avetaranian's life; how his experiences mirrored some of my own, though mine in no way reached the intensity of his. I too left the religion I was raised in, though it was Roman Catholicism, and I did this simply as a response to the truth of Jesus, the message of the gospel, and His call to "follow Me". He leads and you follow, and you just do not know where you will end up, but that does not matter. You follow Him because it is right to do so; He is good and it is salvation to trust Him.

Although I believe this story is for everyone, my hope is it might make its way back to the Turkish people some day. It was Avetaranian's hope and desire to see the gospel reach his own people, and if the account of his own life helps in some way towards this, it would be the most fitting end to his story, a final chapter only Jesus can write, and I trust Him for this. It may have been a long time, but it is certainly not too late.

"God delays; he does not neglect."[1]

---

[1] A Turkish Proverb (see the *Missionary Herald for the year 1880*, p. 254).

APPENDICES

A. Glossary of Geographic References	200
B. Glossary of Who's Who and What's What	210
C. Established Dervish Orders Mentioned by Avetaranian	233
D. What the Sunni Call the Yologhli	234
E. What the Yologhli Call Themselves	235
F. The Twelve Imams According to the Yologhli	236
G. American Missionaries Based in Erzerum in 1881 and 1882 under the American Board of Commissioners for Foreign Missions	237
H. Exchange Rates to the US Dollar in the 1880s and 1890s. What the US Dollar Could Buy Back in the 1880s and 1890s	238
I. Bible Passages	239
J. Koran Passages	246

Appendix A
Glossary of Geographic References

Adana	Still Adana, Turkey; this was also a province of the Ottoman Empire.
Adrianople	Now Edirne, Turkey.
Afghanistan	This region at the time of this story was more or less the same as present-day Afghanistan, its boundaries having been established in the late nineteenth century in the context of the rivalry between Britain and Russia known as 'The Great Game'.
Africa	In regards to geography, the same as today though at that time the object of colonisation by a number of European powers.
Aksakmaral	Still Aksakmaral, China.
Akstafa	Also Agstafa; now Aghstafa, Azerbaijan.
Aksu	Still Aksu, China.
Alashkerd	Also Alashgird; now Toprakkale, Eleshkirt district, Agri province, Turkey; population in 1990: 1,841.
Albania	The most western region of the Ottoman Empire in Europe along the Adriatic and Ionian Seas; the modern-day country of Albania makes up a little over half of the territory which was originally ascribed to it under the Ottomans; it became independent of the Ottoman Empire in 1912.
Alexandretta	Now Iskenderun, Turkey.
Altyn-kopri	Now Altun Kupri, Iraq.
America	The United States of America, though throughout the time of this story it consisted of less than the 50 states that currently make it up.
Amu River	Also Amu-daria or Amu Darya; in eastern Turki: *darya* = *river*; it runs from the Pamirs through Central Asia to empty into the southern end of the Aral Sea; formerly the Oxus River of the ancient Greeks and the Jayhun River of the Arabs.
Andidjan	Now Andijon or Andizhan, Uzbekistan.
Antioch	Also Antaki; now Antakya, Turkey.
Arabia	Also the Arabian Peninsula; an area bounded by the Red Sea on the west and south-west, the Gulf of Aden on the south, the Arabian Sea on the south and south-east, and the Gulf of Oman and the Persian Gulf on the north-east.
Ararat, Mount	In Turkish: *Agri Dagi*; an extinct volcanic massif in extreme eastern Turkey overlooking the point at which the frontiers of Turkey, Iran, and Armenia converge; it consists of two peaks, the highest of which is 16,854 feet (5,137 metres) above sea level.
Aras River	The river that runs eastward from south of Erzurum for 274 miles (441 kilometres) along the northern border of Iran until it flows into the Kura River; formerly the Araxes River of the ancient Greeks.
Arbil	Still Arbil, Iraq.
Armenia	A rather indefinite area which in the nineteenth century comprised eastern Turkey, south-western Caucasia and north-western Persia.
Ashkabad	Now Ashgabat, Turkmenistan.
Asia	This is the traditional reference to the Asian continent which covers the Near East of Western Turkey all the way to China, bounded by the Arctic Ocean on the north, the Pacific Ocean on the east, the Indian Ocean on

	the south, and Europe, the Black Sea, the Greek Archipelago, the Mediterranean, and the Red Sea on the west.
Asia Minor	The western peninsula of Asia, formed by an imaginary line running from the Gulf of Iskenderun on the Mediterranean Sea to the vicinity of Trabzon on the Black Sea; it is washed by three seas, the Black Sea on the north, the Mediterranean on the south, and the Aegean on the west.
Askala	Now Askale, district town, Erzurum province, Turkey; population in 1990: 15,494.
Avrenli	Now Övenler, Pasinler district, Erzurum province, Turkey; population in 1990: 388; Avetaranian's father's native village and where Behjet Khanum lived.
Azerbaijan	This is actually a reference to southern Azerbaijan, the extreme north-western region of modern-day Iran.
Bad Nauheim	Still Bad Nauheim, Germany.
Bagdad	Now Baghdad, Iraq.
Baiburt	Now Bayburt, Turkey.
Bajavut	Now Topalcavus, Askale district, Erzurum province, Turkey; population in 1990: 804.
Baku	Still Baku, Azerbaijan.
Balkan Mountains	The chief mountain range of the Balkan Peninsula and of Bulgaria, which runs east and west through the centre of Bulgaria.
Balkans, the	Also the Balkan Peninsula; the former European part of the Ottoman Empire which today comprises the modern states of Slovenia, Croatia, Bosnia and Herzegovina, Yugoslavia (Serbia and Montenegro), Macedonia, Albania, Bulgaria, Romania, and Moldova as well as Albania, northern Greece, and the small portion of Thrace that remained under Turkish control.
Baltchik	Now Balchik, Bulgaria.
Batum	Now Batumi, Georgia.
Beirut	Still Beirut, Lebanon.
Berlin	Still Berlin, Germany.
Berlin-Steglitz	A southern district of Berlin, Germany.
Bitlis	Still Bitlis, Turkey.
Black Sea	Still the Black Sea.
Bokhara	Now Bukhara, Uzbekistan.
Bosnia	A province of the Ottoman Empire covering modern Bosnia and some of the surrounding areas of Croatia and Serbia.
Bosnia-Herzegovina	That area which forms the north-western corner of the Balkan Peninsula; the Treaty of Berlin, on 13 July 1878, granted Austria the right to occupy and govern this province though in name it remained a part of the Ottoman Empire.
Bosporus, the	The strait running through Istanbul connecting the Black Sea to the Sea of Marmara.
Bulgaria	A region in the north-eastern part of the Balkan Peninsula bounded by the Black Sea, the Rhodope Mountains, Serbia, and the Danube; it gained partial independence from Ottoman rule in 1878 and finally gained independence for all of its territory in 1885 and became a European kingdom in 1908.
Cairo	Still Cairo, Egypt.
Caspian Sea	Still the Caspian Sea.
Caucasia	The region of the Caucasus Mountains and the country immediately to the north and south.
Caucasus, the	The Caucasus Mountains, which run between the Black Sea and the Caspian Sea.

Central Asia	The region of Asia, located in the centre of the Eurasian land mass and extending from the Caspian Sea in the west to the border of western China in the east; Central Asia consists of the republics of Kazakstan, Turkmenistan, Uzbekistan, Kyrgyzstan, and Tajikistan.
Chevermeh	Possible Ovachevirme, Hinis district, Erzurum province, Turkey; population in 1990: 781; at that time the location of an American High School started by missionaries from the American Board of Commissioners for Foreign Missions and where Avetaranian first went to learn Armenian.
China	That is, the Chinese Empire; at that time it included China proper or the Eighteen Provinces; Manchuria, theoretically a subject territory; and the dependencies: Mongolia, Sin-kiang (now Xinjiang), and Tibet; its boundaries were: on the north, Siberia; on the west, Russian Turkistan; on the south, British India; on the south-east, Burma and Tongking (a region of North Vietnam); on the east, the Pacific Ocean; on the north-east, Korea.
Cilicia	The ancient district of southern Anatolia bounded on the north and west by the Taurus Mountain Range, on the east by the Anti-Taurus, and on the south by the Mediterranean Sea.
Circassia	The north-west region of Caucasia, situated north of the eastern part of the Black Sea; roughly the area between the Black Sea, the Kuban River, and the Caucasus Mountains; in 1829 the Ottoman Turks were forced to cede Circassia to Russia.
Congo Free State	The name given to the Belgian colonisation of the Congo (1885-1908), which was carried out under the guise of an international association headed by Leopold, the king of Belgium.
Constantinople	Now Istanbul, Turkey.
Constantza	Also Kustendje; now Constanta, Romania.
Damascus	Still Damascus, Syria.
Danube River	The major river in central Europe, which stretches from southern Germany through Austria and the Balkans to the Black Sea.
Darvaz	Now Darwaz, Tajikistan; also a khanate (within the khanate of Bokhara) in the central part of what is today Tajikistan where it borders the northern tip of Afghanistan.
Dedeagach	Now Alexandroúpolis, Greece.
Diarbekir	Now Diyarbakir, Turkey.
Dorpat	Now Tartu, Estonia.
Dzhumaia	Some older maps show it as Eski Dzhumaia; now Targovishte, Bulgaria.
East Turkestan	Also Chinese Turkestan; that part of Turkestan under Chinese control which today comprises the Xinjiang-Uygur region; it is bounded on the north by Siberia, on the west by what was Russian Turkestan and India, on the south by Tibet, and on the east by Mongolia and the Chinese province of Kansu.
Egypt	The country in the north-east corner of Africa as well as a reference to the ancient kingdom along the Nile River referred to in the Old Testament and the Qur'an.
Ephesus	The ruins of the ancient Greek city, which are located near Selçuk, Turkey.
Erivan	Now Yerevan or Jerevan, Armenia.
Erzerum	Also Erzeroom or Erzeroum; now Erzurum, Turkey; this was also a province of the Ottoman Empire.
Erzingan	Now Erzincan, Turkey.
Europe	The continent that goes from the Bosporus in Turkey along the Mediterranean, including the Mediterranean islands, up the Atlantic coast including the British Isles and on into Scandinavia; the Urals in central

	Russia and the Caspian Sea have always marked the eastern end of Eastern Europe.
Finland	At the time of this story Finland was officially a part of the Russian Empire though it did enjoy a certain amount of autonomy; Finland gained its independence from Russia in 1917.
France	Still France.
Frankfurt (am Main)	Still Frankfurt (on the Main), Germany.
Germany	The Germany of the early twentieth century was larger territorially than it is today and included land that today makes up parts of France, Denmark, and Poland.
Haidari	Possibly Derebogaz, Ilica district, Erzurum province, Turkey; population in 1990: 1,203; the village where Avetaranian was born.
Halle (an der Saale)	Still Halle (on the Saale), Germany.
Harmanli	Now Kharmanli, Bulgaria.
Hassan Kala	Now Pasinler, district town, Erzurum province, Turkey; population in 1990: 19,144.
High Asia	A term used in the nineteenth century to describe the alpine region of Asia including the Pamirs and the eastern Hindu Kush, the Kunlun Mountains, the Tien Shan, the Gissar and Alay ranges, the Plateau of Tibet, the Karakoram Range, and the Himalayas.
Holland	Also The Netherlands; still Holland.
India	That is British India which at that time comprised the peninsula itself, Burma, Aden, the Laccadive, Maldive, Andaman, and Nicobar Islands, though not Ceylon (Sri Lanka), which was a crown colony and politically distinct.
Indus River	Still the Indus River in northern India; it rises in south-western Tibet and runs for 1,800 miles (2,900 kilometres) to empty into the Arabian Sea.
Irkeshtam	Still Irkeshtam, Kyrgyzstan.
Ishtib	Now Štip, FYRO Macedonia.
Jezireh	Now Cizre, Turkey.
Kaisarieh	Also Cesarea; now Kayseri, Turkey.
Karahasan	Still Karahasan, Askale district, Erzurum province, Turkey; population in 1990: 645.
Karakala	Now Merkezkarakale, province centre, Kars province, population in 1990: 570; the site of a community of Protestant Armenians and some Molokans which was established in the early 1880s in territory that had recently been ceded to the Russian Empire from Turkey.
Karakoram Mountain Range	Also Kara-korum; a group of parallel mountain ranges extending for about 770 miles (480 kilometres) from the eastern edge of Afghanistan into Jammu and Kashmir; the Karakorum Range forms a great barrier between India and Central Asia.
Karakoyunly	Now Karakoyunlu, Tasburun district, Kars province, population in 1990: 4,110.
Kars, fortress of	Known today as the Kars Kalesi near Kars, Turkey; it was probably originally an old Ottoman fortress built in the late sixteenth century, though it had been destroyed and rebuilt several times since then.
Kashgar (city of)	Now Kashi, China.
Kashgar River	Also Kashgar-daria or Kashgar Darya; in eastern Turki: *darya* = *river*; now the Kashgar He; in Chinese: *he* = *river*; it rises in the eastern end of the Tien Shan mountains and flows down into the Tarim Basin where it joins with the Yarkand River and eventually the Aksu River to form the Tarim River.
Kashmir	The northernmost region of the Indian subcontinent.
Khanarik	Also Khan-arik; now Hanerik, China.

Kharkov	Now Kharkiv, Ukraine.
Kharput	Also Harpoot; now Harput, Turkey; the location of an American theological seminary, founded in 1859 by the American Board of Commissioners for Foreign Missions, and the Euphrates College founded in 1878.
Khoi	Also Khoy; now Khvoy, Iran.
Khotan (city of)	Now Hotan or Ho-t'ien, China.
Khotan River	Also Khotan-daria or Khotan Darya; in eastern Turki: *darya = river*; now the Ho-t'ien River or He; in Chinese: *he = river*; it rises in the Karakoram Range and flows north through the centre of the Takla Makan Desert, emptying into the Tarim River, though it does not flow the whole distance all year round.
Khynis	Now Hinis, district town, Erzurum province, Turkey; population in 1990: 16,005; at that time it was a district as well as a town.
Khynis, fortress of	The fortress near Hinis, Turkey.
Kizil-Arvat	Now Gyzylarvat, Turkmenistan.
Kokand (city of)	Also Khokand; now Khujand or Khudzhand, Uzbekistan.
Kokand (khanate of)	The realm centred in the Fergana Valley in what is modern-day Uzbekistan and Tajikistan (a khanate is an area ruled over by a khan); the Kokand khanate was annexed by Russia in 1876.
Krasnovodsk	Now Turkmenbashi, Turkmenistan.
Kristiania	Now Oslo, Norway.
Kristinehamn	Still Kristinehamn, Sweden.
Kuen-lun Mountains	Also Kwen-lun; now the Kunlun Mountains; the mountain range that extends east to west some 1,240 miles (2,000 kilometres) from the Pamirs in Tajikistan on the west along the southern edge of the Tarim Basin.
Kur River	Now the Kura River; it rises in extreme eastern Turkey and after travelling northward it curves back to the southeast and empties in the Caspian Sea; formerly the River Cyrus of the ancient Greeks.
Kurdistan	This comprised an area, which included large parts of what are now eastern Turkey, northern Iraq, and north-western Iran and smaller parts of northern Syria and Armenia.
Lailik	Possibly Sheytden, China; according to Hedin, in eastern Turki: *lailik = the dirty clayey place* (see *Through Asia*, p. 452).
Lebanon	Located on the east end of the Mediterranean Sea and a part of the region of Syria; from 1861 it became an independent province within the Ottoman Empire.
Leipzig	Still Leipzig, Germany.
Leyden	Now Leidin, Holland.
Lom Palanka	Now Lom, Bulgaria.
London	Still London, England.
Lop-nor	Also Lob-nor; now Lop Nor or Lop Nur; formerly a salt lake, now a salt-encrusted lake bed at the eastern end of the Takla Makan Desert.
Lovatz	Now Lovech, Bulgaria.
Macedonia	The region in the south-central part of the Balkan Peninsula that comprised northern and north-eastern Greece, the south-western corner of Bulgaria, and the independent Republic of Macedonia; it remained a part of the Ottoman Empire until the Balkan Wars in 1912-13.
Manchuria	A north-eastern division of the Chinese Empire from where the Manchu dynasty (China's last imperial dynasty) came.
Maral-bashi	Now Bachu, China.
Margelan	Now Marghilon, Uzbekistan.

Maritza River	Now the Maritsa River; it rises in the Rila Mountains south of Sofia, runs south through Bulgaria and forms the border between Greece and Bulgaria and Greece and Turkey; it empties into the Aegean Sea.
Mecca	In Arabic: *Makkah*; still Mecca, Saudi Arabia.
Mediterranean Sea	Still the Mediterranean Sea.
Merket	Now Markit, China.
Merv	Also Mery; now Mary, Turkmenistan; founded by the Russians in 1884 and named after the ruined city of Merv which was located 18.5 miles (30 kilometres) west of the new site; the name of the city remained Merv until 1937.
Mesopotamia	The region of the Middle East that falls between the Euphrates and Tigris Rivers.
Middle East	In this book I have used this more modern term to refer to the region comprising Egypt, Turkey, Iran, Arabia, Iraq, Syria, Lebanon, Jordan, Israel, the West Bank and Gaza when the context of the story seemed to imply a restricted sense of the word *Orient*, which is the term that appears throughout the German edition.
Mingyol	Still Mingyol, China.
Monastir	Now Bitola, FYRO Macedonia.
Mongolia	The aggregate area known as Inner and Outer Mongolia; at that time it was a part of the Chinese Empire; Outer Mongolia (the Mongolia of today) gained its independence from China in 1921.
Montenegro	At that time a kingdom in the Balkan Peninsula on the east coast of the Adriatic Sea; formerly a part of the Ottoman Empire, it gained its independence in 1878.
Mosul	Still Mosul, Iraq.
Munich	Still Munich, Germany.
Mush	Also Moosh; now Mus, Turkey.
Mustafa Pasha	Now Svilengrad, Bulgaria.
Mustagh Ata	Also Mus-tagh-ata; now Muztagata; in eastern Turki: *mus-tagh-ata = father of the ice mountains*; a mountain in China in the Karakoram Range, 24,757 feet high (7,546 metres).
Nicopolis	Now Nikopol, Bulgaria.
Odessa	Still Odessa, Ukraine.
Oksalur	Now Ohsalur, China.
Omsk	Still Omsk, Russia.
Orient	In the context of this story, this refers to Asia in the widest possible sense or any part therein: Near East, Middle East, or Far East.
Oryakhovo	Also Rahova or Rahovo; still Oryakhovo, Bulgaria.
Oryekhovica	Possibly Gorna Oryakhovitsa, Bulgaria.
Osh	Still Osh, Kyrgyzstan.
Osman Bazar	Now Omurtag, Bulgaria.
Pamirs, the	The high plateau region centred in modern-day Tajikistan from which several south-central Asian mountain ranges radiate; these ranges include the Hindu Kush, the Karakoram Range, the Kunlun Mountains, and the Tien Shans; this region is also known to the tribes of the region as *Bam-i-Dunya* or 'Roof of the World'; Hedin described the Pamirs as "broad, level, waterless valleys, bounded by low mountain-chains, rounded and greatly worn" (see *Through Asia*, p. 384).
Paris	Still Paris, France.
Pashmakly	Now Smolyan, Bulgaria.
Patmos, island of	An island which today belongs to Greece; the island to which the apostle John was exiled.

Peking	Now Beijing, China.
Persia	At that time this ancient kingdom had been reduced to roughly the territory of present-day Iran.
Perza	That is, Perzor.
Perzor	Possibly Mezrea, Askale district, Erzurum province, Turkey; population in 1990: 432.
Philippopolis	Now Plovdiv, Bulgaria.
Plevna	Now Pleven, Bulgaria.
Potsdam	Still Potsdam, Germany.
Rakhova	Now Ryakhovo, Bulgaria.
Rasgrad	Now Razgrad, Bulgaria.
Rhodope Mountains	A mountain system in the Balkan Peninsula, which lies mainly in south-western Bulgaria, but also reaches into northern Greece.
Romania	Also Rumania; a kingdom in the Balkan Peninsula, the borders of which at that time were the Black Sea, the Danube, the Carpathian Mountains, and the Pruth River; the area that it covered then was only a part of the Romania of today; Romania first gained its independence from the Ottoman Empire in 1878.
Russia	That is, the Russian Empire, the borders of which were being extended throughout the nineteenth century as it increased its political and economic influence in Central Asia and annexed the former khanates that existed there.
Russian Turkestan	See West Turkestan.
Rustchuk	Now Ruse, Bulgaria.
Samarkand	Now Samarqand, Uzbekistan.
Saribaba	Still Saribaba, Askale district, Erzurum province, Turkey; population in 1990: 121.
Serbia	Also Servia; a European kingdom in the north-western part of the Balkan peninsula; it gained its independence from the Ottoman Empire in 1878; the borders of Serbia changed quite considerably during the time of Avetaranian's story.
Sert	Now Siirt, Turkey.
Sevlievo	Also Selvi; still Sevlievo, Bulgaria.
Shabchi	Possibly Daheci, China.
Shanghai	Still Shanghai, China.
Shemakha	Now Šamaxi, Azerbaijan; the site of an evangelical work amongst the Armenians started back in the 1840s and still in existence when Avetaranian was there in the 1880s.
Shumla	Now Shumen, Bulgaria.
Shusha	Also Shoosha; now Šuša, in the disputed territory between Armenia and Azerbaijan.
Siberia	At that time a Russian possession in Asia which formed the northern third of that continent and one of the regions used by the Russian government as a place of exile for convicts; the region extended from the Ural Mountains to the Pacific Ocean and from the coast of the Arctic Ocean to about 50 degrees north latitude.
Sistova	Now Svishtov, Bulgaria.
Smyrna	Now Izmir, Turkey.
Sofia	Still Sofia, Bulgaria.
Sofininki	An unidentified Kirghiz village located somewhere between the Terek Davan and Osh in what is present-day Kyrgyzstan.
Somovit	Still Somovit, Bulgaria.
St Petersburg	Now back to being called St Petersburg, Russia after being called

	Leningrad for seventy years.
Stambul	Also Stamboul; the old section of Istanbul; that part of Constantinople which lies on the European side of the Bosporus.
Stara Zagora	Older maps show it as Eski-Sagra; still Stara Zagora, Bulgaria.
Stettin	Now Szczecin, Poland.
Stockholm	Still Stockholm, Sweden.
Südfriedhof	The cemetery in Wiesbaden where Avetaranian is buried; it is also where Manfred von Richthofen, *aka* the Red Baron, is buried.
Sung-Qaraghol	Also Sogun-karaol; possibly Ayaqsugun, China; in eastern Turki: *karaol* or *qarawal* = *observation post* or *watch-house*.
Sweden	Still Sweden.
Syr River	Also Syr-daria or Syr Darya; in eastern Turki: *darya = river*; it runs from the eastern Fergana Valley to the north-eastern shore of the Aral Sea; formerly the Jaxartes River of the ancient Greeks and the Sayhun River of the Arabs.
Syria	A term used by American missionaries to denote the region of the Ottoman Empire which comprised a narrow strip of land, 500 miles long by 93 wide (805 by 150 kilometres), lying between Asia Minor, Egypt, the Mediterranean, and the Arabian Desert, an area that today is made up of Syria, Jordan, Israel, and Lebanon, as well as the West Bank, the Gaza Strip, and a substantial portion of south-eastern Turkey; by the nineteenth century Syria under the Ottomans was divided into three administrative districts which after 1864 consisted of three *vilayets* (Aleppo, Damascus, and Beirut); the province of Jerusalem; and the *mutasarrifiya* of Mount Lebanon.
Tabriz	Still Tabriz, Iran.
Takla Makan Desert	Still the Takla Makan Desert or Taklimakan Shamo (Chinese); the great desert of Central Asia which occupies the central part of the Tarim Basin; in eastern Turki *takla makan* means, "go in and you won't come out" (see Hopkirk's *Foreign Devils on the Silk Road*, p. 12).
Tarim Basin	Still the Tarim Basin or Tarim Pendi (Chinese); the great basin which falls between the Tien Shan and Kunlun mountain systems in western China.
Tarim Desert	A small portion of the Takla Makan Desert, which is situated west of the Yarkand River.
Tarim River	Also Tarim-daria or Tarim Darya; in eastern Turki: *darya = river*; still the Tarim River or He; in Chinese, *he = river*; it runs the whole length of the Takla Makan Desert along the northern edge of the Tarim Basin in western China.
Tarsus	Also Tersoos; still Tarsus, Turkey.
Tashkent	Also Tashkend; now Toshkent or Tashkent, Uzbekistan.
Tatar Bazardjik	Now Pazardzhik, Bulgaria.
Taz-Kharab	An unidentified place of pilgrimage; according to Avetaranian it was renown for its springs; possibly Orta Kharab, Iraq.
Tchataldcha	Now Çatalca, Turkey.
Teheran	Now Tehran, Iran.
Terek Davan	Literally, 'Poplar Pass', which, at 13,000 feet (3,962 metres) above sea level, lay on a direct route from Osh to Kashgar over the western Tien Shan Mountains; in eastern Turki: *davan = mountain pass*.
Terim	Also Terem; now Terembazar, China.
Thrace	The ancient and modern region of the south-eastern Balkans; modern Thrace is bounded by the Néstos River to the west, the Rhodope Mountains to the north, and the Maritsa River to the east and corresponds to the southern part of Bulgaria, the Greek province of Thrace, and European Turkey, including the Gallipoli Peninsula.

Tiflis	Now Tbilisi, Georgia.
Tirnova	Now Veliko Turnovo, Bulgaria.
Trebizond	Now Trabzon, Turkey.
Tripoli	Also Tripolitania; a region in North Africa which now makes up the northwest part of Libya; it was acquired by the Italians from Turkey in 1912 after the Italo-Turkish War.
Tuman River	Still the Tuman River or He; in Chinese: *he = river*; modern-day Kashgar is situated on its southern bank.
Turkey	The Turkish or Ottoman Empire which at its height included most of south-eastern Europe to the gates of Vienna, including modern Hungary, Serbia, Bosnia, Romania, Greece, and Ukraine; Iraq, Syria, Israel, and Egypt; North Africa as far west as Algeria; and most of the Arabian Peninsula; but in Avetaranian's day the Ottoman Empire had lost control of considerable territory in Europe and the Balkans, Caucasia, and North Africa.
Tyan Shan Mountains	Also Tian-shan; now the Tien Shan Mountains; in Chinese, *tien shan = celestial mountains*; this mountain range stretches for 1,550 miles (2,500 kilometres) and is bounded to the north by the Dzungarian and southern Kazakstan plains and to the south-east by the Tarim Basin.
Ulugchat	Now Ulugqat, China.
Urfa	Now Sanliurfa, Turkey.
Urumiah	Also Oroomiah; now Orumiyeh, Iran.
Uskup	Now Skopje, FYRO Macedonia.
Usun-ada	Also Uzun Ada; now Uzun-Ada, Ostrov, Turkmenistan.
Van	Still Van, Turkey.
Varna	Still Varna, Bulgaria.
Vienna	Still Vienna, Austria.
Vrtsel	Possibly Voditsa, Bulgaria.
West Turkestan	Also Russian Turkestan; a region that extended from the Caspian Sea to the border of China and from Siberia to Persia and Afghanistan and comprised modern-day Turkmenistan, Uzbekistan, Kyrgyzstan, Tajikistan, and sometimes Kazakhstan.
Widdin	Now Vidin, Bulgaria.
Wiesbaden	Still Wiesbaden, Germany.
Yangi-hissar	Also Yanghi-hissar; now Yengisar, China; according to Bayard, a *yangi-hissar* is just a town provided with a *yangi shahar* or 'cantonment' (see *Central Asia*, p. 236).
Yangi-shahr	Also Yanghi-shahr; the Chinese quarter of Kashgar; now Shule, China; in his *My Life as an Explorer* (p. 100) Sven Hedin described the place as a walled city about 7 miles (11 kilometres) from Kashgar; in eastern Turki: *yangi shahar = new town* (*yangi = new*; *shahar = town*); it denoted a cantonment which housed Chinese troops and would be situated about 4 to 5 miles (6.5 to 8 kilometres) outside of a city—a practice that went back to Marco Polo's time (see Bayard's *Central Asia*, p. 236).
Yarkand (city of)	Now Shache, China.
Yarkand River	Also Yarkand-daria or Yarkand Darya; in eastern Turki: *darya = river*; now the Yarkant River or He; in Chinese: *he = river*; it rises in the Karakoram Pass in the Karakoram Range in Kashmir and flows into the Tarim River.
Zakhu	Still Zakhu, Iraq.

Geographic Resources Consulted:

AA Road Atlas Europe © 2000

Armenia and Azerbaijan, © ITMB Publishing Ltd. 2000
Bulgaria © Cartographia 1998
Central Asia © GiziMap 1999
China © Karto+Grafik
Countless other web sites
Eastern Turkey © EuroMap 1990
Encyclopedia Britannica, Britannica 2001Delux Edition CD-ROM © 2001
Global Gazetteer: Worldwide Directory of Cities and Towns. Presentation Copyright © 1998-2000. by Falling Rain Genomics, Inc
Iraq © Gita Shenassi
Map of the Tarim Basin from Huntington's The Pulse of Asia © 1907
Maps of Russian and Chinese Turkestan from Hedin's *Through Asia*, Volumes I and II © 1899
Microsoft Encarta World Atlas © 2001
Middle East © Map Link 1998
Rand, McNally & Co.'s Atlas of the World: Turkey in Europe © 1887
Rand, McNally & Co.'s Atlas of the World: Turkey in Asia © 1887
The Century Atlas: Turkey in Europe © 1897 and 1902
The Century Atlas: Turkey in Asia © 1897
The Century Atlas: Asia © 1897
The Catholic Encyclopaedia © 1909 by Robert Appleton Company
The Catholic Encyclopaedia, Online Edition Copyright © 1999 by Kevin Knight
Turkey © Kartographie

Appendix B
Glossary of Who's Who and What's What

(European, American, and Armenian names are listed surname first; Oriental names are in the order given)

Abdul Hagk, Sheikh	A priest from Bagdad and a member of the Holy Islamic League; he was responsible for writing an inflammatory article in 1903 declaring Islam's stand against Europe and its Christianity.
Abdul Hamid II, the Sultan (1842-1918)	Also Abdülhamid II; the sultan of the Ottoman Empire from 1876 to 1909 when he was eventually deposed by the Young Turks after a brief return to power following the Turkish Revolution.
Abdul-Fazl	A tea merchant in Samarkand who was an exponent of the Babi teaching.
Abel	In Arabic: *Habil*; according to the Bible, the second son of Adam and Eve who was murdered by his brother Cain; he is also referred to in the Qur'an.
Abraham	In Arabic: *Ibrahim*; according to the Bible, the father of Ishmael and Isaac (the father of Jacob or Israel as he was later called); he is mentioned frequently in the Qur'an.
Abrahamian	Avetaranian's first choice for a new name; in Armenian it means, 'son of Abraham'.
Acts of the Apostles	The fifth book of the New Testament relating to God's work through the apostles and the first church.
Adam (the first man)	In Arabic: *Adam*; the first man, according to the biblical creation story; he is also referred to in the Qur'an and considered by Islam to be one of the six great prophets.
Adana Massacre, the	The second series of large-scale massacres of Armenians in the Ottoman Empire which occurred in April 1909; these massacres primarily took place in the prosperous province of Adana, the most severe disturbances taking place in the city of Adana; although the reactionary elements of the Ottoman Empire were suspected of instigating the massacres, the Young Turks were also implicated.
Adhem Ruhi	The editor-in-chief of the *Balkan* newspaper in Bulgaria.
ael aelae ael haqqa	Unidentified language: 'hand in hand and hand to God'; the belief that the people needed the spiritual leadership of the *saiyids* to reach God.
aerkan	According to Avetaranian, one name for the ceremonial stick used as part of the Yologhli worship service.
Agha, Hohannes	An Armenian evangelical believer and teacher in Erzerum; he was later based in Bitlis and became a member of the city council there.
Agha, Malo	The Armenian with whom Avetaranian stayed in Chevermeh while studying Armenian; an early leader of the Protestant Armenian church in Chevermeh.
Ahmed Aga	A Muslim who became a Christian and escaped to Bulgaria after being persecuted in Turkey.
Akhmed Keshaf, Sheikh	The sheikh of the foremost order of Rufai dervishes in Macedonia who became a Christian through reading the Scriptures; originally from Pashmakly, he later joined with Avetaranian in Philippopolis; he died of tuberculosis in Potsdam in 1912.
aksaqal	Also *aksakal*; eastern Turki: 'white beard'; a leader, chief, or elder.
alei	'Ten thousand'; possibly Ottoman Turkish or derived from the Arabic; in

	Arabic: *alf* = *thousand*, *alef* = *thousands*, and *ashera alef* = *ten thousand*.
Alei-Muftisi-Fakhred-din	An army priest in Adrianople and an avid defender of the Young Turk's pan-Islamic ideal.
algan	Eastern Turki: 'taken' (past indefinite).
algen	Uzbek Turkish: 'taken' (past indefinite).
Ali (Muhammad's cousin) (AD 600-661)	Also 'Ali; cousin and son-in-law of Muhammad; the fourth caliph, he was murdered in AD 661.
Ali Beg	A friend of Avetaranian's father whose son Avetaranian taught.
Ali Ziya Efendi, His Excellency	The mufti from Rakhova who wrote articles in the *Balkan* attempting to defend Islam against Avetaranian.
Allah	Arabic: 'God'; the standard Arabic word for God used by Arab Christians (of the Assyrian Church) as well as Muslims.
Allah karim dir.	Arabic: 'God is gracious'.
amban	Chinese (Manchu): minister, official; a local Chinese governor or senior official; Avetaranian spelled this word *ambal*.
American Bible House (in Constantinople)	The central point of the evangelical work in Constantinople for the American Board of Commissioners for Foreign Missions; this building was situated in Stamboul and was a place from where Bibles in many different languages were distributed and sold and two religious papers, a weekly and a monthly, were issued.
American missionaries in Erzerum	Missionaries with the American Board of Commissioners for Foreign Missions which first sent missionaries to Turkey in 1836; the work in Erzerum amongst the Armenians was started in 1840 by William C. Jackson and his wife; see Appendix G for a list of all the missionaries based in Erzerum at the time when Avetaranian was introduced to them.
Amirkhaniantz, (Pastor/Reverend) Abraham (1838-1913)	Avetaranian's co-worker and close friend in Tiflis and Varna; a great linguist who translated the Bible into several Near Eastern languages (e.g., into the Turki of the Tartar Turks and into Ararat Armenian) and a missionary to the Muslims; he was the son of Mirza Farruch; see *Mizan ul-Haqq*.
Amirkhaniantz, Mrs	Abraham Amirkhaniantz's wife.
amulet	In Arabic: *hamah'il* = *anything suspended*; a talisman or charm.
Andidjani	Uzbek; a member of a Central Asian people found mainly in Uzbekistan, but also in other parts of Central Asia and Afghanistan; this also denoted someone or something from West Turkestan (see Hedin's *Through Asia*, p. 846).
Andidjani Turkish	See Uzbek Turkish.
Andrae-Roman, Mr	A man Avetaranian met in Stettin while on a lecture tour; he introduced Avetaranian to his future father-in-law, Mr von Osterroht.
Andreas, Professor/Doctor (Friedrich Karl) (1846-1930)	The orientalist and linguist who helped Avetaranian proofread his Kashgari translation of the Gospels; he was appointed to the "Chair of Western Asian Languages" at the University of Göttingen in 1903.
Antichrist	In a Christian context *antichrist* refers to anyone moving in Christian circles who denies or opposes Christ; it also refers to a specific person, of whom it is prophesied in the Old and New Testaments, who will appear before the second coming of Christ and will seek to deceive the world. In the Islamic traditions he is called *Al-Masihu 'D-Dajjal* (Arabic: 'the Lying Christ').
Anwár-i-Suhaylí	Also *Anvar-e Soheyli: The Lights of Canopus*; composed by Husayn Wá'iz-i-Káshifi (also Hoseyn Wa'ez-i-Kashefi) of Herat (he died in 1505); this is an elaborate prose paraphrase of *Kalila wa-Dimna*.
Apostles, the twelve	Twelve men whom Jesus chose from amongst his disciples; see Matthew 10:2-4, Mark 3:16-19, and Luke 6:13-16.
apostle	From the Greek: αποστολος: *apostolos* = *person sent*; this could be any one of the twelve whom Jesus chose, or other disciples, like Paul, who

	came along later but who likewise was sent out to minister the Word of God in a similar fashion; the concept of an apostle is also found in Islamic teaching; in Arabic: *rasul* = *apostle* or *messenger* and is applied to Muhammad, in particular in the Kalimah, whereas the Qur'an refers to the apostles of Jesus as *hawari*, which is either derived from *hawar*, 'to be white' or *hawryra*, 'to go' or 'to be sent'.
Aqtaghliq	Eastern Turki: 'People of the White Mountain'; one of two powerful factions of Kashgari Khojas.
Arabshah	A mullah in Kashgar whom Högberg used to check Avetaranian's translation of the Gospels; the mullah declared it to be a good translation.
Arakelian, Hagop	One of Avetaranian's Armenian pupils from Khoi who stayed with Avetaranian and his wife in Philippopolis.
Arakelian, Sahak	One of Avetaranian's Armenian pupils from Khoi who stayed with Avetaranian and his wife in Philippopolis; he later got married and moved to Sofia.
Ararat Armenian	Also Eastern Armenian; one of the two main dialects of the modern Armenian language; it was spoken primarily in Transcaucasia.
Armenian Deportations of 1915 and 1916, the	The last and worst single massacre of Armenians which took place during World War I; in response to the threat that Russia would try to organise the Turkish Armenians against the Ottoman Empire during World War I, the Turkish government ordered the deportation of about 1,750,000 Armenians to Syria and Mesopotamia; in the course of this forced exodus about 600,000 Armenians died of starvation or were killed by Turkish soldiers and police while en route in the desert.
Armenian evangelical	See Protestant, Armenian
Armenian National Church	A state church established around AD 300 when, according to tradition, the whole kingdom of Armenia became Christian; this came about when St Gregory the Illuminator converted the Arsacid king, Tiridates III to Christianity.
Armenian-Lutheran Church (in Shemakha)	The church formed out of the evangelical work of Sarkis Hampartzumian after it had been expelled from the Armenian Orthodox Church on Pentecost, 1861 and was then severely persecuted. In 1866 it received permission to go over to the established evangelical Lutheran Church on condition that it gave up all its connections with the Basel Mission.
Arshak	Avetaranian's childhood friend; the one who first gave him the name, *John*.
Arushanian, Hagop	The blacksmith who lived with Sarkis Assadur in Tiflis; he also came out to China as a Bible distributor with Mr Morrison while Avetaranian was in Kashgar.
Aslan Caravansary	The caravansary where Avetaranian stayed when he first came to Tiflis.
Assad Pasha, Wali (or Vali)	The pasha of Erzerum from about 1831 to January 1838; Avetaranian's maternal grandfather served him as his Keeper of the Seal; *wali* in Arabic or *vali* in Ottoman Turkish is a governor of a province.
Assadur, Bses	Sarkis Assadur's father.
Assadur, Sarkis	The Armenian Bible distributor with whom Avetaranian stayed in Tiflis after leaving the Aslan Caravansary.
atropine	A poisonous crystalline substance used chiefly in ophthalmology.
Avetaranian, Helene	John Avetaranian's wife; see also von Osterroht, Miss Helene.
Avetaranian, John (1861-1919)	Muhammed Shükri Efendi's adopted Armenian name; in German: *Johannes Awetaranian*; the actual Armenian for *John* could have been rendered *Hohannes*, *Hovaness*, or *Hovhannes*.
azan	Also *adhan*; Arabic: 'announcement'; the Muslim's call to Friday public worship and to the five daily hours of prayer.
Azerbaijani-Turkish	A Turkish dialect now known as Azeri and spoken by people living in the Republic of Azerbaijan and in the region of Azerbaijan in north-western Iran.

Azizi	That is, Azizi-Al Muhhamed Nasifi, a fourteenth-century Persian mystical writer.
Bab, the	The name given to Mirza Ali Mohammad, a merchant's son whose claim to be the *Bab* ('gateway') to the hidden *imam* gave rise to the Babi religion.
Babites	Also Bahis; members of a Muslim sect who profess a privileged access to final truth via one person who is called the *Bab* or 'gateway'.
Bädeker, Doctor Friederich Wilhelm (1823-1906)	An itinerant German evangelist who travelled in Russia and Eastern Europe; he was noted for reaching out with the Scriptures to Russian prisoners and those exiled to Siberia and southern Russia.
Bagdasariantz, Sembad	An Armenian preacher and evangelical brother in Tiflis.
Baha' Ullah	Arabic: 'Light of God' or 'Glory of God'; the name given to Mirza Husain Ali, founder of the Babi religion.
bakhshi	Eastern Turki; one who exorcises spirits (see Hedin's *Through Asia*, p. 472).
balaban	Possibly Ottoman Turkish: 'trumpet'.
balabanyi	Possibly Ottoman Turkish: 'trumpeter'; like a town crier.
Balkan	A Muslim newspaper produced in Bulgaria.
Balkan Express Train	In German: *Balkanzug*; the express train that ran from Berlin to Constantinople and back; it arrived in Constantinople for the first time on 17 January 1916.
Balkan League, the	The short-lived alliance of Serbia, Bulgaria, Greece, and Montenegro which was formed against the Ottoman Empire; the league was formed to take Macedonia away from Turkey but fell apart over the question of dividing Macedonia.
Balkan War, the first (1912)	The war between the Balkan League and the Ottoman Empire over control of Macedonia.
Balkan War, the second (1913)	The war that came about when Serbia and Greece quarrelled with Bulgaria over the division of Macedonia after the first Balkan War; Bulgaria attacked Serbian and Greek forces in Macedonia but was defeated; Romania then invaded Bulgaria from the north, and Turkey reoccupied Thrace from the south; a peace treaty was signed on 10 August 1913 with Bulgaria gaining little additional territory from the two Balkan wars.
bashi-bazouks	Turkish: 'corrupted head' or 'leaderless'; Turkish mercenary soldiers belonging to the skirmishing or irregular troops of the Ottoman Empire; they were notorious for their indiscipline, plundering, and brutality.
Bayaziden Bestam	Also Abu Yazid al-Bistami; a Persian Muslim mystic who spoke of the mystic's ascension to heaven; he died in AD 874.
Beckström, Miss	One of the Swedish Bible-women working in Tiflis.
beg	Also *bey* or *bai*; eastern Turki: 'chief'; also Turkish: the title of a local Turkish chief or prince.
Behjet Khanum	Avetaranian's stepmother's sister-in-law; the sister of Khadijé's second husband, Sheikh Raejaeb Baba; it was at her home that Avetaranian first came across a copy of the Gospels in Turkish.
Beklund, Missionary	A Swedish missionary in Kashgar.
berat	Turkish: 'testament letter' or 'official order'.
Bey, Daniel	The Armenian Christian brother and lay-preacher who befriended Avetaranian in Erivan; a childhood friend of Abraham Amirkhaniantz.
Beyan-ul-Hakk	Arabic: *Expression of Truth*; a liberal Islamic weekly religious newspaper in Constantinople.
Bible distributor	This translator's rendering of 'colporteur'; someone employed by a religious or Bible society to sell and distribute Bibles and other religious tracts.
Bible, the	The Christian scriptures, which comprises the thirty-nine books of the

	Jewish inspired writings (the Old Testament) and the twenty-seven books of the Christian inspired writings (the New Testament).
Bible-woman	A woman missionary who would distribute and teach the Bible to women, often in circumstances where it would have been improper for a man to do so; this practice first began in 1858 amongst the poor in London, England.
black stone, the	In Arabic: *al-Hajaru 'l-Aswad*; the stone located in the eastern corner of the Kaaba; it is believed by Muslims to be able to take away the sin of those pilgrims who kiss and touch it.
Blumhard, General	A Finnish general living in Tiflis who testified to Avetaranian's character before the justice of the peace.
(Huis ten) Bosch	Dutch: 'House in the Wood'; the royal country residence in Holland situated on the northeast side of The Hague.
brazhnik	Actually *prazdnik*; Cyrillic: *праздник*; Russian: 'holiday' or 'festival'.
British and Foreign Bible Society	The first full Bible Society founded on 7 March 1804; the society was responsible for commissioning Avetaranian's Kashgari New Testament and may have been responsible for printing and distributing the Gospel that Avetaranian found at Behjet Khanum's home.
Buhaira	A Nestorian monk whom Mohammed met when he was twelve years old on a mercantile journey to Syria with his paternal uncle, Abu Talib; this monk is purported to have recognised the first signs of Mohammed's prophetic calling, advising Abu Talib: "Return to your home with this youth and guard him from the Jews; for great dignity awaits your nephew."
Bulgarian Orthodox	A member of the Bulgarian Orthodox Church; this Church was first established in the tenth century AD as the national Church of the Bulgarian people connected with the Eastern Orthodox communion; it ceased to exist after 1393 with the invasion of the Turks but was re-established as an exarchate in 1870.
Bunyan, John (1628-1688)	The celebrated English minister and preacher and author of *Pilgrim's Progress*.
Cain	In Arabic: *Qabil*; the eldest son of Adam and Eve according to the Bible; he is also referred to in the Qur'an.
caliph	Also *khalifah*; from *khalf*, Arabic: 'to leave behind'; the title given to the successor to Muhammad; the religious and secular head of Islam.
Capitulations, the	The exemption from criminal prosecution in Ottoman Turkey of foreigners and those Ottoman citizens protected by foreign consuls.
caravansary	Also caravanserai; a public building found along Asian caravan routes and used for sheltering the members and animals of a caravan as well as other travellers.
Central Powers, the	The World War I coalition of the German Empire and Austria-Hungary, with the Ottoman Empire joining on 29 October 1914 and Bulgaria on 14 October 1915.
Chambers, Mr	Either Robert or William N. (brothers); probably William N.; an American missionary in Erzerum who helped Avetaranian; William was later stationed in Adana and was there during the Armenian massacres in 1909.
Chartak	An unidentified Persian literary work, which had been translated into Kashgari.
Chitjian, Garekin	A student at Euphrates College in Kharput who taught Armenian to Avetaranian during his second stay in Chevermeh; a close friend to Avetaranian.
Chokti Rashid	One of two Buddhist kings of the country of Khotan in the Tarim Basin around the tenth or eleventh century AD; Huntington has Nuktereshid-Chuktereshid as one person (see *The Pulse of Asia*, p. 165).
Chragadin, Doctor	The English physician from India who was in Kashgar and was consulted

	concerning Avetaranian's broken leg.
Christendom	A term no longer in use which once indicated the part of the world in which Christianity prevailed.
"*Chto takoe?*"	Cyrillic: "что такое?"; Russian: "What is this?".
colporteur	Bible distributor; someone employed by a religious or Bible society to sell and distribute Bibles and other religious tracts.
Commands of the Saints, The	One of the writings of the Yologhli.
Corinthians, The Second Letter of Paul to the	The second of two epistles in the New Testament, which Paul addressed to the Christians in the city of Corinth.
Cornelius	The first Gentile convert to Christianity; see the Bible, Acts of the Apostles 10.
daedae	Also *dada*; Turkish: 'grandfather' or 'elder'; a title given to the heads of some dervish communities.
daotai	Also *taotai*; Chinese; a Chinese procurator or circuit commissioner; according to Hedin, *daotai = the man who shows the right way* (see *Through Asia*, p. 233); for the Daotai of Kashgar, see Li Tsung-pin.
Darugham	The family with whom Avetaranian stayed while he was in Shabchi.
"*Davai den'gi!*"	Cyrillic: "давай деньги!"; Russian: "Give me my money!"; *davai* = give (imperative form); *den'gi* = money.
David	In Arabic: *Dawud*; the second king of Israel after Saul; Muslims regard him as a prophet.
dervish	Persian; in Arabic: *darwish* or *faqir*: literally, 'one who goes from door to door'; a religious mendicant; any member of a Sufi fraternity.
Devil, the	A generic term for Satan.
Dolang	Also *Dolans*: 'People of the Forest'; a Turkic people living in the Tarim Basin along the Yarkand River; according to Hedin, in eastern Turki *dolan = a wild wooded tract* (see *Through Asia*, p. 440).
Dozy, Professor Reinhart Pieter Anne (1820-1883)	A Dutch arabist and professor at the University of Leiden who published several books on Islamic history including *Het Islamisme* (*History of Islam*, 1863).
Dr Lepsius' Orient-Mission in Potsdam	The missionary society which Johannes Lepsius registered in 1919 after leaving his previous society (the German or Deutsche Orient-Mission) in 1917; he left on account of the board of the German Orient-Mission disagreeing with him over his handling of the German government's complicity in the Armenian massacres of 1915 and 1916; Avetaranian joined Lepsius at this new mission in July 1918.
dragoman	Arabic; an official interpreter in countries where Arabic, Turkish, and Persian are spoken.
Durra i Munajia i Massihia	Arabic: *Pearls of Christian Salvation*; a small Christian work written by an unknown Muslim author; according to Avetaranian, the book's aim was to bring salvation in Christ closer to Muslims.
Egyptians	The people in the Bible responsible for enslaving the children of Israel; the land of Egypt is also referred to several times in the Qur'an.
Ekman, Doctor A. J.	The chairman of the Swedish Missionary Society when Avetaranian was one of their missionaries in the 1890s.
Elijah	In Arabic: *Ilyas*; a prophet in the Old Testament of the Bible; he is also mentioned several times in the Qur'an.
Emir Shir Ali Nava'i (1441-1501)	A Turkish poet of the fifteenth century who wrote in Persian and especially in the eastern Turkic dialect of Chagatai.
Emrah Khojah	A fellow novice with Avetaranian's father.
Engvall, Missionary	A Swedish missionary whom Avetaranian met in London.
Epistles	The books in the New Testament, which consist of open letters from Paul, Peter, John, James, Jude and the writer of the letter to the Hebrews; they are addressed to churches and individuals and give advice,

	instruction, admonition, and exhortation.
esrar	A form of prepared cannabis resin.
Euphrates College	The college founded in Kharput by Charles H. Wheeler in 1878; though it was under a separate board of trustees, it was closely affiliated with the American Board of Commissioners for Foreign Missions.
Eve	In Arabic: *Hawwa*; the first woman according to the biblical creation story; she is also referred to in the Qur'an.
exarch	Cyrillic: екзарх; a bishop of the Orthodox Church who is lower in rank than a patriarch and has jurisdiction wider than the metropolitan of a diocese.
Faber, Pastor	A German pastor with whom Avetaranian had a brief association after coming back from Kashgar.
Fatima (AD 605-633)	Also Fatimah; daughter of Muhammad and wife of 'Ali.
Fatma Aga	Ahmed Aga's wife.
fatwa	Arabic; in Islamic law, a formal legal opinion; a religious or judicial sentence pronounced by the *caliph* or by a *mufti* or *qadi*.
Ferdinand, King (1861-1948)	The king of Bulgaria who was elected as prince of Bulgaria on 7 July 1887; he assumed the title of king or *tsar* on 5 October 1908; after the defeat of the Central Powers in World War I, he was obliged to abdicate on 4 October 1918.
Fleischmann, Pastor Paul	A professor at the seminary in Potsdam, which was opened in 1909 by the mission board of the German Orient-Mission.
franc	The currency of France which in regard to exchange was on a 1:1 ratio with the Bulgarian lev by virtue of the Latin Monetary Union between France, Belgium, Switzerland, Italy, and Greece; Bulgaria joined this union in 1867; the franc was worth about US $.0196 in the 1880s, 1890s, and early 1900s.
Fungshang	A Chinese friend of Adam Ignatovich.
Furnadjieff, Pastor	An evangelical Bulgarian pastor in Sofia.
Fushang Daloy	The translator for the Chinese governor of Kashgar.
Gabriel, Angel	In Arabic: *Jibra'il*; the angel of revelation in the Qur'an who is supposed to have been the medium by which Muhammad received his revelation; this angel also appears in the book of Daniel in the Old Testament and the Gospel of Luke in the New Testament; see the Bible, Luke 1:26.
Galatians	A reference to Paul's Letter to the Galatians in the New Testament; in New Testament times, Galatia was a region in central-eastern Turkey on the Black Sea.
Galitzin, Kniaz	A Russian prince who travelled through Kashgar on his way to St Petersburg; he had his leg amputated after breaking it.
Garabed, Master Usta	The Armenian who taught the tailor's craft to Avetaranian and who later introduced Avetaranian to the Armenian Protestants in Erzurum.
Gegham	A teacher at the Gregorian Armenian school in Chevermeh who helped Avetaranian learn Armenian.
Genadieff, Mr	The secretary of King Ferdinand and a brother of a Bulgarian minister.
Genesis, the book of	That is, the 'book of beginnings'; the first book of the Old Testament.
German Orient-Mission	In German: *Deutsche Orient-Mission*; the mission conceived by Dr Johannes Lepsius in 1895, originally under the name of *Deutsche Armenierhilfe*, with the aim of running orphanages for Armenian children who had survived the massacres in Turkey; Avetaranian joined the society in 1900, and it was this society which was responsible for sending him and his wife to Bulgaria.
Ghanizade Ali	Avetaranian's father and Khadijé's third husband.
Ghazar	Avetaranian's fellow student at the mission school in Tabriz; he later became his first choice as co-worker who would accompany him and Höijer to Kashgar; Ghazar only got as far as Baku before turning back.

ghazi	Arabic: *hero* or *warrior*; one who fights in the cause of Islam.
ghrish	Also *kurush* or *qurush*; also known as the *piaster*; formerly a monetary unit of Turkish currency; worth about US $.0435 in the 1880s.
giaour	Turkish; unbeliever, infidel, or non-Muslim.
Gordon, Pastor	According to Avetaranian, a learned Jew who became a Christian.
Gospel	A word derived from the Anglo-Saxon, *god-spell* which means 'good story'; this in turn was a rendering of the Latin *evangelium* or the Greek *euangelion* which means 'good news' or 'good telling'; the Christian testimony of the salvation of God as it is revealed in the life, teachings, death, and resurrection of Jesus, and testified to by his disciples.
Gossner, Johannes Evangelista (1773-1858)	A revivalist preacher, missionary, and writer; he was raised and educated in the Catholic Church and was an effective preacher to whom people from all walks of life responded though he was persecuted by the Jesuits; he went to St Petersburg in 1820 where he met with his greatest success as a preacher; he came over to the evangelical church on 23 July 1826; he was also founder of the Gossner Mission which specialised in sending out missionaries without theological training.
gözji	According to Avetaranian, the ones who stood guard during a Yologhli worship service.
gradonachal'nik	Cyrillic: градоначальник; Russian; governor of a town.
Grand Mufti	See *Sheikh al-Islam*.
Greco-Turkish War, the	The first of two military conflicts between Greece and Turkey, also known as the "Thirty Days' War", this conflict took place in 1897.
Gregorian	A member of the Armenian National Church; this term refers to Gregory the Illuminator (AD 240-332); see Armenian National Church.
Gunesh	Turkish: 'sun'; Avetaranian's weekly newspaper, which started in January 1909.
Häckel, Professor Doctor Ernst Heinrich Philipp August (1834-1919)	A German professor at Jena from 1865 to 1909; he was a zoologist and an ardent evolutionist but also dabbled in other areas which included attacks on what he perceived to be entrenched religious ideas.
Haemrah	Also Hamrah; Avetaranian's dog when he was in Kashgar.
hafiz	Arabic: 'guardian' or 'protector'; the title of one who has committed the whole of the Qur'an to memory.
Hafiz Effendi	A Muslim whom Avetaranian met in Sistova.
Hagar	In Arabic: *Hajar*; according to both Islamic tradition and the Bible she was the slave wife of Abraham and the mother of Ishmael.
Hagia Sophia	*Church of the Holy Wisdom*; originally a Byzantine cathedral built at Constantinople under the direction of Justinian I and completed in AD 537; it was converted into a mosque in 1453 and was finally turned into a museum in 1935.
haji	Also *hajji*; from *hajj*, Arabic: 'to set out'; a Muslim who has performed the *hajj* or pilgrimage to Mecca.
Haji Ali (in Kashgar)	A Muslim in Kashgar.
Haji Ali (in Sofia)	An Arabic gentleman in Sofia who, as a supporter of Kiamil Pasha, had fled from Constantinople to Bulgaria; he wrote to Avetaranian and asked for Avetaranian's publications which he then passed on to his teacher, a famous *ulema*.
Hajji Bektash Wali	The founder of the Bektashi order of dervishes in the mid fourteenth century.
Hampartzumian, Sarkis	Also Sarkis Hambarzumoff; a teacher who established an evangelical work amongst the Armenians in Shemakha from 1842 onwards; this work had its roots in the work of the Basel missionaries which began in the region in the 1820s; the missionaries were forced by the Russian government to leave Caucasia, Zaremba being the last to go in April 1838; Sarkis was still active when Avetaranian started working there in

	1885.
Hansen, Pastor	A German pastor in Tiflis.
hanun Hor yev Vorto yev Hokuin Srpo	Ancient Armenian: "in the name of the Father and of the Son and of the Holy Spirit"; part of the Armenian Orthodox Church liturgy.
Hargrave, Mr A. A.	An American missionary with the Presbyterian Board of American Foreign Missions; he worked in Persia from 1883 to 1887 and accompanied Avetaranian from Alashkerd into Persia.
Hasan (Ali's son) (AD 624-669)	Also al-Hasan; grandson of Muhammad; elder son of 'Ali and Fatimah; the fifth caliph; he was poisoned in AD 669.
Hashim Akhund	Avetaranian's second servant in Kashgar who accompanied him when he went with Hedin to the Takla Makan Desert.
Haskell, Missionary Reverend Doctor Edward B.	An American missionary with the American Board of Commissioners for Foreign Missions in the European part of Turkey; he and his wife first joined the work there in December 1891.
Hedin, Doctor Sven Anders (1865-1952)	A Swedish explorer who led a series of expeditions through Central Asia and Tibet; these expeditions resulted in important archaeological and geographical findings in the area but also opened the door to the "theft" of many ancient artefacts from western China by subsequent explorers.
Hemlandsposten	A Swedish newspaper, which ran an article by Lector Waldenström regarding the academic inquiry into Avetaranian's Kashgari translation.
Hendricks, Father	A Dutch Catholic missionary who came to Kashgar from Russia in 1885 or 1886; he was a favourite of the Europeans who passed through Kashgar; he died in 1906.
Herrick, Reverend (Doctor George F.)	A missionary to Muslims with the American Board of Commissioners for Foreign Missions who worked in Western Turkey for over 50 years starting in 1859.
Herzbüchlein	German: *Little Book of the Heart;* also *The Heart of Man*; a book by Johannes Evangelista Gossner which contains 10 emblematic illustrations and portrays the human heart from many angles and its need for salvation.
hidayat	Also *hidayah*; Arabic: '(divine) guidance'.
History of Islam	In Dutch: *Het Islamisme*; a book by Professor Reinhart Dozy published in 1863, which gave one of the first academic portrayals of Islamic history.
Högberg, Missionary L. E.	The Swedish missionary who, with his wife and young daughter, joined Avetaranian in China in 1894; Högberg was the one who later objected to Avetaranian's Kashgari translation of the New Testament.
Höijer, Missionary Nils Fredrik (1857-1925)	A Swedish missionary and founder of the Swedish Slavic Mission who worked with Avetaranian in Caucasia and travelled out to China with him in 1891.
Höijer, Mrs Anna	Nils Höijer's wife who taught Swedish to Avetaranian when he was in Caucasia.
Holy Islamic League	An unidentified organisation in existence at the beginning of the twentieth century; one of many such groups formed for the defence of Islam.
Holy War	In Arabic: *jihad*; literally, an 'effort' or 'striving'; a religious war with those who are unbelievers in the mission of Muhammad.
host	The communion wafer used in orthodox Christian services to represent the bread of the Lord's Supper.
Hotel Denchov	The venue in Baltchik where Avetaranian and his co-workers held Gospel meetings for the Muslims in 1904.
Husain (Ali's son) (AD 626-680)	Also al-Husain or Husayn; grandson of Muhammad and son of 'Ali and Fatimah; the third caliph; he was slain in AD 680.
Husain Aga	A Muslim who became a Christian and was martyred in prison in the 1880s.

Husain Nasifoff (Nathanael)	A Muslim born in Philippopolis and abandoned by his parents; after being educated, he rose to the post of *muezzin* at his local mosque; through his contact with the two mullahs and Avetaranian he eventually came to believe in Christ and after many trials was baptised in 1914 in the Maritsa River.
ibn	Arabic: 'son'.
Ignatovich, Adam	Also Adam Ignatieff, according to Hedin; Father Hendricks' Polish travelling companion; he died around 1895 or 1896.
Ilaah'naa wa Ilaah'kum waahidun wa nahnu lahu muslimun	A quote from the Qur'an in Arabic using Roman letters, which translated literally states: "(O Muslims, say to the people of the Book:) Our God and your God is one God and it is to Him we bow"; see Surah 29:46.
ilham	Arabic: 'inspiration', 'revelation', or 'vision'.
Ilieff	A Bulgarian Muslim teacher from Ishtib who gave a lecture defending Islam; this lecture then formed the basis of an article in the *Balkan* aimed at refuting Avetaranian's articles.
imam	Arabic: 'one whose leadership or example is to be followed'; a designated political and administrative successor to Muhammad; a religious leader.
Imams, the twelve	According to the Shi'ahs, they are the twelve leaders of their sect whom they call the true imams; the Shi'ahs do not use the title of *caliph*; see Appendix D for a full list.
Immanuel Church	The church in Stockholm, Sweden where Avetaranian was consecrated for missionary service.
Indian Red Crescent	The national humanitarian agency in India that represents the same service as the Red Cross, which was founded in 1863; the use of the name Red Crescent in Muslim countries was insisted upon by the Ottoman Empire in 1906.
Injil	From the Greek: Εὐαγγέλιον: *evangel*; the Qur'anic reference that generally refers to the whole of the New Testament.
Isaiah	An Old Testament prophet and one of the books of the Old Testament; he is not referred to in the Qur'an.
ishan	Arabic: Muslim religious leader.
Ishmael (Hagar's son)	In Arabic: *Isma'il*; the eldest son of Abraham whom he had by his slave wife, Hagar; the progenitor of the Arabian race.
Ishmael Efendi	According to Avetaranian, the son of a famous Turkish writer from Erzerum.
Ishmael Hakki	A famous Muslim preacher from Monastir at the Hagia Sophia; he was also a member of the high counsel in Constantinople.
Islam	Arabic: 'resignation to the will of God'; the word used by Muslims to refer to their religion; this resignation takes the form of five duties or "pillars": bearing witness that there is but one God, reciting the daily prayers, giving the legal alms, observing the Ramazan or month's fast, and making the pilgrimage to Mecca once in a lifetime.
Islam (Baï)	Hedin's servant from Osh who joined him in February 1894 at Margelan and travelled with him for several years in the Tarim Basin and northern Tibet.
Israel	In Arabic: *Isra'il*; a biblical reference to the Jewish nation; the term 'children of Israel' occurs frequently in the Qur'an.
Israel, Pastor	The pastor who married John Avetaranian and Helene von Osterroht.
Javad Sami Bey	A writer for the *Beyan-ul-Hakk* newspaper.
Jeremiah	A prophet in the Old Testament and the author of two of its books.
Jessup, Reverend Henry Harris (1832-1910)	A missionary in Tripoli, Abeih, and Beirut who entered the work in Syria with his wife in 1855; he was originally with the American Board of Commissioners for Foreign Missions and then with the Board of Foreign Missions of the Presbyterian Church when that organisation took over

	the work in Syria from the American Board.
Jesus Christ	In Arabic: *Isa 'l-Masih*; to Christians, the Messiah, the Son of God, and the Word of God who is the full revelation of God to man, and the one through whom God has accomplished salvation for man; to Muslims, one of the six great prophets.
Jevdet Abdullah, Doctor	A Kurd and military medic who was there at the inception of the first organisation of the Young Turks known as the Committee of Union and Progress.
Joachim III, Patriarch	The patriarch of Constantinople from 4 October 1878 to 30 March 1884 and from 26 May 1901 to 13 November 1912; he died in 1912.
John (the apostle)	A disciple of Jesus and one of His twelve apostles; he is responsible for one of the Gospels in the New Testament as well as three epistles and the book of Revelation.
John the Baptist	In Arabic: *Yahya*; the prophet in the New Testament who heralded the coming of Christ; he is also mentioned three times in the Qur'an.
John, Gospel of	One of the four Gospels in the New Testament.
Joseph	Jacob's son; one of the Old Testament Patriarchs; see the Bible, Genesis 37, and Genesis 39 to Genesis 47; an inspired prophet, according to the Qur'an.
Juma	One of the large local mosques in Philippopolis.
Kaaba	Also Ka'bah; Arabic: 'cube'; a small shrine located near the centre of the Great Mosque in Mecca and considered by Muslims everywhere to be the most sacred spot on earth.
kadi	Also *qadi* or *qazi*; Arabic; a minor Muslim magistrate.
kaeshish	Possibly Arabic: 'priest'; probably derived from the Arabic *qas* or *qasis* = *priest*; a Nestorian or Assyrian priest was known as a *kasha*.
kafir	Arabic: literally, 'the coverer', that is, one who covers up the truth; an infidel.
khan	A local chieftain or man of rank in some countries of Central Asia.
Kalilah Damina	Also *Kalila and Dimna*; Arabic: *Kalila wa-Dimna*; a famous collection of classical Indian animal fables (*Pancha-tantra*) translated by the Persian, Ibn al-Muqaffa' (died *c.* AD 756), from Pahlavi (Middle Persian) into Arabic; the Persian version was composed by Nasr Allah ibn Muhammad around AD 1144.
Karlsson, Mrs	A woman who cared for Avetaranian in Sweden when he was sick.
Kashgari	One of the dialects of eastern Turki spoken in the Tarim Basin; these dialects are now known collectively as Uyghur [pronounced "we-gar"].
Kassim Bey	The Kurd in Alashkerd who intended to report Avetaranian's whereabouts to the police.
kavass	Turkish; an interpreter and courier employed in the Middle East for liaising between Europeans and Orientals and conducting negotiations.
Kaya	One of Avetaranian's pupils in Saribaba where Avetaranian was the mullah.
Kaygusuz Abdal	A popular fifteenth-century mystical poet associated with the Bektashi order of dervishes.
Kazandjieff, Pastor	A retired pastor in Philippopolis.
Kean, Reverend Doctor William	The superintendent of the British and Foreign Bible Society for the Russian Empire based in St Petersburg; he took up this post in 1897.
ketgan	Uzbek Turkish: 'gone away' (past indefinite).
ketgen	Eastern Turki: 'gone away' (past indefinite).
Kevorkian, Mrs	Pastor Krekor Kevorkian's wife.
Kevorkian, Pastor Krekor	An Armenian pastor from Turkey who ministered in Shemakha and worked with Avetaranian in Caucasia until he was deported back to Turkey; later on he worked with him in Bulgaria, living in Rustchuk with

	his wife.
Khadijé	Avetaranian's maternal aunt and stepmother.
Khan Khudayar	Also Khodiar; the ruler of the khanate of Kokand from 1845 to 1858, from 1862 to 1863, and from 1865 to 1875 when he died.
kharabati	Arabic: 'wine shop' or 'tavern'; men fleeing the world; mystical term for members of the society of spiritual directors of any religious order (*murshid*).
Khatib Jahid Efendi	The Muslim priest at the Juma, the large local mosque in Philippopolis.
Khayri Bey	One of the members of the military court in Constantinople.
khoja	Also *hoca* or *hojja*; Turkish: 'teacher'.
Khoja Baehav ed-Din	Omar Akund's father.
Khojas, the	A race of princes that supplied East Turkestan with its kings from the sixteenth to the nineteenth century.
Khurshid	Persian: 'sun'; the new name that Avetaranian gave to his weekly newspaper, *Gunesh*.
khutba	Also *khutbah*; Arabic; the sermon or oration delivered in the mosque on Fridays or on the two great festivals.
Kilgour, Reverend Doctor R.	The editorial superintendent of the publication department for the British and Foreign Bible Society in London.
kitaykafsh	Eastern Turki: 'Chinese shoes'; *kafsh* = *shoes*; *kitay* seems to be derived from the same word as *Cathay*, the medieval term for Northern China; *kitaykafsh* was the nickname the locals in Kashgar gave to Father Hendricks.
kopeck	Also *copeck*; Cyrillic: копейка = *kopejka*; Russian currency; one hundred kopecks = one rouble; worth about US $.0079 in the 1880s.
Koran	Also Qur'an; Arabic: 'recitation'; the holy book of Islam.
Krikorian, Professor	A preacher and editor of a Christian newspaper in Constantinople and friend of Avetaranian.
Kurban Bairam	Also *Kurban Bayram*; in Arabic: *'Idu 'l-Azha*: 'Feast of Sacrifice'; the Islamic festival that falls on the tenth and the following three days of the last month of the Islamic year, *Zu 'l-Hijjah*; this festival, according to Islam, commemorates the ransom of Ishmael with a ram.
Kurian, Evangelist Khachadur Agha	The evangelist and manager of the Bible depot in Shumla for the German Orient-Mission.
La ilaha illa 'llah: Mohammed-er-Rasul-Allah	The *Kalimah*; Arabic: the 'word'; the Muslim creed: "there is no god but God: Muhammad is his messenger".
Lamentations of Jeremiah, The	The book in the Old Testament by the prophet Jeremiah who is lamenting the suffering that befell Jerusalem when Nebuchadnezzar captured the city in 586 BC.
Landsmann, Missionary	A learned Jew who became a Christian; a missionary to the Jews who was working with the Swedish Missionary Society.
Last Judgement, the	The judgement of mankind before God at the end of the world; according to Christianity, this will happen at Christ's second coming; in Arabic: *al-Qiyamah* = *the Standing Up*, that is, the Day of Resurrection.
Lazarus	A friend of Jesus and the brother of Mary and Martha; he was raised from the dead by Jesus; see the Bible, John 11. See also Omar Akhund.
Lepsius, Doctor Johannes (1858-1926)	The founder of the Deutscher Hülfsbund Mission and the German Orient-Mission (Deutsche Orient-Mission); he was involved in supporting Christian Armenians in the Near East after the persecutions in Turkey in the 1890s; he also did extensive research into the German government's complicity in the Armenian massacres of 1915 through its embassy in Constantinople; he died in Merano, Italy on 3 February 1926.
Li Tsung-pin, the acting daotai of Kashgar (1833/1834-1898/1899)	The Chinese procurator of Kashgar until he died in late 1898 or early 1899; according to a British Foreign Office report dated 19 February 1894, which recommended him for the position of daotai in Aksu, he was

	a man of 60 and a native of Hupeh; he had taken up the post as acting daotai of Kashgar 2½ years before; the report praises him as a man "with great ability"; Hedin called him Shang and said his jurisdiction covered the cities and environs of Kashgar, Maral-bashi, Yarkand, Khotan, Keriya, and Cherchen (see *Through Asia*, p. 234).
London Balkans Committee	An organisation set up to distribute gifts to the prisoners of war during the first and second Balkan Wars.
Lord's Prayer, the	The example that Jesus gave to his followers to show them how they should pray; see Matthew 6:9-13 and Luke 11:1-4.
Lord's Supper, the	Also Communion; the taking of bread and wine which is an act performed by Christians to remember the death of Jesus.
Luther, Martin (1483-1546)	The German priest and scholar whose questioning of certain practices of the Roman Catholic Church led to the Protestant Reformation.
Lutheran Church, the (in Tiflis)	The Lutheran Church which was established throughout Caucasia amongst the German colonists who migrated, on the invitation of Catherine II, to southern Russia in the latter half of the eighteenth century.
Macartney, Mr George (He became Sir George Macartney in 1913)	The British representative in Kashgar for 28 years; he first came to Kashgar as a Chinese interpreter for Lt. (later Col. Sir) Francis Younghusband in November 1890; Macartney was an important player in what has become known as *The Great Game*, an expression coined by Captain Arthur Conolly to describe the struggle for empire and influence in Central Asia between Russia and Great Britain during the nineteenth century; Macartney left Kashgar for good in 1918 and died in 1945.
Maghrabi	A work printed at the printing shop in Shumla; possibly a work by Muhammad Shirin Maghribi (AD 1350-1407), a Persian poet whose work reflected the influence of Sufi mysticism.
Mahdi, the	The messianic deliverer who is to appear in the last days according to Islamic eschatology; the twelfth Imam who disappeared in AD 878; see Appendix F, Mahdi-al-Hadi.
Mahmud	The Persian man from Khoi who joined Avetaranian's caravan on its way back into Turkey and whose presence thwarted a plan to murder him.
Maksum Akhund	The Kashgari scholar and teacher of Turkish who taught Mirza Abd-ul-Karim Akhund.
Manchu	A person from Manchuria in northern China; Manchuria supplied China with its final dynasty that ruled from 1644 to 1911.
mark, German	German currency; worth about US $.243 in the 1880s.
Mark, Gospel of	One of the four Gospels in the New Testament.
Marsh, Missionary (Reverend George D.)	An American missionary with the American Board of Commissioners for Foreign Missions in Philippopolis; he first came to Bulgaria as a missionary in 1872.
Mary	In Arabic: *Maryam*; Jesus' mother; she is also mentioned in the Qur'an.
Matthäikirche	St Matthew's Church, built in 1846; the church in Berlin where Avetaranian and Helene were married.
Matthew, Gospel of	One of the four Gospels in the New Testament.
Mécheroutiette	A newspaper published in Paris by Sherif Pasha criticising the politics of the Young Turks.
medrese	Turkish; in Arabic: *madrasah* = *school*; a theological seminary and law school in Muslim countries with a curriculum centred on the Qur'an; in addition to theology and law, Arabic grammar and literature, mathematics, logic, and, in some cases, natural science were studied.
Mehmed Kiamil Pasha	Also Mehmed Kâmil Pasha; a Turkish army officer who was Grand Vizier of the Ottoman Empire four times; he was forced to resign for the last time in 1913 as a result of Enver Pasha's coup d'état.
Melchizedek	The king of Salem in the book of Genesis in the Old Testament who was

	both a king and a priest; he came and blessed Abraham and received a tithe offering from him; see Genesis 14:18-20.
Methodists (in Bulgaria)	Members of the Methodist churches in Bulgaria which arose from the missionary activity of the American Methodist Episcopal Church; this work commenced in 1857 but had an erratic existence; by 1906 they had one foreign missionary and sixteen native workers with four hundred and thirty-two members and probationers; they worked primarily in northern Bulgaria.
mihrab	Arabic; a semicircular niche in a mosque reserved for the imam from where he leads the prayer.
mile	A Swedish mile = 6.2 English miles or 10 kilometres; a German mile = 3 English miles or 4.8 kilometres; an English mile = 1.609 kilometres.
mimbar	Also *minbar*; Arabic; the pulpit in a mosque from where the *khutba* ('sermon') is recited; this pulpit consists of a set of steps.
minaret	In Arabic: *manarah = beacon*; in Islamic religious architecture, the tower from which the faithful are called to prayer five times each day by a *muezzin*, or crier.
mirovoi sud'ia	Cyrillic: мировой судья; Russian: 'justice of the peace'.
Mirza Abd-ul-Karim Akhund	Avetaranian's secretary in Kashgar who helped him with his translation of the New Testament.
Mirza Fazel Beg	Petrovsky's secretary from Darvaz.
Mirza Husain Ali (1819/1820-1850)	Also Mirza Ali Mohammad; the founder of the Babi religion.
Mirza Ibrahim	A Christian from amongst the Muslims in Shumla who witnessed Vadia's baptism.
Mirza Mukhtar	A Christian from amongst the Muslims in Shumla who witnessed Vadia's baptism; he was also the mission printer at Shumla.
Mirza Yahyah	Avetaranian's Bible distributor in Shumla.
Mirza Yussuf	Mirza Joseph, according to Hedin; a Persian doctor who converted to Christianity and came with the Swedish missionaries who joined Avetaranian in Kashgar.
Mirza, young (Vadia)	A 16-year-old Persian boy who was sent back with Avetaranian to learn the Gospel when Avetaranian returned to Bulgaria from his Persian trip in 1901; the boy later became a Christian and was baptised.
Mizan ul-Haqq	Arabic: *Balance of Truth*; a nineteenth-century Christian apologetic response to Islam composed in the 1830s by Karl Gottlieb Pfander, a missionary with the Basel Mission in Shusha, with the help of Mirza Farruch.
Mnatsagan	A young Armenian who accompanied Avetaranian and Höijer to Kashgar.
Mohammed (570-632 AD)	Also Muhammad or Mahomet; the founder of the religion of Islam and the Muslim community; considered by Muslims to be the last in a line of prophets, the most eminent being Adam, Noah, Abraham, Moses, and Jesus.
Mohammed Zeki Efendi	The first secretary of the Grand Mufti in Sofia.
Molokans	Also *Malakans*; Cyrillic: молокани = *Molokani*; Russian: 'milk eaters'; a Quaker-like Christian sect which had existed in Russia since the seventeenth century.
Morrison, Mr Michael A.	The agent of the British and Foreign Bible Society for southern Russia until 1895 who was based in Tiflis and Odessa and then transferred to Berlin; he arranged the commissioning of Avetaranian's translation of the Gospels into Kashgari.
Moses	In Arabic: *Musa*; the Old Testament prophet who led the children of Israel out of their Egyptian captivity; author of the first five books of the Old Testament; one of the six great prophets, according to Islam.

Mudafea	Possibly Arabic: *Refutation*; a book written by a pasha, which dealt with a disputation that he had had with an English missionary.
muderis	The title for a teacher of religion in Bosnia.
muezzin	Also *mu'azzin*; Arabic; in Islam this is the caller of the *azan* or 'summons to prayer' which is made on Fridays; he also makes the call to daily prayer five times a day.
mufti	Arabic; a professional jurist who interprets Islamic law.
Muhammed Nesimi Effendi	The professor of Muslim theology of the first order who became a Christian through reading the Scriptures; originally from Pashmakly, he later joined with Avetaranian in Philippopolis; he died in 1917.
Muhammed Shükri Efendi	Avetaranian's given and family name.
mujtahid	Arabic: literally, 'one who strives'; a chief mullah and leading Islamic jurist.
mullah	Also *mollah*; the Persian form of the Arabic, *maulawi*: 'learned man' or 'scholar'; a Muslim teacher or interpreter of the religious law.
Mullah Hassan	A local mosque in Philippopolis.
Mullah Nasreddin	Also Khoja Nasreddin; he is believed to be a legendary figure by some, others insist that he was a real person though the exact details of his actual life have not been proven; it is generally accepted that he was born in a Turkish village in 1208 and died around 1284; he is attributed with hundreds of comical stories that reveal a keen, common-sense insight into social issues and human nature.
Münifé	Avetaranian's mother who died when he was three.
munshi	Also *moonshee*; a secretary or language teacher in the Indian subcontinent.
Munshi Abdurrahman	An Indian man whom Avetaranian got to know in Kashgar; he helped Avetaranian with copying out his translation of the Gospels into Kashgari.
Munshi Ahmed ed-Din	Mr Macartney's Indian secretary.
murid	Arabic: literally, 'one who is desirous or willing'; a novice or disciple of a Muslim order of mystics (Sufi).
Musaddiqan limaa maAAakum	A quote from the Qur'an in Arabic using Roman letters which states that the Koran was sent down in order to affirm the Bible; see Surah 2:41.
Muslim Missions Conference, the (in Cairo)	The full name of this conference was the "First Missionary Conference on behalf of the Mohammedan World"; this conference was held in Cairo, Egypt from the 4 to 9 April 1906 and was intended to bring together all the Christian missionary organisations that were working amongst Muslim peoples, so they each could see what the others were doing and what was going on throughout the Muslim world.
nachal'nik	Cyrillic: начальник; Russian: 'chief', 'director', or 'supervisor'.
namaz	Persian; in Arabic: *salat*; the Muslim liturgical prayer performed five times a day.
nasha	Eastern Turki; in Arabic: *hashish* = *dried herb*; the plant known as *Cannabis sativa* or Indian Hemp; *nasha* is also a Central Asian reference to flat cakes of cannabis resin prepared from hemp; in eastern Turki: *nas* = *snuff*.
Nasif Husseinof	The foster father of Husain Nasifoff.
Nathan	The prophet at the time of David who condemned David for his adultery with Bathsheba and for the murder of her husband, Uriah; see the Bible, 2 Samuel 12.
Nathanael	A disciple of Jesus mentioned in the Gospel of John; see the Bible, John 1:45-51; see also Husain Nasifoff.
nephritis	*Glomerulonephritis*; also known as *Bright's Disease*; inflammation of certain parts of the kidneys.
Nerses	An Armenian from Constantinople who was the mission typesetter at the

	printing shop in Shumla.
Nestorian	Also Assyrian; a member of a Christian sect originating in Asia Minor and Syria out of the condemnation of Nestorius and his teachings by the Councils of Ephesus (AD 431) and Chalcedon (AD 451); in its heyday the Nestorian Church stretched from Arabia through Persia and Central Asia into India and China; the area in which this church was active was then sharply curtailed with the invasions of Tamerlaine in the fourteenth century.
Niaz Akhund	An elderly mullah and former minister of Yakub Beg who helped to critique Avetaranian's Kashgari translation of the New Testament.
Nicodemus	A Pharisee from the time of Jesus who used to visit him in secret; see the Bible, John 3:1-21.
Nirani Sultan	An unidentified mystical writer held in high regard by the Yologhli.
Nükti Dakshid	One of two Buddhist kings of the country of Khotan in the Tarim Basin around the tenth or eleventh century AD; Huntington has Nuktereshid-Chuktereshid as one person (see *The Pulse of Asia*, p. 165).
Nur Hajim	A printer in Kashgar who was trained in India in the art of lithography.
Nuri Bey	The assistant editor of the *Balkan* newspaper.
Nyström, Miss Anna	The Swedish missionary and Bible-woman who worked in Persia and came with other Swedish missionaries in 1894 to join Avetaranian in China.
ogul	Also *oghal*; eastern Turki: 'son'.
Omar Akhund (Lazarus)	Mirza Fazel Beg's cousin who became Avetaranian's first servant in Kashgar; Avetaranian later baptised him in the Tuman River, and he adopted the name Lazarus.
Orient-Express, the	A luxury train and Europe's first transcontinental express that ran from Paris to Constantinople for more than 80 years (1883-1977).
Osmanli	Anything pertaining to the Ottoman Empire, the name is derived from Osman (AD 1258-1324), the founder of the Ottoman Empire.
Osmanli Turkish	The language of the Ottoman Empire and of Turkey until 1923 when it was eventually replaced by modern Turkish.
Osmanlidom	A term coined in this context to describe the theoretical realm of all Ottoman Turks.
pan-Islamism	This concept originated from the claim of the Ottoman Sultan that he had religious jurisdiction over Muslims outside his territories (a claim that went as far back as the Treaty of Küçük Kaynarca with Russia in 1774); this claim was used by Abdul Hamid II as a threat to deter European powers from pressing him too hard, lest he create dissension amongst the Muslims within their own territories.
pasha	Turkish: 'lord'; a title of a man of high rank or office in the Ottoman Empire and North Africa.
patriarch	In the Eastern Orthodox Church, the highest ranking bishop in a city which is designated to have a patriarchal seat, e.g., Constantinople, Jerusalem, Moscow, etc.
Patriarchs, the	The men of the Old Testament: Abraham, Isaac, Jacob, and Jacob's sons.
Paul (the apostle)	An apostle of Jesus and former Pharisee who had persecuted the early Church before becoming a follower of Christ; his ministry was primarily to preach the gospel to the Gentiles (non-Jews).
Peter (the apostle)	A disciple of Jesus and one of his twelve apostles; along with the rest of the twelve, his ministry was primarily to the Jews.
Petko, Daedo	A Bible distributor for Avetaranian in Bulgaria.
Petros	A young Armenian teacher who wrote out for Avetaranian the confession of faith based on the Nicene Creed.
Petrovsky, Nikolai Feodorovitch	The Russian Consul General in Kashgar for over twenty years from 1882; according to Hopkirk, he was the chief Russian authority in the

	region and intimidated both Muslim and Chinese alike while collecting intelligence on behalf of the Russian government (see *The Great Game*, pp. 434-435).
pfennig	A German coin; one hundred pfennig = one mark; it was worth about US $.00243 in the 1880s.
Pharaoh	In Arabic: *Fir'aun*; the ruler of Egypt in the time of Moses who tried to keep the children of Israel from leaving their captivity in Egypt; he is considered by Muslims to be the personification of wickedness.
Pharisees	Members of a Jewish religious party that flourished in Palestine from 515 BC to AD 70; one of the groups that regularly challenged Jesus and against whose practices Jesus spoke out.
piastre	Also *piaster*; also known as the *ghrish* or *kurush* or *qurush*; a former unit of currency in Turkey; worth about US $.0435 in the 1880s.
pilaf	Also *pilau*; Persian; a dish of seasoned boiled rice, mutton, and sliced carrots.
Pilgrim's Progress	A Christian allegory written by John Bunyan, which tells the story of Christian who leaves the City of Destruction to go to the Heavenly City and of what he encounters on the way.
pir	Also *peer*; Persian: 'elder'; the spiritual head of a dervish order.
Polo, Marco (1254-1323/1324)	The famous Venetian adventurer whose book about his travels and time spent in the Orient gave medieval Europe a vivid description of the East.
Pomaks	Bulgarian Muslims who speak a Bulgarian dialect as opposed to Turkish Muslims in Bulgaria.
pound, Turkish	Also *lira*; equal to 100 piastres; worth about US $4.37 in the 1880s.
pristav	Cyrillic: пристав; Russian: 'bailiff' or 'official escort', especially for foreigners; 'inspector'; 'warden'.
Proclamation of Freedom	In Turkish: *Hurriyetin Ilani*; a term very popular during the second period of constitutional monarchy in Turkey which followed the 1908 revolt; the reinstitution of the constitution in Turkey was proclaimed in Monastir on 23 July 1908 and in Constantinople on the 24th; at this time Sultan Hamid II was compelled to instigate such freedoms as religious freedom, freedom of speech, and freedom of the press, that is, doing away with the oppressive censorship of the old regime.
Protestant, Armenian	In Armenian terms, a member of the Armenian evangelical community, which was seeking to reform the Armenian Orthodox Church away from the observance of its established church traditions and back to a simple adherence to the gospel; this movement was first organised in Turkey as its own denomination on 1 July 1846.
Psalms	In Arabic: *Zabur*; the book of sacred songs in the Old Testament; it is referred to three times in the Qur'an.
qalon	Also *ghalin*; a musical instrument which looks like a zither but sounds like a piano; a type of psaltery or small harp.
Qarataghliq	Eastern Turki: 'People of the Black Mountain'; one of two powerful factions of Kashgari Khojas.
qotaz	Also *kutaz*; eastern Turki: 'yak'.
qum yaghar	Eastern Turki: "It is raining sand"; a phrase denoting a sand storm or the fallout after a spate of heavy winds.
Radoslavov, Prime Minister Vasil (1854-1929)	The prime minister of the kingdom of Bulgaria from 1914 to 1918.
Raejaeb Baba, Sheikh	Khadijé's second husband and Behjet Khanum's brother.
rajah	A prince or chief in India.
Ramazan	Also *Ramadan*; the ninth month of the Muslim year; the month of fasting.
Raquette, Missionary (Doctor Gustav)	A Swedish missionary in Kashgar who translated many religious works into eastern Turki and who helped with the later edition of the Kashgari

	New Testament.
raya	Also *rayah* or *rayat*; Turkish: 'subject'; non-Muslims e.g., Christians, Jews, etc.; the Ottoman Turkish law code for the raya basically kept them as second-class citizens.
Redeemed One, the	According to Yologhli tradition, she was the one sent by God who was married to Seth and gave birth to all the prophets and the Yologhli people.
Redeemed People, the	A name that the Yologhli used to indicate themselves and which refers to their origin stemming from the union between Seth and the Redeemed One.
Reichsboten	A German newspaper.
Revelation to John, The	Also the book of Revelation; the final book of the New Testament written by the apostle John, which deals with the end times, the return of Christ, and the final Judgement.
Ritson, Reverend John Holland (1868-1953)	One of two general secretaries of the British and Foreign Bible Society in London; he was appointed to the position in 1900.
Rohrbach, Doctor Paul	A professor at the seminary in Potsdam, which was opened in 1909 by the mission board of the German Orient-Mission.
Romans, The Letter of Paul to the	The sixth book of the New Testament, which was a letter from Paul to the Christians in Rome.
Rosenberg, Doctor	According to Avetaranian, a Jewish doctor from Varna who became a Christian and was baptised at the Methodist Chapel in Shumla in the spring of 1902.
Rosenstein, Pastor	According to Avetaranian, a learned Jew who became a Christian.
rouble	Also *ruble*; Cyrillic: рубль; the basic monetary unit in Russia; worth about US $.796 in the 1880s.
Rousseau, Jean-Jacques (1712-1778)	A French philosopher, writer, and political theorist who inspired the leaders of the French Revolution and the Romantic generation.
Russian Orthodox	A member of the Russian Orthodox Church, the Russian form of the Eastern Orthodox Church, which is ecclesiastically independent; it was established in the tenth century AD.
Russo-Turkish War, the (1877-1878)	The last of a series of wars between Russia and the Ottoman Empire that saw the Ottoman Empire lose control of most of its territory in the Balkans.
Sabil-ur-Rashad	Arabic: 'the right road'; formerly the Islamic weekly religious newspaper, *Siratul-Mustaqim*.
Sadducees	Members of a Jewish priestly sect that flourished for about two centuries before the destruction of the Second Temple of Jerusalem in AD 70; one of the groups that regularly challenged Jesus and against whose practices Jesus spoke out.
saiyid	Also *sayid* or *sayyid*; Arabic; a descendant of Muhammad from his daughter Fatima by Ali.
Saiyid Ahmed (John)	A Muslim who converted to Christianity but who gave Avetaranian a lot of trouble because he continued to practise *taqia*; the name given to him at his baptism was *John*.
Saiyid Hasan	The *pir* of Saribaba where Avetaranian was the mullah; also a close friend to Avetaranian.
Saiyid Ismael	A friend of Avetaranian's father.
Salim Divana	Possibly Jalal al-Din Muhammad ibn As'ad Davvani (AD 1427-1501), a Persian poet and moralist.
Sarkis (Effendi Kasabian)	A young Christian whom Baron Sevortian introduced to Avetaranian and who helped Avetaranian while he was in Erzerum; a teacher at the Protestant High School in Erzerum.
Satan	In Arabic: *Shaitan*; according to Christian tradition, the archangel who rebelled against God; he is also referred to in the Qur'an.

Saul	The apostle Paul's name before he became a Christian and changed it to *Paul*.
Schäfer, General Secretary Richard	The General Secretary of the German Orient-Mission who worked with Johannes Leipsus for 33 years and with Avetaranian for 19 years; he was responsible for completing and publishing the second edition of Avetaranian's autobiography in 1930.
Schlagintweit, Adolf (1829-1857)	One of three German brothers all of whom were well-known explorers in the 1800s; he was put to death on 26 August 1857 in Kashgar by the insurgent chieftain and emir of Kashgar, Vali Khan Tura.
Scriptures, the	Also the Scripture; literally, the 'writings'; an alternative reference for the Bible.
sema	The music and whirling dance performed as part of the Yologhlis' (and other dervish orders') worship service.
Serbo-Turkish War in Montenegro, the	The war of independence involving Serbia and Montenegro against Turkey; it began on 30 June 1876 and ended when an armistice was signed on 31 October 1876; one of the conflicts that Ghanizade Ali was involved in as a soldier.
Sermon on the Mount	The passage of Jesus' teaching in the Gospel of Matthew; see the Bible, Matthew 5-7.
setar	A long-necked lute played with a bow; a type of zither.
Seth	In Arabic: *Shis*; the third son of Adam and Eve according to the Bible; he was classed by Muhammad as an inspired prophet.
seventy-two religious communities, the	According to the traditions, Muhammad is said to have prophesied that his people would be divided into seventy-three sects; every one of these sects would go to Hell except one; in fact the number of sects had certainly exceeded seventy-three by the nineteenth century.
Sevortian, Baron	The Armenian bookseller in Erzerum who sold Avetaranian his Bibles; in Armenian: *Baron = Mr*.
shaengaeng	Also *shen-kan* or *hsien-kuan*; head or district commissioner of the regional Chinese Office of Foreign Affairs (see *Tsung-li Yamen*).
Shahid-ül-Haqaiq	Arabic: *Witness of Truth*; the first Turkish monthly periodical that Avetaranian started publishing in Shumla.
Shahveled, Pastor Hagop	The preacher at the evangelical Armenian Church in Sophia who also worked with Avetaranian.
Shari'ah	Also *Sheriet*; Arabic: literally, 'the path leading to the watering place'; the fundamental religious concept of Islam; the law, including both the teaching of the Qur'an and the traditional sayings of Muhammad.
sheikh	Also *shaikh*; Arabic: 'elder' or 'venerable old man'; a superior of an order of dervishes.
Sheikh al-Islam	The chief *maulawi* or 'learned man' of major Muslim cities, e.g., Constantinople, Cairo, Damascus, etc.
(Mehmed) Sherif Pasha	Also Mehmed Cherif Pasha; the former Turkish ambassador in Stockholm who left Constantinople in 1909 to live in Paris where he published the newspaper, *Mécheroutiette*, in which he criticised the politics of the Young Turks.
Shiites	Also Shi'ahs; Arabic: 'followers'; the smaller of the two major branches of Islam; the faction of Islam that supports the power of 'Ali.
Show (Robert Shaw)	Probably Robert Shaw, an English merchant based in India who headed for Kashgar in 1868 to try to establish trade links with the new country of Kashgaria created by the then conqueror, Yakub Beg.
Shung-chi	Possibly Yung-chi, the Manchurian ruler of the Juchen state of Chin in northern China from AD 1208 to 1213; one of the emperors of the Chin dynasty (AD 1115-1234).
Siratul-Mustaqim	Arabic: 'straight path' or 'right way'; an Islamic weekly religious newspaper.

sledovatel'	Cyrillic: следователь; Russian: 'investigator' or 'examining magistrate'.
Solomon	In Arabic: *Sulaiman*; in the Old Testament he is the third king of Israel; David's son; he is celebrated in the Qur'an for his wisdom.
St Elisabeth's Hospital	In German: *Elisabethkrankenhaus*; founded in 1849 on the Lützowstraße in Berlin; the second oldest hospital in Berlin.
St Nicholas Church	The oldest building in Berlin; the church where the two mullahs, Sheikh Akhmed Keshaf and Muhammed Nesimi Effendi, were baptised by Avetaranian on 10 October 1909.
Steinbrecher, Mr	An agent of the British and Foreign Bible Society in Tiflis in the 1890s.
Stoïleff, General	The local military commander for Sophia during the second Balkan War.
Sublime Porte, the	The government of the Ottoman Empire; this term comes from a French reference to the gate which gave access to the block of buildings in Constantinople where the principal state departments were housed.
Sufi	A Muslim mystic; one who professes the mystic principles of *tasawwuf*, a word used to sum up the doctrines of the Sufis and Muslim mystics.
Suleiman Efendi	Avetaranian's maternal grandfather and the Keeper of the Seal to Wali Assad Pasha.
Sundqvist, Mrs	The woman in Sweden who took Avetaranian in and cared for him when he developed his eye inflammation.
sungaq-chi	Eastern Turki: 'one who works on bones'.
Sunni	Also Sunnite; Arabic: 'one of the path'; an orthodox Muslim; an Islamic traditionist; adherents of the *Sunna*, or 'practices', of the Prophet.
surah	Also *sura*; Arabic: 'row' or 'series'; a chapter of the Qur'an.
suyukash	An eastern Turkestani dish which consists of noodle soup with vegetables and some meat.
Swedish Missionary Society	In Swedish: *Svenska Missionsförbundet*; founded in 1881 by Doctor Paul Waldenström.
tagia	Possibly Persian; the Shiite teaching that it is permitted to deny one's religion in cases of extreme danger.
tajwid	Also *'ilmu 't-tajwid*; Arabic; the science of reading the Qur'an correctly, that is, out loud and with the correct intonation.
tariq	According to Avetaranian, one name for the ceremonial stick used as part of the Yologhli worship service.
Tashjian, Pastor Hagop	An Armenian from Cesarea and a graduate of the Marsovan Seminary which was run by the American Board of Commissioners for Foreign Missions; he was the pastor of the Armenian Protestant Church in Erzerum, a position he first took up on a temporary basis (for one year) in 1876 but which was extended due to the Russo-Turkish War; he received his formal ordination to that post in September 1879.
Ten Commandments	A reference to the laws which Moses received from God on Mount Sinai; see the Bible, Exodus 20:2-18 and Deuteronomy 5:6-21.
tenga	Also *tengeh*; a monetary unit used in Eastern Turkestan; worth about US $.05 in the 1890s.
ter Asaturoff, Markara	Avetaranian's fellow student from Caucasia who was with him at the Swedish mission school in Kristinehamn.
Testament, New	The second part of the Bible containing the Christian scriptures of the Gospels, the Acts of the Apostles, the Epistles, and the book of Revelation; this book is also held in high regard by Muslims and referred to as the *Injil*.
Testament, Old	The first part of the Bible containing the Jewish scriptures in thirty-nine books which depict God's dealings with the Jews prior to Jesus and prophesies the coming of God's Messiah; this book is held in high regard by Muslims.
Theodoroff, Pastor	The preacher at the Bulgarian Methodist Church in Varna.

Thirty-two Disputations of the Artisans, The	A Kashgari work printed at the printing shop in Shumla.
Timothy	One of the Christians who accompanied Paul on his missionary trips and who worked as an evangelist; there are two letters in the New Testament to him from Paul.
Todoroff, Pastor	A Christian who was with Avetaranian during his 1904 trip to Sistova.
Toff, Missionary	According to Avetaranian, a learned Jew who became a Christian.
toman	Persian currency; worth about US $1.68 in 1885.
traditions, Islamic	In Arabic: *Hadis* or *Hadith*; the uninspired record of the inspired sayings of Mohammad which accompany the Qu'ranic teachings.
Trinity	In Christian doctrine this refers to the unity of Father, Son, and Holy Spirit as three persons in one Godhead; Muhammad refers to the concept of the Trinity twice in the Qur'an, though in the context of advising his followers against such a belief.
Tripolitanish War, the (1911-12)	Also the Italo-Turkish War; a war undertaken by Italy to gain colonies in North Africa by conquering the Turkish provinces of Tripolitana and Cyrenaica (modern Libya); Italy eventually forced Turkey to concede its rights over these provinces.
Tsung-li Yamen	Also *Tsungli Yamen* or *Tsung-li-yamen*; Chinese: 'Office for General Management', that is, the Chinese Office of Foreign Affairs; it was created in 1861 to conduct all dealings with foreign nations and foreigners.
Tumayan, Professor	Also Tumajan; the specialist and translator consulted in 1911 for the printing of Avetaranian's Kashgari New Testament.
Turka, sitting *à la*	To kneel down and then sit back on one's heels.
Turkdom	A term coined in this context to describe a theoretical realm of all Turkish people, though primarily pertaining to Osmanli Turks.
Turkish Revolution, the	A revolt lead by the Committee of Union and Progress; the revolt started on 3 July 1908 in Resna and quickly spread throughout the Ottoman Empire; on 23 July Abdul Hamid, the Ottoman sultan, was forced to announce the restoration of the 1876 constitution and recall the Turkish parliament.
Tzakoff, Pastor	The local evangelical Bulgarian pastor in Philippopolis.
ulema	Also *ulama*; Arabic: 'the ones who know'; the learned of Islam; those who possess the quality of *'ilm*, that is, 'learning', in its widest sense.
Urateba Caravansary	The caravansary in Kashgar where Avetaranian stayed.
Uriah	Bathsheba's first husband; see the Bible, 2 Samuel 11.
Utro	Cyrillic: утро; Bulgarian or Russian: 'morning'; a daily newspaper in Sofia.
Uzbek Turkish	One of three Turkish dialects spoken in the part of Central Asia formerly known as West Turkestan.
Vali Khan Tura, King	Also Wali Khan Torah; the insurgent chieftain who in 1857 captured Kashgar and other cities in the area; he was responsible for having Adolf Schlagintweit killed that same year; *wali* in Arabic or *vali* in Ottoman Turkish is a governor of a province.
Van Duzee, Miss Cyrene O.	An American missionary in Erzerum with the American Board of Commissioners for Foreign Missions; she transferred to the Presbyterian Board of American Foreign Missions and worked with them at Urumiah from 1886 onward; she accompanied Avetaranian from Alashkerd into Persia.
vasiyadt	Possibly Turkish: 'name'.
Voice from the Homeland	An Armenian periodical that Garekin Chitjian published while he was in America.
Voltaire (1694-1778)	A French writer of worldwide repute, whose work propagated the ideal of progress.

von Blücher, Miss Henriette	A German supporter of the German Orient-Mission who helped to provide funds for a new printing press for the mission in Philippopolis.
von Oertzen, Pastor Detwig (1876-1950)	The German missionary sent out by the German Orient-Mission to work amongst the Kurds.
von Osterroht, Miss Helene	Avetaranian's wife's maiden name.
von Osterroht, Mr	Avetaranian's father-in-law.
"Vy Evrei!"	Cyrillic: "вы еврей!"; Russian: literally, "You, Jew!"; *vy* = *you* (plural or formal form); *Evrei* = *Hebrew* or *Jew*.
Wa hiya walaahnwa laghaiyrahi	Arabic; this is taken from the Kullabiyya, a teaching that derives its name and origin from Abu 'Abdi'llah ibn Kullab, a ninth-century Islamic theologian (he died in AD 855); ibn Kullab's actual saying went: "I do not say that His attributes (*sifat*) are He (God) (*sifatuhu hiya Huwa*), nor that they are other than He (*wa la hiya ghairuhu*)."
Wa maa unzila min qablika	A quote from the Qur'an in Arabic using Roman letters which according to Avetaranian states that those ones who are led by God believe not only in the Koran but also in the Holy Scriptures; see Surah 2:4.
Waldenström, Doctor Paul Peter (1838-1917)	The director of the Swedish Missionary Society; a Swedish preacher and politician who was one of the main promoters of the Mission Covenant of Sweden.
Warneck, Professor Gustav (1834-1910)	The foremost professor of missions at the University of Halle (1897-1908) and a pioneer of missiology as an academic discipline.
Warns, Johannes (1874-1937)	The son of a Lutheran pastor in Ostfriesland; in 1904-1905 while in Schildesche, near Bielefeld, he experienced the revival that took place in the parish there; in 1905 he became a teacher at the Bible School for Home and Foreign Missions in Berlin and became rector there in 1919; he prepared the illustrations for Avetaranian's Turkish version of Gossner's *Herzbüchlein*; he was also the writer of several books including one on Christian baptism, its history, and importance for today: *Die Taufe. Gedanken über die urchristliche Taufe, ihre Geschichte und ihre Bedeutung für die Gegenwart*.
Whipple, Mr (Reverend W. L.)	A missionary in Urumiah with the Presbyterian Board of American Foreign Missions from 1872 to 1879; after that he was an agent for the American Bible Society in Persia until 1896; he escorted Avetaranian from Urumiah to Tabriz.
Wilson, Mr (Reverend Samuel Graham) (1858-1916)	A missionary in Persia with the Presbyterian Board of American Foreign Missions; in 1882 he was appointed principal of a small school for boys in Tabriz which ten years later became the Memorial Training and Theological School.
World War, the First	Also known as the Great War; an international conflict that from 1914 to 1918 embroiled most of the nations of Europe along with Russia, the United States, the Middle East, and other regions.
Wright, Doctor	The director of the British and Foreign Bible Society in London.
Yakub Beg (1820-1877)	The Muslim adventurer, born in Biskent (now Piskent, Uzbekistan) in the then khanate of Kokand, who took advantage of anti-Chinese sentiment amongst the Muslims in Eastern Turkestan to establish the kingdom of Kashgaria in what is today China's Xinjiang province; he ruled over Kashgaria from 1864 to 1877.
Yamini, book of	Possibly a work by the Persian poet, Ibn Yamin, that is, Amir Fakhr al-Din Mahmud (AD 1286-1368).
yapunja	Possibly Armenian; a Caucasian coat.
yarim-pasha	Eastern Turki: 'half-prince'; the name that the Kashgaris gave to Kniaz Galitzin.
Yoldash	Also Yolldash; one of the dogs which accompanied Hedin; in eastern Turki: *yuldash* = *travelling companion*.
Young Turks	The coalition of various reform groups that led a revolutionary movement against the authoritarian regime of Ottoman sultan Abdul

	Hamid II, which culminated in the establishment of a constitutional government in 1908.
Yussuf Kadrkhan Ghazi	The Arab invader who in the late tenth or early eleventh century AD conquered Kashgar and other cities of the Tarim Basin; Ellsworth cites one local source stating that he was king of Kashgar in 1000 AD (see *The Pulse of Asia*, p. 164).
zaki	According to Avetaranian, the drinking ceremony, which was a part of the Yologhli worship service.
Zamzam	The sacred well within the precincts of the mosque at Mecca; it is supposed to be the identical spring from which Hagar and Ishmael drank in the wilderness; see the Bible, Genesis 21:19.
Zehni	Khadijé's first husband; the city secretary and, according to Avetaranian, a famous Muslim poet.
zikr	Also *dhikr*; Arabic: 'reminding oneself'; the ritual prayer or litany practised by Muslim mystics for the purpose of glorifying God and achieving spiritual perfection.
Zornitsa	*Morning Star*; the weekly and monthly religious newspaper in Bulgarian published in Philippopolis by the American missionaries of the American Board of Commissioners for Foreign Missions; this paper was first issued in 1866 and appeared weekly from 1876 to 1948.
Zwemer, Doctor Samuel Marinus (1867-1952)	A missionary to the Islamic world, especially amongst Arabs, from 1890 onwards; he authored or co-authored at least 48 books in English.

Appendix C
Established Dervish Orders Mentioned by Avetaranian

Bektashi	Also Bakhtashi; an order of dervishes founded by Hajji Bektash Wali in the mid fourteenth century AD.
Kadiri	Also Qadiri; an order of dervishes founded by Abdu 'l-Qadir Jilani in the twelfth century AD.
Nakshibendi	Also Naqshbandi; an order of dervishes founded by Pir Muhammad in the early fourteenth century AD.
Rufai	Also Rüfai; an order of dervishes founded by Saiyid Ahmad Rufai in the late twelfth century AD.
Tarikh-i-Nazaenin	An unidentified order of dervishes.

Appendix D
What the Sunni Call the Yologhli

Kitabsiz	'People without the book'.
Chirasöndüren	'Extinguishers of the light'.
Kizilbash	Also Qizilbash: 'Redheads'—a reference to the red headgear that they wore.
Rafizi	Arabic: literally, a 'forsaker' or 'heretic'.
Distant Turk	That is, barbarian.
Turkmans	Also Turcomans; Turkic people living mainly in what is today Turkmenistan, but also in Iran and Iraq.
Shabak	Possibly a reference to a Kurdish tribe in what is today central Iraq.
Shahsavan	Possibly a reference to a tribe in what is today north-eastern Iran.
Alallahi	Also Ali-Allahis; 'followers of God'.
Tsairakli	Unidentified reference or meaning.
The ones outside the seventy-two religions	According to the traditions, Muhammad is said to have prophesied that his people would be divided into seventy-three sects; every one of these sects would go to Hell except one; in fact the number of sects had certainly exceeded seventy-three by the nineteenth century; this name seems to mean that the Yologhli were even outside of these sects.

Appendix E
What the Yologhli Call Themselves

Yologhli	'Sons of the way'; Avetaranian's sect of dervishes.
Yolushaghi	'Children of the way'.
Erenler	'The brave men'.
Gerchekler	'The truthful ones'.
Uryankhusurli	Possibly 'the awakened, imperfect ones'.
Aghu-ichendi	Possibly 'those within the net'.
Baba-mansuri	Meaning unknown.
Quraishi	Possibly a figurative reference to the Quraish, the Arabian tribe from which Muhammad was descended; this tribe occupies a very prominent place in the Qu'ran and in Muhammadan history.
Inj-Yolli	'The ones who go by the narrow way'.

Appendix F

The Twelve Imams According to the Yologhli

Ali (AD 600-661)	Also 'Ali; cousin and son-in-law of Muhammad; the fourth caliph; he was murdered in AD 661.
Hasan (AD 624-669)	Also al-Hasan; grandson of Muhammad; elder son of 'Ali and Fatimah; the fifth caliph; he was poisoned in AD 669.
Husain (AD 626-680)	Also al-Husain or Husayn; grandson of Muhammad and son of 'Ali and Fatimah; the third caliph; he was slain in AD 680.
Zain-ul-Abidin	Also 'Ali Zayn al-'Abidin; he died in AD 712.
Mohammed-Baghir	Also Muhammad al-Baqir; he died in AD 731.
Jafar-Sadik (AD 699/700 or 702/703-765)	Also Ja'far as-Sadiq or Ja'far ibn Muhammad; he died in AD 765.
Musa al-Kazim	Also Musa-Kazim; he died in AD 799.
Ali-Riza (AD 765/768/770-818)	Also 'Ali ar-Riza or 'Ali ar-Rida; he died in AD 818.
Mohammed-Tagi	Also Muhammad al-Jawad; he died in AD 835.
Ali an-Naqi	Also Ali Nagi or 'Ali al-Hadi; he died in AD 868.
Hasan al-'Askari	Also Hasan-Askari; he died in AD 874.
Mahdi-al-Hadi (the Mahdi)	Also Muhammad al-Mahdi al-Hujjah; the messianic deliverer who is to appear in the last days according to Islamic eschatology; the twelfth Imam who disappeared in AD 878.

Appendix G

American Missionaries Based in Erzerum in 1881 and 1882 under the American Board of Commissioners for Foreign Missions

Miss Mary E. Brook

Robert Chambers (arrived in Turkey on 7 November 1879)

Mrs Elizabeth L. Chambers (arrived in Turkey on 7 November 1879)

William Nesbit Chambers (arrived in Turkey on 7 November 1879)

Mrs Mary F. Chambers (born Miss Mary Bliss, arrived in Turkey in October 1878; she died on 28 May 1881)

Royal M. Cole

Mrs Lizzie Cole

P. Moses Parmelee M.D.

Mrs Julia F. Parmelee

Miss Harriet G. Powers (arrived in Turkey in September 1868)

Miss Cyrene O. Van Duzee (arrived in Turkey in September 1868)

Appendix H

Exchange Rates to the US Dollar in the 1880s and 1890s

Currency:	$	Source:
German mark	0.2633	US Dictionary - 1885
German pfennig	0.0026	US Dictionary - 1885
British pound	4.8600	US Dictionary - 1885
British shilling	0.2300	US Dictionary - 1885
British pence	0.0192	US Dictionary - 1885
Turkish pound	4.3700	US Dictionary - 1885
Turkish piastre	0.0435	US Dictionary - 1885
Persian toman	1.6840	Hedin/Wilson
Russian rouble	0.7960	US Dictionary - 1885
Russian kopeck	0.0079	US Dictionary - 1885
Turkestani tenga	0.0518	Hedin
French franc	0.1960	US Dictionary - 1885
Bulgarian lev	0.1960	LMU-tied to the franc in a 1:1 ratio

What the US Dollar Could Buy Back in the 1880s and 1890s

According to:	in:		cost:
The Missionary Herald	1881	a Bible in Turkey (2 roubles)	$1.59
Hedin	1895	a camel in Kashgar	$21.16
Hedin	1895	a camel in Yarkand	$26.45
Hedin	1895	a camel in Kargalik	$29.90
Sears, Roebuck and Co.	1894	a 24 piece cutlery set	$2.05
Sears, Roebuck and Co.	1894	a classical guitar	$6.00
Sears, Roebuck and Co.	1894	a sewing machine	$10.00
Sears, Roebuck and Co.	1894	a bicycle	$11.90
Sears, Roebuck and Co.	1894	an English football	$2.00

Appendix I

Bible Passages

Passages of the Bible to which Avetaranian refers (in the order that they are referred to in the story):

All passages are taken from the New American Standard Version (1995 Updated Edition).

New American Standard Format Notes:

Italics are used in the text to indicate words not found in the original Hebrew, Aramaic, or Greek but implied by it.

Passages, which appear in all capital letters in the New Testament, indicate Old Testament quotations or obvious references to Old Testament texts.

An asterisk (*) is used to mark verbs that are historical presents in the Greek, which have been translated with an English past tense in order to conform to modern usage.

These brackets [ ] in the text indicate words probably not in the original writings.

1. Matthew 1:1-17

The record of the genealogy of Jesus the Messiah, the son of David, the son of Abraham:

Abraham was the father of Isaac, Isaac the father of Jacob, and Jacob the father of Judah and his brothers.

Judah was the father of Perez and Zerah by Tamar, Perez was the father of Hezron, and Hezron the father of Ram.

Ram was the father of Amminadab, Amminadab the father of Nahshon, and Nahshon the father of Salmon.

Salmon was the father of Boaz by Rahab, Boaz was the father of Obed by Ruth, and Obed the father of Jesse.

Jesse was the father of David the king. David was the father of Solomon by Bathsheba who had been the wife of Uriah.

Solomon was the father of Rehoboam, Rehoboam the father of Abijah, and Abijah the father of Asa.

Asa was the father of Jehoshaphat, Jehoshaphat the father of Joram, and Joram the father of Uzziah.

Uzziah was the father of Jotham, Jotham the father of Ahaz, and Ahaz the father of Hezekiah.

Hezekiah was the father of Manasseh, Manasseh the father of Amon, and Amon the father of Josiah.

Josiah became the father of Jeconiah and his brothers, at the time of the deportation to Babylon.

After the deportation to Babylon: Jeconiah became the father of Shealtiel, and Shealtiel the father of Zerubbabel.

Zerubbabel was the father of Abihud, Abihud the father of Eliakim, and Eliakim the father of Azor.

Azor was the father of Zadok, Zadok the father of Achim, and Achim the father of Eliud.

Eliud was the father of Eleazar, Eleazar the father of Matthan, and Matthan the father of Jacob.

Jacob was the father of Joseph the husband of Mary, by whom Jesus was born, who is called the Messiah.

So all the generations from Abraham to David are fourteen generations; from David to the deportation to Babylon, fourteen generations; and from the deportation to Babylon to the Messiah, fourteen generations.

2. John 10:34-36

Jesus answered them, "Has it not been written in your Law, 'I SAID, YOU ARE GODS'?

"If he called them gods, to whom the word of God came (and the Scripture cannot be broken),

do you say of Him, whom the Father sanctified and sent into the world, 'You are blaspheming,' because I said, 'I am the Son of God'?"

3. John 1:1,14

In the beginning was the Word, and the Word was with God, and the Word was God.

And the Word became flesh, and dwelt among us, and we saw His glory, glory as of the only begotten from the Father, full of grace and truth.

4. John 3:11

"Truly, truly, I say to you, we speak of what we know and testify of what we have seen, and you do not accept our testimony."

5. Luke 18:31

Then He took the twelve aside and said to them, "Behold, we are going up to Jerusalem, and all things which are written through the prophets about the Son of Man will be accomplished."

6. Matthew 5:17

"Do not think that I came to abolish the Law or the Prophets; I did not come to abolish but to fulfill."

7. Matthew 8:17

This was to fulfill what was spoken through Isaiah the prophet: "HE HIMSELF TOOK OUR INFIRMITIES AND CARRIED AWAY OUR DISEASES."

8. Isaiah 53:4

Surely our griefs He Himself bore,
And our sorrows He carried;
Yet we ourselves esteemed Him stricken,
Smitten of God, and afflicted.

9. Matthew 6:9-13

"Pray, then, in this way:
'Our Father who is in heaven,
Hallowed be Your name.

'Your kingdom come.
Your will be done,
On earth as it is in heaven.

'Give us this day our daily bread.

'And forgive us our debts, as we also have forgiven our debtors.

'And do not lead us into temptation, but deliver us from evil. [For Yours is the kingdom and the power and the glory forever. Amen.]'"

10. Matthew 11:28

"Come to Me, all who are weary and heavy-laden, and I will give you rest."

11. Romans 8:26

In the same way the Spirit also helps our weakness; for we do not know how to pray as we should, but the Spirit Himself intercedes for *us* with groanings too deep for words...

12. Romans 1:3-4

concerning His Son, who was born of a descendant of David according to the flesh,

who was declared the Son of God with power by the resurrection from the dead, according to the Spirit of holiness, Jesus Christ our Lord...

13. Acts 10:25-26

When Peter entered, Cornelius met him, and fell at his feet and worshiped *him.*

But Peter raised him up, saying, "Stand up; I too am *just* a man."

14. Revelation 19:10

Then I fell at his feet to worship him. But he *said to me, "Do not do that; I am a fellow servant of yours and your brethren who hold the testimony of Jesus; worship God. For the testimony of Jesus is the spirit of prophecy."

15. Exodus 20:1-17

Then God spoke all these words, saying,

"I am the LORD your God, who brought you out of the land of Egypt, out of the house of slavery.

"You shall have no other gods before Me.

"You shall not make for yourself an idol, or any likeness of what is in heaven above or on the earth beneath or in the water under the earth.

"You shall not worship them or serve them; for I, the LORD your God, am a jealous God, visiting the iniquity of the fathers on the children, on the third and the fourth generations of those who hate Me,

but showing lovingkindness to thousands, to those who love Me and keep My commandments.

"You shall not take the name of the LORD your God in vain, for the LORD will not leave him unpunished who takes His name in vain.

"Remember the sabbath day, to keep it holy.

"Six days you shall labor and do all your work,

but the seventh day is a sabbath of the LORD your

God; *in it* you shall not do any work, you or your son or your daughter, your male or your female servant or your cattle or your sojourner who stays with you.

"For in six days the LORD made the heavens and the earth, the sea and all that is in them, and rested on the seventh day; therefore the LORD blessed the sabbath day and made it holy.

"Honor your father and your mother, that your days may be prolonged in the land which the LORD your God gives you.

"You shall not murder."

"You shall not commit adultery."

"You shall not steal."

"You shall not bear false witness against your neighbor.

"You shall not covet your neighbor's house; you shall not covet your neighbor's wife or his male servant or his female servant or his ox or his donkey or anything that belongs to your neighbor."

16. Genesis 3:21

The LORD God made garments of skin for Adam and his wife, and clothed them.

17. John 6:37

"All that the Father gives Me will come to Me, and the one who comes to Me I will certainly not cast out."

18. Matthew 13:7

"Others fell among the thorns, and the thorns came up and choked them out."

19. Mark 4:7

"Other *seed* fell among the thorns, and the thorns came up and choked it, and it yielded no crop."

20. Luke 8:7

"Other *seed* fell among the thorns; and the thorns grew up with it and choked it out."

21. Matthew 20:1-16

"For the kingdom of heaven is like a landowner who went out early in the morning to hire laborers for his vineyard.

"When he had agreed with the laborers for a denarius for the day, he sent them into his vineyard.

"And he went out about the third hour and saw others standing idle in the market place;

and to those he said, 'You also go into the vineyard, and whatever is right I will give you.' And *so* they went.

"Again he went out about the sixth and the ninth hour, and did the same thing.

"And about the eleventh *hour* he went out and found others standing *around*; and he *said to them, 'Why have you been standing here idle all day long?'

"They *said to him, 'Because no one hired us.' He *said to them, 'You go into the vineyard too.'

"When evening came, the owner of the vineyard *said to his foreman, 'Call the laborers and pay them their wages, beginning with the last *group* to the first.'

"When those *hired* about the eleventh hour came, each one received a denarius.

"When those *hired* first came, they thought that they would receive more; but each of them also received a denarius.

"When they received it, they grumbled at the landowner,

saying, 'These last men have worked *only* one hour, and you have made them equal to us who have borne the burden and the scorching heat of the day.'

"But he answered and said to one of them, 'Friend, I am doing you no wrong; did you not agree with me for a denarius?

'Take what is yours and go, but I wish to give to this last man the same as to you.

'Is it not lawful for me to do what I wish with what is my own? Or is your eye envious because I am generous?'

"So the last shall be first, and the first last."

22. Matthew 28:19-20

"Go therefore and make disciples of all the nations, baptizing them in the name of the Father and the Son and the Holy Spirit,

teaching them to observe all that I commanded you; and lo, I am with you always, even to the end of the age."

23. James 3:1

Let not many *of you* become teachers, my brethren, knowing that as such we will incur a stricter judgment.

24. Matthew 10:33

"But whoever denies Me before men, I will also deny him before My Father who is in heaven."

25. 1 John 2:19

They went out from us, but they were not *really* of us; for if they had been of us, they would have remained with us; but *they went out*, so that it would be shown that they all are not of us.

26. Acts 1:11

They also said, "Men of Galilee, why do you stand looking into the sky? This Jesus, who has been taken up from you into heaven, will come in just the same way as you have watched Him go into heaven."

27. Acts 9:4

and he fell to the ground and heard a voice saying to him, "Saul, Saul, why are you persecuting Me?"

28. Matthew 1:1

The record of the genealogy of Jesus the Messiah, the son of David, the son of Abraham...

29. Matthew 4:3

And the tempter came and said to Him, "If You are the Son of God, command that these stones become bread."

30. Genesis 21:19

Then God opened her eyes and she saw a well of water; and she went and filled the skin with water and gave the lad a drink.

31. Romans 10:17

So faith *comes* from hearing, and hearing by the word of Christ.

32. Matthew 13:3-9

And He spoke many things to them in parables, saying, "Behold, the sower went out to sow;

and as he sowed, some *seeds* fell beside the road, and the birds came and ate them up.

"Others fell on the rocky places, where they did not have much soil; and immediately they sprang up, because they had no depth of soil.

"But when the sun had risen, they were scorched; and because they had no root, they withered away.

"Others fell among the thorns, and the thorns came up and choked them out.

"And others fell on the good soil and *yielded a crop, some a hundredfold, some sixty, and some thirty.

"He who has ears, let him hear."

33. Matthew 16:24

Then Jesus said to His disciples, "If anyone wishes to come after Me, he must deny himself, and take up his cross and follow Me."

34. Acts 10:47

"Surely no one can refuse the water for these to be baptized who have received the Holy Spirit just as we *did*, can he?"

35. Acts 8:38

And he ordered the chariot to stop; and they both went down into the water, Philip as well as the eunuch, and he baptized him.

36. Romans 6:3-4

Or do you not know that all of us who have been baptized into Christ Jesus have been baptized into His death?

Therefore we have been buried with Him through baptism into death, so that as Christ was raised from the dead through the glory of the Father, so we too might walk in newness of life.

37. 1 Corinthians 9:20-22

To the Jews I became as a Jew, so that I might win Jews; to those who are under the Law, as under the Law though not being myself under the Law, so that I might win those who are under the Law;

to those who are without law, as without law, though not being without the law of God but under the law of Christ, so that I might win those who are without law.

To the weak I became weak, that I might win the weak; I have become all things to all men, so that I may by all means save some.

38. Numbers 13:25-33

When they returned from spying out the land, at the end of forty days,

they proceeded to come to Moses and Aaron and to all the congregation of the sons of Israel in the wilderness of Paran, at Kadesh; and they brought back word to them and to all the congregation and showed them the fruit of the land.

Thus they told him, and said, "We went in to the land where you sent us; and it certainly does flow with milk and honey, and this is its fruit.

"Nevertheless, the people who live in the land are strong, and the cities are fortified *and* very large;

and moreover, we saw the descendants of Anak there.

"Amalek is living in the land of the Negev and the Hittites and the Jebusites and the Amorites are living in the hill country, and the Canaanites are living by the sea and by the side of the Jordan."

Then Caleb quieted the people before Moses and said, "We should by all means go up and take possession of it, for we will surely overcome it."

But the men who had gone up with him said, "We are not able to go up against the people, for they are too strong for us."

So they gave out to the sons of Israel a bad report of the land which they had spied out, saying, "The land through which we have gone, in spying it out, is a land that devours its inhabitants; and all the people whom we saw in it are men of *great* size.

"There also we saw the Nephilim (the sons of Anak are part of the Nephilim); and we became like grasshoppers in our own sight, and so we were in their sight."

39. 1 Thessalonians 5:21

But examine everything *carefully*; hold fast to that which is good…

40. Luke 10:25-37

And a lawyer stood up and put Him to the test, saying, "Teacher, what shall I do to inherit eternal life?"

And He said to him, "What is written in the Law? How does it read to you?"

And he answered, "YOU SHALL LOVE THE LORD YOUR GOD WITH ALL YOUR HEART, AND WITH ALL YOUR SOUL, AND WITH ALL YOUR STRENGTH, AND WITH ALL YOUR MIND; AND YOUR NEIGHBOR AS YOURSELF."

And He said to him, "You have answered correctly; DO THIS AND YOU WILL LIVE."

But wishing to justify himself, he said to Jesus, "And who is my neighbor?"

Jesus replied and said, "A man was going down from Jerusalem to Jericho, and fell among robbers, and they stripped him and beat him, and went away leaving him half dead.

"And by chance a priest was going down on that road, and when he saw him, he passed by on the other side.

"Likewise a Levite also, when he came to the place and saw him, passed by on the other side.

"But a Samaritan, who was on a journey, came upon him; and when he saw him, he felt compassion,

and came to him and bandaged up his wounds, pouring oil and wine on *them*; and he put him on his own beast, and brought him to an inn and took care of him.

"On the next day he took out two denarii and gave them to the innkeeper and said, 'Take care of him; and whatever more you spend, when I return I will repay you.'

"Which of these three do you think proved to be a neighbor to the man who fell into the robbers' *hands*?"

And he said, "The one who showed mercy toward him." Then Jesus said to him, "Go and do the same."

41. Genesis 32:24-25

Then Jacob was left alone, and a man wrestled with him until daybreak.

When he saw that he had not prevailed against him, he touched the socket of his thigh; so the socket of Jacob's thigh was dislocated while he wrestled with him.

42. John 3:19-21

"This is the judgment, that the Light has come into the world, and men loved the darkness rather than the Light, for their deeds were evil.

"For everyone who does evil hates the Light, and does not come to the Light for fear that his deeds will be exposed.

"But he who practices the truth comes to the Light, so that his deeds may be manifested as having been wrought in God."

43. John 3:3

Jesus answered and said to him, "Truly, truly, I say to you, unless one is born again he cannot see the kingdom of God."

44. Acts 20:24

"But I do not consider my life of any account as dear to myself, so that I may finish my course and the ministry which I received from the Lord Jesus, to testify solemnly of the gospel of the grace of God."

45. John 1:47

Jesus saw Nathanael coming to Him, and *said of him, "Behold, an Israelite indeed, in whom there is no deceit!"

46. Psalm 100:1-5

Shout joyfully to the LORD, all the earth.

Serve the LORD with gladness;
Come before Him with joyful singing.

Know that the LORD Himself is God;
It is He who has made us, and not we ourselves;
We are His people and the sheep of His pasture.

Enter His gates with thanksgiving
And His courts with praise.
Give thanks to Him, bless His name.

For the LORD is good;
His lovingkindness is everlasting
And His faithfulness to all generations.

47. Psalm 101:1-8

I will sing of lovingkindness and justice,
To You, O LORD, I will sing praises.

I will give heed to the blameless way.
When will You come to me?
I will walk within my house in the integrity of my heart.

I will set no worthless thing before my eyes;
I hate the work of those who fall away;
It shall not fasten its grip on me.

A perverse heart shall depart from me;
I will know no evil.

Whoever secretly slanders his neighbor, him I will destroy;
No one who has a haughty look and an arrogant heart will I endure.

My eyes shall be upon the faithful of the land, that they may dwell with me;
He who walks in a blameless way is the one who will minister to me.

He who practices deceit shall not dwell within my house;
He who speaks falsehood shall not maintain his position before me.

Every morning I will destroy all the wicked of the land,
So as to cut off from the city of the LORD all those who do iniquity.

48. 1 John 4 & 5

Beloved, do not believe every spirit, but test the spirits to see whether they are from God, because many false prophets have gone out into the world.

By this you know the Spirit of God: every spirit that confesses that Jesus Christ has come in the flesh is from God;

and every spirit that does not confess Jesus is not from God; this is the *spirit* of the antichrist, of which you have heard that it is coming, and now it is already in the world.

You are from God, little children, and have overcome them; because greater is He who is in you than he who is in the world.

They are from the world; therefore they speak *as* from the world, and the world listens to them.

We are from God; he who knows God listens to us; he who is not from God does not listen to us. By this we know the spirit of truth and the spirit of error.

Beloved, let us love one another, for love is from God; and everyone who loves is born of God and knows God.

The one who does not love does not know God, for God is love.

By this the love of God was manifested in us, that God has sent His only begotten Son into the world so that we might live through Him.

In this is love, not that we loved God, but that He loved us and sent His Son *to be* the propitiation for our sins.

Beloved, if God so loved us, we also ought to love one another.

No one has seen God at any time; if we love one another, God abides in us, and His love is perfected in us.

By this we know that we abide in Him and He in us, because He has given us of His Spirit.

We have seen and testify that the Father has sent the Son *to be* the Savior of the world.

Whoever confesses that Jesus is the Son of God, God abides in him, and he in God.

We have come to know and have believed the love which God has for us. God is love, and the one who abides in love abides in God, and God abides in him.

By this, love is perfected with us, so that we may have confidence in the day of judgment; because as He is, so also are we in this world.

There is no fear in love; but perfect love casts out fear, because fear involves punishment, and the one who fears is not perfected in love.

We love, because He first loved us.

If someone says, "I love God," and hates his brother, he is a liar; for the one who does not love his brother whom he has seen, cannot love God whom he has not seen.

And this commandment we have from Him, that the one who loves God should love his brother also.

Whoever believes that Jesus is the Christ is born of God, and whoever loves the Father loves the *child* born of Him.

By this we know that we love the children of God, when we love God and observe His commandments.

For this is the love of God, that we keep His commandments; and His commandments are not burdensome.

For whatever is born of God overcomes the world; and this is the victory that has overcome the world—our faith.

Who is the one who overcomes the world, but he who believes that Jesus is the Son of God?

This is the One who came by water and blood, Jesus Christ; not with the water only, but with the water and with the blood. It is the Spirit who testifies, because the Spirit is the truth.

For there are three that testify:

the Spirit and the water and the blood; and the three are in agreement.

If we receive the testimony of men, the testimony of God is greater; for the testimony of God is this, that He has testified concerning His Son.

The one who believes in the Son of God has the testimony in himself; the one who does not believe God has made Him a liar, because he has not believed in the testimony that God has given concerning His Son.

And the testimony is this, that God has given us eternal life, and this life is in His Son.

He who has the Son has the life; he who does not have the Son of God does not have the life.

These things I have written to you who believe in the name of the Son of God, so that you may know that you have eternal life.

This is the confidence which we have before Him, that, if we ask anything according to His will, He hears us.

And if we know that He hears us *in* whatever we ask, we know that we have the requests which we have asked from Him.

If anyone sees his brother committing a sin not *leading* to death, he shall ask and *God* will for him give life to those who commit sin not *leading* to death. There is a sin *leading* to death; I do not say that he should make request for this.

All unrighteousness is sin, and there is a sin not *leading* to death.

We know that no one who is born of God sins; but He who was born of God keeps him, and the evil one does not touch him.

We know that we are of God, and that the whole world lies in *the power of* the evil one.

And we know that the Son of God has come, and has given us understanding so that we may know Him who is true; and we are in Him who is true, in His Son Jesus Christ. This is the true God and eternal life.

Little children, guard yourselves from idols.

49. Revelation 12:9-11

And the great dragon was thrown down, the serpent of old who is called the devil and Satan, who deceives the whole world; he was thrown down to the earth, and his angels were thrown down with him.

Then I heard a loud voice in heaven, saying, "Now the salvation, and the power, and the kingdom of our God and the authority of His Christ have come, for the accuser of our brethren has been thrown down, he who accuses them before our God day and night.

"And they overcame him because of the blood of the Lamb and because of the word of their testimony, and they did not love their life even when faced with death."

50. Acts 16:9

A vision appeared to Paul in the night: a man of Macedonia was standing and appealing to him, and saying, "Come over to Macedonia and help us."

Appendix J
Koran Passages

Passages of the Koran to which Avetaranian refers (in the order that they are referred to in the story):

All passages are taken from the 1946 Abdullah Yusuf Ali edition of the Koran.

1. Surah 15:29

"When I have fashioned him
(In due proportion) and breathed
Into him of My spirit,
Fall ye down in obeisance
Unto him."

2. Surah 3:2-3

God! There is no god
But He,—the Living,
The Self-Subsisting, Eternal.

It is He Who sent down
To thee (step by step),
In truth, the Book,
Confirming what went before it;
And He sent down the Law
(Of Moses) and the Gospel
(Of Jesus) before this,
As a guide to mankind,
And He sent down the Criterion
(Of judgement between right and wrong).

3. Surah 2:31-32

And He taught Adam the nature
Of all things; then He placed them
Before the angels, and said: "Tell Me
The nature of these if ye are right."

They said: "Glory to Thee: of knowledge
We have none, save what Thou
Hast taught us: in truth it is Thou
Who art perfect in knowledge and wisdom."

4. Surah 91:9

Truly he succeeds
That purifies it,

5. Surah 4:169-171

Except the way of Hell,
To dwell therein for ever.
And this to God is easy.

O mankind! the Apostle
Hath come to you in truth
From God: believe in him:
It is best for you. But if
Ye reject Faith, to God
Belong all things in the heavens
And on earth: And God
Is All-knowing, All-wise.

O People of the Book!
Commit no excesses
In your religion: nor say
Of God aught but the truth.
Christ Jesus the son of Mary
Was (no more than)
An apostle of God,
And His Word,
Which He bestowed on Mary,
And a Spirit proceeding
From Him: so believe
In God and His apostles.
Say not "Trinity": desist:
It will be better for you:
For God is One God:
Glory be to Him:
(Far Exalted is He) above
Having a son. To Him
Belong all things in the heavens
And on earth. And enough
Is God as a Disposer of affairs.

6. Surah 10:94

If thou wert in doubt
As to what We have revealed
Unto thee, then ask those
Who have been reading
The Book from before thee:
The Truth hath indeed come
To thee from thy Lord:
So be in no wise
Of those in doubt.

7. Surah 2:38-41

We said: "Get ye down all from here;
And if, as is sure, there comes to you
Guidance from Me, whosoever
Follows My guidance, on them
Shall be no fear, nor shall they grieve.

"But those who reject Faith
And belie Our Signs,
They shall be Companions of the Fire;
They shall abide therein."

O Children of Israel! call to mind
The (special) favour which I bestowed
Upon you, and fulfil your Covenant
With Me as I fulfil My Covenant
With you, and fear none but Me.

And believe in what I reveal,
Confirming the revelation
Which is with you,
And be not the first to reject
Faith therein, nor sell My Signs
For a small price; and fear Me,
And Me alone.

8. Surah 2:2-4

This is the Book;
In it is guidance sure, without doubt,
To those who fear God;

Who believe in the Unseen,
Are steadfast in prayer,
And spend out of what We
Have provided for them;

And who believe in the Revelation
Sent to thee,
And sent before thy time,
And (in their hearts)
Have the assurance of the Hereafter.

9. Surah 29:45-46

Recite what is sent
Of the Book by inspiration
To thee, and establish
Regular Prayer: For Prayer
Restrains from shameful
And unjust deeds;
And remembrance of God
Is the greatest (thing in life)
Without doubt. And God knows
The (deeds) that ye do.

And dispute ye not
With the People of the Book,
Except with means better
(Than mere disputation), unless
It be with those of them
Who inflict wrong (and injury):

But say, "We believe
In the Revelation which has
Come down to us and in that
Which came down to you;
Our God and your God
Is One; and it is to Him
We bow (in Islam)."

Bibliography

The works read or consulted for the translation into English of Johannes Awetaranian's *Geschichte eines Muhammedaners der Christ wurde* and the compiling of the appendices:

A myriad of web sites.
Anderson, Gerald H., *Biographical Dictionary of Christian Missions*. Grand Rapids, USA, Cambridge, UK, 1998.
Anderson, Rufus, *History of the Missions of the American Board of Commissioners for Foreign Missions of the Oriental Churches*, Vols. I and II. Boston, 1872.
Arberry, A. J. Litt. D., F.B.A., *Classical Persian Literature*. London, 1958.
Armajani, Yahya, Ricks, Thomas M., *Middle East Past and Present*. Englewood Cliffs, New Jersey, USA, 1986, 1970.
Articles written by John Avetaranian, Khatib Djahid, Ali Zija, El Hadj Mustafa Zehni, and others originally published in the *Balkan* and *Gunesh* in 1908. English translator unknown. Found in the archives of the Swedish Missionary Society by John Quanrud.
Awetaranian, Johannes, *Geschichte eines Muhammedaners der Christ wurde*. (Die Geschichte des Johannes Awetaranian), 1905.
Awetaranian, Johannes, *Geschichte eines Muhammedaners der Christ wurde*. (Die Geschichte des Johannes Awetaranian). Completed after his death by Richard Schäfer, Potsdam, 1930.
Ayliffe, Rosie, Dubin, Marc, Gawthrop, John, *Turkey, The Rough Guide*. London, 1997.
Barnham, Henry D. (trans.), *The Khoja, Tales of Nasr-ed-Din*. New York, 1924.
Bayard, Taylor (compiled and arranged by), *Central Asia: Travels in Cashmere, Little Tibet and Central Asia*. New York, 1883.
Bloomingdales Illustrated 1886 Catalog. Mineola, New York, 1988.
Broadbent, E. H., *The Pilgrim Church*. London, Glasgow, 1931, 1935, 1946, 1950, 1956, 1963, 1974, 1978, 1981.
Browne, Edward G., *A Literary History of Persia: Modern Times (1500-1924)*, Vol. IV. Cambridge, 1959.
Canton, William, *The Story of the Bible Society*. London, 1904.
Carroll, H. K., LL. D., *Missionary Growth of the Methodist Episcopal Church*. New York, 1907.
Catholic Encyclopaedia, The. 1909.
Census of Population, 1990, (Turkey). 1990.
Compton's Home Library, The Complete Reference Collection. 1997.
Encyclopaedia Britannica, Britannica 2001 Deluxe Edition CD-ROM. 2001.
Encyclopaedia Britannica, Britannica 2002 DVD Edition. 2002.
Eppler, Paul, *Geschichte der Basler Mission, 1815-1899*. Basel, 1900.
Fritzon, Ann-Charlotte, *Passion for the Impossible, The Life of the Pioneer Nils Fredrik Höijer*, trans. by John and Lynne Quanrud. Malmö, Sweden, 1998.
Goodsell, Fred Field, *You Shall Be My Witnesses*. Boston, 1959.
Greene, F. V., *Report on the Russian Army in 1877-1878*. Nashville, 1879, 1996.
Hedin, Sven, *Through Asia*, Vols. I and II. New York, London, 1899.
Hedin, Sven, *My Life as an Explorer*, trans. by Alfhild Huebsch. Garden City, New York, 1925.
Heier, Edmund, *Religious Schism in the Russian Aristocracy, 1860-1900: Radstockism and Pashkovism*. The Hague, 1970.
Historical Sketches of the Missions under the Care of the Board of Foreign Missions of the Presbyterian Church U.S.A. Philadelphia, 1897.

Hopkirk, Peter, *The Great Game, The Struggle for Empire in Central Asia*. New York, Tokyo, London, 1990.
Hopkirk, Peter, *Foreign Devils on the Silk Road, The Search for the Lost Cities and Treasures of Chinese Central Asia*. Oxford, New York, 1980.
Hughes, Thomas Patrick, B.D., M.R.A.S., *A Dictionary of Islam, Being a Cyclopædia of the Doctrines, Rites, Ceremonies, and Customs, Together with the Technical and Theological Terms, of the Muhammadan Religion*. London, 1885.
Huntington, Ellsworth, *The Pulse of Asia*. Boston, New York, 1907.
Inalcik, Halil, *The Ottoman Empire, The Classical Age 1300-1600*. London, 1973.
Kieser, Hans-Lukas, "Some Remarks on Alevi Responses to the Missionaries in Eastern Anatolia (19th-20th cc.)", *Columbia International Affairs Online*. Columbia University Press, March 2001.
Knight, Kevin, *The Catholic Encyclopaedia, Online Edition*. 1999.
Latimer, Robert Sloan, *Dr. Baedeker: and His Apostolic Work in Russia*. London, 1907.
Latimer, Robert Sloan, *Under Three Tsars, Liberty of Conscience in Russia, 1859-1909*. London, 1909.
Lepsius, Dr Johannes (ed.), *Ex Oriente Lux. Jahrbuch der Deutschen Orient-Mission*. Berlin, 1903.
Lewis, Raphaela, *Everyday Life in Ottoman Turkey*. London, New York, 1971.
Macartney, Lady, *An English Lady in Chinese Turkestan*. Oxford, New York, 1985.
Merriam-Webster's Collegiate Dictionary, Tenth Edition, 2001.
Missionary Herald for the year 1880, Vol. 76, Cambridge, USA, 1880.
Missionary Herald for the year 1881, Vol. 77, Cambridge, USA, 1881.
Missionary Herald for the year 1882, Vol. 78, Cambridge, USA, 1882.
Missionary Herald for the year 1883, Vol. 79, Boston, 1883.
Missionary Herald for the year 1903, Vol. 99, Boston, 1903.
Missionary Herald for the year 1908, Vol. 104, Boston, 1908.
Missionary Herald for the year 1909, Vol. 105, Boston, 1909.
Mistele, Liane, *Christliche Gemeinden unter der türkischsprachigen Minderheit in Bulgarien. Ein Beitrag zum ökumenischen Lernen im Religionsunterricht*. Heidelberg, 1995.
National Geographic, The Complete, 110 Years (1888-1998). Washington, D.C., 1999.
Oxford English Dictionary, Encyclopaedia Britannica 2001 Deluxe Edition CD-ROM. Oxford, 2001.
Pfander, C. G., D.D., *The Mizan-ul-Haqq* (Balance of Truth), trans. into English and revised and enlarged by W. St. Clair Tisdall, M.A., D.D. Villach, Austria, 1910.
Polo, Marco, *Voyages and Travels*. London, 1894.
Revised New American Dictionary of the English Language, The. New York, 1884.
Schlatter, Wilhelm, *Geschichte der Basler Mission*, Vol. I. Basel, 1916.
Sears, Roebuck & Co. Consumer Guide for 1894.
Segal, Louis, M.A., Ph.D. (Econ.), P.Phil., *The Complete Russian-English Dictionary*. London, 1943.
Webster's New World Dictionary of American English. New York, London, Toronto, Sydney, Tokyo, Singapore, 1994.
Whitaker, H., F.R.G.S., *Eastern Turki*. Chaubattia, India, 1909.
Willoughby, W. W., *Indian Hemp. Opium as an International Problem: The Geneva Conferences*. Baltimore, 1925.
Wilson, S. G., Rev. M.A., *Persian Life and Customs*. New York, Chicago, Toronto, 1896.
Wingate, R. O., *The Steep Ascent: The Story of the Christian Church in Turkestan*. London, 1949.
Zwemer, S. M., F.R.G.S., *Two Pioneer Missionaries in Bulgaria. The Moslem World*, Vol. 17. New York, 1927.
Zwemer, S. M., F.R.G.S., Wherry, E. M., D.D., Barton, James L., D.D. (ed.), *The Mohammedan World of Today, Being Papers Read at the First Missionary Conference on*

behalf of the Mohammedan World held in Cairo April 4th-9th, 1906. New York, Chicago, Toronto, London, Edinburgh, 1906.

Maps

Avetaranian's World	252
Avetaranian's Anatolia and Caucasia	253
Avetaranian's Turkestan	254
Avetaranian's Balkans	255

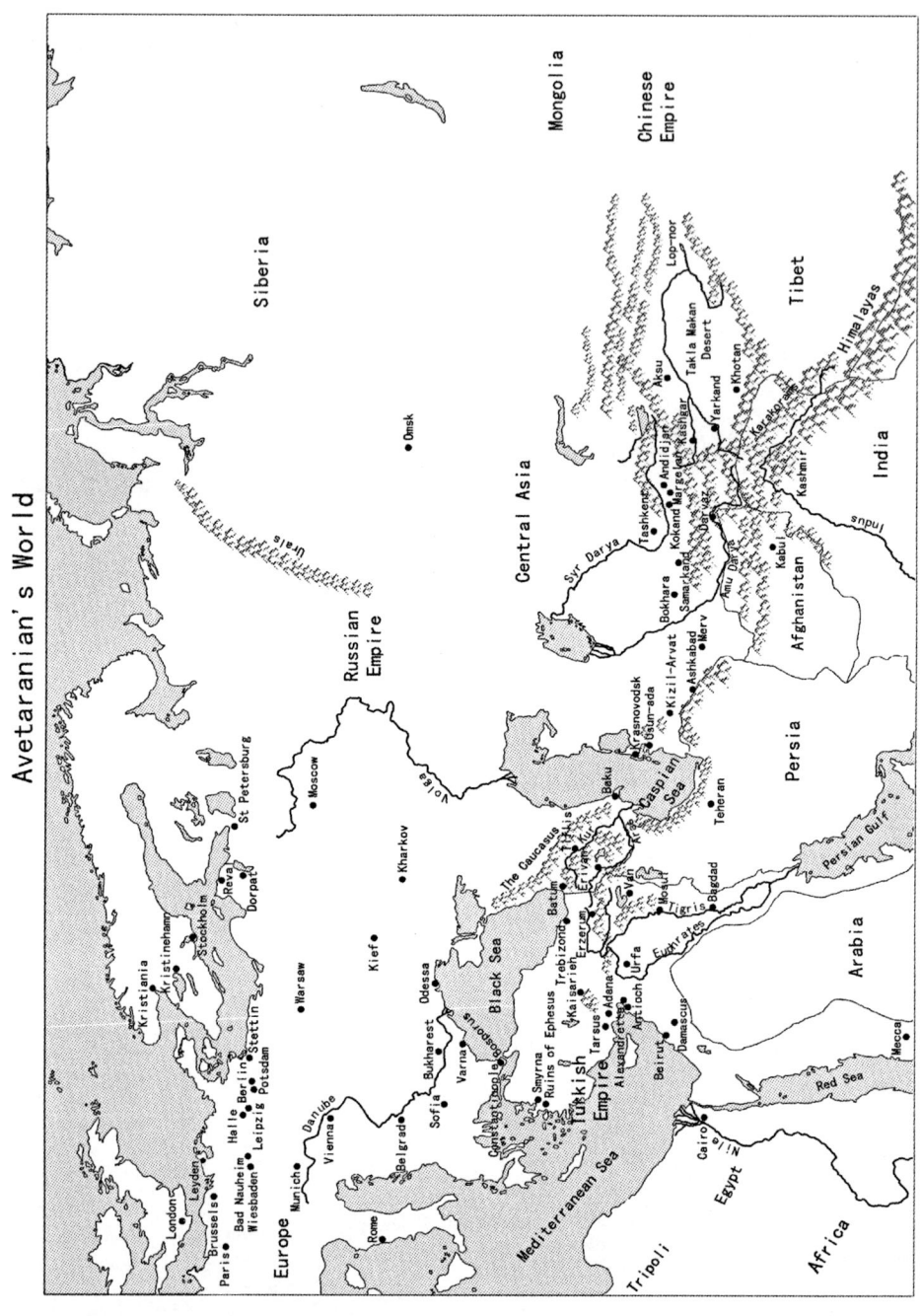

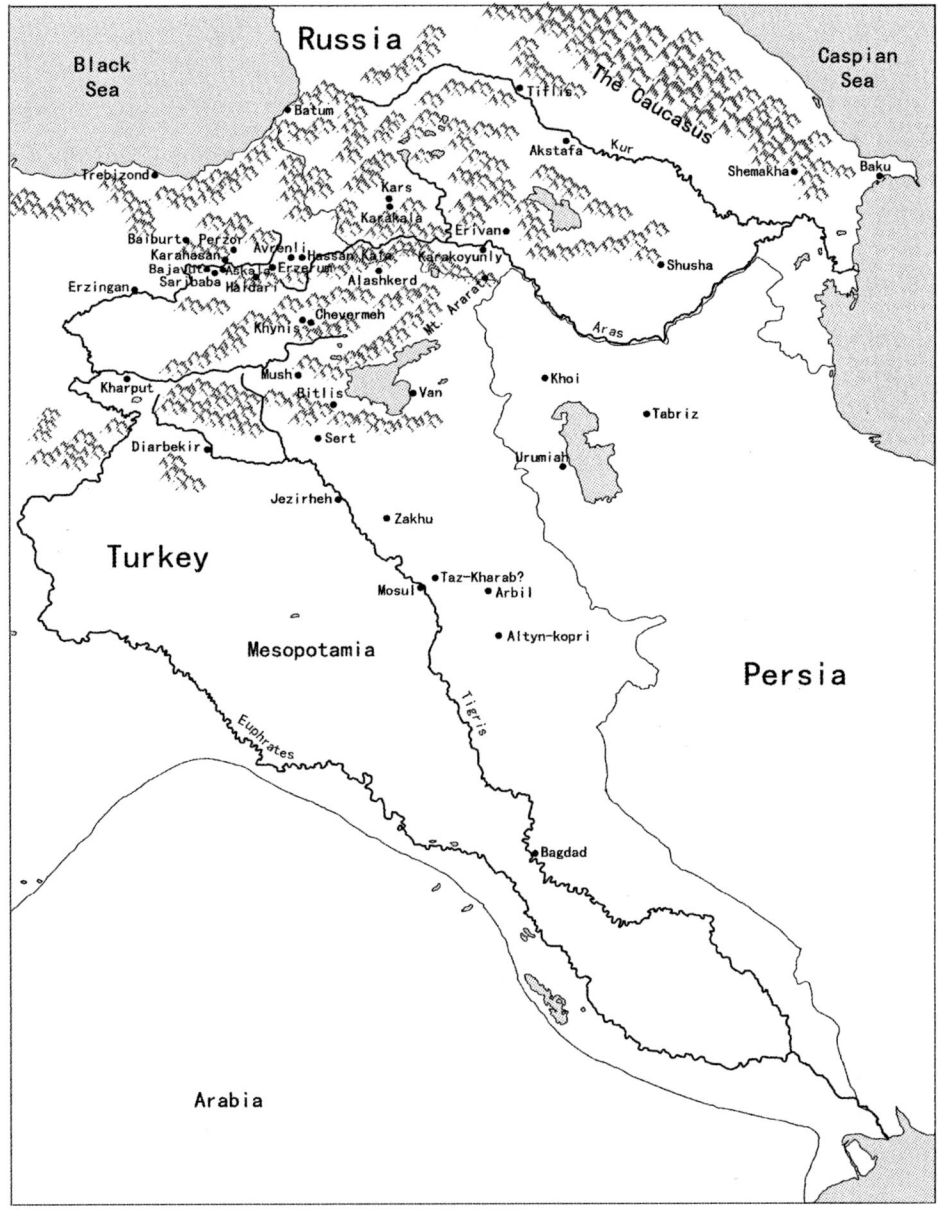

Avetaranian's Anatolia and Caucasia

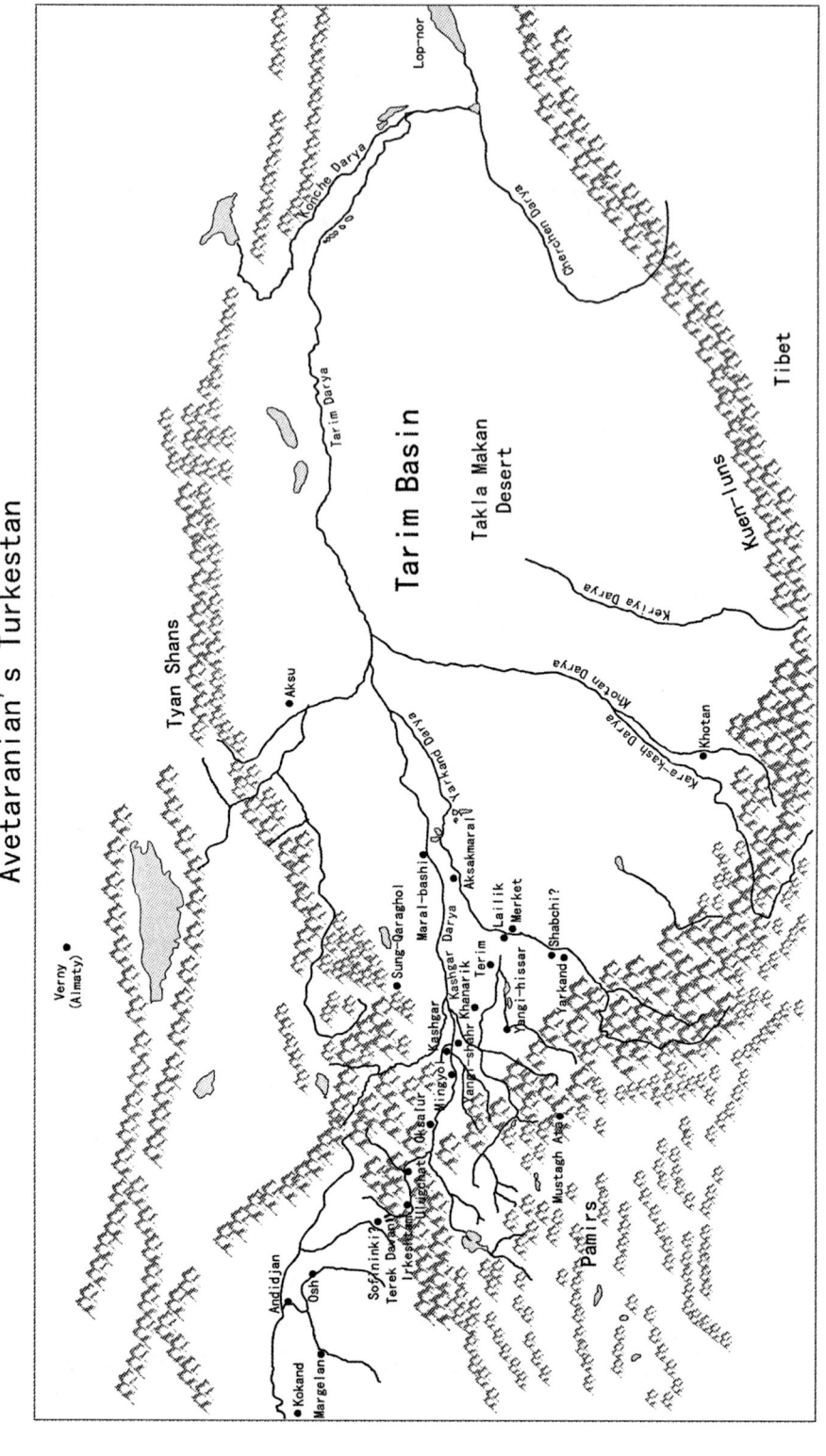

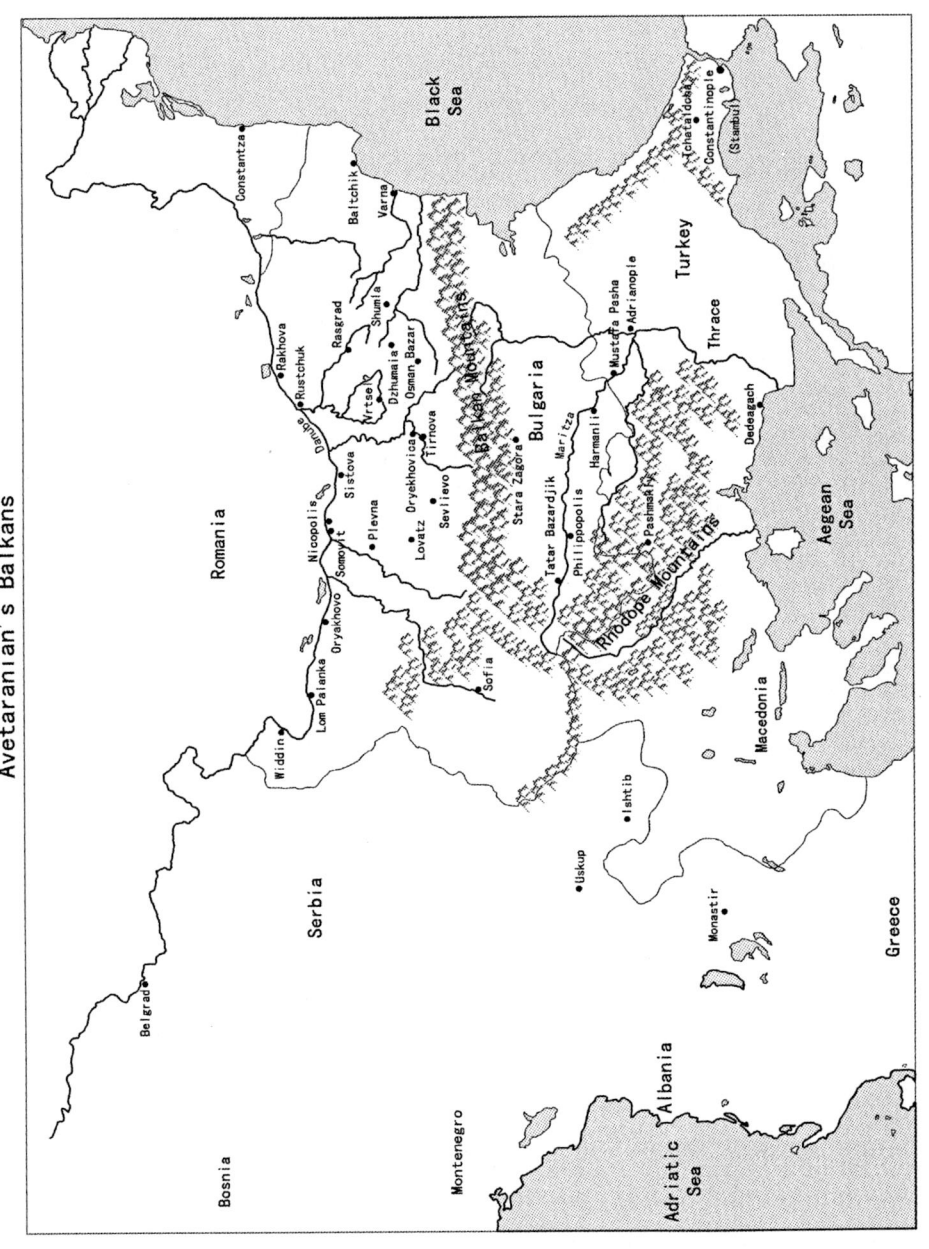

Index

Abdul Hagk, Sheikh, 136
Abdul Hamid II, the Sultan, 151, 157, 158
Abdul-Fazl, 68
Abel, 13
Abraham, 34, 44, 68
Abrahamian, 44
Acts of the Apostles, 18, 24, 89
Adam (the first man), 11, 13, 24, 105, 133
Adana, 155, 158
Adana Massacre, the, 155, 158
Adhem Ruhi, 150, 168, 172
Adrianople, 168, 170, 176, 178, 180
ael aelae ael haqqa, 36
aerkan, 10
Afghanistan, 170
Africa, 60, 137, 159, 170
Agha, Hohannes, 31
Agha, Malo, 42
Aghu-ichendi, 7
Ahmed Aga, 46
Akhmed Keshaf, Sheikh, 156, 158, 165, 181
Aksakmaral, 100
aksaqal, 69, 98, 101, 103
Akstafa, 62
Aksu, 100, 104
Alallahi, 7
Alashkerd, 43, 44, 45, 46, 48, 51, 52
Albania, 164
alei, 170
Alei-Muftisi-Fakhred-din, 170, 171
Alexandretta, 155
algan, 80
algen, 80
Ali (Muhammad's cousin), 10, 11, 12, 13, 32, 33
Ali an-Naqi, 12
Ali Beg, 17, 29, 32
Ali Ziya Efendi, His Excellency, 151
Ali-Riza, 12
Allah, 111, 134, 138
Allah karim dir, 112
Altyn-kopri, 5
amban, 69
America, 45, 55
American Bible House (in Constantinople), 129
Amirkhaniantz, (Pastor/Reverend) Abraham, 52, 53, 54, 55, 56, 57, 58, 61, 62, 67, 116, 120
Amirkhaniantz, Mrs, 56
Amu River, 73

amulet, 2, 19, 21, 35, 105, 131
Andidjan, 79, 89
Andidjani. *See* Uzbek Turkish
Andrae-Roman, Mr, 119
Andreas, Professor/Doctor (Friedrich Karl), 116, 117, 118, 119
Antichrist, 12
Antioch, 191
Anwár-i-Suhaylí, 80
apostles, the twelve, 37, 41, 129
Aqtaghliq, 80
Arabia, 165, 166
Arabshah, 119, 120
Arakelian, Hagop, 144
Arakelian, Sahak, 144, 188
Ararat Armenian, 52
Ararat, Mount, 126
Aras River, 126
Arbil, 5
Armenia, 158, 164, 165, 191
Armenian Deportations of 1915 and 1916, the, 158
Armenian evangelical. *See* Protestant, Armenian
Armenian National Church, 17, 52
Armenian-Lutheran Church (in Shemakha), 113
Arshak, 40
Arushanian, Hagop, 55, 78
Ashkabad, 67
Asia, 39, 127
Asia Minor, 1, 169
Askala, 30, 38
Aslan Caravansary, 54
Assad Pasha, Wali, 1
Assadur, Bses, 56
Assadur, Sarkis, 54, 55, 56
atropine, 59
Avetaranian, Helene, 174
Avetaranian, John, 1, 40, 42, 43, 44, 55, 57, 58, 59, 61, 65, 66, 106, 117, 118, 120, 144, 145, 146, 148, 150, 151, 152, 154, 155, 156, 157, 158, 159, 160, 161, 162, 165, 166, 169, 175, 184, 185, 188, 189, 190, 191, 192, 193, 194
Avrenli, 1, 3, 15
azan, 35
Azerbaijan, 47
Azerbaijani-Turkish, 148
Azizi, 11

Bab, the, 68
Baba-mansuri, 7

Babites, 67, 68
Bad Nauheim, 185, 186, 187, 188, 191, 192
Bädeker, Doctor Friederich Wilhelm, 61
Bagdad, 3, 136
Bagdasariantz, Sembad, 55, 63
Baha' Ullah, 68
Baiburt, 1, 3
Bajavut, 19, 21, 29
bakhshi, 103
Baku, 67, 95, 110, 113, 126
balaban, 142
Balkan, 150, 157, 165, 166, 167, 168, 169, 170, 171, 172
Balkan Express Train, 188
Balkan League, the, 174, 176
Balkan Mountains, 176
Balkan War, the first, 175, 176, 177, 182
Balkan War, the second, 175, 176, 182
Balkans, the, 46, 167, 174
Baltchik, 141
bashi-bazouks, 176, 177
Batum, 66, 67
Bayaziden Bestam, 124
Beckström, Miss, 65
beg, 79, 80, 87, 101
Behjet Khanum, 6, 15, 17
Beirut, 147, 164
Beklund, Missionary, 88, 118
Bektashi, 4, 5, 7, 180
berat, 138
Berlin, 116, 117, 118, 119, 120, 121, 190
Berlin-Steglitz, 158
Bey, Daniel, 52, 53, 55
Beyan-ul-Hakk, 170, 171, 173
Bible distributor, 54, 55, 78, 128, 141, 144, 178
Bible, the, 12, 29, 30, 31, 37, 38, 41, 44, 52, 55, 56, 64, 67, 68, 78, 79, 82, 102, 105, 115, 116, 118, 174, 188, 189
Bible-woman, 59, 95
Bitlis, 5, 43
Black Sea, 141, 191
black stone, the, 125
Blumhard, General, 65
Bokhara, 67, 71, 168, 170
Bosch (Huis ten Bosch), 191
Bosnia, 147, 168
Bosnia-Herzegovina, 168
Bosporus, the, 46
brazhnik, 113
British and Foreign Bible Society, 52, 55, 78, 108, 113, 114, 116, 117, 118, 119, 162, 163, 179
Buhaira, 174
Bulgaria, 41, 45, 46, 121, 122, 127, 130, 136, 141, 144, 145, 148, 156, 157, 159, 160, 161, 162, 163, 165, 167, 168, 169, 174, 175, 176, 178, 179, 180, 184, 185, 186, 191
Bulgarian Orthodox, 132, 143
Bunyan, John, 136, 144

Cain, 13
Cairo, 145, 147, 172
caliph, 151, 155, 167, 170
Capitulations, the, 170
caravansary, 53, 55, 62, 68, 77, 78, 87, 111, 112
Caspian Sea, 113, 126
Caucasia, 60, 61, 63, 66, 67, 115, 148, 166, 167, 168
Caucasus, the, 46, 75, 78
Central Asia, 132, 137, 160
Central Powers, the, 184
Chambers, Mr (Either Robert or William N.), 47
Chartak, 80
Chevermeh, 42, 44, 48
China, 58, 60, 76, 90, 170
Chirasöndüren, 7
Chitjian, Garekin, 44, 45, 46
Chokti Rashid, 71
Chragadin, Doctor, 109
Christendom, 144, 158, 159, 190, 194
Cilicia, 155
Circassian, 167
Commands of the Saints, The, 12
Congo Free State, 58
Constantinople, 12, 119, 129, 131, 136, 141, 142, 146, 147, 151, 152, 154, 155, 156, 158, 159, 161, 167, 168, 170, 171, 172, 173, 179, 183, 185
Constantza, 126, 168
Corinthians, The Second Letter of Paul to the, 162
Cornelius, 30

daedae, 8
Damascus, 102, 164
Danube River, 139
Daotai, the (Li Tsung-pin), 80, 83, 96
Darugham, 106
Darvaz, 77
David, 11, 33
Dedeagach, 186
dervish, 1, 2, 3, 4, 5, 7, 13, 20, 21, 40, 126, 135, 156, 158, 165, 180
Devil, the, 13
Diarbekir, 191
distant Turk, 7
Dolang, 101, 104
Dorpat, 58
Dozy, Professor Reinhart Pieter Anne, 172, 173, 174
dragoman, 79, 86
Durra i Munajia i Massihia, 147
Dzhumaia, 141

East Turkestan, 90, 111
Egypt, 13, 145, 159, 170, 172
Egyptians, 13
Ekman, Doctor A. J., 58, 88, 106, 108, 116,

257

117, 119
Elijah, 12
Emir Shir Ali Nava'i, 76
Emrah Khojah, 20
Engvall, Missionary, 116
Ephesus, 191
Epistles, 28, 162
Erenler, 7
Erivan, 52, 56, 115
Erzerum, 1, 3, 4, 5, 15, 17, 29, 35, 41, 42, 48, 51, 63, 125
Erzingan, 3
esrar, 4, 5, 9
Euphrates College, 44
Europe, 45, 74, 76, 79, 88, 91, 96, 108, 109, 117, 119, 136, 137, 152, 167, 170
Eve, 13
exarch, 61

Faber, Pastor, 115, 116, 117, 119
Fatima, 12
Fatma Aga, 46
fatwa, 166
Ferdinand, King, 179
Finland, 65
Fleischmann, Pastor Paul, 158
franc, 130, 149, 171, 172
France, 72
Frankfurt (am Main), 188
Fungshang, 87
Furnadjieff, Pastor, 179
Fushang Daloy, 80, 81, 82

Gabriel, Angel, 11, 12
Galatians, 7
Galitzin, Kniaz, 109, 110
Garabed, Master Usta, 3, 17, 31, 32, 37, 38, 42, 43
Gegham, 43
Genadieff, Mr, 179
Genesis, the book of, 79
Gerchekler, 7
German Orient-Mission, 120, 121, 145, 146, 157, 158, 160, 162, 184, 185, 187
Germany, 78, 115, 116, 117, 120, 121, 129, 144, 145, 146, 158, 159, 160, 162, 163, 175, 180, 185, 187, 191
Ghanizade Ali, 1, 2, 3
Ghazar, 49, 67
ghazi, 71
ghrish, 18, 37
giaour, 39
Gordon, Pastor, 132
gospel, 1, 16, 35, 40, 41, 50, 52, 57, 58, 61, 63, 83, 92, 93, 103, 121, 127, 131, 132, 141, 142, 145, 146, 150, 151, 152, 153, 155, 156, 160, 162, 165, 169, 172, 178, 179, 180, 181, 183, 184, 189, 194, 195
Gospel, 12, 15, 16, 17, 18, 19, 21, 23, 24, 25, 26, 28, 29, 30, 31, 34, 35, 36, 37, 38, 40, 41, 42, 43, 44, 45, 48, 49, 68, 69, 81, 87, 88, 126, 132, 133, 134, 135, 149, 150, 154, 174, 175, 181
Gospels, 18, 29, 108, 113, 116, 119, 120, 162, 178
Gossner, Johannes Evangelista, 178
gözji, 8, 9
gradonachal'nik, 188
Grand Mufti. *See Sheikh al-Islam*
Greco-Turkish War, the, 165
Gregorian (Armenian Orthodox), 31, 32, 33, 41, 42, 43, 44, 53, 55, 67, 125
Gunesh, 154, 156, 157, 158, 159, 160, 165, 166, 169, 170, 171, 172, 173

Häckel, Professor Doctor Ernst Heinrich Philipp August, 173, 174
Haemrah, 98, 99, 104
hafiz, 140, 141
Hafiz Effendi, 140, 142
Hagar, 125
Hagia Sophia, 173
Haidari, 1
haji, 111
Haji Ali (in Kashgar), 87
Haji Ali (in Sofia), 179
Hajji Bektash Wali, 12
Halle (an der Saale), 159
Hampartzumian, Sarkis, 58
Hansen, Pastor, 115
hanun Hor yev Vorto yev Hokuin Srpo, 25
Hargrave, Mr A. A., 46
Harmanli, 176
Hasan (Ali's son), 12
Hasan al-'Askari, 12
Hashim Akhund, 80, 98, 99, 100, 101, 104
Haskell, Missionary Reverend Doctor Edward B., 147
Hassan Kala, 4, 5
Hedin, Doctor Sven Anders, 84, 93, 94, 97, 98, 99, 100, 101, 102, 103, 104, 106
Hemlandsposten, 118
Hendricks, Father, 77, 78, 83, 84, 85, 104, 109
Herrick, Reverend Doctor George F., 146
Herzbüchlein, 178
hidayat, 148, 149
High Asia, 73
History of Islam, 172
Högberg, Missionary L. E., 63, 87, 88, 95, 96, 97, 103, 104, 106, 108, 110, 118, 119, 120
Höijer, Missionary Nils Fredrik, 58, 62, 63, 67, 69, 70
Höijer, Mrs Anna, 58
Holland, 188, 191, 192
Holy Islamic League, 136
Holy War, 138, 139, 164, 184
host, communion wafer, 25, 84
Hotel Denchov, 142

258

Husain (Ali's son), 10, 12
Husain Aga, 46
Husain Nasifoff (Nathanael), 181, 182

ibn, 120
Ignatovich, Adam, 77, 78, 83, 84, 85, 86, 87
Ilaah'naa wa Ilaah'kum waahidun wa nahnu lahu muslimun, 149
ilham, 148
Ilieff, 166
Imams, the twelve, 4, 12
Immanuel Church, 60
India, 72, 76, 77, 82, 92, 99, 105, 109, 137, 159, 170
Indian Red Crescent, 175
Indus River, 73
Injil, 16
Inj-Yolli, 7
Irkeshtam, 69, 111
Isaiah, 23, 24, 29
ishan, 111
Ishmael (Hagar's son), 125
Ishmael Efendi, 35, 36
Ishmael Hakki, 173
Ishtib, 164, 166
Islam, 1, 2, 4, 7, 8, 18, 20, 71, 76, 78, 79, 88, 89, 90, 93, 112, 136, 137, 138, 139, 143, 144, 145, 146, 148, 149, 150, 151, 152, 154, 155, 156, 157, 158, 159, 163, 164, 165, 166, 167, 168, 169, 171, 172, 173, 174, 182, 184, 186, 189, 190, 194, 195
Islam Baï, 93, 99, 100, 101, 103, 104
Israel, 13, 45, 68, 132
Israel, Pastor, 121

Jafar-Sadik, 12
Javad Sami Bey, 170
Jeremiah, 164
Jessup, Reverend Henry Harris, 146
Jesus Christ, 4, 16, 21, 23, 24, 25, 26, 27, 28, 30, 32, 33, 35, 36, 37, 38, 39, 40, 41, 43, 44, 46, 48, 49, 55, 57, 58, 62, 64, 68, 85, 86, 89, 92, 102, 125, 126, 127, 128, 131, 132, 133, 134, 135, 137, 140, 141, 142, 146, 147, 148, 152, 155, 164, 166, 169, 178, 180, 182, 183, 190, 194
Jevdet Abdullah, Doctor, 172, 173
Jezireh, 5, 191
Joachim III, Patriarch, 171
John (the apostle), 30, 36
John the Baptist, 12, 40
John, Gospel of, 16, 18, 23, 35, 36, 105, 122
Joseph, 36
Judgement Day. *See* Last Judgement, the
Juma, 169

Kaaba, 125
kadi, 43, 44, 113
Kadiri, 7
kaeshish, 33
kafir, 49, 173
Kaisarieh, 42, 186
Kalilah Damina, 136
Karahasan, 24, 29
Karakala, 52
Karakoram Mountain Range, 73
Karakoyunly, 115
Karlsson, Mrs, 59, 60
Kars, fortress of, 52
Kashgar (city of), 67, 70, 71, 72, 73, 74, 75, 76, 77, 78, 80, 82, 83, 84, 87, 89, 90, 92, 93, 95, 96, 97, 98, 99, 100, 101, 103, 104, 105, 106, 107, 108, 109, 110, 116, 117, 118, 119, 136, 147, 162, 163, 174, 180, 186, 192
Kashgar River, 73
Kashgari, 69, 71, 72, 74, 77, 78, 79, 80, 82, 85, 87, 90, 97, 103, 117, 120, 136, 147, 148, 151, 154, 162, 163, 174, 180, 186, 188, 191, 192, 193
Kashgaris, 71, 73, 74, 75, 76, 77, 78, 79, 80, 84, 85, 87, 114
Kashmir, 106
Kassim Bey, 51
kavass, 178
Kaya, 35
Kaygusuz Abdal, 11, 13
Kazandjieff, Pastor, 182
Kean, Reverend Doctor William, 116
ketgan, 80
ketgen, 80
Kevorkian, Mrs, 67
Kevorkian, Pastor Krekor, 58, 66, 113, 128, 132, 160, 163, 164, 178, 185
Khadijé, 1, 2, 3, 4, 6
Khan Khudayar, 72
Khanarik, 98, 106
kharabati, 5
Kharkov, 63
Kharput, 42, 44, 45
Khatib Jahid Efendi, 169
Khayri Bey, 161
Khoi, 49, 188, 191
khoja, 24, 140
Khoja Baehav ed-Din, 89, 90
Khojas, the, 89, 90
Khotan (city of), 71, 87, 104
Khotan River, 73
Khurshid, 165, 166, 167, 168, 169, 171, 172
khutba, 123
Khynis (district of), 42
Khynis, fortress of, 5
Kilgour, Reverend Doctor R., 162
Kitabsiz, 7
kitaykafsh, 83
Kizil-Arvat, 67
Kizilbash, 7
Kokand (city of), 72, 111
Kokand (khanate of), 90
kopeck, 53, 55, 56

Koran, 10, 12, 16, 17, 19, 20, 21, 23, 25, 26, 41, 49, 54, 77, 123, 133, 134, 135, 140, 148, 149, 156, 158, 159, 166, 167, 174
Krasnovodsk, 113
Krikorian, Professor, 183
Kristiania, 59
Kristinehamn, 58, 59
Kuen-lun Mountains, 73
Kur River, 57
Kurban Bairam, 122, 141, 164
Kurdistan, 146, 152, 164, 191
Kurian, Evangelist Khachadur Agha, 164, 180

La ilaha illa 'llah Mohammed-er-Rasul-Allah, 19, 20
Lailik, 100, 101, 103, 104, 105
Lamentations of Jeremiah, The, 164
Landsmann, Missionary, 118, 132
Last Judgement, the, 14, 26, 36
Lazarus, 92, *See* Omar Akhund
Lebanon, 164
Leipzig, 116, 117, 119, 162
Lepsius, Doctor Johannes, 119, 120, 145, 154, 156, 157, 158, 160, 165, 167, 185, 187, 188, 189, 190, 191, 192, 194
Lom Palanka, 141
London, 45, 113, 114, 115, 116, 117, 118, 119, 162
London Balkans Committee, 177
Lop-nor, 73, 97
Lord's Prayer, the, 24, 26, 27, 50, 79
Lovatz, 141
Luther, Martin, 168
Lutheran Church (in Tiflis), 66

Macartney, Mr George, 80, 81, 83, 84, 85, 91, 92, 96, 103, 104, 105, 106
Macedonia, 155, 156, 165, 168, 176, 177, 181, 186
Maghrabi, 136
Mahdi-al-Hadi (the Mahdi), 12
Mahmud, 50
Maksum Akhund, 80
Manchu, 79, 82
Manchuria, 80
Maral-bashi, 98, 99, 105
Margelan, 111
Maritza River, 182
mark, German, 18, 25, 49, 79, 95, 110, 113, 117
Mark, Gospel of, 31, 151
Marsh, Missionary Reverend George D., 147, 177
Mary, 12, 64, 134
Matthäikirche, 121
Matthew, Gospel of, 16, 23, 27, 31, 108, 120, 133
Mecca, 111, 122, 138, 147
Mécheroutiette, 167
Mediterranean Sea, 191

medrese, 156
Mehmed Kiamil Pasha, 179
Melchizedek, 68
Merket, 98, 101, 103, 105
Merv, 67
Mesopotamia, 119, 191
Methodists (in Bulgaria), 122, 128, 130, 132
Middle East, 139, 141, 166
mihrab, 122, 141
mimbar, 122
minaret, 35, 181
Mingyol, 70
mirovoi sud'ia, 65, 66
Mirza Abd-ul-Karim Akhund, 80, 82
Mirza Fazel Beg, 77, 78
Mirza Husain Ali, 68
Mirza Ibrahim, 128
Mirza Mukhtar, 128, 136, 141
Mirza Yahyah, 128, 130
Mirza Yussuf, 95, 96, 97, 106, 107
Mirza, young (Vadia), 127, 128
missionaries, American (in Bulgaria), 136, 141, 147, 175, 177
missionaries, American (in Persia), 46, 47, 48, 49, 63, 66, 184
missionaries, American (in Turkey), 31, 41, 42, 43, 44, 45, 46, 47, 48, 49, 51, 52, 63, 136, 183
missionaries, Baptist, 51, 61
missionaries, Swedish, 59, 60, 70, 83, 87, 88, 89, 93, 95, 96, 97, 116, 118, 120, 162, 163, 174
missionary, Arab, 71
missionary, Catholic, 77, 78
missionary, English, 140
Mizan ul-Haqq, 56
Mnatsagan, 67, 69, 70
Mohammed, 4, 10, 11, 12, 17, 19, 20, 23, 25, 26, 38, 41, 49, 50, 72, 124, 135, 138, 144, 155, 165, 166, 173, 174, 195
Mohammed Zeki Efendi, 169
Mohammed-Baghir, 12
Mohammed-Tagi, 12
Molokans, 58, 63
Monastir, 168, 173
Mongolia, 83
Montenegro, 3
Morrison, Mr Michael A., 78, 79, 117, 118, 120
Moses, 12, 13, 25, 26
Mosul, 5, 40
Mudafea, 140
muderis, 147, 157
muezzin, 123, 181
mufti, 2, 19, 134, 138, 139, 140, 150, 151, 168
Muhammed Nesimi Effendi, 157, 158, 165, 181
Muhammed Shükri Efendi, 1, 2, 3, 40, 42, 156, 165, 166, 179
mujtahid, 68, 136
Mullah Hassan, 181
Mullah Nasreddin, 190

Munich, 188
Münifé, 1, 2, 3
Munshi Abdurrahman, 99, 105, 106
Munshi Ahmed ed-Din, 81, 97
murid, 1
Musa al-Kazim, 12
Musaddiqan limaa maAAakum, 149
Mush, 5
Muslim Missions Conference, the (in Cairo), 145, 146
Mustafa Pasha, 176
Mustagh Ata, 93, 94, 97

nachal'nik, 112, 113
Nakshibendi, 7
namaz, 4, 62, 122, 124
nasha, 76
Nasif Husseinof, 181
Nathan, 33
Nathanael, 182, 183, *See* Husain Nasifoff (Nathanael)
nephritis, 190
Nerses, 129
Nestorian, 173, 174
Niaz Akhund, 80
Nicodemus, 23, 144
Nicopolis, 141
Nirani Sultan, 12
Nükti Dakshid, 71
Nur Hajim, 82
Nuri Bey, 167
Nyström, Miss Anna, 59, 65, 95, 97, 106

Odessa, 46, 175, 186
ogul, 120
Oksalur, 95
Omar Akhund (Lazarus), 77, 80, 89, 90, 91, 92, 93, 98
Omsk, 83, 85
Orient-Express, the, 146
Oryakhovo, 141
Oryekhovica, 141
Osh, 69, 111
Osman Bazar, 141
Osmanli, 171, 184
Osmanli Turkish, 77
Osmanlidom, 171

Pamirs, the, 73
pan-Islamism, 159, 167, 170, 171, 172
Parable of the Good Samaritan, 133
Parable of the Sower, 127, 133
Paris, 167
pasha, 1, 140, 167, 176, 179
Pashmakly, 157, 175
Patmos, island of, 191
Patriarchs, the, 24
Paul (the apostle), 28, 102, 125, 154, 160, 163
Peking, 72, 73

Persia, 61, 63, 66, 106, 113, 115, 118, 119, 126, 127, 129, 131, 136, 148, 159, 160, 191
Perzor, 17, 43
Peter (the apostle), 86
Petko, Daido, 141
Petros, 28
Petrovsky, Nikolai Feodorovitch, 70, 72, 77, 83
pfennig, 79, 105
Pharaoh, 13
Pharisees, 130
Philippopolis, 46, 138, 146, 147, 148, 151, 156, 157, 159, 160, 162, 163, 166, 167, 168, 169, 173, 174, 175, 176, 177, 178, 180, 181, 182, 185, 186, 187, 188, 191, 192
piastre, 31, 37
pilaf, 74
Pilgrim's Progress, 136, 144, 148, 160
pir, 8, 9, 10, 17, 29, 32
Plevna, 141
Polo, Marco, 71
Pomaks, 182
Potsdam, 145, 157, 158, 159, 165, 181
pound, Turkish, 31
pristav, 64, 65, 66, 112, 113
Proclamation of Freedom, 172
Protestant, Armenian, 17, 18, 24, 25, 30, 32, 41, 42, 43, 45, 52, 53, 66, 122, 150, 155
Protestant, Bulgarian, 132, 133, 148, 167, 168, 181
Protestant, English, 83
Protestant, German, 66
Psalms, 12, 31, 192

qalon, 76
Qarataghliq, 80
qotaz, 69
qum yaghar, 73, 74
Quraishi, 7

Radoslavov, Prime Minister Vasil, 187
Raejaeb Baba, Sheikh, 1, 20
Rafizi, 7
rajah, 99
Rakhova, 151
Ramazan, 93, 122, 123
Raquette, Missionary Doctor Gustav, 88, 162, 163
Rasgrad, 163, 164
raya, 157
Redeemed One, the, 13
Redeemed People, the, 13
Reichsboten, 132
Revelation to John, The, 28, 30
Rhodope Mountains, 176
Ritson, Reverend John Holland, 162
Rohrbach, Doctor Paul, 158
Romania, 126, 132, 168, 175
Romans, The Letter of Paul to the, 28, 110
Rosenberg, Doctor, 132

Rosenstein, Pastor, 132
rouble, 55, 56, 58, 84, 85, 104, 108, 110, 111
Rousseau, Jean-Jacques, 144
Rufai, 7, 156
Russia, 3, 15, 41, 51, 62, 63, 69, 73, 113, 116, 119, 131, 165, 167, 170
Russian Orthodox, 83
Russian Turkestan, 93
Russo-Turkish War, the, 15, 138
Rustchuk, 126, 128, 131, 132, 133, 135, 139, 140, 141, 163, 178

Sabil-ur-Rashad, 173
Sadducees, 130
saiyid, 4, 20, 35, 36, 62, 72, 156
Saiyid Ahmed (John), 62
Saiyid Hasan, 32, 35, 36, 37, 38, 40
Saiyid Ismael, 21
Salim Divana, 10
Samarkand, 67, 68, 71, 77, 111, 112, 113
Saribaba, 29
Sarkis (Effendi Kasabian), 30, 31, 32, 37, 38, 41, 42, 43
Satan, 4, 13, 36
Saul, 102
Schäfer, General Secretary Richard, 185
Schlagintweit, Adolf, 72
Scriptures, the, 15, 16, 26, 30, 31, 33, 34, 36, 43, 46, 51, 59, 62, 89, 105, 114, 116, 128, 129, 130, 134, 135, 141, 145, 147, 148, 156, 178, 179, 191, 193
sema, 9
Serbia, 175, 180
Serbo-Turkish War in Montenegro, the, 3
Sermon on the Mount, 31, 78, 127, 133
Sert, 5
setar, 76
Seth, 13
seventy-two religions, the ones outside the, 7
seventy-two religious communities, the, 13
Sevlievo, 141
Sevortian, Baron, 29, 30, 31
Shabak, 7
Shabchi, 105, 106
shaengaeng, 95, 96
Shahid-ül-Haqaiq, 129, 131, 136, 141, 142, 144, 147, 148, 150, 153, 154, 158, 160, 169, 179
Shahsavan, 7
Shahveled, Pastor Hagop, 122, 127, 141, 142, 164, 178, 182, 183, 185
Shanghai, 88
Shari'ah, 151, 159
sheikh, 1, 2, 6, 20, 126, 127, 135, 138, 156, 165
Sheikh al-Islam, 157, 158, 166, 169
Shemakha, 58, 63, 66, 113
Sherif Pasha, 167
Shiites, 49, 50, 61
Show (Robert Shaw), 71

Shumla, 45, 127, 129, 130, 131, 132, 141, 142, 145, 146, 163, 164, 166, 178, 180
Shung-chi, 81
Shusha, 52, 58, 62, 113
Siberia, 61, 64, 65, 66, 83, 84, 160
Siratul-Mustaqim, 170, 173
Sistova, 139, 141
sledovatel', 64
Smyrna, 183
Sofia, 127, 163, 164, 169, 172, 175, 176, 178, 179, 182, 187, 188
Sofininki, 111
Solomon, 10, 11, 13
Somovit, 141
St Elisabeth's Hospital, 190
St Nicholas Church, 158
St Petersburg, 110, 116, 168
Stambul, 46, 51
Stara Zagora, 179
Steinbrecher, Mr, 113
Stettin, 119
Stockholm, 58, 59, 60, 88, 116, 117, 120, 167, 174, 177, 186, 192
Stoïleff, General, 176
Sublime Porte, the, 138
Südfriedhof, 193
Sufi, 157, 158, 179, 180
Suleiman Efendi, 1, 2
Sundqvist, Mrs, 59
sungaq-chi, 109
Sung-Qaraghol, 70
Sunni, 5, 7, 8, 12, 15, 21, 61
suyukash, 74
Sweden, 58, 67, 89, 95, 98, 100, 106, 108, 118, 120
Swedish Missionary Society (Svenska Missionsförbundet), 58, 61, 63, 67, 88, 117, 118, 162, 163, 192
Syr River, 73
Syria, 155

Tabriz, 47, 48, 49, 53, 62, 63, 66, 67, 88, 95
tagia, 61, 62
tajwid, 54
Takla Makan Desert, 73, 98, 99, 101, 104
Tarikh-i-Nazaenin, 7
Tarim Basin, 73
Tarim Desert, 100
Tarim River, 73
tariq, 10
Tarsus, 191
Tashjian, Pastor Hagop, 32
Tashkent, 72
Tatar Bazardjik, 147, 176, 179
Taz-Kharab, 5
Tchataldcha, 176
Teheran, 95, 136
Ten Commandments, 31, 36
tenga, 105

ter Asaturoff, Markara, 58, 60
Terek Davan, 69
Terim, 98, 101
Testament, New, 12, 15, 16, 17, 18, 24, 35, 77, 78, 79, 97, 108, 113, 114, 117, 120, 140, 146, 147, 151, 160, 162, 163, 180, 181, 186, 190, 191, 192, 193, 194
Testament, Old, 16, 17, 24, 77, 131
Theodoroff, Pastor, 122, 127
Thirty-two Disputations of the Artisans, The, 136
Thrace, 176, 178, 180
Tiflis, 46, 52, 55, 57, 61, 63, 65, 67, 78, 95, 108, 113, 115, 131, 160
Timothy, 154
Tirnova, 141
Todoroff, Pastor, 140
Toff, Missionary, 132
toman, 49
traditions, Islamic, 20, 134, 135, 148, 159
Trebizond, 183
Trinity, 8, 137, 166, 167, 190
Tripoli, 164, 165
Tripolitanish War, the, 165
Tsairakli, 7
Tsung-li Yamen, 93
Tuman River, 87, 92
Tumayan, Professor, 162
Turka, sitting *à la*, 123
Turkdom, 171
Turkestan, 112, 168
Turkey, 47, 63, 66, 118, 136, 146, 151, 152, 153, 154, 159, 160, 161, 164, 165, 167, 168, 169, 170, 172, 176, 180, 181, 183, 184, 186
Turkish Revolution, the, 151
Turkmans, 7
Tyan Shan Mountains, 73, 89
Tzakoff, Pastor, 182, 183

ulema, 179
Ulugchat, 69
Urateba Caravansary, 77, 84
Urfa, 191
Uriah, 33
Urumiah, 46, 47, 48, 131, 191
Uryankhusurli, 7
Uskup, 168
Usun-ada, 67
Utro, 175
Uzbek Turkish, 79, 80

Vadia. *See* Mirza, young (Vadia)
Vali Khan Tura, King, 72

Van, 191
Van Duzee, Miss Cyrene O., 46
Varna, 119, 121, 122, 126, 127, 132, 146
Vasiyadt, 138
Vienna, 185, 188
Voice from the Homeland, 45
Voltaire, 144
von Blücher, Miss Henriette, 151
von Oertzen, Pastor Detwig, 146, 151, 152
von Osterroht, Miss Helene, 121
von Osterroht, Mr, 119
Vrtsel, 141

Wa hiya walaahnawa laghaiyrahi, 134
Wa maa unzila min qablika, 149
Waldenström, Doctor Paul Peter, 118, 119, 120, 162
Warneck, Professor Gustav, 159
West Turkestan, 69, 79, 111
Whipple, Mr (Reverend W. L.), 47
Widdin, 141
Wiesbaden, 185, 191, 192, 193
Wilson, Mr (Reverend Samuel Graham), 47, 49, 55
World War, the First, 184, 195
Wright, Doctor, 116

Yakub Beg, 72, 73, 79, 80, 90
Yamini, book of, 11
Yangi-hissar, 93, 95
Yangi-shahr, 72, 98
yapunja, 64
yarim-pasha, 110
Yarkand (city of), 71, 100, 101, 103, 105, 106, 107, 108
Yarkand River, 73, 101, 105
Yoldash, 99
Yologhli, 5, 6, 7, 8, 10, 11, 12, 13, 15, 17, 20, 21, 23, 33, 35, 36, 39
Yolushaghi, 7
Young Turks, 129, 130, 151, 152, 153, 155, 158, 167, 168, 169, 170, 171, 172, 184
Yussuf Kadrkhan Ghazi, 71

Zain-ul-Abidin, 12
Zakhu, 5
zaki, 10
Zamzam, 125
Zehni, 1, 3
zikr, 111
Zornitsa, 182
Zwemer, Doctor Samuel Marinus, 146

Photographs

An old dervish	265
Avetaranian as a dervish	265
Young dervishes	265
Persian dervishes	266
A street in Kashgar	267
Indian Muslims in the assembly of Kashgari begs. By Dr Chragadin and Munshi Ahmed ed-Din	267
The old Russian consulate in Kashgar. (Picture taken by John Quanrud in November 2001)	268
A market stall in Kashgar. (Picture taken by John Quanrud in November 2001)	268
Fushang Daloy	269
Avetaranian with the translation of the New Testament into Kashgari	270
Ancient Samarkand—Timur's tomb	270
The missionaries Abraham Amirkhaniantz and John Avetaranian in 1900	271
John Avetaranian and his wife Helene, born von Osterroht (1900)	272
In the court of the mission-house in Varna	273
The printing shop in Shumla	274
Avetaranian's mission-house in Shumla	274
Philippopolis	275
Mimbar and mihrab in a Muslim house of God	275
Pastor Kevorkian and John Avetaranian (Rustchuk 1904)	276
Johannes Lepsius and John Avetaranian (1906)	276
Avetaranian with two mullahs who became Christians (1909)	277
Avetaranian at his work (Philippopolis 1908)	277
Mr and Mrs Avetaranian with the literature work	278

An old dervish.

Avetaranian as a dervish.

Young dervishes.

Persian dervishes.

A street in Kashgar.

Indian Muslims in the assembly of Kashgari begs.
By Dr Chragadin and Munshi Ahmed ed-Din.

The old Russian consulate in Kashgar.
(Picture taken by John Quanrud in November 2001. Used with permission.)

A market stall in Kashgar.
(Picture taken by John Quanrud in November 2001. Used with permission.)

Fushang Daloy

Avetaranian with the translation of the New Testament into Kashgari.

Ancient Samarkand — Timur's tomb.

The missionaries Abraham Amirkhaniantz and John Avetaranian in 1900.

John Avetaranian and his wife Helene, born von Osterroht (1900).

In the court of the mission-house in Varna.

The printing shop in Shumla.

Avetaranian's mission-house in Shumla.

Philippopolis

Mimbar and mihrab in a Muslim house of God.

Pastor Kevorkian and John Avetaranian (Rustchuk 1904).

Johannes Lepsius and John Avetaranian (1906).

Avetaranian with two mullahs who became Christians (1909).

Avetaranian at his work (Philippopolis 1908).

Mr and Mrs Avetaranian with the literature work.

Printed in the United Kingdom
by Lightning Source UK Ltd.
93071